OREGON ARGONAUTS

*Merchant Adventurers
on the
Western Frontier*

By

ARTHUR L. THROCKMORTON

1961

OREGON HISTORICAL SOCIETY

PORTLAND, OREGON

Edition limited to 1,000 copies

Library of Congress Catalog Card Number 61-64035

Copyright 1961
Oregon Historical Society
Portland, Oregon

Printed in U.S.A. by Abbott, Kerns & Bell Co.

TO FLO

PREFACE

This book is an account of the role of the frontier merchant in the economic development of Oregon and the Pacific Northwest from 1839 to 1869. The entrepreneurial activities of George Abernethy, Henry W. Corbett, and Henry Failing, whose business careers have been selected for the purposes of this study, demonstrate the processes of business and trade which assured Oregon's frontier communities the supply of manufactured goods necessary to sustain them. Wholesale merchants established regular facilities for credit in New York and San Francisco and goods flowed to the Oregon frontier by sea. Successful merchants ultimately used their accumulated profits of trade as capital for the development of the resources of the Pacific Northwest. Some, like Corbett and Failing, made the transition from pioneer merchants to bankers and financiers.

Part I of this study presents the history of Oregon's isolated Willamette community during the first decade of settlement. My purposes in this section are to define the role of the Hudson's Bay Company in the process of settlement; to evaluate the contributions of the Methodist Mission to the economic development of the Willamette Valley; to identify the economic problems that beset the new community; and to give a fresh synthesis of Oregon's development during the crucial decade of the 1840s.

The supply problem and measures taken for its solution provide a major theme for this study. From the beginnings of settlement, facilities for supply existed but they became woefully inadequate during the 1840s owing to the limited export market. Thus an acute supply problem arose which threatened the very existence of the Willamette community. The idea of frontier self-sufficiency is essentially a myth; for it is hard to conceive how the Willamette community could have survived had it not been for the fortuitous circumstance of the California gold rush.

The impact of California gold upon the development of Oregon, which is thoroughly treated in Part II of this study, has been slighted or neglected in the general histories of the Pacific Northwest. It solved Oregon's most pressing economic problems by creating a market for lumber and provisions. It thus created opportunities for profit and stimulated every branch of pioneer enterprise. It was largely responsible for the establishment of regular trade routes via Cape Horn and Panama from New York to San Francisco and Oregon, and for the growth of river navigation and the rise of towns in Oregon.

Gold indeed was the principal sustaining element in Oregon's economy. As shown in Parts III and IV of this study businessmen and farmers depended upon the markets created by the succession of gold rushes in California and the Pacific Northwest from 1849 through the 1860s. I quite agree with the late Professor Joseph Schafer's conclusion that had it not been for gold civilization in the far Northwest quite likely would have retrogressed. While the economy was subject to cycles of inflation and depression owing to too great a dependence upon the uncertainties of mining, the gold that remained in the region in various forms of capital contributed vitally to the sounder more diversified economy which emerged as the region settled into its post-frontier development.

For the period 1849 to 1869, this study focuses upon Portland in relation to the development of its expanding hinterland. While San Francisco exerted an economic hegemony throughout the Far West and thus overshadowed Portland, the latter was the entrepôt for Oregon and an important distribution center in its own right. Corbett and Failing and other of Portland's leading merchants purchased in New York and had relatively little business with merchants in San Francisco. Because San Francisco was practically the only market for Oregon products outside the region, however, the dependent relationship persisted at least until the beginning of Oregon's foreign grain trade in 1869.

This is regional history but it is not intended to be narrowly so. A conscious effort has been made to place the region's development from 1839 to 1869 within the context and broad perspectives of American history. The Oregon boundary controversy, the California gold rush, the long line of commerce from New York to Oregon, New York as the metropolis serving an expanding nation, the effect of the Civil War upon business in the Far West provide some of the connecting themes. It is my hope, moreover, that as case studies the business careers of Abernethy, Corbett and Failing may contribute to a better understanding of frontier merchant-capitalism in the American West.

A. L. T.

Lewis and Clark College
Portland, Oregon
September, 1959

ACKNOWLEDGMENTS

I wish to express my appreciation to the following authors whose substantial studies on the economic history of the Far West have so greatly aided me in writing this book: Professors John S. Galbraith of the University of California at Los Angeles, James H. Gilbert of the University of Oregon, Dorothy O. Johansen of Reed College, John H. Kemble of Pomona College, Rodman W. Paul of the California Institute of Technology, and Oscar O. Winther of Indiana University.

I am deeply indebted to Professor Ernest S. Osgood, of the University of Minnesota, for his helpful and encouraging guidance throughout all stages of this study. I am also indebted to the late Professor Dan E. Clark of the University of Oregon for helping me to define the topic and for his many kindly suggestions. I appreciate the ideas of Professor Charles M. Gates of the University of Washington on urbanization and the frontier which were partly responsible for directing my attention to a study of Portland. I owe much to the late Professor Albert Ray Newsome of the University of North Carolina, who first instructed me in the techniques of the historian's craft.

I wish to acknowledge the many kindnesses and helpful services of members of the staffs of the Oregon Historical Society, the University of Oregon Library, and the Portland Public Library. Miss Priscilla Knuth, research associate at the Oregon Historical Society, Mr. Martin Schmitt, curator of the Special Collections Library of the University of Oregon, and Mr. Thomas Vaughan, Director of the Oregon Historical Society, have been especially helpful. I appreciate the editorial suggestions of Miss Knuth and Professor Kenneth Johnson of Lewis and Clark College who at one time or another read the entire manuscript. I also appreciate the comments of Professor Walter J. Mead, formerly of the Department of Economics of Lewis and Clark College and now of the University of California at Santa Barbara, on the sections having to do with special aspects of economic development. A further word of appreciation is due the Danforth Foundation for providing the modest grant necessary for the preparation of the manuscript in its final form. To the Western Imprints Fund of the Oregon Historical Society I want to express thanks for the publication of this book.

My deepest debt of gratitude is to my wife, Flo, for her help, understanding, and sacrifice as this study progressed.

TABLE OF CONTENTS

ILLUSTRATIONS

LIST OF TABLES

PART I

Early Days, 1839-48

The Hudson's Bay Company in Oregon

The fur trade prepared the way for the permanent development of the Oregon Country as it did elsewhere on the American frontier. Rival traders from several nations had operated along the coast since late in the eighteenth century, but after 1813 the men of the British North West Company with their several interior posts gained the strongest foothold. After the merger of the Hudson's Bay and North West companies in 1821, the new and revitalized Hudson's Bay Company sought to defeat its American and Russian rivals and to monopolize the trade. By 1839, on the eve of the advance of American settlers into the region, it had achieved these purposes without question; also it had developed various subsidiary industries. Its profits, derived primarily from the exploitation of a single resource, were not used for the region's improvement, but flowed to England to enhance the accumulations of capitalists there. For the Company to have acted otherwise would have been contrary to the very nature and purpose of the fur trade.

The Company nevertheless contributed to the process of settlement. By providing essential goods and services it immeasurably aided the American settlers who arrived in increasing numbers during the 1840s. This significant relationship between the giant British fur trading company and the settlement of Oregon is treated in the first section of this book. The growth of the Company's economic power in the region prior to 1839 is the subject of this introduction.

The Company's Columbia Department was practically coterminous with the vast wilderness known as the Oregon Country prior to the division of the territory in 1846. The Columbia Department embraced the entire Pacific slope from the Rockies to the sea and from Mexican California to the southern and eastern limits of Russian America in the far north. It was the western frontier of the Company's extensive trading domains, and precisely because it was a zone of conflicting trading and international interests it called for extraordinary men and measures. Like the Company's other frontiers the Columbia Department, especially the southern part, served as a protective zone for the important fur preserves to the north and east. While the Hudson's Bay Company carried forward its economic policies it also served the imperial interests of Great Britain for, as the sole representative of British authority in northern and western North America, it was the only effective agent of empire in this vast region.[1] The Columbia Department, on the western edge of this territory, for many years prior to 1839 had been the most difficult administrative unit within the Company's entire organization. Here the challenges of competition required able leadership and masterful trading techniques. Here appeared men of the stature of John McLoughlin, James Douglas and Peter Skene Ogden. The challenges of the Columbia Department also had not a little to do with the fame attained by Governor George Simpson.

Fort Vancouver, located on the north bank of the Columbia River one hundred miles from the sea, served as principal headquarters for this department and entrepôt for the Company's network of interior trade routes and posts, as well as for the extensive coastal operations. The site of Fort Vancouver had been carefully chosen by Governor George Simpson in 1824 with regard to the river and the spacious lands adaptable for the development of agriculture and stock raising in the vicinity. It was to have served as entrepôt only temporarily, however. Simpson had planned to locate the permanent headquarters at the mouth of the Fraser, but upon discovering the unsuitability of that river as a route to the interior he had dropped the plan. London officials of the Company revived this idea in 1834, and repeatedly urged, for reasons of economy and convenience, the establishment of a more centrally located entrepôt on the coast farther to the north. Fort Vancouver nevertheless remained the principal headquarters; and the Columbia, in spite of the hazards of navigation at its mouth, continued to be the main avenue for trade into the interior.

The location of Fort Vancouver also served a political purpose. Fort George, formerly called Astoria and the headquarters for the trade prior to 1824, was on the south side of the river near its mouth, in that part of the region certain to go to the United States in any settlement of the boundary question. British negotiators in 1824 seemed determined to hold for British possession the territory north of the Columbia to the forty-ninth parallel, the specific area then in dispute between the governments of the United States and Great Britain. Thus, fully expecting the Columbia River to become the boundary, the Company for practical reasons as well as in response to pressure from the British foreign office located Fort Vancouver and most of its other expensive establishments north of the river. Actual occupation of the disputed territory, it was thought, would give greater strength to British arguments in the boundary negotiations.

Monopoly in the Columbia Department was not easily achieved. With the merger of the North West and Hudson's Bay companies in 1821 the long period of strife existing between the two companies east of the mountains came to an end. The new organization incorporated the best practices of the two companies and under the leadership of Governor George Simpson the trade was revitalized throughout the extended domains of the Hudson's Bay Company.* Prior to 1821 only the North West Company had operated west of the Rockies where declining returns and increasing expenses in the fur trade had been so great that the new Company seriously considered abandonment of the Columbia district. These conditions were due to inefficient management and not to inadequacy of the fur resources, however. Governor George Simpson inspected the Columbia posts in 1824 and as a result of his vigorous reorganization of the trading operations and the efficient management of Chief Factor John McLoughlin, whom Simpson placed in charge of the Columbia Department, the fur trade became profitable throughout all its branches. Agriculture, flour and lumber milling, stock raising, and the fisheries were developed to sustain or bolster the fur trade and were considered legitimate branches of the

---

*The Deed Poll of 1821 effected a partnership system by which all field officers, twenty-five chief factors and twenty-eight chief traders, were to form a central administrative council for the Northern Department of Rupert's Land and to share the profits. The proprietors in London were to receive 60 per cent and the field officers 40 per cent of the annual profits from the total operations. The 40 per cent was to be divided into 85 equal shares annually with two eighty-fifths for each chief factor and one eighty-fifth for each chief trader. Seven eighty-fifths were to be placed in a retirement fund.

total operation. The products of these enterprises also became important items in the limited commerce of the North Pacific.

The Hudson's Bay Company had to prepare for American competition. The Convention of 1818 guaranteed equal privileges to American citizens and British subjects in the entire region even though the negotiators had narrowed the disputed territory to the area lying between the Columbia River and the forty-ninth parallel. The license of 1821 from the British government granting exclusive trading privileges to the Hudson's Bay Company in the region west of Rupert's Land specifically provided that these privileges applied only against British subjects in the area west of the Rockies. It was therefore expedient for the Hudson's Bay Company to exhaust as far as possible the fur resources of that part of the region most certain to go to the United States since the "joint" privileges guaranteed in the Convention of 1818 were due to expire in 1828.[2]

The principal zone of conflict with the Americans was the Snake River country where the North West Company had prepared the way and where for six years beginning in 1824 Peter Skene Ogden led his famed annual expeditions. Hudson's Bay officers took advantage of every weakness of the Americans: their limited capital resources; their individualistic methods of trading; and the friction between them and the Indians. The principal weapon of the Hudson's Bay Company was underselling, at a loss if necessary, in order to drive out the competitor. The returns from the Snake Country had produced sizeable profits during the mid and late 1820s, and Company officials had breathed a sigh of relief when in 1827 the new convention between Great Britain and the United States renewed "joint occupation" indefinitely. With greater zeal the Company sought to exterminate the fur bearing animals in the region south of the Columbia, and returns from the Snake expeditions steadily declined, reflecting the effectiveness of the methods used. American competition became less serious and then virtually disappeared by the mid-thirties. For three years after Ogden gave up the command in 1829, Chief Trader John Work led the Snake expeditions. The returns for 1831-32 declined so much that Simpson ordered abandonment and the Snake

6

Country was now pronounced a virtual "fur desert." The expeditions concentrated thereafter in other parts of the region south of the Columbia in the direction of California.[3]

The notable expeditions of Nathaniel Wyeth from Boston, by land and sea in 1832 and again in 1834 to compete in the fisheries and the fur trade, were somewhat anti-climactic. In addition to bad luck, he lacked sufficient capital resources to combat the Hudson's Bay Company and failed utterly against its entrenched monopoly. Fort Hall, which he established in the "fur desert" on the Snake on his second expedition, was sold to the Hudson's Bay Company in 1836.[4]

The Americans were defeated in competition and their further intrusion forestalled. The Company had successfully protected its fur preserves, particularly those in the far northern part of the region known as New Caledonia. A major purpose of this policy was also to prevent or delay settlement, for Company officials well knew that settlers inevitably followed the American fur traders. Thus, the Company succeeded in guarding a crucial frontier both of the trade and of the British empire.[5]

Competition in the coastal trade was far more severe. Here Americans traded from their ships and furnished supplies to the Russian-American Company in the north. The American sea otter trade, with the important outlet at Canton, although especially lucrative in the early part of the century, had become insignificant by the early twenties. American sea captains, however, continued their quest for furs on the Northwest Coast and their practice of supplying the Russian posts. They threatened the New Caledonia district where the Hudson's Bay Company sought to establish its monopoly. To win it McLoughlin built a chain of four posts from Puget Sound to 54° 40′ between 1827 and 1833, and kept one or more ships constantly employed in the coastal trade. The "Bay" man used three tariffs for the New Caledonia trade with the highest prices paid for furs at or near the coast, the lowest in the relatively safe interior, and one in between for the intermediate area high enough to deter the Indians from making the trip to the coast. By these means the Company finally drove its competitors away. The day of the famous Yankee traders, which had begun with the adventures of

7

Captains Robert Gray and John Kendrick in 1787, had practically ended by the mid-thirties.

McLoughlin had also encountered serious opposition in 1829 when Captain John Dominis, representing the Boston firm of Marshall and Wildes, with two ships, the *Owhyhee* and the *Convoy*, entered the Columbia itself. Dominis offered high prices for furs and the Hudson's Bay Company strained to meet the competition. McLoughlin feared shortage of supplies since the Company's brig *William and Ann* had been lost at the mouth of the Columbia. While his supplies actually were adequate, he did wish the Columbia district to show a profit. Rather than to continue the competition with the prices of furs steadily rising, McLoughlin violated Company policy by attempting to buy out Dominis and to rid himself of this annoying competition. Dominis did not accept but left the Columbia in 1830 to bring a none-too-profitable venture to a close. Company officials in London viewed the Columbia district as expendable and disapproved of McLoughlin's attempted deviation from underselling as the standard method of meeting competition.

In the far north the Hudson's Bay Company met the competition and hostility of the Russians. Governor George Simpson sought transit privileges from the Russian-American Company across the Alaska panhandle into the rich fur country to the east in the vicinity of the Stikine River, and to restrict the Russian traders "to their own proper territory." Also, in order to undermine the American competitive position, he sought permission from the Russian company in 1828 for the Hudson's Bay Company to provide the provisions and other supplies needed to supplement those brought to Sitka in the Russian company's annual ship. While the Russians found American competition in the trade as annoying as did the Hudson's Bay Company, they saw the activities of the latter as the greater threat. The Russians refused Simpson's proposal in 1828, and for ten years thereafter he was unable to negotiate a satisfactory arrangement with them. While the Stikine area had become a zone of conflict, the aim of the Hudson's Bay Company was to confine the Russians rather than to eliminate them as they wished to do with the American traders. Finally, after the Americans had all but disappeared and with the prospect

8

that the Hudson's Bay Company could amply supply them with provisions from Fort Vancouver and goods from England, the Russian company became disposed to settle its differences with its British rival.[6]

In 1839 Governor George Simpson and Rear Admiral Baron Ferdinand Wrangell negotiated a mutually satisfactory agreement on matters in dispute between the two companies. The Russians agreed to discontinue their trading activities in the Alaskan strip and to lease it for a ten-year period to the Hudson's Bay Company for an annual payment of 2,000 land otter skins. The British Company agreed to supply the Russians annually with some 5,000 additional skins and various quantities of agricultural produce at stipulated prices. Hudson's Bay ships were to transport consignments of other supplies and equipment from England to Alaska at specified freight rates. Now Fort Ross, the Russian post in California upon which they had relied for provisions, was unnecessary. It might be added that the men of the Hudson's Bay Company had been fully prepared to force their way into the Stikine area if agreement had not been reached.[7] With this peaceful settlement, however, they had finally achieved their complete monopoly on the Northwest Coast.

The Russian agreement was in part responsible for the formation of the Puget Sound Agricultural Company at London in 1838-39. Agricultural production at Fort Vancouver was insufficient to meet the new export demand imposed by the Russian contract, and a separate but dependent company was planned to develop farms and herds of cattle and sheep as a large-scale industry. Expansion of agriculture for the purpose of supplying the Russian outposts as a part of the Hudson's Bay Company's regular business had been considered in 1828, when Governor Simpson first sought a Russian agreement. In 1832 Chief Factor John McLoughlin had urged the formation of an independent company to develop the hide and tallow trade. The plan to develop agriculture and stock raising on a large scale had been seriously considered again in 1834. McLoughlin, while he had confidence in an independent venture, thought that one sponsored by the Company would fail.

9

Political considerations contributed to the Company's decision to establish the subsidiary company. In 1837 the Governor and Committee applied for the renewal of the license of 1821, due to expire in 1842, for their exclusive trading privileges west of Rupert's Land. To meet the usual criticisms against the Hudson's Bay Company as an archaic, mercantilistic institution, and its failure to develop other resources than the fur trade or to encourage settlement, Company officials now asserted their intention to promote agriculture and stock raising and to sponsor colonization in the area north of the Columbia. Such measures, it was hoped, would secure this area for Great Britain and counteract the new threat of American settlement. They were particularly alarmed by Senator Linn's bill in 1838 demanding the assertion of American sovereign rights in Oregon. While it and successive Oregon bills failed in the Senate, there had been considerable support for the measure. The Company's trading privileges, exclusive against other British subjects west of the Rockies, were renewed and the Hudson's Bay Company prepared to hold the territory between the Columbia and Puget Sound and to continue operations in the Columbia Department as a buffer for the protection of the vast fur country to the north and east.

In carrying out this policy, the Governor and Committee intended to promote emigration from Great Britain and to induce the retired servants of the Company then residing in the Willamette Valley to move to the lands of the agricultural company north of the Columbia. The Company would provide each head of family with a house, 100 acres of cleared land, twenty cows, 500 sheep, eight oxen, six horses, some hogs, and provisions for the first year. Each farmer would receive one-half the increment of his stock and one-half of his crop each year, but could not gain full title to his land.

In spite of these attractions the plan was only partially successful. There were no settlers from abroad, and Father Blanchet, the new priest appointed to serve the French Canadians of the Willamette Valley, failed to persuade his parishioners to accept conditions that would not permit full proprietorship. Twenty-one families of English half-breeds and French Canadians, a total of 116 persons, migrated from the Red River settlements to the lands of the Puget Sound

Agricultural Company. After their arrival in the summer of 1841, fourteen families were sent to farms near Fort Nisqually on Puget Sound, and seven to Cowlitz Farm in the Cowlitz Valley. Those at Nisqually soon became dissatisfied and within two years all fourteen families had moved to the Willamette Valley. Those at Cowlitz Farm appear to have remained. Simpson and Company officials soon lost their enthusiasm for colonization, abandoned plans for further emigration, and for the most part assigned the care of the lands and flocks of the subsidiary company to regular servants of the Hudson's Bay Company.[8]

Thus the colonization scheme failed and at times the Company was hard-pressed to fulfill the Russian contract. The basic reason for the failure, according to Professor Galbraith, was the ill-advised system which would have placed the settler in a permanently dependent status. He concludes that since the fur trade was the antithesis of free settlement, "The Company cannot be criticized for failure to act in a manner alien to its being," and "any colonization project undertaken under its auspices was foredoomed to failure."[9]

The Hudson's Bay Company was more successful in developing commercial relationships between the Columbia River and the Hawaiian Islands. American traders, whalers and missionaries had made the islands a Pacific mart of considerable importance during the 1820s and 1830s. In addition to the products of the whale fishery, island exports included sandalwood and coarse sugar products. A wide variety of goods and provisions had to be imported to sustain these enterprises. Although the market was limited, the Company found a profitable outlet there for lumber, flour, salmon and other provisions from the Columbia River. A regular Hudson's Bay station was established at Honolulu in 1833 and the twenty to twenty-five-day run from the Columbia to the islands became an important leg in the Company's widening pattern of trade.[10]

Not a little of the success of the Company in its many enterprises was due to Dr. John McLoughlin, chief factor in charge of the Columbia Department, who stood at the zenith of his career as a fur trader in 1839. He had had the able assistance of James Douglas, Peter Skene Ogden, and others of the Company's commissioned officers. McLoughlin knew the fur

11

trade well and served diligently in carrying out the policies of the Governor and Committee and Governor George Simpson. Now, at the age of fifty-five, the white-haired giant and his assistants ruled the vast region encompassed within the Columbia Department somewhat like benevolent feudal barons. So long as the fur trade was conducted on a monopoly basis, peace prevailed between trader and native. Efficiency was maintained in all branches of the trade as Simpson's dictum that "every pursuit tending to leighten the Expence of the Trade is a branch thereof . . ."[11] had been put into effect faithfully. In 1836, in recognition of McLoughlin's outstanding service, the Governor and Committee had awarded him a special emolument of £1,100. While on furlough in London in 1838 and 1839 he had impressed them favorably with advice on important matters of policy. He was now given the additional responsibility of administering the affairs of the Puget Sound Agricultural Company in Oregon. For this he was to receive a salary of £500 per annum in addition to his regular share of the profits from the fur trade.[12]

After 1839 the general depression of the fur market affected the Hudson's Bay Company adversely. Gradually silk had been substituted for fur in the manufacture of hats during the 1830s and by the midforties the preference in fashionable circles had definitely turned away from the beaver hat. The wholesale price for northern beaver in New York fell from $4.50 per pound in 1839 to $3.50 per pound in 1840. The dividend rate of the Hudson's Bay Company fell from 25 and 23 per cent in 1838 and 1839 to 15 per cent for each of the succeeding three years and 10 per cent for 1843. While the Company's operations remained generally remunerative in all its territories, the fur returns from the Columbia Department's southern zone of operation declined not only in value but also in quantity during the early 1840s.[13]

But the year 1839 marks the apogee of the Hudson's Bay Company's ascendancy in Oregon. It achieved monopoly of the trade in this frontier region and thus protected the more lucrative fur areas from the incursions of rival traders. By sponsoring colonization and agricultural development its leaders hoped to promote the interests of the fur trade, to counteract American settlement, and to aid the British government in securing the disputed territory between the Columbia River and the 49th parallel on the grounds of actual British occupation. The Company had dealt effectively with its competitors in the trade but it had no real defense against the men who came for land, whether British or American. Although there were few settlers in the region in 1839, with British settlers almost equal in number to the Americans, Chief Traders Douglas and Ogden were already apprehensive. They believed that the fur trade and settlement could not exist together—a view they shared with several of the Company's London officials.[14] McLoughlin, however, sought to adjust the Company's interests to the conditions of settlement, and his later career as a Company officer is largely identified with the history of the relations between the Oregon settlers and the Hudson's Bay Company.

Chapter I

Missionaries

"The germe of a Great State . . ."

No sooner had the Hudson's Bay Company secured its monopoly and the promise of a larger share in the commerce of the Pacific in the late 1830s than the process of American settlement threatened its position. In spite of the Company's success against American traders in the 1830s, a few mountain men, roving farmers and missionaries had settled in the Willamette Valley to spearhead the advance of the American frontier and to form the nucleus of an American colony. By 1838 the American settlement included eighteen heads of families on farms in the valley, and the preachers, teachers and other secular personnel of the Methodist Mission which, including families, totaled thirty people. Twenty-three families of French Canadians, retired servants of the Hudson's Bay Company, also resided in the Willamette Valley on the rich farm land of French Prairie. Altogether fifty-one adult males resided in the Willamette Valley. Both groups of farmers, Americans and French Canadians, depended upon the Company for their supplies and their market, receiving goods on a barter basis at 50 per cent advance upon first London cost in exchange for wheat at three shillings per bushel. The missionaries received goods at an advance varying from 70 to 100 per cent upon first London cost.[1] While this small dependent community in itself constituted no particular problem for the Company, the rising agitation in the United States for the occupation of Oregon after 1838 threatened the Company's ascendancy in the region. This agitation presaged the more rapid growth of the settlement which would occur when pioneer farmers came to the distant valley in successive waves after 1842.

Although the process of settlement had just begun, Chief Trader James Douglas in 1838 predicted the ultimate doom of the fur trade in the vicinity of the lower Columbia and noted the condition of the Willamette settlement:

The interests of the Colony [the Willamette settlement], and Fur Trade will never harmonize, the former can flourish, only, through the protection of equal laws, the influence of free trade, the accession of respectable inhabitants; in short by establishing a new order of things, while the fur trade, must suffer by each innovation.

The only perceptible effect yet produced on our affairs, by the existence of the Settlement, is a restless desire, in the Company's servants, to escape from our service to the colony, but in the present state of the country, when the Settlers are so entirely dependent on us, that every man must go down to Vancouver, to sharpen his share, his coulter, and his Mattock, we have no reason to fear desertion, however, when the introduction of foreign capital terminates this dependence such events may be expected; and our general influence will decline as the wants of the Settlement find a provision in other sources. The feelings of the colonists generally are now favourable to the Company, the Canadians being attached from habit and association, identify as far as possible their interest with ours; the vagrant Americans respect power and integrity; but I fear that the Methodists nourish secret views, at variance with our interests.[2]

The Reverends Jason and Daniel Lee, the Methodists who aroused the suspicions of Douglas, were the first missionaries to arrive in the region. They had accompanied Wyeth on his second expedition in 1834, and had established their principal mission, with McLoughlin's encouragement, in the Willamette Valley near the French Canadian settlements ten miles north of the present site of Salem. Their supplies arrived on board Wyeth's brig, the *May Dacre,* in September 1834. By drawing bills on the Missionary Society in New York they obtained additional supplies, as needed, from the Hudson's Bay Company.

The Lees were zealous and devoted as they sought to improve the Indians by teaching religion, morality, and the arts of civilization. Amid severe hardships and disappointments they remained dedicated to these high purposes as they struggled to maintain themselves in the wilderness. There were few Indians in the immediate vicinity of their mission, however, and these few were among the most diseased and debilitated natives of the region. The Lees, nevertheless, established a school which by 1836 some twenty-two Indian and half-breed children attended. They also produced substantial crops of wheat, potatoes, oats, barley, and peas during the 1835 and 1836 seasons.

An example of their industry and enterprise was their participation in 1836 with other American and French Canadian settlers in obtaining cattle from California. Lieutenant William A. Slacum of the United States navy, an official representative of the United States government who visited Oregon in 1836, thought the little colony's most serious handicap was its lack of an independent supply of cattle. The Hudson's Bay Company let cattle out on loan but would not sell to the settlers. Slacum encouraged the settlers to form an association and to subscribe money to purchase cattle in California. He offered to convey a few settlers on board his ship free of charge to California where they could purchase some 500 head of cattle to be driven overland to the Willamette Valley. The settlers subscribed $1,600 of which $500 was advanced by Slacum to Jason Lee as the mission's share. The venture proved eminently successful as the settlers laid the foundations of the large cattle herds of the Willamette Valley. Stock raising thus became one of the mission's early enterprises.

In 1836 Jason Lee urged the Missionary Society to send him a substantial reinforcement. His reports pictured Oregon as a fair field for missionary endeavor, and as a result the society acted favorably and sent out two preachers, four women teachers, a physician, and two men for other secular positions. Those having families brought their wives and children. This, the first reinforcement, arrived at Fort Vancouver in 1837 in two groups, one on board the *Diana* and the other on the *Sumatra* after long Cape Horn voyages via the Hawaiian Islands. Supplies shipped out on both vessels for the missionaries had to be transported by canoe upstream some seventy miles from Fort Vancouver to the Willamette mission. The mission family now numbered thirty including wives and children. There was about an equal number of natives at the mission, or as Bancroft puts it, "one civilizer to every savage." The Rev. Daniel Lee now established a branch station at the Dalles of the Columbia, where he soon reported that he had baptized some 500 natives, the most noteworthy achievement of the Methodist Mission during its entire Oregon history.

Jason Lee, superintendent of the Oregon mission, and his associates at the mission headquarters developed agriculture, stock raising, milling and other mechanical arts to sustain them in the field. Douglas, as we have seen, suspected them, especially after the reinforcement of 1837, of having colonization as their main purpose, an aim "at variance" with the fur trade as he suggested. While Lee may have formulated his colonization aims by this time, the purpose of the various secular enterprises was to make the mission as self-sustaining as possible. His original purpose for locating his principal mission on the fertile prairie lands of the Willamette Valley was to provide the best possible base for a wide zone of missionary activity throughout the region. Regardless of his motives, he and his associates were to play a vital role in the colonization and early development of Oregon.

Meanwhile a second group of American missionaries had arrived. After a strenuous overland journey, missionaries of the American Board of Commissioners for Foreign Missions representing the Presbyterian, Congregationalist, and Dutch Reformed churches arrived in 1836. They established two stations at locations recommended by the Rev. Samuel Parker who had come to Oregon the previous year: one at Waiilatpu, near the Hudson's Bay Company's post at Fort Walla Walla, with Dr. Marcus Whitman in charge; and the other at Lapwai, farther to the north and east in the Nez Perce country, in charge of Whitman's assistant, the Rev. Henry H. Spalding. Like the Methodists the missionaries of the American Board were zealous and devoted. They were also ardent advocates of the American colonization of Oregon and their letters and reports like those of the Methodists helped to arouse the Oregon fever in the United States. They voluntarily pledged not to engage in the fur trade, and while they developed agriculture and milling to make their stations as self-sufficient as possible, their secular activity was not nearly as extensive as that of the Methodists. Consequently they did not threaten the operations of the Hudson's Bay Company in the interior. Like their Methodist colleagues they could purchase supplies from the Company with bills of exchange drawn on the American Board.[3]

Catholic missionaries, the Reverend Fathers F. N. Blanchet and M. Demers, secular priests from the Archdiocese of Quebec arrived in 1838. They came to the Oregon Country to serve the French Canadian settlements at French Prairie and Cowlitz Farm under the auspices of the Hudson's Bay Company. An additional purpose was to counteract the Methodist influence. They were to serve these purposes well and to become the Company's strongest allies. In 1842 Fathers Bolduc and Langlois arrived to reinforce the Catholic missionary effort. The presence of these priests in Oregon aroused the resentment, fear and never-ending wrath of both Protestant groups of missionaries, who thoroughly subscribed to the anti-Catholic nativist doctrine rampant in the United States.

Catholic and Protestant men of God now engaged in an uncompromising contest for the souls of natives and settlers. Missionaries on each side denounced their adversaries as the un-Christian agents of the devil, and proclaimed their own monopoly of the truth. Blanchet and Demers, in their official reports, refer to their opponents with such epithets as "ministers of error," "false prophets," and "Bible colporteurs," and to the Protestant doctrine as "damnable," "deplorable," and "scandalous." Protestant ministers were equally or even more intolerant in their vitriolic denunciations of "Popery" as a doctrine of "superstition and ignorance." While the natives were undoubtedly bewildered by conflicting interpretations of Christianity wherever Catholic and Protestant missionaries competed for their salvation, the priests seem to have enjoyed greater success by readily adapting to wilderness conditions and to have pursued their mission with greater zeal among the natives of the vast region. With the favor of the Hudson's Bay Company, the Catholic priests gained the advantage of direct access to remote Indian tribes in the vicinities of the Company's numerous outlying posts.[4]

Since 1824 the Hudson's Bay Company had reluctantly encouraged the missionary effort throughout its territories. The rising tide of humanitarianism in England in that decade had dictated this general policy. The Company could not risk being charged with failure to promote the moral and spiritual betterment of the natives if it were to remain secure in its monopoly. Early in his career George Simpson had thought that missionary work would detract from the efficient conduct of the fur trade; but on this matter the Governor and Committee made the policy, and Simpson

18

accepted the decision. He therefore encouraged missions when he thought their establishment was feasible. Consistent with this policy John McLoughlin welcomed the missionaries, both Protestant and Catholic, to Oregon, and encouraged them in their efforts to propagate the faith.[5] While the Catholic missionaries did not threaten the Company's economic ascendancy, the colonization efforts and nationalistic aims of the Methodists caused considerable apprehension among its officials.

The fame of Jason Lee, founder of the Methodist Mission in Oregon and its superintendent from 1834 to 1844, rests largely on his work as a colonizer. By 1837 or 1838, it appears that he had become convinced that all attempts to civilize the debilitated Indians of the Willamette Valley would fail. He was alarmed by the appearance of Catholic missionaries in the area in 1838 and sought to counteract their influence. An American colony where Methodism could spread and thrive under the dictates of the Gospel and the laws of the United States became his ideal. He was typical of the American frontier missionary so aptly described by de Tocqueville: "If you converse with these Missionaries of Christian civilization you will be surprised to hear them speak so often of the goods of this world, and to meet a politician where you expected to find a priest." American occupation of Oregon and the establishment of a Methodist commonwealth strong enough to withstand the corrupting influences of civilization apparently became a holy cause for Jason Lee. He wrote in 1843, after settlement had begun, "that the growth and spread, and rise, and glory and triumph of Methodism, in the Walamette [sic] Valley is destined to be commensurate with the growth and rise and prosperity of our new infant but flourishing and rapidly increasing settlement . . ."[6] Lee thus merged his religious, political and economic purposes. He was at once a zealous preacher and moralist, an ardent American nationalist, and a prophet of Manifest Destiny.

Lee looked to the future. Oregon's abundant resources and its advantages for ocean commerce were bound to attract settlers. He feared the possibility that they might be reckless and intemperate men from the mountains or, worse, renegades from foreign lands. The ideal settler for

19

his ideal Methodist commonwealth had to be a sober, moral and industrious American pioneer. To assure this outcome the advantages of Oregon had to be advertised. The authority of the laws of the United States had to be established in this distant land in order to attract the type of settlers desired by giving assurance of valid land titles and orderly government. Lee was the author of the first of many petitions from Oregon to the Congress of the United States praying for these benefits. A few American and French Canadian settlers signed this petition on March 16, 1838, and Lee himself carried it across the plains. On his arrival in Washington early in 1839, he delivered it personally to Senator Lewis F. Linn of Missouri, who a short time earlier, in December, 1838, had introduced the first of his several bills calling for the extension of American authority to Oregon. This marks the revival of congressional interest in Oregon reflecting the land hunger of people of the Mississippi Valley states and the commercial interests of New England. The Oregon Question was soon to become a major political issue in the United States.

James Douglas well understood Lee's motives at the time of the latter's departure for the United States. In Douglas' mind competition between the Hudson's Bay Company and a missionary society was a frightening possibility. He reported to the Governor and Committee as follows:

> The Revd. Mr. Lee . . . returned . . . to the United States, to make arrangements for importing goods. A vessel is, there-fore, expected, in the course of the next year, freighted by the Missionary Society, solely, or, in part, with other adven-turers, who may be deceived by false hopes of gain. It is difficult to anticipate their real intentions, and perhaps un-fair to question them; but I am naturally anxious about the designs of a body of men, who have the power of seriously injuring our business, and whose conduct may justify suspi-cion. It is my opinion, they will engage directly or indirectly in trade and their interference will be more detrimental to our interests, than the efforts of the most active commercial body. I really wish, such an event could be averted, by means of a settlement with them; but if that cannot be done, we . . . take the field . . . against them. It is a contest from which we can derive nether [sic] honour nor advantage. I know our motives and conduct will be misrepresented. If the eager spirit of rivalry should unfortunately beget a mu-tual hostility, their cause will attract general sympathy, and

by raising the cry of persecution against us, they may perhaps rouse the attention of government to the subject.[7]

Lee did much to arouse the Oregon fever. He preached the "gospel of Oregon" to prospective settlers in numerous churches in the western states on his way east in 1838. His petition soon became a part of Massachusetts Congressman Caleb Cushing's thorough report on Oregon. "We flatter ourselves that we are the germe of a great State," the petition reads, "and are anxious to give an early tone to the moral and intellectual character of its citizens." It emphasized the commercial advantages of the territory with respect to trade with China, Russia and other parts of the Northwest Coast, and especially with the Hawaiian Islands. The economy of the latter, which would soon be based upon a growing production of tropical products such as sugar and coffee, would nicely complement that of Oregon. At Newburyport, Massachusetts, he urged members of the Cushing family, veterans of the Pacific trade, to expand their commercial enterprises to include the Columbia, a suggestion that was soon to be followed. He persuaded the Missionary Society of the Methodist Church at New York, in spite of the apprehensions of some of its members, to send out another reinforcement of personnel and to provide more money and supplies for the Oregon mission. Everywhere he spoke he gave careful and encouraging explanations of the advantages of settling in Oregon. He thus became an effective agent of Manifest Destiny.[8]

Lee simply reasserted the well-known and often repeated American dream of commerce and empire. The idea of continental expansion coupled with Pacific commerce had survived, especially in the minds of New England men of commerce, since the days of the sea otter trade, the Lewis and Clark expedition, and the grandiose plans of John Jacob Astor. Acquisition of Pacific ports to facilitate the development of Pacific commerce had long been a major aim of American diplomacy.[9] The sea would automatically assure market outlets for a flourishing Oregon settlement, enthusiasts believed, and bring it into direct contact with the alleged riches of the Far East.

Hall J. Kelley, the New England schoolmaster who since 1829 had become the most noted propagandist for the settlement of Oregon, emphasized the expansion theme in his numerous tracts. After learning all he could about Oregon, Kelley became obsessed with the idea of a settlement there and in 1829 organized the American Society for Encouraging the Settlement of the Oregon Territory. Although Kelley's plan for an overland emigration in 1832 failed to materialize, he seems to have exerted some influence upon Wyeth and others who went on Wyeth's first expedition. Wyeth, a member of Kelley's society for a time, gained information about Oregon from him for the purpose of launching a trading expedition; but he had little interest in Kelley's comprehensive colonization plan. Lee first learned of Oregon from Kelley.

It was somewhat of a coincidence that Wyeth, Lee and Kelley were all at Fort Vancouver during the same season in 1834. Kelley had come by way of Mexico and California and had arrived at Fort Vancouver ill and destitute. He had joined Ewing Young's party going north from California and, because certain members of this party were accused by the governor of northern California of horse thievery, McLoughlin suspected the entire party for a time. Although he received proper care at Fort Vancouver, Kelley felt that he had been ostracized by the Hudson's Bay Company and neglected by his own countrymen. His unhappy experiences at Fort Vancouver contributed to the growth of his persecution complex, and account for his numerous false or prejudiced statements against the Hudson's Bay Company, written after his return to the United States. But through his writings and petitions to Congress he did much to inspire the Oregon fever.[10]

Kelley's writings inspired a group of preachers in Lynn, Massachusetts, to form the Oregon Provisional Emigration Society in 1838. Its purpose was to promote a systematic yearly emigration of 200 settlers and their families to Oregon. They requested assistance, information and supplies from the Hudson's Bay Company in return for their own guarantee not to engage in the fur trade. The Company assured them that they could expect friendship and assistance but that a formal agreement defining the particulars would be desirable. Like New Englanders before them, in explaining their plan to Caleb Cushing in 1839, they hesitated to embark without assurances in advance that the United States would provide government and security of land titles. The group intended to civilize and Christianize the Indians as a principal purpose but they also intended to develop the resources. The secretary of the society explained:

> Having reached the territory we shall seek such points of settlement as will afford the greatest facilities for intercourse with the tribes; for agriculture, manufactures, and commerce; and also for defense. . . . For our own emolument, we shall depend principally upon the flour trade, the salmon fishery, the culture of silk, flax, and hemp, the lumber trade, and perhaps a local business in furs. We shall establish a regular commercial communication with the United States, drawing supplies of men and goods from thence; and ultimately, we shall contemplate the opening of a trade with the various ports of the Pacific.[11]

Obviously the resources of Oregon were well known in New England. The society failed to put this plan into effect but their aims and Lee's, particularly those concerning commerce, soon became current in the halls of Congress and in newspapers throughout the country. The tiny group of Methodist missionaries in Oregon attempted to put them into effect.

The Methodist Missionary Society granted Lee's request for additional personnel in spite of the misgivings of some of its members. Fifty-one people, known as the "Great Reinforcement" and probably the largest missionary group ever to leave New York up to that time, sailed on board the *Lausanne* in 1839. After the long Cape Horn voyage they arrived on the Columbia in the spring of 1840. The group included five preachers, four women teachers, and eight men for specific secular jobs; the others were wives and children. They were cordially received at Fort Vancouver where they stopped briefly before hurrying on to the Willamette mission. The Methodist "family" in Oregon now numbered seventy-seven.

One of the members was George Abernethy, the new mission steward, who was destined to become chief executive of Oregon's Provisional Government and one of its most important early businessmen. He had been an accountant with considerable experience in the New York business community before his departure for Oregon. After arriving at

Fort Vancouver he stayed there for some time supervising the storage and trans-shipment of the *Lausanne's* cargo, valued at $13,000 or $14,000. Included in the cargo was the machinery for Lee's new grist mill.

Under Lee's supervision, Abernethy was charged with the duty of keeping accurate accounts of allowances, requisitions for goods, returns from the various secular enterprises, and all general expenses. Within a year, three new branch stations of the Methodist Mission in addition to the one already at the Dalles of the Columbia had been established: at Clatsop, at Nisqually, and at Willamette Falls. New headquarters were also established at Chemeketa, the present site of Salem and ten miles south of the old mission, where missionaries and secular personnel were soon busily engaged in farming, stock raising, milling and other secular activities, as well as in the education of a few Indians.

Although the mission group maintained their religious zeal, dissent and discord arose among them. Some of them resented the colonization effort since it caused them to neglect their missionary duties. This neglect was noticed by Lieutenant Charles Wilkes, of the United States Exploring Expedition, the American settlers, and Hudson's Bay officials. McLoughlin in 1844 reported that "since their large reinforcement came in 1840, these men have acted more as political partisans than as Missionaries." But to Lee, it seems, the interests of God and the imperial mission of the United States were one and the same. The Mission Board and some of Lee's own colleagues in the field could not reconcile these purposes so easily, and their refusal to do so became the source of much difficulty for the prophet of Manifest Destiny. Actually the Mission Board strictly charged the missionaries "to abstain from all unnecessary traffic and other secular affairs," and required the secular personnel to engage only in such enterprises as were necessary to sustain the missionary effort. They had no intention of sponsoring a program of colonization. While Lee expanded the zone of missionary activity among the Indians, preparation for the spread of Methodism among the expected settlers seems to have been a more important consideration.[12]

Lee's various sins, according to some of his colleagues, included not only the colonization purpose but speculation, maladministration and incompetence. Dr. Elijah White, a member of the 1837 reinforcement, broke with Lee as a result of a disagreement and returned to the United States in 1840 on board the *Lausanne,* with an adverse report to the Mission Board. Other criticisms of Lee's administration from dissatisfied missionaries followed. One of his disgruntled colleagues, the Rev. W. W. Kone, stationed at Clatsop, wrote in 1841 with reference to the Rev. Father F. N. Blanchet, that "one Roman Catholic Priest is doing more than all our missionaries." Another part of his report reads:

> From all that I can see I am prepared to assert that there is no possible necessity for my remaining in the country as a missionary, there are too many here already. Several families in the interior have abandoned their field, some are going home, and others are becoming farmers in the lower country. Within the bounds of our Mission the Indians are few in number, and *not prepared to receive the Gospel.* Mr. Lee is extremely desirous of keeping in the field all who are now here.

These reports tended to confirm the convictions of some members of the Mission Board that the "Great Reinforcement" of 1840 had been unwise.

While much of this dissent was no doubt due to the general unpreparedness of the missionaries for wilderness conditions, part of it resulted from Lee's poor administrative methods. He was imaginative and zealous but somewhat impractical. Distribution of supplies was needlessly difficult and expensive. Goods which had been transported upriver to the Willamette mission at Chemeketa had to be returned downriver to reach destinations at the branch stations. The Rev. J. P. Richmond at Nisqually on Puget Sound found it far less expensive to purchase supplies from the Hudson's Bay Company than to draw them from the distant Willamette mission. The Rev. Daniel Lee found that in order to obtain needed goods he must himself make the 160-mile trip from The Dalles to Chemeketa. The Rev. J. H. Frost, Kone's associate at Clatsop, noted the same difficulty and complained bitterly about the work involved in getting supplies and in building his station while all the secular personnel remained at the mission headquarters. "And it is not only the time of the missionary that is spent," he observed, "but his bodily strength is thus exhausted and his health impaired which must disqualify him for future usefulness." Frustrated and ineffective in his missionary work, he became convinced that his mission to the coastal Indians was useless and that religion could flourish only in a civilized society.[13]

Lee, lacking the knowledge necessary to manage the financial affairs of the mission, failed to delegate enough authority to Abernethy to assure greater efficiency. He allowed indiscriminate distribution of supplies without proper requisition or record. Thus Abernethy found the performance of his special duties impossible. "I had made up my mind," the steward wrote in July, 1841, "that if another Cargo of goods should come to this place and be disposed of as the Lausanne's Cargo had been—that it would be good for me to go home as I cannot possibly render an account of goods that are taken without my knowledge." Lee failed to submit the regular financial reports required by the Mission Board and explained that this was due partly to the fact that he was "not sufficiently acquainted with Bookkeeping to . . . report intelligibly the fiscal state of this Mission." He also refused the secular members of the mission a voice in the management of temporal affairs.

Lee faced many hardships. He had suffered the loss of both his first and second wives who had fallen victim to the ardors of frontier life. Unexpected sieges of sickness struck the mission community, and there was the constant hard physical work in which he willingly engaged. There was a severe fire at the mission headquarters and its new milling machinery broke down. As has been noted, throughout this period of hardship Lee had to contend with the dissent and dissatisfaction of some of his trusted colleagues who in his judgment were either unwilling to face wilderness conditions or were lacking in the proper qualifications for the work. As to their charges against him regarding his sponsorship of secular enterprises, was this really inconsistent with Methodism? John Wesley himself had taught the advancement of the material well-being of the individual and the divine proprietorship of wealth, and had seen no antithesis between religion and business.

In 1841 Lee permitted Abernethy to locate the mission store at the falls of the Willamette, a more convenient location twenty-five miles above the river's juncture with the Columbia. This was also the most promising industrial site in the territory. Now the steward believed that he could keep "the temporal affairs of the Mission on system." When the settlers came, the mission store was there to serve them with goods and credit; but its primary function was to serve the missionaries in the field, who were to receive goods at New York retail prices.[14] It was the first American mercantile establishment in the Willamette Valley to figure significantly in the process of settlement.

Abernethy was careful in his relations with Vancouver, for in spite of their generally hostile attitude toward the Hudson's Bay Company, the missionaries were in a great measure dependent upon its good offices. Some purchases paid for in drafts on the Mission Board in New York had to be made at the fort.[15] In 1839 one of the mission's bills on Messrs. Sands, Hodgson, Turner, and Co. for £1,000 was at first refused but ultimately paid after considerable delay, to the great annoyance of the Governor and Committee. They laid down the following general policy to McLoughlin in the same year:

> While these Missionaries confine themselves strictly to the avowed objects of their residence in the country we have no objection to their being supplied from our stores with such absolute necessaries in clothing &c. as they may require if they be in condition to pay for the same, but certainly not with goods for the purpose of dealing with Indians or our retired servants, nor to promote or facilitate the settlement of emigrants from the United States. . . .

McLoughlin considered the mission store as a competitor of some consequence. He was aware that the capital of the Methodists was derived from charitable sources but mistakenly believed that no account of its expenditure had to be rendered. The mission store at Willamette Falls was in a far better location to tap the trade of the few farmers of the upper valley than was Fort Vancouver.

But this was the only advantage. By contrast, the facilities of the fort were commodious indeed. Lieutenant Wilkes of the United States Exploring Expedition observed in 1841:

> Everything may be had within the fort: they have an ex-
> tensive apothecary shop, a bakery, blacksmiths' and coopers'
> shops, trade-offices for buying, others for selling, others
> again for keeping accounts and transacting business; shops
> for retail, where English manufactured articles may be
> purchased at as low a price, if not cheaper, than in the
> United States, consisting of cotton and woolen goods, ready
> made clothing, shipchandlery, earthen and iron ware, and
> fancy articles; in short, every thing, and of every kind and
> description, including all sorts of groceries.

Wilkes received goods at the fort at an advance of 80 per
cent on first London cost and assumed that this was the
standard mark-up. With regard to the exploring expedition,
McLoughlin thought it was good policy not "to take advantage of their wants" and to avoid being charged with "selling
at an exorbitant price."[16]

The Methodists were first to utilize the industrial potential of the falls of the Willamette. A group of settlers, most
of whom were members of the Methodist Mission, formed
the Island Milling Company in 1841. The following year
they erected a grist mill and a saw mill at the falls on the
small island in the river, soon known as Abernethy Island.
As early as 1829 the Hudson's Bay Company had asserted a
claim to the entire site bordering the falls on the east side
of the river, including the island, but had done nothing to
develop it beyond blasting a canal and cutting a small quantity of timber. Both Simpson and McLoughlin had realized
its potential and the latter thought possession on the part
of the Company would prove a valuable long-term investment. The Methodists had obtained permission from
McLoughlin to locate their mission buildings at the site
but, in 1841, Simpson ordered McLoughlin to build mills
there in keeping with the Hudson's Bay Company's practice
of meeting all competition and retaining control of the
import-export trade. Simpson observed that "it appears very
desirable that the Company should retain command of the
import and export business of this settlement, as long as
possible, to the exclusion of strangers. . . ." It was not until
1843 that McLoughlin built a saw mill and a grist mill on
the river bank opposite the island. In the meantime the
members of the Willamette Falls mission, in charge of the

Rev. A. F. Waller, were actively engaged in their own milling and building enterprises.

Wilkes, noting the advantages of the site, thought the Hudson's Bay Company was not unfair in trying to retain the trade. He observed: "I cannot help feeling it is quite unsuited to the life of a missionary, to be entering into trade of any kind. To embark in traffic must I think, tend to destroy the usefulness of the missionary; or divert his attention from the great cause in which he is engaged."[17]

A new effort to compete with the Hudson's Bay Company in the Oregon Country was undertaken in 1843 by J. P. Cushing and Company of Newburyport. With a fortune made in the China trade, the Cushings decided to investigate the commercial possibilities of Oregon, particularly the salmon fishery. They already had played a leading role in the expansion of America's maritime frontier. Their Oregon venture was no doubt influenced by Jason Lee's visit to Newburyport in 1839, but the traditions of the Northwest coastal trade were still alive and current among New England seamen and men of commerce.[18]

Whatever the reasons for the more recent failures of Wyeth and others, Captain John H. Couch of the brig *Maryland,* a representative of the Cushing firm, arrived on the Columbia in the fall of 1840. His was the first American trading vessel to enter the river since the arrival of Wyeth's *May Dacre* in 1834. He found that the native fishermen were unwilling to supply salmon to anyone but Hudson's Bay men, so his first effort was a failure. But this adventuresome Yankee explored the rivers thoroughly and carefully observed the possibilities for development of trade. He took his brig up the Willamette as far as the falls at a time when the river was unusually high. Although he discovered that the navigation of the river for that distance was impractical, he became convinced that any ship that could be navigated across the dangerous bar at the Columbia's mouth could safely reach a point on the Willamette twelve miles below the falls at any time of the year. At this point on the heavily wooded west bank he later made his claim for 640 acres. Here was the future site of Portland, a town Couch had a share in founding as a direct result of his experience on the river in 1840. In 1841 he sailed to Honolulu, sold his ship there, and returned to Newburyport on board a whaler.

Initial failure did not deter the Cushings from their plan to extend their commercial enterprise to Oregon, and Couch re-appeared on the river in 1842, as captain of the *Chenamus* and with a sizeable cargo of goods. Couch was the first American tradesman, except for Abernethy, whose business career, first at Oregon City and later at Portland, was identified with the early development of the region.[19] He established a store at Willamette Falls, soon to be called Oregon City.

Thus facilities to supply the new demands shortly to be created by the immigrations of 1842 and 1843 existed in Oregon. Most important was the Hudson's Bay Company with its ample stock of merchandise, its reliable source of supply, and its contacts with established avenues of commerce. But the mission store and Couch's new establishment were also to provide merchandise, credit, and employment for the new settlers. Agricultural production had begun and the mills of the mission and the Hudson's Bay Company could provide flour and lumber for the new settlers. Lee's "germe of a Great State" had taken root indeed.

Chapter II

Oregon Pioneers
and
McLoughlin

"To civilize and endure . . ."

The annual overland migrations to Oregon of the 1840s present a phenomenon unique in the history of the American frontier up to that time. Hitherto the westward march had been generally to contiguous areas. Now families in wagons drawn by oxen marched across plains, deserts and mountains to reach new homes and farms in the distant Willamette Valley near the Pacific Ocean. They came by the now reasonably well-defined Oregon Trail which provided an outlet for the pressures existing on the Missouri frontier.

In Missouri and elsewhere in the western states depression conditions following the panic of 1837 prevailed. Western farmers, particularly those of Missouri, suffered from over-production and low prices. They depended upon the Mississippi River as their only outlet, for East and West were not as yet knitted into a single economic unit by a network of railroads. Jesse Applegate, an Oregon immigrant of 1843, asserted that he had sold a steamboat load of bacon and lard in Missouri for only $100, and that bacon was so plentiful it was used on Mississippi steamboats for fuel. Produce from the western states glutted the New Orleans market and the future was not at all promising. Applegate and others also objected to slavery in Missouri and the economic system that forced independent farmers to compete with slave holders. Oregon's resources and prospects for the development of Pacific markets appealed to serious minded men who could afford the overland trip. The fertile land of the Willamette Valley, Oregon's mild, humid climate, its abundant timber, and its sea outlet were attractive, indeed, when compared with the treeless prairies and unnavigable rivers immediately to the west of the Missouri frontier. These advantages had been well advertised by Oregon enthusiasts, like Hall J. Kelley and Jason Lee, and soon appeared in the numerous emigrant guide-books. One major disadvantage in Oregon when compared with the Mississippi Valley, the authors of the guide-books admitted, was the unsuitability of its climate for growing corn. Weighed against this was the fact that elaborate facilities for the storage of hay and fodder for cattle during the winter months were unnecessary in Oregon.[1]

Thus economic considerations largely motivated emigration to Oregon. A British observer, Lieutenant William Peel of the H.M.S. *America* writing in 1845, while noting the economic problems in Missouri, wrote that some of the immigrants "come merely from speculation and a habit of restlessness," and others "either to receive or get rid of their debts or to escape justice."[2] Captain Avery Sylvester, an associate of Captain John H. Couch and another representative of the Cushing firm, saw American expansionism as an inherent attribute of the Anglo-Saxon "race." This perceptive sailor wrote as follows concerning the "Great Migration" of 1843:

> Whilst we were here, a large party of Americans, mostly Missourians, [arrived]. . . . They are well adapted for pioneering, and to this end to civilize and endure, and devote their attention. As soon as schools and churches make their appearance, and the chase becomes scarce, they sell their lands for the most that they can get, and retire to the West, where they take up new lands, shove back the Indians, and prepare the way for more advanced civilization. In this way this roving class of people . . . descendants of those who first landed in America . . . have been making gradual progress from the Eastern boundary of the United States to the western shores of Oregon. What turn they will make is more than I can tell, but one thing is sure, this place will hold but few of them, and that few the most civilized. The others will sift out to California and form a new Texas, most likely. In this way the U. S. will be enabled to take honorable possession of a great part of Mexico. O, Thou grasping, cool, calculating Anglo-Saxon race; is it thus thou dost intend to reduce all other races of men to thy subjection?[3]

The spirit of Manifest Destiny also motivated settlers who made the long trek to Oregon. This, simply stated, meant that the people of the United States were divinely predestined to preserve and extend American civilization and the democratic institutions of the United States upon the continent of North America and beyond. Manifest Destiny was thus an expression of American nationalism and democratic idealism, and as it grew in tempo during the 1840s, it was a force of some consequence in the expansionism of that decade.[4] No doubt many of Oregon's pioneers were emotionally inspired by ideals of patriotism, religion and duty.

The migrations of the early forties brought between 5,000 and 6,000 people to the Willamette Valley. Dr. Elijah White, the erstwhile colleague of Jason Lee and now official United States sub-Indian agent for Oregon, led the first important migration of some 100 to 150 pioneers across the plains in 1842. The Great Migration of 1843 followed when between 800 and 900 people reached the new land of promise. Successive waves of 1,400 and 3,000 immigrants arrived in the Willamette Valley in 1844 and 1845.[5]

Oregon's Provisional Government had been established only a few months when the Great Migration of 1843 arrived. The movement for government dates back to 1841, when owing to the circumstance of the death of Ewing Young, who died intestate, a series of meetings initiated by members of the Methodist Mission were held to consider the advisability of government. The movement culminated in the famous meeting at Champoeg on May 2, 1843, when the settlers by a close vote decided to organize. Several committees prepared reports and on July 5, 1843, the settlers adopted organic laws for the "Territory" of Oregon. These laws, in addition to a bill of rights, established a legislature of nine members, an executive committee of three, and a judiciary composed of one supreme court, a probate court and justices of the peace. A land provision allowed settlers to make individual claims of 640 acres but prohibited any settler from making claim to town sites or "extensive water privileges." It made a special concession to the Methodist Mission by granting "any claim of any mission of a religious character made previous to this time of an extent not more than six miles square." Further the Organic Act was to be in force "until such time as the USA extend their jurisdiction over us," and it specifically stated that the statutes of the Territory of Iowa were to be the laws of Oregon "in all cases

33

not otherwise provided for." The Hudson's Bay Company, Catholic missionaries, and most of the French Canadians opposed the government in this form. In 1844, when Applegate and others of the immigration of 1843 provided new leadership, the organic laws were amended so as not to jeopardize the allegiance or land claims of British subjects. Chief Factor John McLoughlin and the French Canadians then agreed to the jurisdiction of the Provisional Government, or to the "organization," as McLoughlin put it. In 1845 a single executive replaced the executive committee and George Abernethy was elected first and only governor of Oregon's Provisional Government.[6] Although defeated in their hope to gain thirty-six square miles of land including the townsite at Willamette Falls, the Methodist missionaries continued to influence the affairs of the Provisional Government, and its establishment may be considered one of their achievements. The new government also evinces the traditional concern of American frontiersmen for law and order and their alacrity in creating government when no other provision for it existed.

The early immigrants, especially those of 1843, seem to have been generally poor and some were actually destitute upon arrival. Most had had scarcely enough resources to finance the journey across the plains for themselves and their stock. The Hudson's Bay Company and the American merchants then in Oregon quickly absorbed the small amounts of money brought by the immigrants in payment for necessities. The immigrant could not replenish his cash supply since the barter economy so essential for the fur trade, prevailed in the area.[7]

As has been noted, a few business establishments existed in Oregon when the early immigrants arrived. In addition to the facilities of the Hudson's Bay Company at Fort Vancouver, there were the stores of the Methodist Mission and John H. Couch at Willamette Falls, or Oregon City, the name now given to the new town. Here, in 1843, F. W. Pettygrove of Maine, representing Benson and Bro. of New York, established a third American mercantile firm. He arrived with $15,000 worth of goods on board the bark *Fama*, which also brought out supplies for the missions. McLoughlin described Pettygrove as an "American shopkeeper, with a few articles suitable for farmers." While McLoughlin treated the newcomer with his usual kindness, he was quite curious about Pettygrove's invoices and intentions. Partly in response to this threat of new opposition McLoughlin stepped up the Company's development at Willamette Falls and established a Hudson's Bay branch store there in 1844.[8]

Humanitarianism and practical considerations dictated McLoughlin's policies toward the early immigrants. Owing to the false statements in some of the Oregon propaganda and the intense nationalism it inspired, many of the immigrants were extremely hostile to the Hudson's Bay Company upon arrival. According to McLoughlin, some even believed that they would have to defend themselves by force of arms against this "foreign monopoly." Shortly, however, responsible Americans realized their dependence upon the Honourable Company for supplies, a market for their produce and the peaceful conduct of the Indians, and their hostility abated. Peter H. Burnett, an immigrant of 1843, wrote:

> Had it not been for the generous kindness of the gentlemen in charge of the business of Hudson's Bay Company we should have suffered much greater privations. The company furnished many of our immigrants with provisions, clothing, seed and other necessaries on credit. Many of our immigrants were unworthy of the favors they received, and only returned abuse for generosity.[9]

McLoughlin considered his assistance to the settlers the only practical course to follow. Fort Vancouver, the entrepot for the entire fur trade west of the Rockies, and other Company property were vulnerable, McLoughlin realized, as Americans, many of whom were hostile, arrived in increasing numbers each year. The vulnerability of Fort Vancouver was one reason, though not the principal one, for the Company's decision in 1843 to establish its headquarters on Vancouver Island as soon as practicable. In defending his policies McLoughlin reported to the Governor and Committee in 1845, as follows:

> I have always found it best to be watchful without appearing to be so, as the appearance of fear incites aggression, and if we had refused assistance to these men, and that driven by their wants they had made an attack upon our property . . . the world, anxious to throw discredit on all our proceedings, would have said we deserved to suffer. . . .

McLoughlin requested Company officials to seek the protection of the British government for the property and personnel of the Hudson's Bay Company on the coast. The Governor and Committee replied that no such protection could be expected, but with the renewed attention given to the Oregon Question by the British government, the sloop of war, H.M.S. *Modeste*, appeared in the Columbia in 1844, and in the following year the fifty-gun frigate H.M.S. *America* began cruising off the Oregon coast.[10]

American merchants, as well as McLoughlin, extended credit to the destitute immigrants of 1843. For reasons already explained, McLoughlin abandoned his former practice of extending credit to Americans only "to the amount of two or three pounds," and by the spring of 1844, he had allowed credit to the amount of £6,606, or about $29,330, to 300 or 400 Americans. Couch and the mission store each also sold about $30,000 worth of goods on credit to the new settlers. In 1845 Couch offered to sell his debts to the Hudson's Bay Company for $30,000; and the mission did likewise, but for $27,000, or $3,000 less than the amount Abernethy took them for in 1846. McLoughlin, of course, refused both these offers.[11] Pettygrove probably granted credit also. But as the supplies of the American merchants approached depletion there was little opportunity for them to replenish their stocks owing to the inadequate export market. This, of course, was no problem for the Hudson's Bay Company since it still practically controlled the import-export business of the region. In any case facilities for supply and credit were available to the early settlers and their situation was not dissimilar to that of their predecessors on the American frontier where such facilities were within reasonable distances.

Sir George Simpson severely criticized McLoughlin's credit policy. In his dispatch to the Governor and Committee of June 20, 1844, Simpson expressed his disapproval as follows:

> An extensive trade in buying & selling seems to be carried on at Ft. Vancouver with the settlers: but although the selling prices are high, say 80 & 100 p. Cent advance on prime cost (grain & furs being payable in goods at 50 p. Cent and a dollar valued at 4/6) we are very doubtful that this is a remunerating business, especially so, as we observe in the Columbia accounts of this year, that credit is taken for a

sum of £6,000 for debts owing by the settlers, many of which, I fear, are doubtful, while others are unquestionably bad.

With this report, Company officials naturally became apprehensive and directed that the practice "should be gradually discontinued and one of prompt payment, either in cash or goods, substituted." Consequently McLoughlin granted little credit in 1844, and none in 1845. Company officials also instructed him to charge all settlers and missionaries one hundred per cent advance upon first London cost on all items. McLoughlin had been regulating his prices according to the competition and the demand, and he thought the Company's new directive would be impossible to carry out. It became the standard practice of his successors after his resignation in 1846, however.

While McLoughlin's credit policy was a relatively minor issue among the several points of disagreement between Company officials and himself, he defended it ably. He thought it eminently sound on practical and humanitarian grounds and justified it accordingly. He had prevented Indian outrages against the immigrants of 1842 and 1843, and the actual starvation of some of "these poor people," he maintained. If he had failed, not only would the fur trade have suffered, but there would have been other dire results. He wrote:

> Such an outcry would justly have been raised against us, that even you in London would have suffered by it, and be blamed for the inhuman conduct of those persons managing the business of which you had the supreme direction, and I believe you would have been among the first to censure my conduct, and in acting as I have done I firmly believe time will prove I have not only fulfilled the dictates of humanity, but most effectually promoted the best interests of the Company, as after all, these men are paying their debts (charged with interest at 6 per cent) and the whole amount will be considerably reduced this year [1845], and though we may and will lose some, still on the whole we will draw in a sufficient sum to pay and leave us a handsome profit on the whole amount, for I must do the Americans the justice to say that as a body they are most anxious to pay their debts. . . .

In meeting American competition McLoughlin followed the same general methods previously used so effectively in the fur trade and fisheries. The specific instruction governing American competition issued by the Governor and Committee in August of 1835 was still in effect. "Whenever they attempt to establish a Post on shore," the instruction states, "we should have a party to oppose them, and to undersell them even at a loss." In 1841, as mentioned above, Simpson had ordered McLoughlin to take measures to hold the import-export business of the Willamette community as long as possible and to develop the Willamette Falls. Again in 1843, McLoughlin had been instructed to follow the same general principles as before in meeting the opposition of Captain Couch, and "to endeavor to defeat the object of the intruder by every fair means within your power, rendering his speculation unprofitable, and selling at a small or even no profit for a time."

In following the letter and spirit of these instructions McLoughlin used every facility at his command to oppose American mercantile, milling, fishing and shipping enterprises. As has been noted, he erected a flour mill and a saw mill at the falls in 1843, and established a branch store there a year later. While he built and operated these establishments as regular Hudson's Bay enterprises, he let the settlers believe that he owned and operated them as his own private business, for fear that, owing to their hostility toward the Company, the settlers would destroy the buildings if these were known to be Company property. The store was soon known to be a Hudson's Bay operation, but since it was most inexpedient for the Company to try to make good a claim for land, McLoughlin maintained his individual claim to the mill and townsite. Although he resided at Fort Vancouver, he operated the mills at Oregon City himself and placed Chief Trader Francis Ermatinger in charge of the store. Warehouses for the storage of wheat were also built at Oregon City and at Champoeg. Until 1846, McLoughlin and Company officials considered all these trading enterprises a part of the regular business of the Columbia Department.[12]

An early attempt by Americans to develop the lumber export trade in competition with the Hudson's Bay Company deserves mention. Henry H. Hunt and Tallmadge B. Wood, immigrants of 1843, established a mill on the lower Columbia some thirty miles upriver from Fort George

(Astoria) expressly for the Hawaiian trade. Hunt had hauled his machinery overland. Albert E. Wilson, who had been employed by the Cushings to manage the Oregon City store in Couch's absence, joined in partnership with Hunt and Wood to give the new concern the advantage of reasonable freight rates on board the Cushing brig *Chenamus,* then under the command of Captain Avery Sylvester. The mill with a daily output of up to 3,000 board feet was in operation early in 1844. Sylvester's cargo of 50,000 board feet of lumber, loaded out in March, brought around $20 per thousand in the island market. James Birnie, who had managed the Hudson's Bay station at Fort George, resigned his post and joined the milling enterprise with a one-fourth interest in 1845.[13] Sylvester's description of the little mill is interesting:

> It is situated on the west bank of the Columbia . . . on a little stream that will carry it about 9 months in a year. This stream has a fall of about 60 ft. The mill is on the precipice or bank, and is carried by an over-shot wheel 20 ft. in diameter. Thirty-six inches of water with this wheel will carry two run of saws. . . . Logs can be had at it two or three years, with little more trouble than to roll them in, and this can be done on each side of the stream.[14]

Sylvester, representing the Cushings, made the run from the Columbia to the Hawaiian Islands at irregular intervals during 1844 and 1845. He exchanged lumber, flour and salmon for coarse sugar, coffee and other mechandise with American merchants there. He attempted to carry out the Cushing plan for the development of the salmon trade and reported having sold 250 barrels of salmon costing not more than $5.00 per barrel on the Columbia at a handsome profit in the islands. Competition with the Hudson's Bay Company in the salmon fishery was difficult, however, because the natives who supplied the fish continued to deal with the Company as a matter of custom. The Company, whose ships made two or more trips to the islands yearly, seem to have had a decided advantage in the limited Hawaiian trade.*

*Sylvester's cargo on board the *Chenamus* bound for the islands in August 1844 included: 293 barrels of salmon, 32,480 board feet of lumber, 36,250 shingles, fifty barrels of flour, three barrels of peas, and a few miscellaneous articles. Edmond S. Meany, Jr., The History of the Lumber Industry in the Pacific Northwest to 1917 (Ph.D. Thesis, Harvard University, 1935), p. 68.

McLoughlin reported the cargo of the bark *Cowelitz* leaving Fort Vancouver for Oahu on July 19, 1845 as "752 Barrels Flour at $5 p. Barrel, 52 M feet Deals

Sylvester left Oregon in September 1845 and the Cushings gave up their Oregon enterprise except for Couch's mercantile business at Oregon City.[15]

Pettygrove became the Hudson's Bay Company's principal American competitor by mid-decade. He and his associates carried on the Hawaiian trade with the same irregularity as had Sylvester, while the greater share of it remained in the hands of the Hudson's Bay Company. Pettygrove also engaged in the fur trade on a small scale, and though he expected to export his returns, he found McLoughlin's prices much higher than he could obtain in New York. Pettygrove, according to his own account, however, competed successfully against the Hudson's Bay Company in his mercantile and grain purchasing enterprises. He built a store and a warehouse for the storage of grain at Champoeg where he purchased large quantities of grain yearly.[16]

Meanwhile the tension between McLoughlin and officials of the Hudson's Bay Company mounted and was soon to reach the breaking point. Since 1841, Sir George Simpson and the Governor and Committee had become increasingly dissatisfied with McLoughlin's administration of the Columbia Department, owing largely to circumstances entirely unrelated to the process of settlement. Fur prices fell during the early forties when, at the same time, there was a constantly decreasing supply. The Governor and Committee expressed their dissatisfaction in a dispatch to Simpson dated June 1, 1843, as follows:

> We cannot indeed contemplate either the present state or future prospects of the fur trade on the west side of the mountains without Anxiety. Although there appears to have been no remission of zeal or exertion on the part of the Gentlemen in charge of the different establishments, the trade has fallen off greatly for two successive years, marking, it is to be feared, a rapidly progressive diminution of the fur bearing animals.

While the department may not have been as remunerative as it had been formerly, available evidence shows that it

at $15 p. M feet, 200 Barrels salt Salmon at $5 p. Barrel, 45 Spars at $5 each, 53 M Shingles at $4 p. M, the amount of the Invoice is $5885, which is a great deal less than half what the cargo will bring, the Deals will sell for about $50 p. M feet the Spars are valued at what they cost to put them on board, but as they are large, several 72 feet long fit for Masts, and in demand, they ought to sell well, but I invoice them low to save duties." McLoughlin to Governor and Committee, July 19, 1845, *McLoughlin's Fort Vancouver Letters*, Third Series, p. 85.

was not unprofitable. McLoughlin estimated the profits for outfits 1841, 1842, and 1843, according to scales provided him by the Company and upon the basis of actual returns, to be £22,974, £16,982, and £21,726, respectively. Douglas' figures for the returns for outfits 1842 and 1844 are £16,126 and £16,868, totals which he expected to be roughly equivalent to the profits for those years. Simpson expected a 25 per cent reduction in price, which would have resulted in losses for 1842 and 1843, but this, apparently, did not materialize. Furthermore, Professor Galbraith states that the annual net profits for the Company's operations south of the 49th parallel alone, for the seven-year period preceding 1846, averaged more than £40,000 of which £30,000 were the profits from the trade and sales at Fort Vancouver.[17] The Company's financial records, which have been unavailable to the present writer, may reveal more precise information as to profits derived from its several enterprises. One would assume from the published correspondence that the Company's business with the American settlers was relatively unimportant in the total picture.

Dissatisfaction with McLoughlin's administration of the Columbia Department derived in great part from his serious quarrel with Sir George Simpson concerning the conduct of the fur trade and more personal matters. These can be only briefly summarized here. McLoughlin and Simpson disagreed about the northern coastal trade, the steamer *Beaver*, the closing of the California station, and the manner in which the investigation of the murder of McLoughlin's son, John McLoughlin, Jr., had been conducted. McLoughlin favored the pursuit of the northern coastal trade through the use of permanent posts, whereas Simpson believed that the Russian agreement of 1839 had rendered the posts, except for one or two, unnecessary. The steamer *Beaver* could carry on the trade on the coast most efficiently, Simpson believed, while McLoughlin nursed a deep prejudice against this little ship. Simpson had become highly skeptical about the California station at the very time it was established in 1841, and became increasingly impatient with McLoughlin's tardiness in closing that branch of the business. McLoughlin grieved over the loss of his son and with extreme bitterness blamed Simpson for mishandling the investigation of the murder which had occurred at Stikine in 1842. On this matter Simpson seems to have been in the wrong with the weight of the argument favoring McLoughlin, but the Governor and Committee, while sympathizing with McLoughlin, could not repudiate Simpson. Another issue between the two men was the difficulty of finding men for employment in McLoughlin's department because of the alleged severity of the discipline prevailing on the west side of the mountains. Consequently some who were employed were renegades who made McLoughlin's administration more difficult. The Governor and Committee became increasingly annoyed with McLoughlin's dispatches defending his conduct and containing long, detailed and repetitious discussions of all aspects of his quarrel with his superior. Simpson, moreover, had come to rely more upon the reports of McLoughlin's subordinates, Chief Factors James Douglas, and Peter Skene Ogden and others, than upon the advice of McLoughlin. Thus, much to his embarrassment and chagrin McLoughlin lost his former prestige in Company circles both in England and America.[18]

One point of difference between McLoughlin and Simpson had very much to do with the American settlement in the Willamette Valley. It grew out of Simpson's decision, in 1841, to develop the Willamette Falls site and the instructions McLoughlin received to meet all American competition in the same manner as he had done previously. These measures led McLoughlin into a controversy with the Methodist missionaries over his claim to the town and water power site at the falls. The Company, the reader will recall, had asserted a claim to this favorable location in 1829, when McLoughlin blasted a canal and cut a few logs there. Nothing further was done owing to the Company's statement of policy, dating from 1824, prohibiting expensive establishments south of the Columbia. Thus Simpson's decision to develop the falls in 1841 was a departure from this long standing policy, when the prospect for a boundary settlement on the Columbia was even less favorable to the British than in 1824. But in 1841, neither Simpson nor McLoughlin seemed to question the propriety of building mills at this site in the name of the Hudson's Bay Company for the purpose of keeping the import-export business of the region under the Company's control.

The Methodists assumed that Oregon was already American territory and that they could lay claim to the soil as American citizens. To be sure, they had obtained permission from McLoughlin when they built their mills, store, and other buildings at Willamette Falls and established their branch mission there in 1841 and 1842. But no one knew how the Hudson's Bay Company would fare in the treaty settlement, and the Methodists knew very well that no corporation could hold land by preemptive right under the laws of the United States. Through their influence, as has been noted, the organic laws of the Provisional Government sanctioned the Methodist claim and thus denied McLoughlin's, but this clause was deleted when the organic laws were revised in 1844. McLoughlin, furthermore, did not reside on his claim until 1846, a weakness in terms of American law that the Methodists did not hesitate to exploit.

McLoughlin, however, had assumed the role of town proprietor at Oregon City in 1843. As has been mentioned, he built mills there in that year and established a branch store there a year later. He declared the mills to be his own private venture in order to protect the property from possible hostile action on the part of the settlers. He surveyed the townsite in 1843 and began selling or renting lots, also as his own individual enterprise. But his position was a constant source of embarrassment since he could not demonstrate his right to a proprietary role nor the validity of the deeds he issued.[19]

In March 1843, McLoughlin requested advice from the Company as to how the claim should be maintained. He thought it should be secured in the name of an individual, but wished to know whether the Company could claim the site, or whether he should claim it for the Company. "If either of these can be done, I will do it at once," he wrote, but "If the Company cannot keep it in their name, nor I cannot keep it for them in mine, I will then keep it in my own name on my own account." Adam Thom, the Company's recorder, explained that the validity of any claim would depend ultimately upon the law code of the new country. This was the only possible legal answer, although there was the possibility that the boundary settlement might grant some concession or guarantee of the

Company's property rights. Thom's opinion did not satisfy McLoughlin. He had proposed three alternatives for asserting the claim and the Company responded with no constructive advice—only an opinion written in legalistic terms which McLoughlin said he could not even understand. Thereafter, as he continued his proprietory role, he seems to have been confused as to which of the three purposes for holding the claim he actually followed.[20]

Meanwhile Simpson lost enthusiasm for the Willamette Falls project and regretted his decision to develop it. As early as 1842 he had begun to suspect that British diplomats would fail to establish the Columbia as the boundary. As the negotiations became more delicate the Company had to recognize the precarious nature of its tenure on lands south of the Columbia as well as the difficulty of recovering debts in a community where its rights could be denied at any time. In view of these considerations, Douglas advised against the maintenance of an expensive outlay at Oregon City. McLoughlin believed, however, that the Americans would respect the Company's property rights in the boundary settlement, and that the Company should take full advantage of the commercial and industrial opportunities at Oregon City at least until the matter of sovereignty was settled.[21]

McLoughlin unwittingly aided Company officials in making their decision to reduce the Oregon City outlay. In 1845 he conveniently offered to purchase the mills there for the amount they had cost and sent drafts on his own personal account, amounting to £4,173 11s. 6d., in payment. His purpose for making the purchase was not clear because of the ambiguity of his offer. It could have been interpreted as a desire on his part for the Company to refuse acceptance of his drafts, or as a sincere offer to purchase the property. Simpson gave the latter interpretation and accepted the drafts as a *bona fide* payment for the property. But Company officials had already decided to relieve McLoughlin of his superintendency, to transfer him to some location east of the mountains, and to end his special salary of £500. Simpson knew these decisions had been made at the time he accepted the drafts, and McLoughlin did not. Simpson also knew, according to McLoughlin, that the absolute conditions upon which

McLoughlin renewed his contract with the Company in 1839 were that he would have the superintendency of the Columbia Department and the special salary of £500.

The contemplated changes in his status were like successive blows to McLoughlin, and his consternation and bitterness seems to have colored his later correspondence with Company officials. He contended that the Company should not have accepted his drafts, since he merely wanted some tangible evidence of a sale having been made, as a "test of proprietorship" to support his claim against the Methodists and other Americans. In defense of his action he also referred to instructions requiring him to meet American competition and to extend British influence. The establishments at Willamette Falls were necessary, he contended, if he were to carry out these instructions and he resented the implication on the part of Company officials that he was lacking in zeal. In any case he would not have submitted his drafts had he known of the impending changes in his status. Since Simpson knew of these changes at the time he accepted the drafts, McLoughlin felt that he should at least have been given the opportunity to reconsider. As it was he was forced to resign in order to attend to a claim that otherwise would have been worthless to him had he not made a substantial investment in it. Perhaps it suited Simpson's purpose to force McLoughlin's resignation under these humiliating circumstances and to end a relationship that had grown difficult. Simpson and Company officials seem never to have understood the predicament in which McLoughlin found himself.[22]

Historians generally have dealt kindly with McLoughlin while placing the Methodists under a cloud of suspicion for their alleged duplicity in their attempt to win the Oregon City land claim. Frances Fuller Victor in the Bancroft history, for example, is unconvincing in her attempt to uphold McLoughlin's position and the nationalistic aims of the Methodists at the same time.[23] The action of the missionaries on this and other matters seems consistent if one grants their nationalistic purpose as a good end. This purpose, it will be recalled, was to establish an American community where Protestantism and the democratic ideals and institutions of the United States would flourish, and one in which the Hudson's Bay Company and its Catholic allies would have little or no influence. The conflicting claims of McLoughlin and the Methodists had little validity in the absence of a law code, but given the fact that both parties knew that it was highly unlikely that the British would be favored in the area south of the Columbia, the Methodist position was superior to that of their adversary even from the legal standpoint.

McLoughlin's action, moreover, provides a case for duplicity or confused judgment. He was caught in a dilemma in trying to preserve the land claim for the Company as a matter of duty while publicly proclaiming it to be his own private venture to the American settlers. Regardless of his intent at the time he purchased the mills, he had been willing previously to hold the claim for the Company in his own name. His reasons for making the purchase can not be determined exactly. Perhaps all he desired was evidence that he had sent the drafts and that otherwise the sale remained fictitious. In view of his growing attachment for Oregon City and his stubbornness in promoting its interests, it seems that the purchase offer was a sincere one at the time it was made; but that he would not have made it if he had known that he was to be deprived of his superintendency and extra emolument.

When McLoughlin purchased the mills, Simpson ordered a gradual curtailment of all the Company's operations south of the Columbia. Hereafter the Company could purchase no more wheat from the settlers than that necessary to supplement its own production and that of its subsidiary, the Puget Sound Agricultural Company, in order to meet the Russian contract plus a reserve to provision whatever ships of the British navy that might call at Fort Vancouver or Fort Victoria. In the fall of 1845 McLoughlin had 44,000 bushels of wheat on hand, or enough to produce the flour necessary for the Russian contract and 6,000 additional barrels, which he hoped to sell in Hawaii. He had already curtailed his purchases, however, and wrote in his last official report of November 20, 1845, that "At present we purchase wheat at 60 cents per bushel payable in goods at 100 per cent advance, but only from a few good customers whom out of policy we cannot cast off."

The Company thus restricted the market for the Willamette Valley's basic staple and the principal commodity having exchange value. The settlers naturally concentrated on wheat production for their own food needs and the growing local market assured by each new wave of immigration appearing in the fall. But surpluses had to be used to purchase goods and the Hudson's Bay Company was the best source of supply. The export market, which the Company practically controlled, could not absorb the surpluses and thus the community suffered a real handicap. McLoughlin, if he had been permitted a free hand at Oregon City in developing the Company's enterprises, would have tried to expand the export market. He was certain that exports of flour, lumber, and salmon would become increasingly profitable in the Hawaiian market. He had already explored the possibilities of a market for provisions in the French colony of Tahiti. These markets were limited and little possibility for their expansion existed.

McLoughlin argued vigorously against the Company's curtailment of its Oregon City enterprises. If he had continued in charge without restriction he would have pursued every trading advantage as long as it was possible to do so. The flour and lumber necessary for export could be produced far cheaper at Oregon City than at Fort Vancouver, he asserted. Owing to the convenience of the location for the settlers, the Company sold its goods at not less than 133 per cent advance upon first cost there. He, therefore, believed it far more economical and profitable for the Company's principal flour and saw mills to be located at the new town, the store there retained, and the entire operation expanded. He felt that the management of the store should be in charge of a commissioned officer rather than a clerk, or an American, as Simpson's new order suggested. Profits from the Company's Oregon City establishments totaled £3,854 in 1845, and McLoughlin believed these would increase in succeeding years if his plans were to be followed. He felt victimized by the Company's reversal of its traditional policy concerning competition and the extension of British influence. Furthermore, he had much more confidence in the Americans than did Simpson. In rebuttal to Simpson's statement that "there

47

is no honor nor honesty among these people," McLoughlin observed that the Americans were paying their debts and seemed quite anxious to do so.[24]

McLoughlin also noted, partly in defense of the Americans, that there were many men of means among the immigrants of 1845. They "brought large herds of cattle," he wrote, "and judging by their appearance, they seem with few exceptions to have been in easy circumstances in their own Country." McLoughlin's observation is corroborated by the following statement of a Missouri resident suggesting that Oregon immigrants enjoyed greater affluence than was usually the case on a new frontier:

> . . . You ask me to account for the mania for Oregon that prevails in Missouri, and seem to think that it does not say much in favor of our State, that so many of our citizens are leaving it . . . and you must know that no very small amount of means is essential to procure the necessary outfit. It may, therefore, he taken for granted, that the emigrants from our state who are seeking a home beyond the Rocky Mountains, belong to the most enterprising and patient and resolute portion of our population, and are very far from being the poorest people in the country. . . . They are rather different from those who acted as pioneers in the Western states, and whose object, in part at least, seems to have been to avoid the restriction of salutary law and order . . . there are many, who are actuated by the very laudable purpose of carrying the principles of our religion and government to that part of the world. . . .[25]

Meanwhile the Methodist Mission suffered new tribulations. McLoughlin reported, probably with considerable satisfaction, that "the Methodists are broken both as a Mission and as Store Keepers." When the settlers arrived, the mission had met the new demands as best it could and had granted an extensive amount of credit; and its various enterprises gave the new immigrants considerable opportunity for employment. But the fact that the missionaries were so extensively engaged in such enterprises as merchandising, milling, farming, stock raising, and the mechanical arts caused the settlers to suspect and to resent them. Although the mission store had an ill-assorted stock, some of which were donation goods not worth the freight charges required to ship them out, its manager, George Abernethy, had expected to clear at least $10,000 on the goods that had been shipped out most recently. These, apparently, were the supplies shipped on board Pettygrove's ship, the *Fama*.

But the Methodist Missionary Board in New York had become increasingly alarmed about the confused state of the Oregon mission particularly as to its secular affairs, reported by returning ministers. They were as apprehensive about bad debts as were the officials of the Hudson's Bay Company. One of several charges made by the Board against Jason Lee was: "The Superintendent of the Oregon Mission has spent $100,000 and no account of disbursements had been rendered." They dismissed him peremptorily in 1844, a fact which Lee learned, to his amazement, in Hawaii while en route to the United States by sea.

In July 1844, Lee appeared before the Mission Board in New York to defend his administration of the Oregon mission. Although he had difficulty explaining his financial policies, he succeeded in his defense and the Board exonerated him on all charges of maladministration. After this ordeal Lee returned to his boyhood home of Stanstead, Canada, where he became ill and died on March 12, 1845. In the meantime the Mission Board had sent the Rev. George Gary to Oregon to succeed Lee as superintendent of the Oregon mission with specific instructions to end its confused state of affairs and to close out the secular business.[26]

After investigating the situation this ill-tempered old minister stopped the credit and employment policies of the mission entirely and thus contributed to the growing resentment of the settlers toward the mission. Gary reported the situation he found as follows:

> Under the former business managements, the prejudice of [this] community was [that] this mission was of a speculative and monopolizing character. Now as our business closes up and it is difficult to get mission drafts from us, we are ruining the country. Formerly when an emigrant came or anyone and wanted employ, the mission had it for him at a high price, and he soon could get a draft and everything went very fine. Now the mission has little or no employ of this kind. . . . Almost everyone, or at least quite a proportion of those who have been in this region for two or more years and are well off have received their foundation or start from the mission. The news of this has spread and people have lately come . . . with the expectation the

Methodist mission will be glad to employ them; but finding it otherwise, they are seriously disappointed. So you see the mission has the curses or rather their superintendent's, Bro. Lee, for monopoly and speculation; his successor for this sudden shock and revulsion in business.[27]

Thus the mission was reduced to a strictly religious project. Gary was anxious to recover the mission's investments as far as possible, and it took about two years to evaluate the assets and liabilities and to close out the business. In most cases the secular members of the mission simply took over the enterprises in which they were already engaged after making financial arrangements with Gary.

Particularly troublesome were the debts owed the mission, which by 1846 were estimated at $30,000. George Abernethy finally agreed to take them over for $20,000 along with $10,000 of the mission's liabilities. He gave security for the balance of $10,000. He had earlier purchased the goods on hand at the rate of 25 per cent advance on cost, except for the old donation goods, which he bought at 50 per cent discount. Three years later he reported: "I can say one thing for the people of Oregon they pay up well though not quick. I shall not lose $2,000 out of the $30,000 I had to collect. I have their notes drawing 10 per cent and allow the Mission six per cent two years I paid no interest to the Mission." In 1846 Abernethy also acquired complete control of the Island Milling Company.[28] Thus he was prepared to go into business on a large scale with a loan of capital originally derived from gifts to the Missionary Society of the Methodist Church.

Settlement of the mission's financial affairs was also involved in the intricacies of the land controversy between McLoughlin and the Methodists over the Oregon City townsite. In order to possess all his claim in 1844, McLoughlin had to pay $500 to the Rev. A. F. Waller, formerly in charge of the Willamette Falls branch of the mission, and $5,400 to the mission itself for lots he had donated. McLoughlin thought the mission should have returned the lots to him, since they were no longer required for the purpose for which he had donated them. "I had to purchase them at an enormous amount," the embittered town proprietor wrote, "and this is the treatment I received from the Methodist Mission in Oregon." He had done his utmost to help the missionaries, he noted, "because I thought they came to teach 'thou shalt not covet thy neighbours house nor his ox nor anything that is his' and that of course they would practice the doctrine they taught."[29]

Owing to circumstances already related, McLoughlin resigned from service with the Hudson's Bay Company and retired to Oregon City in 1846. He continued his proprietory role while operating the flour mill as his own business and renting the saw mill to an American. He retained all his benefits as a retired officer of the Hudson's Bay Company but lost his special annual emolument of £500, after May 1846. He received his full chief factor's share of the profits until June 1, 1850, and a half-share for another five years. That he was cut off from all benefits after his resignation and that the Company deducted the debts owed it by Americans from his personal account are legends now happily disproved. Estimates of these fictitious debts, varying from $30,000 to $100,000, appear in contemporary accounts and are repeated in several histories of the Pacific Northwest. McLoughlin probably originated these legends at a time when he had reason to complain of the injustices done him by the Company and when he did not know what action regarding these matters its officials would take. Americans, apparently, repeated these tales, and McLoughlin let them go uncorrected.

The crowning blow came in 1850, when the eleventh clause of the Donation Land Act, passed by Congress, "the special Methodist provision," deprived McLoughlin of his entire land claim, though he had fulfilled all obligations of American law by declaring his intention of becoming an American citizen. He was never dispossessed of his property and continued to operate his mill and to carry on other business activities at Oregon City from 1846 until his death in 1857. His later life was filled with bitterness and disappointment however. The provision dispossessing him of his property seems to have been a severe measure of injustice and ingratitude to Oregon's first great businessman. The Oregon legislature made restitution for the loss of the property to the McLoughlin heirs in 1862, in belated recognition of McLoughlin's positive role in the process of settlement.[30]

The Methodist Mission remained a strong force in molding the structure of the new community. Its members had laid important foundations for the area's economic development and as far as it was possible for them to do so, had set the religious and moral tone of the community. Through their political leadership they promoted the steady flow of petitions to the United States, led in the movement to establish the Provisional Government, and played a dominant role in it until the advent of territorial government in 1849. George Abernethy, a prominent member of the mission group, held the office of provisional governor from 1845 to 1849 and discharged his duties in a creditable manner. Through the Provisional Government the missionaries prohibited the manufacture and sale of liquor, which in effect was a continuation of the Hudson's Bay Company's practice of preventing the distribution of liquor in order to assure peaceful relations with natives.[31] Although the influence of the Methodists was great, and perhaps sufficient for Bancroft to refer to the new community as the "Missionary Republic,"[32] Oregon hardly became the religious commonwealth envisaged by Jason Lee. If the settlement of Oregon was important in the fulfillment of America's national destiny, however, the Methodists deserve considerable credit for their part in the achievement of this goal.

Chapter III

An Isolated American Community

"This feeble and distant portion . . ."

Serious questions of survival faced the small American community in the Willamette Valley in the later 1840s. Although agricultural development assured a measure of self-sufficiency and Abernethy's and McLoughlin's mills evinced industrial progress, the community lacked a money supply and an adequate export outlet for its commodities. The Hudson's Bay Company remained in the region only to gain as much as possible from the "possessory rights" guaranteed under the Oregon treaty before making its final retreat.[1] That this was to take a considerable length of time was a boon to Oregon settlers. As mentioned above the fur trade was basically incompatible with settlement and had become generally less profitable in the region south of the forty-ninth parallel. In spite of its aim to withdraw entirely the Company, in the years between the Oregon treaty and the California gold rush, seems to have adjusted to the changed conditions of the territory. Sales to the settlers became an increasingly important source of profit. Goods were exchanged for cash brought in by immigrants and for limited amounts of wheat. Responsible settlers recognized the important role of the Hudson's Bay Company and feared that the community would face ruin should its facilities be withdrawn suddenly.

Lieutenant Howison of the U. S. Schooner *Shark,* writing in 1846, explained the Company's position as follows:

> Although it is well known that furs are not so abundant as formerly, they nevertheless still form an important article of trade and this is entirely monopolized by the company. Nearly every dollar of specie which comes into the country—and there is more of it than might be supposed—finds its way sooner or later into the company's chests; keeping, as they do, a very large stock on hand of all those articles most necessary to the new settler. Indeed, so extensive and well selected are their supplies, that few country towns in the United

States could furnish their neighbors so satisfactorily. An annual ship load arrives from London, which, with the old stock, makes an inventory of one hundred thousand pounds. Goods are invariably sold at an advance of one hundred per cent on London prices; which taking their good quality into consideration, is cheaper than they are offered by the two or three Americans who are engaged in mercantile business in the country.[2]

American merchants, while generally successful, were unable to establish the trade relationships necessary to assure a regular flow of supplies to the new community. This and most other economic problems facing the pioneer settlement were due directly or indirectly to the inadequacy of the export market. The only Pacific markets for wheat or flour were the Russian outposts and the Hawaiian Islands and these were limited. The Hudson's Bay Company monopolized the former under the contract of 1839, but shared the latter with the Americans. The costs of transportation and the abundance of wheat and flour in other parts of the world prevented shipment elsewhere. Actually flour selling at $5.25 per barrel in the United States could be shipped to the Hawaiian Islands for about the same price, or at a lower rate, as flour shipped from the Columbia.[3] Under such unfavorable conditions for commerce American tradesmen could not risk sea voyages of 20,000 miles via Cape Horn in order to supply the region in competition with the Hudson's Bay Company. Thus while this distant colony had advanced beyond its most primitive stage of development, isolation and the possible withdrawal of the British fur company threatened to deprive it of the necessary material goods upon which its survival and development depended, if it were not to revert to the backwardness characteristic of other isolated communities. It even seemed to be forsaken by the federal government after the boundary settlement, owing to the delay of almost three years in the establishment of territorial government.

Again Howison, who urged government assistance, explained the situation succinctly:

The granaries are surcharged with wheat; the sawmills are surrounded with piles of lumber as high as themselves; the grazier sells his beef at three cents per pound to the merchant, who packs it in salt and deposits it in a warehouse, awaiting the tardy arrival of some vessel to take a portion of his stock at what price she pleases, and furnish in return a scanty supply of tea and sugar and indifferent clothing, also at her own rate. I feel it particularly my duty to call the attention of government to this subject. This feeble and distant portion, of itself, is vainly struggling to escape from burdens which, from the nature of things, must long continue to oppress it, unless parental assistance comes to its relief. The first measure necessary is to render the entrance and egress of vessels into the mouth of the Columbia as free from danger as possible . . .

American seamen knew of the dangers to navigation at the mouth of the Columbia and dreaded the voyage to Oregon. Owing to this added risk freight and insurance rates rose, and higher prices for the few goods imported by Americans at infrequent intervals resulted.[4]

Shortage of supplies had become acute. Fewer goods were available in 1846 than in 1843, it was alleged, and the territory had attracted no new merchants in spite of the growth of population. Oregon City, the only important town, now had 500 residents, and here the stores of Pettygrove, Couch, Abernethy, and the Hudson's Bay Company still attempted to meet the demands of the growing Willamette community.[5] According to Joel Palmer the American merchants charged "whatever their avarice demands, and the necessity of the purchaser will bear." Prices were higher than they had been before the arrival of the American merchants, he asserted, and would have reached even higher levels if the field had been left open to them alone.

> The settlers are labouring under great disadvantages on account of not being able to obtain a sufficient amount of farming implements. The early settlers were supplied at the Hudson Bay Company's store, and at prices much less than those now charged for the same articles. At that time the supply was equal to the demand; but since the tide of emigration has turned so strongly to this region, the demand is much greater than the supply. This may be said of almost every kind of goods . . .

Palmer and Howison agreed that the presence of the Hudson's Bay Company had a generally salutary effect by giving the economy whatever stability it had.[6]

Prices for merchandise were exorbitant. Many of the farmers complained about the high price of goods and the low price of wheat and thought the Hudson's Bay Company was to blame for both. The fact was, however, that they were plagued with an over-supply of wheat. While American merchants usually carried short, poorly assorted stocks of merchandise with few of the articles most in demand on hand, they were sometimes overstocked with useless or unsaleable goods.[7] The Hudson's Bay Company had a complete line of merchandise, but it now could sell only for cash or in exchange for strictly limited quantities of wheat. In 1846 the price of nails was from 20 to 25 cents per pound; chopping axes, $4.00 to $6.00 each; cross-cut saws, $8.00 to $12 each; stoga shoes, $4.50 a pair; coarse boots, $6.00 to $8.00 a pair; calico, 31 to 87 cents a yard; and flag handkerchiefs, purchasable in Cincinnati at only 5 cents, 50 cents each. "The prices imposed in selling to the consumer are enormously high," Howison noted, "and these he must pay from the produce of his labor, or dispense with the most necessary articles of clothing, cooking utensils, groceries and farming implements." In addition to wheat at 60 cents to $1.00 per bushel, settlers bartered beef at $6.00 and pork at $10 per hundredweight, hides at $2.00 apiece, butter at 20 to 25 cents per pound, potatoes at 50 cents per bushel, lumber at from $15 to $25 per thousand board feet, and shingles at $4.00 to $5.00 per thousand in exchange for manufactured goods or other commodities. Chief Factor James Douglas of the Hudson's Bay Company noted that while the settlers never hesitated to complain about the Company's practice of taking a fair share of profit on wheat, they failed to blame the American merchants for the high cost of goods.[8]

The community needed more merchants and more capital. This, according to Palmer, would provide the necessary stimulus for trade and go far toward correcting the economic problem. "There is scarcely any branch of business that might not be carried on successfully in Oregon," he noted. "Flouring mills, saw mills, carding machines, fulling and cloth dying, tin shops, potteries tanyards . . . would all be profitable," he observed, and all were much needed. Another observer wrote that Oregon now had in operation, excluding the facilities of the Hudson's Bay Company, six saw mills, five flour mills, six stores, two tan yards, six blacksmith shops, numerous carpenter shops and "Lawyers, Doctors, and Preachers by the dozen . . ."[9]

Wages were high. Unskilled and skilled workmen had no difficulty obtaining work as there were many jobs created by the process of settlement. Mills, houses and warehouses were under construction in Oregon City and elsewhere on the Willamette and Columbia rivers. The mission and McLoughlin had given employment to American carpenters and laborers. Immigrants arriving in the fall could always find work splitting logs or doing other tasks for the farmers already in the valley. Mechanics, carpenters and unskilled workmen also found work to a limited extent in the existing small industries: lumber and flour milling, the fisheries, boat transportation, ship repair and others. It cost two dollars to get a pair of shoes or boots half-soled, $1.25 per hundred for cutting and splitting rails, and from 75 cents to $1.00 for cutting a cord of wood. Carpenters received from $2.00 to $3.00, and laborers from $1.00 to $2.00 per day. Ship building, surprisingly enough, was unimportant; only the schooner *Star of Oregon,* and the sloop *Calapooya,* were built for the river traffic during the entire decade.[10]

Desertion from the few American merchantmen that arrived in Oregon was common because of the high wages paid for mechanics' labor. Ship captains took the extra precaution of hiring Kanaka seamen in Hawaii before making the Columbia voyage. Ten of Howison's own men deserted from the U.S.S. *Shark,* and though he offered a liberal reward for their apprehension only two were returned.[11]

In 1845 Pettygrove had received a large cargo of merchandise, shipped by Benson and Brother of New York on board the bark *Toulon,* with Captain Nathaniel Crosby in command and Benjamin Stark as supercargo. Another cargo, consigned to Stark, arrived on board the *Mariposa* in 1846. These were two of only five ships* that arrived on the Columbia with cargoes of goods direct from the United States during the five-year period, 1843-48.[12] These cargoes, while not alleviating the supply problem appreciably, gave

*These ships were the *Fama,* 1843; *Chenamus,* 1844; *Toulon,* 1845; *Mariposa,* 1846; and *Henry,* 1847. The *Toulon's* cargo was the largest supply down to the close of 1845. The items are listed in *Oregon Spectator,* February 5, 1846, and seem to represent a well assorted cargo.

Pettygrove and his associates a distinct advantage in competition. The mercantile and shipping enterprise, now styled F. W. Pettygrove and Company, expanded further in 1846 when Dr. McLoughlin added $20,000 to the capital resources of the firm as a partner's share for his son, David McLoughlin. Howison called Pettygrove "the principal commercial man in the country."[13]

Of the three American merchants Pettygrove was most active during the mid-forties. In addition to his store at Oregon City and his trading station and granary at Champoeg, he established a new store on the left bank of the river "12 miles below" the falls at the head of navigation on the Willamette. Here, alongside Couch's claim, Pettygrove and Asa L. Lovejoy founded the new town of Portland in 1845. Pettygrove, after winning the toss of a coin, named it after the principal city of his home state of Maine. He now gave most of his attention to the new store which was conveniently located with respect to both the river and the farming community on the Tualatin Plains to the west. By 1846 some twelve or fifteen houses stood at this place and others were being built. It was the only promising townsite other than Oregon City in the country. Though Pettygrove's store seems to have flourished, the growth and development of Portland was relatively insignificant prior to 1849.[14]

Pettygrove and Stark now used the two ships under their control in the Hawaiian trade. They drew some supplies from Hawaii for themselves but refused to import goods for their Oregon competitors. For instance, Stark loaded out a cargo of lumber to the islands for George Abernethy in 1846, but refused to bring back goods for him, or for Couch, except at exorbitant freight rates. The normal high rate had been around $16 or $17 per ton, but on this occasion Stark asked $24 per ton and $3.00 per barrel, and would ship goods for his prospective customers only if they promised a minimum cargo of 1,000 barrels. He loaded one ship with goods for Pettygrove's stores but rather than accommodating Abernethy or Couch the other ship returned to the Columbia in ballast. Stark's freight rates were almost as high as those from New York to the Columbia. He and Pettygrove evidently sought a monopoly of as much of the Oregon trade as they could get at a time when the Honolulu market was glutted with merchandise. Many goods retailed there at less than New York cost in 1846. But the quantity of goods and island products imported from Hawaii could not be increased easily as long as Oregon products met a limited market there. The Hudson's Bay Company also refused to ship goods from Hawaii for its American competitors, except for the purpose of filling out a cargo. The rates, though high, were uniform.[15]

In 1846, Pettygrove and Stark arbitrarily raised the price of salt in an attempt to gain control of the salmon trade. The supply of salt, which sold normally at 62½ cents per bushel, had run short at Fort Vancouver in 1845. The price soon reached $2.00 per bushel at the Hudson's Bay store at Oregon City, while Pettygrove, with a large supply of his own, refused to sell at any price. Most settlers, however, continued to believe that "monopoly" was something peculiarly British.[16]

The region's barter economy continued. For the Willamette settlement wheat was still the medium of exchange and its value was fixed by the Hudson's Bay Company in accordance with the existing demands. Its price ranged as high as $1.00 per bushel, but for most of the decade to 1848, it stayed at 60 to 62½ cents per bushel. The normal price of flour sold to the immigrants was four cents per pound. In 1845, by act of the Provisional Government, wheat, orders on solvent merchants, and treasury notes became legal tender along with gold and silver for the payment of debts, taxes, and the fulfillment of contract obligations. Orders on solvent merchants were certificates for stipulated amounts in dollars and cents, which represented the value of wheat deposited in designated warehouses belonging to merchants. A treasury draft was based upon the credit of the Provisional Government, and therefore indirectly upon wheat, since it was the medium used for the payment of taxes.[17] No large amounts of cash came in and, as explained above, that which did soon found its way to the coffers of the Hudson's Bay Company. The lack of adequate exterior markets, the concentration upon the production of a single commodity, and the dominating position of the Hudson's Bay Company were the principal factors which made the barter system necessary and prevented the inward flow of a money supply.

The existing currency was indeed heterogeneous. The orders of the Hudson's Bay Company were generally redeemable at par and had a reputation for reliability, whereas those of the American merchants fluctuated. On one occasion an American merchant offered only grindstones for the redemption of his own orders. Abernethy tried to foist off his poorest goods, or those not really wanted, upon his customers, and sometimes refused to honor his own orders at par. There were many currencies and such terms as "Vancouver money," "Abernethy money," "Couch money" or "Ermatinger money" came into common usage.[18]

Abernethy is noted for the novel device of using rocks to make change because of the lack of fractional coins. He found flints at a nearby deposit where Indians obtained their arrowheads, pasted pieces of paper on them with his name and figures to indicate the denomination, and allowed them to circulate. The term "pocket full of rocks" soon became an appropriate expression.[19]

Cash was always favored. Howison noted that approved bills were discounted at the rate of twelve per cent at Oregon City in 1846, although the Hudson's Bay Company accepted bills on Baring Brothers at par. A premium favoring cash over the ordinary currency of the country prevailed from 1846 to 1848. For example, the Hudson's Bay Company sold flour at $3.00 per hundredweight for currency and at $2.50 for cash in the winter of 1847. The rate was low, however, and the price of flour only recently had fallen to two and one-half cents per pound cash. Normally the exchange rate was $33\frac{1}{3}$ per cent.[20]

Real or imagined hardships due to the inadequate market for wheat led to a movement in 1846 and 1847 among the farmers of the Tualatin Plains to establish their own cooperative import-export company. One purpose was to combat the alleged "extortionist" practices of the Hudson's Bay Company, now called the "Monster," and those of the unscrupulous American merchants as well. Outstanding indebtedness was considerable, but there was no real danger of an over-extension of credit since wheat had a legal tender quality and since the area was poorly supplied.[21] Farmers needing more supplies realized that their real problem was the inadequate export market for their wheat which, in turn, prevented an inflow of supplies. They complained about the fixed price of wheat and alleged that the merchants were conspiring to defraud them. Their plan called for a joint stock company under their own control which would purchase vessels and seek the markets of the world, particularly those of the Pacific islands and California. If that much were accomplished, one advocate of the project asserted, "Who will then be in favor of praying Congress to drive the Hudson's Bay Company away, to make room for Jews and sharpers?"[22] The farmers' resolutions breathe distinct distrust of business practices, and reveal a profound confidence in the ideals of an agrarian society and in the doctrines of physiocracy. One resolution reads: "That those who are not producers in the blessings of life are a burden to the human family, and in the same proportion as they are able by intrigue and extortion to amass and monopolize the blessings of this world."[23]

A similar movement had occurred on the Missouri frontier in 1822 for the purpose of obtaining better facilities for the export of produce.[24] The parallel is interesting, because the similar predicaments of the settlers of the two frontiers inspired essentially the same idea. The Oregon movement was handicapped for want of proper organization, lack of capital, and an inadequate knowledge of the ways of business. Interest in the project subsided with the improvement of market and supply facilities.

Encouraging news of a market for Oregon produce in California reached the Willamette settlement in the spring of 1847. Twenty thousand barrels of flour, quantities of wheat for seeding, lumber and potatoes would be needed by fall, and it was anticipated that the demand would exist for two years. It arose, not because California could not produce these items, but because of a crop failure, increased immigration, and the war operations in southern California. During the previous winter the price of flour in California had reached $25 to $30 per barrel. The *Toulon's* cargo, shipped down by Pettygrove in the spring, sold at $15 per barrel netting a profit of $10 per barrel. The price of potatoes was $2.50 per bushel, lumber, $50 per thousand board feet; shingles, $5.00 per thousand, and butter, 50-62½ cents per pound. All these products could be exchanged for cash.[25] Figures available for the month of April 1847, show that 1,736 barrels of flour, 171,000 board feet of lumber, and 96,000 shingles were exported from Oregon to markets in Hawaii, California and Alaska. These represent a small beginning but a great improvement over the conditions of 1846. Although the California demand was light, seven American trading vessels called at the Columbia occasionally during 1847 and 1848 for cargoes of lumber and flour for California or the islands. Few of them brought in goods, however.[26]

Unlike Oregon, California's external trade had long been dominated by Americans. After the sea otter trade had declined on the North West Coast, the hide and tallow business of the California coast had risen to command the attention of American tradesmen in the Pacific. California hides helped to sustain the New England shoe industry and became the basis of a flourishing commerce. For the procedure, adventure and dull humdrum of the hide and tallow trade as it was carried on on the coast from San Francisco to San Diego during the 30s, one needs only to turn to Richard Henry Dana's classic *Two Years Before the Mast*. The Russian-American Company had also penetrated California with a station at Fort Ross, mainly for the purpose of getting provisions to sustain their far northern operations. After their agreement with the Hudson's Bay Company in 1839, the further maintenance of Fort Ross was unnecessary. Other fur traders, both American and British, had been active in California during the 1820s and 1830s. The Hudson's Bay Company had a station at San Francisco from 1841 to 1845, which was unsuccessful largely because of a serious misunderstanding among McLoughlin, Simpson, and the Governor and Committee concerning its purpose. But it was American tradesmen who had reduced Mexican California to a condition of dependence and had prepared the way for the American conquest by settlement and by the war which was now taking place.[27]

Oregon's economic horizons became somewhat brighter. In addition to the California market, the local market for produce improved when some 4,500 immigrants, many of whom were of "comfortable means," arrived in the fall of 1847. This, the largest immigration of the decade, was probably due to the settlement of the boundary question and the prospects of early legislation concerning territorial government and a land policy for Oregon. Cash received in payment for provisions sold in California or to the new immigrants was now more plentiful. Wheat soon became scarce and sold for $1.00 per bushel cash in December, 1847, as a result of the new demands.[28] Thus provisions as well as goods became high. The new supply of cash led the Provisional Government on March 4, 1848, to repeal that part of the currency act which made wheat and orders on solvent merchants legal tender. Only gold, silver and treasury notes could have this quality.[29]

The scarcity of needed supplies and the general prevalence of high prices persisted as major problems. The few American trading vessels engaged in the California trade came for cargoes of produce, and only one brought in a cargo of goods from the United States during 1847. This was the new venture of Captain William K. Kilbourne of the brig *Henry* of Newburyport, who established a store at Oregon City. The *Henry's* cargo contained much second-hand merchandise, particularly furniture and stoves, and the cabinet-maker employed to repair the furniture asserted that it was so nearly in pieces that he charged more for its repair than it was worth. He also said that "It was just like coining money to sell that off. Stoves sold for $45 and $60." Almost all available articles of clothing were selling at 100 to 200 per cent advance on New York retail prices in 1847.[30]

The immigrants of 1847 brought in many necessary items of goods, as well as a greater supply of cash. Due to the publication of guides for travel on the Oregon Trail like that of Palmer, the immigrants, it seems, had planned their wagon cargoes more carefully in terms of their own needs in the new country and the exigencies on the trail. Abernethy noticed that they had brought a considerable assortment of hollow ware, cooking utensils, crockery, groceries, and dry goods.[31]

First mention of business in the hinterland of the upper Willamette Valley, except for the small trading post at Champoeg, appears in 1847. Thomas Cox brought out goods overland in that year, a unique feat in itself, and established a small store at Salem. Cox is an example of the pioneer entrepreneur who marched westward with the frontier. He was born in Virginia and made successive stops in Ohio, Indiana and Illinois between 1811 and 1834. At each stop he established a small merchandising and manufacturing enterprise and now he was ready to repeat the process in Oregon. His day-book for the fall of 1847 shows extremely small sales at high prices. He received from 25 to 37½ cents per yard for ordinary cotton cloth, 62 to 75 cents per pound for tobacco, $2.50 for shoes, and $4.00 to $4.50 for boots. He retailed from his small supply of goods on a cash or barter basis. One entry for December shows that he received wheat at 90 cents per bushel in payment of an account. Other entries for 1847 and 1848 show that he received lumber, butter, pork, skins and oats, as well as wheat, in payment. He made trips to Oregon City to replenish his supplies but nothing resembling a wholesale business had yet developed.[32]

The supply problem became more acute in 1848. There was a tremendous demand for ordinary merchandise, especially good cotton cloths, which had "scarcely found their way" to Oregon in appreciable amounts. Abernethy reported that he had no groceries and but few ill-assorted dry goods in store, while such items as hats, saddles, and large ploughs for which there was little demand "still hang on and all very very slow." Captain Kilbourne brought in a small cargo of goods worth $6,000 from California on board the brig *Henry* early in the year. He sold his goods readily at prices regarded as exorbitant but his supply hardly dented the demand. Coffee sold at 33⅓ cents per pound; calico at three yards for $1.00; saleratus (baking soda) at 50 cents per pound; nails at 20 and 25 cents per pound; and other items in proportion.[33] In May the supply problem was aggravated further when the Hudson's Bay Company's bark *Vancouver* went down at the mouth of the Columbia with a cargo of dry goods, agricultural implements and other merchandise having a total value, according to Bancroft, of £30,000. Prices were reported generally at 300 to 400 per cent advance on the retail prices of the frontier states of the Mississippi Valley. In March 1848, one observer noted that advances on first cost ranged between 100 and 1,000 per cent.[34]

Abernethy faced many difficulties in business. He experienced a disadvantage in competition, for his rivals, by owning or controlling their own ships, at least had access to markets in California and Hawaii. He was sustained in business by his mills, and was able occasionally to ship out lumber and flour on one of the few ships that entered the river. He considered the freight rates to California, $2.00 per barrel and $20 per thousand board feet, "outrageously" high. The local market was important, but he could sell flour in the spring of 1848, when he had it, only at the low price of $4.50 per barrel currency or at $3.00 per barrel cash.

He was also handicapped by lack of capital and his indebtedness to the mission. He was obliged to pay an annual installment on his debt to the mission of $2,000 currency and $500 cash, and to meet it he depended largely upon his collections of the old debts of the settlers to the mission. Although these payments came in slowly, he had easily paid more than the $2,000 currency installment in 1847. But he had failed to make the cash payment; and there was little prospect that he could do so in 1848. He still had to collect $12,000 from the settlers. For lack of cash he had to borrow from the mission to meet a $1,100 cash obligation at Fort Vancouver. "There is an honest buisness [sic] like promptness in his manner of doing buisness which I like," wrote the Rev. William M. Roberts, third superintendent of the Oregon Methodist Mission, concerning Abernethy, "and altho he cannot just now meet all his engagements with the Mission . . . I have no doubt he will be able to do so when he shall have struggled through the toils of the present year."

Financial uncertainties prevented Abernethy from requesting credit from New York firms and from entering partnerships with Captain Roland Gelston of the bark *Whiton* or Edward F. Folger of the New York firm, Folger, Alford, and Company, both of whom visited Oregon in 1847. He urged them to send out goods in 1848 and to provide him with a vessel for the California trade. The first vessel from the States could not avoid "doing well," he asserted.[35]

In spite of the difficulties he confronted in his several business enterprises, Abernethy had confidence in the future prosperity of Oregon. The exterior market had improved and the immigration fever had not as yet abated. The wheat harvest for 1848 looked promising. Territorial government could not be postponed much longer, and with it the new government installations would provide work and an additional market for lumber and provisions, he thought. He looked forward to the day when the government would give valid titles to land. "My property is increasing in value very fast," he observed in the spring of 1848, "and if I should make nothing in business it will make me independent in a very few years unless there is a change. . . ."[36]

In the meantime, early in December, 1847, news of the Whitman massacre shocked the Willamette community. Now the colony's meagre economic resources were strained to meet the exigencies of its first serious Indian war. Dr. Marcus Whitman, his wife, Narcissa, and some eight or ten others had been brutally murdered by Cayuse Indians at Waiilatpu on November 29-30. The immediate cause of this disaster was suspicion on the part of some of the Indians that Whitman had used poison instead of a cure for the measles, a disease which was then decimating the tribe. McLoughlin had warned Whitman as early as 1841 of the danger at Waiilatpu, telling him that the Cayuses sometimes killed their own medicine men. Actually Whitman had known for some time that his position in the interior was untenable.

Basically the Indians were apprehensive and increasingly restive about the annual migrations that crossed their hunting grounds. They had little respect for the trail-weary Americans as warriors but knew well enough that they had come for land. Whitman had often asserted that the authority of the United States would shortly be established and with it would come government officials, white warriors, and a land policy. But such authority was not forthcoming— only the immigrants, whom the Indians held in contempt.

They respected the resolute methods of the Hudson's Bay Company, however. The fur trader, they knew from experience, provided for many of their greatest needs and did not threaten their lands. When Chief Factor Peter Skene Ogden received the news of the massacre, he immediately exerted the influence of the Hudson's Bay Company to effect the release of the prisoners still in Cayuse hands. No other force in Oregon could have accomplished so much at the time.[37]

The Willamette settlers responded to the Indian threat immediately. The governor and legislature of the Provisional Government called for volunteers and before the year was out a small force was beyond the Cascades. Prompt measures were taken likewise for the establishment of a commissary department, a peace commission, and a loan commission. Force alone would command the respect of the Indians, the settlers reasoned. Immigrants would need protection now more than ever before, and the little colony itself was exposed. The war aims were to obtain and punish the Indians responsible for the crime, and to prove to the interior tribes that the settlers had the power to protect themselves. It was also necessary to prevent the unification of the interior tribes. Operations east of the mountains in the spring of 1848 had the desired effects, but two years passed before the Indians surrendered five of the murderers. These were tried at Oregon City in May, 1850, and subsequently hanged.[38]

Provisioning the army of some 600 to 1,000 men in the interior taxed the resources of the little settlement. The legislative assembly authorized a board of loan commissioners composed of Jesse Applegate, A. L. Lovejoy and George L. Curry to float a loan not to exceed $100,000 on the credit of the Provisional Government.[39] Without much hope for success this board applied for a loan from the Hudson's Bay Company on the credit of the Provisional Government with the virtual certainty that the United States would ultimately pay it. Chief Factor James Douglas politely explained that he could under no circumstances exceed his instructions to the extent of granting a loan, but pledged the support of the Company in every other way. Consequently the loan commissioners had to fall back upon the colony's own resources. Governor Abernethy, the commander-in-chief, required the volunteers to provide their own clothing, blankets, arms and as much other equipment as they could. Settlers willingly subscribed wheat, wheat orders and other materials, but little cash, in return for the bonds or treasury notes of the Provisional Government. Though it was difficult to get cash to purchase goods directly from the Hudson's Bay Company, some was obtained at a premium of from 25 to 33⅓ per cent. Wheat was exchanged for flour and other provisions from the Company and the American merchants. The Company sold a few large consignments of supplies to the governor, loan commissioners, and the commissary-general on their own personal notes. Commissary-general Joel Palmer had the difficult task of getting supplies to the upper country. Though he accomplished it with a high degree of efficiency under the circumstances, there was considerable suffering among the volunteer soldiers during the winter and spring of 1847-48.[40]

Only a small part of the actual cost of the war was raised by subscription. The total bond issue was slightly less than $15,000. Payments to soldiers and various other expenditures had to be met, so in August, 1848, the entire debt was refunded and new scrip issued. Payable to the bearer with interest at 10 per cent, this scrip had a legal tender quality. It rested upon the reasonable assurance that the total cost of the Cayuse War would be assumed by the United States. Ultimately Congress appropriated $100,000 in 1851, and $75,000 in 1854 to discharge the debt. In the meantime the Oregon scrip circulated as currency, though sometimes at a discount.[41]

Governor George Abernethy reached the height of his political career during the Cayuse War. He acted promptly in December, 1847, promoting the war effort by every means at his command. Like a few other prominent citizens of Oregon, he purchased supplies on his own account. He vainly sought military aid from those in command of American forces in California and sent a special appeal to President Polk describing the situation in Oregon. Devoted to the cause of law and order, he earnestly promoted and anxiously awaited the establishment of territorial government in Oregon.[42]

News of the Whitman massacre had a direct bearing upon the passage of the Oregon territorial bill in 1848. The provisional legislature had immediately dispatched Joseph L. Meek to the national capital overland with the news and documents. Earlier, in October, 1847, Abernethy had sent J. Quinn Thornton to Washington by sea to represent the interests of the colony. The anti-mission faction alleged, however, that Thornton was sent to represent mission interests rather than those of the colony's entire population. At any rate both Meek, the former mountain man, and Thornton, a learned lawyer, pressed for the passage of the territorial bill.[43]

This and the discovery of gold in California in 1848 were events of great portent for the isolated Oregon colony. James Marshall made his discovery in January and President Polk signed the Oregon territorial bill in August. Before the year ended gold had revolutionized Oregon's pioneer economy; and in March 1849 the sovereign jurisdiction of the United States was finally established. California gold gave Oregon a money supply, a market and better communications. With American authority came territorial government, American law, a custom-house, ocean mail service, military protection, Indian agents, and a beneficent land policy. This fortuitous combination of circumstances inaugurated a new stage in the development of Oregon's pioneer economy. The economic ascendancy of the Hudson's Bay Company ended and the day of the fur trader gradually came to a close in Oregon.

Chapter IV

The Hudson's Bay Company in Retreat

"The interests of the Colony and the Fur Trade will never harmonize"

The fur trader had to retreat or adjust to new conditions as the pioneer farmer advanced. The Hudson's Bay Company had gone far toward making this adjustment in Oregon as it aided in the process of settlement. It continued its positive assistance throughout the decade even after the settlement of the boundary dispute in 1846. The Oregon treaty, in addition to defining the boundary on the 49th parallel from the Rocky Mountains to the channel separating the mainland from Vancouver Island, guaranteed the "possessory rights" of the Hudson's Bay Company and confirmed the right of the Puget Sound Agricultural Company to possession of its lands south of the forty-ninth parallel. The treaty also guaranteed free navigation of the Columbia to the Company and to other British subjects.[1] It seems that the Hudson's Bay Company by utilizing these privileges could have continued its adaptation to the changing economic situation in the region if its governors had desired to do so. They chose, however, to abandon the region as soon as they could dispose of their "possessory rights" in a favorable settlement with the United States government.

The pressure of American settlement had little to do with the Company's decision to retreat. While Company officials did debate about the wisdom of remaining in the area in the face of American settlement prior to 1846, the actual decision came only when they learned that the Company's interests had been sacrificed by the provisions of the Oregon treaty. Lord Aberdeen, British foreign secretary in the Peel ministry, surrendered all the territory that had been in dispute, except the tip of Vancouver

Island. Aberdeen conveniently interpreted the establishment of Fort Victoria on the tip of Vancouver Island, in 1843, and the Company's stated purpose to make it the principal headquarters of the Hudson's Bay Company on the coast, as evidence of retreat and willingness on the part of Company officials to abandon the disputed territory north and west of the Columbia River and south of the 49th parallel.

Such was not the Company's purpose, however. As early as 1835, and subsequently, Company officials had ordered McLoughlin to seek out a more suitable entrepôt on the coast than provided by Fort Vancouver. Douglas finally located the site of Fort Victoria for this purpose in 1842. By this time Sir George Simpson had begun to doubt that Great Britain could gain the Columbia River as the boundary in any negotiation with the United States. This factor and the vulnerable position of Fort Vancouver after large numbers of American settlers began arriving in 1843 made the issue more urgent. On January 1, 1845 Simpson recommended that McLoughlin keep no more goods in depot at Fort Vancouver than absolutely necessary; that he keep the reserved outfits for the Columbia in depot at Fort Victoria and all goods intended for the coastal trade at Fort Simpson; that the furs be collected at Fort Victoria instead of Fort Vancouver; and that the ships from England go directly to Victoria with all reserve outfits. While the pressure of settlement was a factor in these decisions, the primary reason for the establishment of Fort Victoria was the need for the more centrally located entrepôt which had been urged repeatedly before American settlers arrived in appreciable numbers.[2]

Prior to 1846 the Hudson's Bay Company actually had no intention of abandoning the Columbia. It had determined to hold its posts south of the 49th parallel for three reasons: (1) profits were still substantial; (2) effective occupation of the disputed territory, its officials believed, would enhance the British position in negotiation; and (3) the entire interior trade west of the mountains still depended upon the Columbia River.

After 1846 the Company retained its posts south of 49° largely to demonstrate the value of its "possessory rights" which, as already mentioned, it hoped to dispose of as quickly as possible in a favorable settlement with the United States government. Even so the interior trade depended upon the Columbia River outlet and for three years after the treaty, Fort Vancouver remained the Company's principal headquarters. Not until 1849 did the Company build a road, a poor one, entirely within British territory to tap the interior trade directly from Fort Victoria. Fort Vancouver retained a degree of its former importance thereafter as entrepôt for the declining interior trade until the Indian wars of the mid-fifties completely disrupted the Company's relationships with the natives east of the Cascades.[3]

The Oregon treaty of 1846 has been variously interpreted. That the settlement of the boundary on the line of 49°, so favorable a solution to the United States, was due primarily to the pressure of Oregon pioneers is now discredited. Few American settlers ventured north of the Columbia prior to 1846, and by the usual test of sovereignty, occupation, the Hudson's Bay Company held the disputed territory for the British empire. But American negotiators since 1818 had consistently demanded the line of 49° as the boundary to assure American control of Puget Sound. While the pressure of settlement had no effect upon the formation of this official American policy, it was the expansionist sentiment within the United States, which had been growing since the days of Jefferson, that largely determined the issue. The settlement of Oregon was only one manifestation of this widespread and pervading force.

From 1842 through 1846 the Oregon Question had been a potent political issue in the United States. Congressional debates during these years reflect the rising pitch of the Oregon agitation as congressmen and senators considered Oregon measures in response to a flood of petitions from the people of the western states. Most of the proposals before Congress concerning Oregon included one or more of the items in Senator Linn's comprehensive Oregon bill of December 19, 1842, calling for land grants, military establishments and territorial government to protect the settlers and to encourage emigration. This bill had succeeded in the Senate but failed in the House in 1843. Congressmen and senators, like the diplomats, also argued about the origin and relative merits of American and British claims to the region. In his inaugural address President Polk asserted the American title to all of Oregon to be "clear and unquestionable" and repeated the assertion in somewhat similar language in his first annual message in December 1845. Now the more enthusiastic "Oregon" politicians from the western states demanded the whole territory to the line of 54° 40′ and threatened war with Great Britain to achieve it. This extreme position failed to gain sufficient support in American public opinion to determine official policy, but the "possession of Oregon to at least the 49th parallel became an *idee fixe* in American society." By 1845 the alternatives were this line and Puget Sound for the United States or war with Great Britain. Debates in Congress from December 1845, through April 1846, concerned the issue of 49° or 54° 40′ and whether notice to the British government of the abrogation of the Convention of 1827 and a possible breakdown in the negotiations would lead to war.[4]

In spite of the war threats on both sides of the ocean in 1845, the Peel government had been anxiously seeking an amicable solution for some time. The low tariff policy of the Polk administration had a mollifying effect upon British Whigs who like many western Democrats in the United States had taken a bellicose attitude on the Oregon Question. Whigs and Peelites, the Tory free trade minority, soon combined to repeal the British Corn Laws. These factors and the attitude of responsible American statesmen who spoke against the unrealistic demand for 54° 40′ reduced the agitation for war and prepared the way for Lord Aberdeen's offer which resulted in the Oregon treaty of 1846. This offer, as has been noted, was not a compromise for it surrendered all that had been in dispute except the tip of Vancouver Island. Aberdeen and Peel had not considered the disputed territory to be of great value and as long as British national honor and property rights were protected they willingly surrendered it in the interest of amicable Anglo-American relations. Had it not been for President Polk's politically-inspired belligerency, the issue would have been settled much more easily, for the Peel government had been ready to accept the 49th parallel in 1844. But President Polk's statements and the rising tempo of the Oregon agitation in the United States made it a question of British national honor in 1845. The settlement was a disappointment for the men of the Hudson's Bay Company who had failed to convince their government of the value of the disputed territory which they as agents of empire had guarded so long.[5] Now they had to contend with the knotty problem of "possessory rights."

What were "possessory rights?" Article III of the Oregon treaty reads: "In the future appropriation of the territory, south of the 49th parallel of north latitude . . . the possessory rights of the Hudson's Bay Company and of all British subjects who may be already in the occupation of land or other property, lawfully acquired within the said Territory shall be respected." The ambiguity of this provision made it practically impossible to interpret its meaning. It seems, as Douglas and Ogden observed, that these rights included the Company's trading privileges, but even so with no guarantee against the operation of the American tariff such privileges might well become meaningless.[6] Did these rights include the free use of unoccupied land or did the Company's property rights include only their posts and improved lands? How could such language as "lawfully acquired" be interpreted when no specific law governing land tenure, except that of the Provisional Government, had existed in the territory? Actually Company personnel had made individual claims to plots of land in and about Fort Vancouver under the land law of the Provisional Government and these claims were later transferred to the Company. The law establishing the Territory of Oregon declared that all acts of the Provisional Government would remain in force until altered by the territorial legislature except those "making grants of land, or otherwise affecting or incumbering the title to lands. . . ." Thus the land law of the Provisional Government became void, and the Donation Act superseded it in 1850. The latter act prohibited persons holding land under the Oregon treaty of 1846 from making claims under its provisions. The vague terms of the treaty provided no specific means for the Company to legally designate its property rights. A question as to whether "possessory rights" included land or just movable property was involved in interpreting the treaty. Settlers, believing the Company had no right to the land, soon laid claims within the very preserves of the Company at Forts Vancouver and Nisqually.[7]

Despite these handicaps and the general decline of the fur trade, profits at Fort Vancouver from 1846 through 1850 were considerable. The net gain from sales and trade there for 1845-46 was £21,263 and, as has been noted, the annual average for the seven years ending in 1846 had been over £30,000. The other trading posts in Oregon during the same period had produced an annual average profit of £10,929. During the trading season of 1849-50, the years of the California gold rush, the total profit for Oregon south of 49° was £35,390 and of this £14,902 was derived from the Fort Vancouver sales shop. Like all branches of business in Oregon, Fort Vancouver felt the stimulus of California gold. Particularly profitable were sales to the United States army, a contingent of which was stationed on or near the post. Total profits for operations south of 49° for 1850-51 were £14,814 but thereafter the trade declined rapidly. Outfit 1851-52 showed a loss of £6,754.[8]

In spite of the decision of Simpson and other Company officials to dispose of the possessory rights of the two companies as soon as possible, there was some sentiment favoring the expansion of the Company's merchandising operations in Oregon. In 1852, Chief Factor John Ballenden, a member of the Board of Management of the Columbia Department, urged the establishment of a Hudson's Bay store in each of the principal towns of Oregon. He pointed to the extremely profitable venture of Allan and McKinlay, former Hudson's Bay men, who had taken over the store at Oregon City. It seems that others, including Governor Eden Colvile, favored expansion of the Company's mercantile enterprises, but Chief Factors James Douglas and John Work, the other members of the Board of Management, ruled against Ballenden's proposal because of the disadvantages of operating within the boundaries of a foreign country. Even so one of the arguments presented before the Anglo-American Claims Commission considering Hudson's Bay claims in 1868, reads:

> But the buying and selling of furs was not its only business, and if the Company had been left unmolested and its rights had been respected its whole trade would have changed with

> the changing circumstances of the Country and have become
> in its new form even more profitable than its old.[9]

As has been noted, such an adaptation seems to have been feasible, but it did not accord with Company policy, already determined in 1846, in favor of retreat as soon as possible. Delay in effecting a settlement with the United States forced the Company to hold on to its posts south of 49° in order to demonstrate their value.

The Company continued its trade but it was hampered increasingly not only by incursions of settlers but by official acts of the United States government. In 1850 Anson Dart, newly appointed Superintendent of Indian Affairs for Oregon, acting upon the instructions of the Commissioner of Indian Affairs attempted unsuccessfully to prevent all trade between the Indians of the interior and the Hudson's Bay Company. The Indian law of 1834, which was extended to Oregon in 1850, prohibited licenses for trading with the Indians to any but citizens of the United States. According to the Indian commissioner the 1850 act extending the earlier law to Oregon superseded the treaty of 1846. Dart understood the conflict between the law and the treaty and urged the United States government to purchase the Company's possessory rights in order to reduce the difficulties he faced. In 1853 Governor Isaac Stevens of Washington Territory, acting upon the same instructions as Dart had received, stated his determination "to break up the ascendancy of the Hudson's Bay Company, and permit no authority or sanction to come between the Indians and the officers of this government."[10]

The Company also had to pay American customs duties. During 1849 John Adair, recently appointed as Oregon's first collector of customs at Astoria, levied $23,000 in duties on goods imported from London, of which $6,800 was paid under protest. Duties on goods intended for the fur trade of the interior north of 49° and those intended for sale to Company employees were paid under protest during 1850 but were later remitted upon appeal to the Secretary of the Treasury. Had it not been for the duties levied upon goods of British manufacture, however, the Company would have enjoyed "an advantage of about 35 per cent . . . over all other importers in Oregon." While this application of the law was justified in the interest of fair competition, it bears out the judgment of Douglas and Ogden regarding the second article of the treaty of 1846 guaranteeing free navigation of the Columbia to the British. Writing in 1847 they termed it "a decitful [*sic*] clause, in the form of a liberal concession, which substantially leaves the Company subject to the revenue and navigation laws of the United States...." In 1851 customs officials on Puget Sound seized two Company ships "on frivolous pretexts" to the extreme annoyance of Company officers. In February 1853, the Hudson's Bay bark *Josephine* brought in a cargo worth more than £17,000, on which $23,782.09 in duties were levied at Astoria. Such exactions of the American government contributed substantially to the losses reported by the Company on its Oregon operations during the early 1850s.[11]

Meanwhile, the Hudson's Bay Company had sought to sell its possessory rights to the United States. In 1846 Sir George Simpson and Sir John H. Pelly, Governor of the Hudson's Bay Company, would have accepted £100,000 for the property and rights of the two companies in Oregon. The British foreign office failed to initiate negotiations on the matter and Simpson went to Washington to negotiate directly. Here he became involved with a notorious "influence man" and professional lobbyist, George N. Sanders, who hoped to lobby a substantial appropriation through Congress for payment of Hudson's Bay claims. According to his plan he would gain a sizeable commission for himself and use various smaller sums to influence legislators directly. Simpson, none too scrupulous himself when promoting the Company's advantage, seemed to think that some such procedure as this was the most effective way to deal with the American government. In January, 1848, Simpson promised Sanders a commission of $10,000 if he could dispose of the Company's rights for $500,000, but Sanders had more grandiose plans. His association with Simpson led to a contract signed in London on April 28, 1848 whereby Sanders agreed to act as the Company's agent for one year. The Company would accept $410,000 in United States bonds at five per cent interest for its claims and Sanders would receive two and one-half per cent of this amount plus whatever payment he could obtain above the $410,000, as well as payment for his expenses. The Company's price was to be kept secret.

Sanders attempted to get $1,000,000 for the Hudson's Bay claims. He had support from Secretary of State Buchanan and Senators Webster, Calhoun, Hannegan, Mangum, Breese, Cass and others. Webster received $5,000 as a fee for legal advice on the matter. Buchanan insisted, however, that the British government should surrender the right of free navigation of the Columbia and be a party to any agreement regarding the possessory rights of the Hudson's Bay Company. In August, 1848, a bill providing for $1,000,000 as payment to the Hudson's Bay and Puget Sound Agricultural companies for liquidation of their claims failed in the Senate. Again in February, 1849 the Senate defeated a bill to purchase the claims of the two companies. Thus the affair with Sanders ended, but Simpson and the Company became involved in a similar arrangement with former Secretary of the Treasury Robert J. Walker. The latter tried to obtain $1,000,000 for the Company in return for a large commission but he also failed.

The right of navigation of the Columbia guaranteed to the British by Article II of the Oregon treaty complicated the issue. As mentioned above Buchanan had insisted that this right be eliminated in any agreement with the British government concerning Hudson's Bay claims. Others argued that since the upper waters of the Columbia, north of 49°, were unnavigable this privilege was useless once the Hudson's Bay Company withdrew from the territory south of that line entirely, and that it had no real relationship to the settlement of the Hudson's Bay claims. Both Buchanan and Webster, Secretary of State in the Fillmore administration, would have negotiated a treaty settling the Hudson's Bay claims for $1,000,000 with the relinquishment of the right of navigation by the British. Lord Palmerston, British foreign secretary, refused to surrender the right of navigation without some concession for Great Britain in return. Lord Malmesbury, foreign secretary in the weak Derby government, thought a treaty could be negotiated without mention of the right of navigation. With the Company's withdrawal there was no point in ceding a right that had ceased to exist, he thought. So the impasse developed.

William L. Marcy, Secretary of State in the Pierce administration, sought to settle the matter on a fair basis. He had learned of the Sanders attempt to bribe senators and thought the amount asked by the Hudson's Bay Company— now $1,500,000 on the assumption that Oregon land values had risen—was entirely too much. In 1855 he offered $300,000 for the claims of the two companies. He held that their rights would end with the expiration of the Hudson's Bay Company's license in 1859, and that the navigation of the Columbia was of no importance. Pierce had urged a settlement of the claims in each of his annual messages in 1854 and 1855, but in March 1855, the Senate rejected an amendment to an appropriation bill authorizing negotiation and payment up to $300,000.[12]

Meanwhile Company operations south of 49° became increasingly unprofitable. Fort Walla Walla was abandoned in 1855 by order of an Indian agent. The Indian wars of 1855-56 hastened the Company's withdrawal from this post because Americans suspected its agents of aiding the Indians. Fort Hall, which had been profitable for some years prior to 1851 from sales of provisions to immigrants, was finally abandoned in 1856. Fort Boise was also abandoned in that year. By mid-decade losses south of 49° had a serious effect upon the fur trade as a whole. Only Fort Colvile, just south of the boundary in Washington Territory, remained profitable, but the Indian wars also disrupted trade in this area.

At Fort Vancouver relations between Company officials and officers of the United States army were cordial and mutually satisfactory during the early 1850s in spite of the growing hostility of settlers. With the Company's permission the army carved out its reservation on Company lands, located Columbia Barracks on the bluff above the fort, and used some of the Company's buildings. As has been noted, the Company profited considerably from army purchases of goods, provisions and lumber. Army officers respected the Company's rights under the Oregon treaty and prevented incursions upon Company lands by land-hungry settlers.

By mid-decade, however, the army tended to ignore the Company's rights and to develop its reservation on the assumption that the lands in the vicinity of Fort Vancouver were, or soon would be, the property of the United States. That these lands had been occupied by permission of the Company was seemingly forgotten. As the army took over more land and buildings in 1858 and 1859, Company officers could do little but protest against this kind of "official claim jumping" as a trespass upon Company property.

On March 3, 1860 Brigadier General W. S. Harney, in command of the Department of Oregon, wrote that "the Hudson's Bay Company is not recognized as having any possessory rights in the soil of the military reserve at this place, in consequence of the expiration of their charter as a trading company on this coast." The Company's charter had expired on May 30, 1859 and the interpretation given by Harney had been held by several American officials since 1846. Harney, who virtually ordered the Company to vacate Fort Vancouver, was sustained in this interpretation by the Secretary of War. In a note to the British government, however, Secretary of State Lewis Cass repudiated Harney's decision upon a question "affecting the diplomatic engagements of this Government," and the war department sent out orders prohibiting further trespassing. Before this order reached Fort Vancouver, A. G. Dallas, who was in charge of the Company's affairs west of the mountains, had ordered the withdrawal of the Company's goods and machinery and had practically evacuated the place in May, 1860. He believed erroneously that Harney had acted upon orders and that any further attempt to maintain the Company's rights at Fort Vancouver would be useless. Thereafter the Company exercised scarcely any of its possessory rights south of 49°, and maintained only Fort Colvile south of that line.[13]

Negotiations on the claims of the Hudson's Bay and Puget Sound companies continued intermittently during the critical years of secession and Civil War in the United States. Secretary of State Cass refused to offer more than $300,000 since the Senate had earlier refused even that amount. The British minister, Lord Napier, conscientiously sought $650,000 but was shocked to learn that the Company would have settled for $410,000 under the Sanders contract. Finally in 1863 Secretary of State Seward negotiated a convention with the British minister, Lord Lyons, to establish a joint commission to settle the issue. It was not until September 1869 that the commission made its award of $450,000 to the Hudson's Bay Company and $200,000 to to Puget Sound Agricultural Company after considering the voluminous evidence presented before it.[14]

The prediction of James Douglas in 1838, that the "interests of the Colony and the Fur Trade will never harmonize" is borne out essentially by the record of the Company's retreat from the area of American settlement. It had to face similar problems in the Canadian West after 1858, when the British government terminated its license for exclusive trade. The decline of the fur trade in importance and the pressure of settlement ultimately forced the Company to change its very nature as it adjusted under a new set of managers to new conditions in Canada.

The day of the "Bay" men, gentlemen capitalists and partners in the giant company, had long since come to a close in Oregon. They all but disappeared from the region south of the 49th parallel, a domain they had once ruled somewhat like feudal barons. Bloody struggles between the Americans and the Indians of the interior replaced their more humane relations with the natives. Except for McLoughlin, who was the unhappy patriarch of Oregon City until his death in 1857, the Company's commissioned officers whose careers had been identified with the fur trade in Oregon remained in the Company's service as it retreated northward. Some of its lesser personnel like Allan and McKinlay, who took over the old Hudson's Bay store at Oregon City, found business opportunities in Oregon. James Birnie, once a diligent Company subordinate, became Cathlamet's outstanding man of business. The 1840s, when the Company positively aided the process of settlement in the Willamette Valley, had given way to a new day of development which saw the rise of American capitalists who were ready and willing to identify their futures and fortunes with the growth of the new commonwealth.[15]

PART II

The Stimulus of Gold, 1848-54

Chapter V

California Gold

"We are left with women and children ..."

Gold—accessible and in vast quantities in California! One can only imagine the electrifying effect of this news as it spread throughout the world in 1848. President Polk's official confirmation of this news in his annual message of December 1848[1] dispelled all doubt as to whether it was fact or wild rumor. In 1849 the grand rush to California began in earnest as thousands of Americans and foreigners responded to the magnetic attraction of gold. Men crowded the dusty overland trails or fought for passage on board the hundreds of ships, many of questionable navigability, that were pressed into service in the eastern coastal cities. Merchants stood to make phenomenal profits if only they could get their goods to the depleted California market and take advantage of the rising prices before competition would serve to balance the demand with an adequate supply at reasonable rates.

Mining operations had begun in California shortly after James Marshall's initial discovery of gold on the American fork of the Sacramento River in January, 1848. Californians abandoned their normal pursuits and took to the gold fields, where mining was in full swing during the summer. Methods were primitive, but according to reports, any industrious, able-bodied man could earn $100 per day. Some obtained $1,500 to $1,800 for a single day's work. By September, gold to the value of $850,000 had flowed into San Francisco. There it fell largely into the hands of a few merchants who, though unprepared to meet the new demands with their scant inventories, realized huge profits as supplies decreased.[2]

Thus the western mining frontier opened. It attracted thousands of adventurers who abandoned their trades and professions temporarily in order to accumulate a fortune or at least to gain sufficient capital for a new start in life. Many were unprepared for the hardships of travel, the hard work, the lack of supplies, and a climate in many ways forbidding.[3] The gold fever persisted, the mining frontier advanced; and in its wake came more stable agricultural, industrial and mercantile enterprises. California's population rose rapidly from a few thousand Mexicans and Americans to almost 100,000 by the end of 1849.[4]

In traditional frontier fashion Americans in California met the challenge of a reckless environment by providing their own methods to preserve law and order. Soon their demand for statehood became a potent factor in the political controversy then raging in the Congress of the United States concerning the extension of slavery into the new territories acquired from Mexico. As an important part of the Compromise of 1850 California was admitted as a free state, only two years after the treaty of Guadaloupe-Hidalgo had confirmed American sovereignty to the great Southwest.

During the next thirty years the mining frontier fanned out from the Sacramento Valley into the entire mountain region of the American West. Skilled prospectors using placer methods scrutinized virtually every crevice and mountain stream in their search for "pay dirt." Some made important strikes which were followed by the inevitable rushes to new el dorados in the mountain region from British Columbia to Mexico. In California and Nevada, after the discovery of deep lodes, mining operations soon required large capital investments for machinery. By the mid-fifties the transition from placer to quartz mining had begun in California and by 1863 one-third of that state's gold production was from quartz.[5] Elsewhere wandering prospectors, many of whom gained their first experience in California, were in the van of the eastward advancing mining frontier.

California gold wrought important economic changes throughout the world. It added to the world's supply of precious metals and thus caused inflation in all countries. It stimulated all branches of commerce and industry in the United States. New York's merchandising houses responded immediately with bustling vigor to meet the new demands. Gold flowed eastward to stimulate America's tremendous industrial effort, just then in its initial stages of development. Men trained in the gold fields of California not only made new discoveries in North America but in other parts of the world as well. Most notable was Edward Hargraves who returned to Australia to set off a chain of rushes there which revolutionized the life and economy of that distant continent for the rest of the century.[6]

Gold provided the principal stimulus for the economic development of the Far West during the entire pioneer period from 1849 to 1869. Here it attracted settlers, and assured an adequate money supply for the first time. Demand created by the mining fever provided incentives for the expansion of agricultural, milling, shipping and mercantile enterprises in California and Oregon. The California market became a natural outlet late in 1848 for Oregon's provisions and lumber and a thriving trade arose between the two frontier communities. This trade relationship persisted throughout Oregon's pioneer period in spite of the fact that agriculture, flour and lumber milling developed in California and in the other mining areas.

While California gold stimulated Oregon's underdeveloped agricultural economy, the rapid growth of the Golden State destined the northern territory for a dependent and secondary role. Prior to 1848, prospects for the scattered American communities in both California and Oregon were generally unpromising in spite of the continued optimism of the pioneers. They were isolated and the limited market conditions plagued their economic development. Contacts with the Orient were few, and the long-hoped-for Asiatic trade failed to materialize. During the 1840s when a few thousand American emigrants had made the trek to the Far West, Oregon had been the goal for most of them. Oregon had been the name most conspicuous in the journals expounding the doctrine of Manifest Destiny. Emigration to Oregon generally had shown marked yearly increases after 1842, but dwindled to a mere 200 to 400 or so in 1849, when not less than 20,000 passed Fort Hall en route to California.[7] Thereafter Oregon's population growth was modestly gradual while that of California was phenomenal.

Oregon's farmers were among the first to catch the gold fever. The news of Marshall's discovery reached the little northern colony early in August, 1848. Captain Newell, who had arrived on board the schooner *Honolulu* from San

Francisco in late July, announced the news after he had purchased all the equipment and provisions his small ship could carry. The fever spread rapidly and by September the exodus of Oregon's able-bodied men by land and sea had fairly begun. Eager to avoid the hazards of winter travel, organized pack and wagon trains moved southward over the little-known trails.[8] On September 4, the Rev. G. H. Atkinson, a Congregational missionary who had just arrived at Oregon City, reported:

> During the last two weeks our town has been in a state of high excitement. Our lawyers are going or gone. Our mechanics have left their shops in many cases. Our three physicians decided to leave. Some of our merchants decided to dispose of their merchandise, or to close business and leave. Several preachers left camp meetings and religious duties to follow their fleeing people. We are left with women and children. No job is taken, except for a few days.[9]

During October pressure for passage on the few ships now arriving on the Columbia was tremendous. As provisional governor, George Abernethy protested against the overloading of the brig *Henry*, a ship of only 155 tons burden, owned by one of his competitors. The 122 deck passengers on board probably faced the hazards of a sea voyage for the first time. Eager to acquire riches, they willingly consented to live and sleep on the open deck through the stormy coastal waters of the North Pacific. These "western people know nothing of sea life," Abernethy observed, "and think, I presume, it is like sailing down the Mississippi on a steamboat . . ." Peter H. Burnett estimated that two-thirds of the men capable of bearing arms left Oregon in the fall of 1848, though many returned for the winter. The percentage of men who left for the mines was even greater in 1849, and consequently fields were either abandoned or neglected. The prospect of a severe labor shortage threatened to bring the agricultural and nascent industrial enterprises of the territory to a complete standstill.[10]

But Oregon reaped her share of the golden harvest. Men returning during the winter of 1848-49 brought with them sums ranging from $1,000 to $10,000 or more, and one laborer, formerly quite poor, was reported worth $100,000. According to estimates $500,000 had poured into Oregon by January, $1,000,000 by March, and $5,000,000 by December, 1849.[11] Gold now began to flow into the hands of Oregon's merchants and farmers in payment of their short supplies of produce.

Few Oregon argonauts intended to settle in California permanently or to follow the life of a prospector or miner. Rather, the promise of easy wealth and a temporary adventure attracted them. Those who did not go immediately were urged by their friends already on the scene to sell everything except their land claims in order to participate in the grand rush. The editor of the *Spectator,* before suspending publication on February 22, 1849, because his printer went to California, vainly urged Oregonians to stay on their farms and reap greater profits from the growing California market. He appealed to America's agrarian tradition by saying: "The earth is the source of all wealth, and those who cultivate it are truly said to be the life and soul of the country." He also urged the development of the mineral resources of Oregon, where coal, iron ore, and even gold in moderate amounts were reported to exist. One report stated that a man could obtain gold in Oregon and earn from $3.00 to $5.00 per day, but that no one would work for so little. More cautious men resisted the California mania and determined to make the best of their situations in Oregon. Of the large number of Oregon farmers who made the trek to California most are assumed to have returned and to have redeemed their land claims, since the increase from 9,083 by Governor Lane's census in 1849 to 13,264 by the official United States census in 1850 is not accounted for by immigration.[12]

Merchants who were prepared to supply the growing California market with goods or produce enjoyed tremendous initial advantages. Prices for some goods at San Francisco, according to reports received in Oregon, rose as high as 100 per cent and in some cases 200 per cent over New York costs by February, 1849. Merchants at Oregon City lost little time in making advantageous adjustments to the changed conditions. Kilbourne, Lawton and Company of Oregon City continued to transport cargoes of lumber and produce in the brig *Henry* for the California market. Hiram Clark, representative of a Boston firm, opened a store at Oregon City in the spring of 1848 and after selling his first cargo of goods, went to California in the spring of 1849. F. W. Pettygrove closed his stores at Oregon City and Portland and left for the greener pastures to the south.[13] Captain John H. Couch, who had returned to Newburyport in 1847, learned of the gold discovery early in 1849 and promptly loaded out a cargo of lumber and mining tools on the bark *Madonna* for the California market. Along with many other ship captains, he braved the tempestuous waters of the Cape Horn route during the southern hemisphere's winter season, and sold his cargo at fabulous prices in San Francisco in July, 1849. Captain Nathaniel Crosby, Lot Whitcomb, and other Oregon pioneer merchants engaged actively in the Oregon-California trade.[14]

The entrepreneurial activity of George Abernethy, whose early business career in Oregon has been discussed in preceding chapters, exemplifies the effect of gold upon the economy of Oregon. As already mentioned, he had sought in 1848 before the news of the gold discovery reached Oregon, to persuade Captain Roland Gelston or Edward F. Folger to enter partnership with him and to send out goods from New York. He needed a vessel to transport flour and lumber to the then improving California market in order to avoid the high freight rates on his competitors' ships to San Francisco. He also wanted credit and requested Gelston to induce someone to ship out "an invoice of goods of not over $5,000 purchased low in New York." To convince his prospective creditor of his solvency he noted that his saw mill produced lumber at the rate of 4,000 or 5,000 feet in twenty-four hours and that the value of his Oregon City property was rising rapidly.

By mid-summer 1848, just before the news of the gold discoveries was known in Oregon, trade conditions had become worse. There was only one ship on the river, Captain Goodwin's bark *Eveline,* taking on a cargo of lumber for Oahu. Kilbourne had gone to California in the brig *Henry* in March and there had been no other ship on the river until the arrival of the *Honolulu* in July bringing the exciting news from the south. Abernethy wrote despairingly: "It is strange that no vessels touch our river this year, we are worse off for goods . . . than we were last year. Grain scythes are not to be had. $10 has been offered and refused for a scythe, coffee 25c sugar 10c nails 18c calico 28c unbleached drilling 20c. These are cash prices." Abernethy was convinced by these conditions that a merchant to be prosperous in Oregon had to own his own vessels as well as his own mills.[15]

The gold rush strengthened this determination. He was unable immediately to take advantage of the rising demand for lumber and flour in California because he lacked control of his own shipping facilities. Nor did he enjoy the advantage of being a representative or an agent of an eastern firm as did some of his competitors. Ships now arrived more frequently than at any time previously but he could not get his freight loaded unless ship captains failed to get full cargoes for his ship-owning competitors. The *Spectator,* a paper alleged to have been under the domination of Abernethy,* reported on October 26, 1848, that "Ships are mints here now, and will remain so for some time." Ship captains refused to take cargoes except as a matter of *"pure grace and favor,"* the editor asserted. Abernethy complained that his lumber had lain on the river bank at Portland for months awaiting shipment, and that in consequence of the lack of shipping facilities he lost from 50 to 100 per cent on the lumber and produce he received in payment for goods. Thus he experienced the same disadvantages as he had earlier in meeting the competition of the Hudson's Bay Company and the few American merchants who controlled their own ships.[16]

Gold, the dynamic element in the rapidly changing economy, enabled Abernethy to go far toward the realization of his new ambitions. He possessed the advantage of a respected and prominent position in the community as well as a favorable location at Oregon City. He had been Oregon's provisional governor since 1845 and had taken a leading role in the community since 1840. He ranked with McLoughlin as one of Oregon's few prominent merchants. As the principal successor to the various enterprises of the Methodist Mission he had a considerable capital outlay in

---

*Abernethy was probably the source of this information since his views were frequently reflected in the paper's editorials. The *Spectator* had a succession of editors during its early existence. George L. Curry resigned in February, 1848, because of the alleged dictatorial policies of the Printing Association and Abernethy's domination and censorship. Curry was followed by Aaron E. Wait from February, 1848, to February, 1849, when the paper suspended publication. It resumed publication on October 4, 1849.

the form of mills, a store, and ill-assorted merchandise. By February, 1849, he had received payments for most of the debts owed by settlers to the mission. As has been noted, with gold flowing freely into the area he expected to lose not more than $2,000 out of the $30,000 he had to collect. He shared with McLoughlin the best water power site for manufacturing in the area at the falls of the Willamette at Oregon City. Here he had both a flour mill and a saw mill which numbered among an estimated eight flour mills and fifteen saw mills in the entire territory in 1848. He had quantities of flour and lumber as well as adequate supplies of wheat and logs on hand when the great demand for Oregon lumber, flour and produce arose in California in the fall of 1848. His store was in short supply but he had reasonable expectations that his efforts to obtain goods directly from New York would soon succeed.

Abernethy shared the general optimism that caught the population during the exciting early days of the gold rush, but at the same time he evinced a cautious, conservative, even apprehensive attitude. He had no desire to go to the mines nor to pull up stakes and establish himself in San Francisco. He was convinced that Oregon offered more certain opportunities for an enterprising businessman and referred to the California rush as a snare. After citing the hard work experienced in mining by many of the returning Oregonians, he suggested that the soft-handed gentlemen of the East who were dreaming about gold "had better practice digging wells at home" before coming to California. In evident contradiction to this line of thought he was apprehensive about the ease with which gold could be obtained. Costs of labor and the prices of produce were bound to rise. Actually he feared that gold might exist in such great quantities in California as to render it a valueless or practically useless commodity. In addition, he anticipated the possible cessation of all farming and milling activity in Oregon and wrote in February 1849: "What will be the consequence? Oregon with California will be ruined in toto. Who will make rails, hew timber, harvest, or do any hard work with $20,000 in their pockets, and when that is gone able to go and pick up $20,000 more." He even feared that the newly appointed territorial officials including the governor would not stay in Oregon, as anyone could make more than the governor's salary in a few weeks in California.[17]

This pessimism was not general. Some people believed all of Oregon's economic ills were to be solved as gold flowed into the territory in return for lumber and produce for the California market. The editor of the *Oregon Spectator* commented:

> Is not a market for your wheat, beef, pork, potatoes, peas, beans, garden vegetables, fish, and lumber, a desirable matter? and will not such mines draw to them a sufficient population to provide you a market for all these articles? Certainly, Oregon is temporarily injured by reason of so many of her citizens having left their farms, and shops for the purpose of gold digging; but only temporarily. The time will come when the population of the gold mines of California and Oregon, (for we believe there are gold mines in Oregon) will be supplied, in part, with provisions from the Atlantic seaboard. Wheat, and most of the other grains, with the exception of Indian corn, can be afforded cheaper in Oregon than in any other part of the Union, and beef vastly cheaper; . . . All that Oregon has wanted was a good market, the facilities for carrying her produce to that market, and the protection and care of the home government.[18]

In spite of this optimism, alleviation of Oregon's supply problem did not immediately follow the discovery of gold. There was a greater scarcity of goods in Oregon in the fall of 1848 than ever before. A principal reason for this, as mentioned earlier, was the loss of the Hudson's Bay Company's yearly shipment of valuable supplies when the *Vancouver* was shipwrecked at the mouth of the Columbia in May, 1848. Further, most available merchandise shipped from the East moved into the San Francisco market, and only gold flowed into Oregon in exchange for produce and lumber. Many staple items of groceries, dry goods and hardware were not on the market at all, and most other goods were in great demand. In February 1849, no cheese and scarcely any butter was on the market, and that available was reported not fit to eat. The Rev. G. H. Atkinson noted that the merchants were "reaping golden harvests with their few goods," making from 200 to 500 per cent on them while the community was nearly destitute.[19] According to the statement of the Rev. William M. Roberts, another frontier minister:

> Not a Blanket, or Kettle, or tin pan or pair of boots or strong
> coat or pants or hat fit to wear or pound of Sal Eratus
> [baking soda] or tea can be bought anywhere in the territory
> that I know of at any price. A few lbs. sugar, some Manilla
> coffee, a little rotten sewing silk &c remain, but I suppose
> the sugar crop is neglected at the Islands and if raised the
> ships are otherwise employed.[20]

The discomfiture of the transplanted Missouri housewife who was now unable to concoct her traditional saleratus biscuits can only be imagined.

Short supply of merchandise in Oregon and the tremendous demand for Oregon products in California provided very attractive business opportunities for men with nominal capital resources. Step by step Abernethy accumulated capital and soon emerged as Oregon's foremost middleman. By January of 1849, he completed a shipping agreement with C. L. Ross of San Francisco whereby the latter's ships would transport consignments of lumber and flour from Abernethy in return for gold or, when possible, merchandise which might be in over-supply at San Francisco. Each would retain one-half the profits on goods sold rather than a regular commission. Ross, incidentally, was a California pioneer of 1847, having come out on board Gelston's bark *Whiton*. During the first year of the gold rush, when he sold Oregon lumber for $300 per thousand, he cleared $110,000 from his merchandising enterprises. In 1850 he made many more thousands in land speculation and rents from choice sites on Montgomery and Washington streets only to be wiped out entirely when a great fire swept San Francisco in 1851.

During 1849, Oregon's flour and lumber industries flourished as never before because of the stimulus of gold. New grist and saw mills appeared, to meet the new demand. For the mill owners of the territory these industries offered the best means for quick profits and capital accumulation.

Abernethy and other merchant-millers gained by the rising price of flour. They had either purchased or contracted for the 1848 crop at the regular rate of 60 to 62½ cents per bushel. The normal price of flour in August 1848, was from $5.50 to $6.00 per barrel, or $2.75 to $3.00 per hundredweight. By December it had reached $10 per barrel, and by February 1849, $12 to $15 per barrel. In December

1848 Oregon flour sold at $25 per barrel at San Francisco and $100 per barrel at the mines. Abernethy and other Oregon merchants thus gained from $4.00 to $10 per barrel, the increase in the Oregon price. The total output of Abernethy's mill can not be estimated, but he reported in February 1849, having 300 barrels of flour on hand which he was selling at $10 per barrel cash, and again in April that he still had enough wheat, which he apparently had purchased at 60 or 62½ cents per bushel, to make 300 barrels more. Thus Oregon farmers failed to benefit from the rising price of flour, but in 1849 those who resisted the lure of quick riches at the mines marketed their wheat at $2.00 per bushel. The 1849 crop was short, however, for so many fields were neglected during that season owing to the exodus of Oregon farmers to California.[21]

The demand for lumber in California was equally strong. Vast quantities were needed for building cabins, stores, sluice boxes, flumes, and for innumerable other purposes. In response to the need, lumbering on a small scale developed almost immediately in the mining region itself, where there were fine stands of timber. But the difficulty of competing with the mines for labor and the problem of an inadequate water supply hampered the development of lumbering in the Sierra area. Conditions were far more favorable in the great forests of the coastal regions. Lumber production developed there as well as in the mining region, and the California industry was well established by 1852. But during the early years of the rush, 1848-49, the California market was highly favorable to the importer, with prices rising to phenomenal heights.[22]

Oregon shared largely in meeting this demand. Abernethy and other Oregon saw mill operators who were prepared to supply lumber for the California market were favorably situated. The Oregon price rose from $16 per thousand board feet in the fall of 1848 to $60 to $75 per thousand during the summer of 1849, and as high as $80 to $100 per thousand in November, 1849.

Abernethy made money in spite of the rising production costs. He had improved his lumber mill at Oregon City so that at maximum capacity its output per 24 hours was 6,000 feet with the saw striking 400 strokes per minute under a full head of water. But with the shortage of manpower, labor costs rose accordingly. Wages were $2.00 to $5.00 per day in February, 1849, and by the end of the year mechanics received $5.00 to $10 per day. To retain his sawyers Abernethy had to pay them at the rate of $10 per thousand for lumber and $15 per thousand for shingles. He paid $24 per ton for boating or rafting his flour and lumber twelve miles downriver to the landing at Portland where it was most convenient for ocean-going ships to load. But as early as July, 1849, he stated that he expected to clear $26,000 on the lumber and flour he had sold as of that time. He also shipped house frames to San Francisco.

Because ocean-going ships could not conveniently navigate the Columbia-Willamette system as far inland as Oregon City, Abernethy decided to locate a lumber mill down on the Columbia closer to the sea. He was still convinced that Oregon City would become the commercial and industrial center of the territory, but for the time being, he needed a more desirable location from the standpoint of availability of timber and of accessibility to the sea. In May, 1849, he sold his mills and all available logs on hand at Oregon City for $35,000 to Judge Bryant, a newly appointed territorial official. This sale apparently also served a more questionable purpose on the part of Abernethy and the mission faction—to deprive Dr. McLoughlin of his claim to Abernethy Island, where Abernethy's mills were located.*

The new saw mill was located at Oak Point on the right bank of the Columbia some fifty miles closer to the sea. Virgin timber in vast quantities stood conveniently at the very site of the mill. Other advantages included an unfailing

---

*The sale of Abernethy Island seems to have been a part of the political maneuvering of the mission faction and Territorial Delegate Samuel R. Thurston which resulted in the enactment of the 11th clause of the Donation Act. This clause deprived McLoughlin of his Oregon City property and nullified his claim to Abernethy Island by specifically confirming title to the island to the milling company currently in possession. *U. S. Statutes at Large,* IX, p. 499.

The relationship between Abernethy's sale of the site and the clause in the Donation Act is not clear. Although he sold it to Judge Bryant, he apparently repossessed it. According to an affidavit signed by Abernethy on February 2, 1852, he had transferred the island to Governor Joseph Lane prior to the passage of the Donation Act. While Abernethy's correspondence reveals no hint of complicity in a nefarious design, Bancroft in *History of Oregon,* II, p. 122, says that Bryant was bribed outright. Abernethy disliked McLoughlin intensely and in a private letter referred to his rival as "a Catholic and one of the most bigoted kind." McLoughlin expressed his bitterness in a letter to the *Milwaukie Star,* April 10, 1851, quoted in "Documents," *OHQ,* 1900, pp. 108-109 as follows: "part of my

water supply to propel the milling machinery and the great depth of the river where sailing vessels could come alongside the wharf and load out the lumber in dry condition. The new mill required an outlay of only $10,000. Abernethy employed skilled craftsmen to run it on a partnership basis and later stationed his brother, A. S. Abernethy, at Oak Point to supervise the operations. Abernethy expected to keep from four to six brigs of about 180 tons each in constant supply on regular runs to San Francisco. Production began in November, 1849, at the rate of 5,000 feet per day.[24]

Oregon lumber sold for phenomenal prices in California and the heavy demand held through 1849 and the early months of 1850. In two years the number of saw mills in Oregon more than doubled, as the California trade brought handsome profits to producers, shippers, and distributors. Oregon lumber wholesaled at San Francisco at $120 per thousand board feet in December, 1848, $325 in July, and $400 in November, 1849. Captain John H. Couch sold his cargo of eastern lumber at $600 per thousand in the summer of 1849. But ship owners operating in the coastal trade had to pay ordinary seamen $150; officers, $250; and captains, $500 per month, and freight charges rose proportionately. The freight charged for Oregon lumber on the Oregon-San Francisco run soon equalled the Oregon cost per thousand.[25]

In spite of the favorable market Oregon lumber producers could not meet the demand in the fall of 1849. Twenty ships waited for cargoes on the Willamette and Columbia in October, and ship captains became discouraged as they discovered the limited sources of supply. Consequently fewer imports flowed into the Oregon market than would have been the case if there had been a greater supply of Oregon commodities. The total lumber export for the two-month period September 1 to November 1, 1849, was

claim which has been jumped, Mr. Thurston persuades Congress to donate Judge Bryant, and the remainder is reserved. I make no comment — the act speaks for itself, but merely observe, if I had no claim to Abernethy Island, why did Mr. Thurston get Congress to interfere and what had Judge Bryant done for the territory to entitle him to the favor of the delegate, Mr. Thurston is exerting the influence of his official situation to get Congress to depart from its usual course, and to interfere on a point in dispute, and donate that island to Abernethy, his heirs and assigns, alias Judge Bryant, his heirs and assigns." See letters of Abernethy to Gelston, May 18, 1849, and to Francis Hall, June 30, 1849 and his affidavit of Feb. 2, 1852, Abernethy Mss, O. H. S., and *McLoughlin's Fort Vancouver Letters*, Third Series, p. lxii.

1,485,000 board feet, which wholesaled on the river at the average price of $100 per thousand.[26]

The price of Oregon lumber in California fell precipitously owing partly to the heavy shipments of eastern lumber to San Francisco in 1850, but mostly to the rapid development of the lumber industry in the Golden State itself. From the winter of 1849-50 to April, 1850, the Oregon price fell from $80-$100 to $75-$80 per thousand. An observer at Astoria noted in June that: "Lumber is so low in California that it don't pay to send it there now, but the price for consumption here is still good, and the mills above pay very well." By the end of the year the price quotations were $40-$50 per thousand, a decline of 50 per cent for the year. By May, 1851, lumber had fallen to $25-$35 per thousand.

The demand for Oregon flour and produce, on the other hand, remained strong in California until 1852, in spite of the development of agriculture there. As noted above, the price of flour in Oregon rose from $10 per barrel in December, 1848, to $12-$15 per barrel in February, 1849. It continued to rise during 1849 and until harvest time in 1850. It sold for $14-$15 per barrel in the fall of 1849; $25 per barrel in December, 1849; and ranged from $18 to $25 per barrel during the spring and summer of 1850. Throughout the next year, from the fall of 1850 to the fall of 1851, the price remained steady at $15 per barrel.[27]

Gold dust was also a source of profit for Oregon merchants. For a time, during the fall of 1848 and the early months of 1849, it sold at an average of $11 to $12 per ounce when the value of gold coin was $16 per ounce. While the Hudson's Bay Company received it for as little as $7.00 per ounce, it fluctuated more generally between $10 for cash and the California price of $16 per ounce in exchange for goods. Miners and traders soon learned to exchange dust for cash at the rate of $16 per ounce before leaving California. They could then buy up gold dust circulating in Oregon at $11 or $12 per ounce, return to San Francisco where they could convert it into cash, and thus make substantial profits from the two transactions. Merchants benefited from the premium favoring cash, but at the same time the fluctuations in price and the inconvenience they experienced in handling gold dust were extremely irritating.[28]

The process of weighing was wasteful and irregular and often the dust itself was mixed with impurities. The general premium favoring cash, however, was sufficient to attract to the territory a heterogeneous metallic currency which included foreign coins of various denominations as well as standard United States currency.

Gold dust was now the principal circulating medium. While its use was inconvenient, it was far superior to the wheat certificates and orders on solvent merchants used previously. In the language of Professor Gilbert it was superior to the former medium "on account of its universally accepted value, its divisibility and portability." But he adds that "it lacked two essentials of a perfect currency—homogeneity and cognizability." Because of these deficiencies losses to the ordinary citizen were considerable. In the public mind, "greedy" merchants reaped the unearned increment from the sale of gold dust since they monopolized the weighing and assaying processes and seemed to dictate its value.

Oregon merchants also experimented with the coinage of money. In order to attract coin to the area the Provisional Government, disregarding the currency clause of the Constitution of the United States, passed its own coinage law in February, 1849. Fine gold was to be converted into coins at the rate of $16.50 per ounce. This law was nullified almost immediately when the authority of the United States was at last established in Oregon in March. But in spite of the constitutional restriction and the presence of territorial officials, the Oregon Exchange Company was organized for the express purpose of weighing and stamping gold. The eight partners were Oregon City businessmen, including William K. Kilbourne and George Abernethy. Dies for both $5.00 and $10 gold pieces were improvised by William H. Rector and Thomas Powell, a blacksmith. The processing and coinage of gold began by primitive methods, indeed; but altogether some $58,500 in five and ten dollar gold pieces were minted during 1849. Conspicuous on the coins were imprints of the letters "O. T., 1849," the name of the company, the initial of the last name of each member of the company on the $5.00 piece but of only six of them on the $10 piece, and the likeness of a beaver. Popularly known as "beaver money," it was under-valued purposely at eight to twelve per cent in relation to standard United States coins of the same denominations. Standard currency by the operation of Gresham's Law gradually drove "beaver money" from circulation, and the establishment of the United States mint at San Francisco in 1855 soon completed the process. But it had served the useful function of attracting standard coinage to the territory.[29] Gold dust continued to be used as a medium of exchange and circulated along with metallic currency. Oregon finally had an adequate money supply. This and the emergence of the reasonably dependable California market outlet in 1849, solved two of her most pressing economic problems.

The supply problem remained acute, however. Scant inventories and high prices continued during the gold rush years through the spring of 1851. Prices for provisions and staple items of general merchandise in continuous supply from the fall of 1849 to the spring of 1851 were either higher at the latter date or at about the same levels. A comparison of the prices quoted on November 1, 1849, with those for March 26, 1851, shows the price of coffee to have risen by 77 per cent; tea from 25 per cent to 50 per cent for the two qualities on the market; and pepper by 66⅔ per cent. On the other hand, the price of butter and brown sugar remained about the same. The best quality tobacco declined from $1.25 per pound to $1.00 per pound, as did the price of nails from 18 and 20 cents per pound to 12 to 15 cents per pound. In some items there had been severe shortages. There was no saleratus on the market at all in December, 1849, and salt was quoted at $6.00 per bushel. In February, 1850, saleratus retailed at $2.00 per pound.[30] Needed to relieve the supply problem were: first, dependable transportation and distribution facilities; and second, competition in the selling market to bid down the prices of goods as supply improved. The former came quickly, but a four-year period was required before a reasonable balance between supply and demand was attained.

During the first year of the gold rush, as we have seen, the market sought the product as Oregon's lumber, flour and provisions flowed to California in exchange for gold. More than fifty ships, many in ballast, arrived on the

Columbia during 1849. But Oregon could not adequately meet the demand for lumber and flour late in that year because of limited production.[31] Further, the demand for merchandise in Oregon could not be met adequately as long as a strong demand for goods from eastern sources existed in the San Francisco market. Thus ship owners engaged in the Oregon trade were frequently deprived of valuable cargoes at lucrative freight rates on the northward leg of the journey.

Abernethy thought direct shipment from New York to Oregon City was the only solution to the supply problem. There had been no ship direct from the United States to Oregon since the *Whiton* arrived in 1847. Although he expected the gold circulating in Oregon to attract goods from San Francisco, he could not visualize California's new metropolis as a permanent supply center for the Oregon frontier. He noted in April 1849, however, "Couch is on his way out. Crosby is running backwards and forwards continually and I think this market will get an overstock of goods this summer from California." He thought it would be to his advantage to obtain a cargo of goods direct from New York before the Oregon market became overstocked with goods from San Francisco. Should this occur, "Unsaleable articles will not be so advantageously got rid of," he observed.

From available evidence Abernethy seems to have been the first independent Oregon merchant to establish his credit and direct business contacts with New York firms. He based his appeal for credit upon the new conditions which promised a profitable trade. He offered to share the profits equally with the eastern firms, a practice that had been followed earlier by the ship captain merchants. He assured his prospective creditors of profits of at least 100 per cent, but noted that sales necessarily had to be on a retail basis. While the great distance would deprive the shipper of the use of his capital from twelve to sixteen months, the expected steamship service to Oregon would lessen the time required to make remittances considerably. "In this country the credit system is entirely abandoned," he wrote confidently, and "Cash on delivery is our way of doing business, this will enable me to do a large and safe business I trust."

101

Abernethy's principal contact in New York was the firm, S. and S. Halsted. Captain Gelston's corroboration of Abernethy's statements concerning his solvency, and the fact, perhaps, that Samuel Halsted had known Abernethy as a fellow churchman in New York in the 1830s were sufficient to establish credit with the firm. S. and S. Halsted agreed to purchase and to ship merchandise for Abernethy and to receive his remittances with interest at seven per cent after eight months. Shipping via Cape Horn normally required six months and remittances via the isthmus now required less than two months. Abernethy received his first goods under this arrangement, various small invoices shipped via San Francisco, in the summer of 1849. The total freight cost was $60 per ton, $25 of which was charged for the San Francisco-Oregon run. Earlier in the year freight on this run had been as high as $40 per ton, and as noted above, the rate for lumber was as high as the Oregon cost per thousand board feet.

Abernethy remitted by shipping gold dust directly to S. and S. Halsted. He also drew bills of exchange on this firm to meet his obligation to other houses. The New York firm took out a blanket insurance policy covering any amount of gold dust up to $20,000 that Abernethy might ship via Panama. Since miners and traders exchanged gold dust for coin before returning to Oregon, it was not easily obtained in Oregon by the summer of 1849. In order to gain the profits on gold dust in New York it was to Abernethy's advantage to exchange cash for dust in San Francisco before making his remittances. He shipped $17,000 in gold dust to S. and S. Halsted in August, 1849, and paid only a two per cent premium to cover freight and insurance via the Panama route. Thus emerged the pattern of trade between Oregon merchants and New York wholesale houses which prevailed until the first transcontinental railroad was completed in 1869.

Meanwhile the San Francisco market became attractive to Oregon buyers. Whenever it became overstocked in any line of merchandise such goods in most instances could be sold profitably in Oregon. Captain Gelston, who was in San Francisco in June 1849, failed to ship to Abernethy several items of goods, notably women's and children's shoes, which were in over-supply there when they would have yielded a profit in Oregon of 300 to 500 per cent. Other items of no particular use to the predominantly male population of California such as calicos, cottons, linen collars and wristbands could be purchased there for as much as 25 per cent below cost. In September 1849, Hiram Clark, Abernethy's new partner, bought a large cargo of merchandise in San Francisco for the Oregon market at prices varying between New York cost and from 25 to 50 per cent above cost. He purchased some goods at less than cost.

Supply in relation to demand remained highly unstable in California, and Oregon merchants could purchase only a few goods so advantageously in San Francisco. Much of the merchandise that did flow to the Oregon market was of poor quality, and Abernethy complained that "goods unsaleable in California are equally unsaleable here." He also complained that he had enough sad irons in stock to last ten years. There was a tremendous over-supply of tobacco in San Francisco in 1850, enough chewing tobacco, it was reported, to last the inhabitants sixty-five years. There were fifty pairs of boots and shoes for every man, woman and child in the vicinity. In 1851 the San Francisco market was glutted temporarily in all lines of merchandise. Until 1853, however, the trade remained profitable for the owners of the great California clippers, and it was not until that date that the San Francisco market became generally overstocked. In Oregon through 1851 at least, the supply problem remained acute and the general paucity of goods was a ruling condition of business.

While Oregon merchants had to be aware of the vagaries of the San Francisco market, Abernethy thought direct transportation of goods from New York to Oregon was the only solution to the supply problem. This was especially true, he believed, since a sufficient number of country stores now existed in Oregon to warrant a wholesale business in general merchandise. He decided to purchase one or more ships in order to import supplies directly from New York and also to engage in the coastwise trade. The latter would be especially profitable, since with the prevailing high freight rates for lumber one could double his profits if he owned his own ships. A ship laden with lumber from his mill, according to Abernethy's calculations, would pay for itself in two trips to San Francisco.

Abernethy was admirably situated, in the summer and fall of 1849, to expand his various business enterprises. As indicated above his new, more advantageously located mill promised continued profits in lumber exports. He had contacts and credit with New York merchandising houses. Available for investment were his recently accumulated capital resources of about $60,000 derived from merchandising, exporting, collection of the mission's old accounts of debts owed by the settlers, and sale of Oregon City property. Hiram Clark, his new partner, added his capital and business ability to Abernethy's firm in August, 1849. After purchasing the large assortment of merchandise mentioned above at San Francisco at low prices in the fall of 1849, Clark sailed promptly for New York with $40,000 of the new firm's ready cash to purchase a ship and cargo. In 1850, James R. Robb brought $50,000 of the $65,000 he had made at the California mines into the firm. Thus, California gold and the opportunities created by it contributed to the establishment and growth of a promising Oregon business institution.[32]

Abernethy at last realized his ambition to own ships and to make direct shipments from New York. Abernethy, Clark and Company, the new shipping firm, landed its first large cargo of goods at Oregon City in November, 1850. A wholesale business was immediately inaugurated—and George Abernethy and Company, the merchandising firm, became the first substantial wholesaling house in the territory. Direct transportation facilities between New York and Oregon seemed to herald a new day in the development of business and to solve the problem of inadequate supply, which had plagued the territory so long. San Francisco now could be by-passed, it was believed, and Oregon merchants would no longer have to depend upon the market there nor pay extra profits to California merchants. The costs and risks of shipping goods from San Francisco including freight, lighterage, insurance and handling charges, which the small Oregon merchants with capital resources ranging from $5,000 to $15,000 could ill afford, would now be reduced.

The editor of the *Spectator* stated:

> It is just as we predicted; the merchants of the interior have
> saved 25 per cent on the original cost, and the freightage
> and risks from California here. Thus, Abernethy, Clark &
> Co., by keeping up a supply, will save the consumer about
> 50 per cent; which instead of leaving the country and passing
> into the hands of San Francisco merchants, remains in the
> Territory, and forms a part of the circulating medium. Good.

In 1851, the bark *Culloma,* one of Abernethy and Clark's
ships, made a 140-day record trip from New York to Astoria,
and in July discharged her cargo valued at $160,000, prob-
ably the largest shipment on board an American ship ever
to arrive on the Willamette up to that time.[33]

Although it was an attractive and promising enterprise
direct shipping from New York was not the answer to Oregon's supply problem. The pattern to be established during
the early fifties was for many Oregon merchants to make all
or most of their purchases in San Francisco, while others who
had made the necessary arrangements purchased in New
York. In either case merchandise flowed to San Francisco
where it was unloaded and later shipped northward to the
Columbia River on board a sailing vessel or steamship
engaged in the coastal trade. Abernethy, Clark and Company made a few shipments direct from New York during
the early 1850s, but by 1853 it was a rare occasion when
anyone advertised a ship "Up for Oregon" in New York.
Although an increasing number of Oregon merchants placed
their orders in New York, the trade throughout the pioneer
period was insufficient to warrant the delay involved in
loading out a cargo large enough for a Columbia-destined
ship. It was faster by far and much more convenient to place
goods ordered by Oregon merchants on board those bound
for San Francisco.[34]

Thus California gold stimulated all branches of commerce
and industry in Oregon. The little colony now had a money
supply and a market for its surpluses. Abernethy's business
activities evince the kind of opportunities available to
enterprising businessmen and the means by which capital
accumulation could be achieved on the frontier. Abernethy
was also an innovator in establishing the new pattern of
trade which now included Oregon. California gold enabled

Oregon to overcome the pressing economic problems which plagued the Willamette community during the 1840s; and indeed the years of the California gold rush mark a distinct stage in Oregon's pioneer development. Gold, as Professor Joseph Schafer suggests, prevented Oregon from becoming a backward pocket of civilization similar to the isolated mountain communities of Kentucky and Tennessee.[35]

Chapter VI

Oregon's "Life-line" by Sea

"Several rising towns just beginning to spring up . . ."

Oregon's development during the 1850s and 1860s depended upon reliable lines of transportation and communication which appeared during the years of the California gold rush. Steamships and sailing vessels operating on lines between San Francisco and the Willamette River connecting Oregon with the Cape Horn and Panama routes decreased the effects of the isolation suffered by the little Oregon colony during the 1840s. California gold, as already explained, provided a new market for Oregon products and a reliable money supply. The stimulus of gold also accounts in great measure for the growth of agriculture and the extension of the cultivated area, the development of steam navigation on the rivers, and the rise of towns and villages in the Willamette Valley. Towns appeared to meet the needs of the small but growing agricultural hinterland and the demand of the California trade. All depended upon Oregon's newly developed "life-line" by sea.

The Emergence of the Ocean Route

As has been noted, sailing vessels plied the coastal route from San Francisco to the Columbia more frequently than ever before in 1849, and were running on a regular basis the following year. Oregon tradesmen purchased ships from the tremendous aggregation of sailing vessels in San Francisco Bay which had resulted from the demands of the California trade. After unloading valuable cargoes from the East, there was little or no ready employment for most of them. Consequently tradesmen purchased several fine new vessels at much less than cost for the Oregon-California coastwise trade. Commission and forwarding merchants appeared in Oregon and by January of 1850, Lot Whitcomb, a pioneer merchant-miller and founder of the town of Milwaukie, advertised himself as agent for a line of vessels running between Oregon City and San Francisco.[1] After relatively little shipping directly from New York, Abernethy, Clark and Company established the Oregon and California Packet Line and settled into the coastwise trade. Popularly known as the Abernethy line it became the leading line of sailing vessels on the San Francisco-Oregon run by mid-decade. Abernethy, Clark and Company established facilities at San Francisco for storage and acted as agent for the trans-shipment of Oregon-bound goods out of New York, as well as receiver for Oregon produce seeking the California market. George Abernethy and Company, the wholesale firm, provided similar services at Oregon City at the other end of the line. The names of the several fine sailing vessels of this almost forgotten line as well as others that frequented the Willamette were once the household words of the inhabitants of the little communities along the lower river.[2] The Pacific Mail Steamship Company, as will be explained, extended its service to Astoria in 1850 and to Portland in 1851. Thus emerged the San Francisco-Oregon run as the final leg of Oregon's vital connection with the outside world.

Oregon, like California, depended upon the Cape Horn and Panama routes. A virtual transportation revolution occurred during the height of the California gold rush, 1849-53, with the advent of steamships and the great clippers to the waters of the North Pacific. It also marked the beginning of steam navigation on the rivers of the Far West. The famous California clippers racing for San Francisco added a stream of the fastest and most majestic sailing vessels ever built. The rapidity of the expansion and development of transportation facilities in response to the California gold rush reflects the dynamics of American capitalism and industry, and is another example of how technology aided and accelerated the advance of the American frontier.

The United States government had already authorized mail service by steamship to the Pacific Coast before the discovery of gold in California. This was largely the result of continuous agitation from 1843 to 1847 on the part of Oregon settlers and friends of Oregon in the United States for the establishment of a reliable mail service to the Far West. The most practicable means for faster communication between the Atlantic and Pacific was to establish two steamship lines, one on either side of the continent, to connect via the portage across the Isthmus of Panama. On March 3, 1847, Congress authorized mail service on steamships via the Panama route and also, by another bill of the same date, required the builders of the new steamships to fulfill certain navy specifications so that they might be used as auxiliary ships of war. Congress granted appropriations to the navy department for these purposes and authorized it to let the mail contracts to the steamship lines. By March, 1848, the navy had completed contract arrangements with the newly incorporated United States Mail Steamship Company, by which it agreed to provide regular mail service at fortnightly intervals in five steamships from New York to the isthmus via New Orleans for an annual subsidy of $230,000.

The navy made arrangements for the service on the Pacific side with Howland and Aspinwall's newly formed Pacific Mail Steamship Company. Three steamships were to run from Panama City to San Francisco and Astoria with several intermediate stops. Aspinwall considered the mail subsidy, an annual payment of $199,000, scarcely sufficient for the costs of operation, but he planned to build a railroad across the isthmus and to develop the trade on the Pacific side of both North and South America. Unforeseen by the promoters of the Pacific Mail Steamship Company, the sudden onrush to California assured the success of a venture previously regarded as rather doubtful.

Thus the dawn of a new era in the ocean navigation of the Pacific coincided with the gold rush. The *California,* the Pacific Mail Steamship Company's first ship in the Pacific, rounded the Horn on her maiden voyage and arrived at Panama City on January 17, 1849. Here she met the clamor of hundreds of American gold seekers demanding passage to San Francisco. During 1849, the facilities of the company's first three ships in the Pacific, the *California,* the *Oregon,* and the *Panama,* were taxed to the limit to accommodate passengers at rates that soon rose to $300 for cabin and $150 for steerage passage from Panama to San Francisco. It was also the heyday for the ticket speculator who could resell steerage tickets for as much as $1,000. By 1851 the Pacific Mail Steamship Company had a fleet of thirteen ships in the Pacific.

The Panama route became the principal avenue for the transportation of mail and express destined for California and Oregon. As a route for travel it was second in importance only to the overland trail. As the Panama railway gradually extended its span of the isthmus after 1850, the volume of the express business steadily increased. After its completion in 1855 most of the lighter, more lucrative freights were diverted away from the Cape Horn ships, a damaging blow to those engaged in trade via the longer route. At least $710,000,000 in gold bullion, the Far West's most important export commodity, flowed eastward via the Panama route during the period, 1849-69. Charges for carrying treasure fell from 2½ per cent of its value in 1850, to one-fourth of one per cent in 1860.[3]

The Pacific Mail Steamship Company held its early monopoly of the traffic between Panama and San Francisco only briefly during the early part of 1849. Rivals soon appeared and competition brought down passenger rates. Those for passengers in May, 1851, were reported as low as $100 for first cabin, $75 for second cabin, and $50 for steerage. During 1850 and 1851 they varied, however, between $100 and $300 for cabin service and between $60 and $125 for steerage depending upon the speed of the ship, its accommodations and competition. In July, 1851, the freight rate from Panama to San Francisco was advertised by the Pacific Mail Steamship Company at $100 per ton. The fascinating story of competition between Aspinwall and Vanderbilt, the giants of steamship navigation via the isthmus, is beyond the scope of this study. Suffice it to say that the pioneer, the Pacific Mail Steamship Company, was destined to perform a long and valuable service for the communities of the Far West during the entire period from 1849 to 1869.

Passage via the Panama route from New York to San Francisco during the early years required from 33 to 35 days, with from 18 to 21 days on the Panama-San Francisco run. The completion of the Panama railroad in 1855 reduced the time for the through trip to 23 to 26 days. With the improvement of ships this time was further reduced. Though some ships could make it in less time, the standard set in 1865 for the whole route was 21 to 21½ days. The standard for the Panama-San Francisco run became 14 days. From 1851 to 1867 the number of passengers westbound over the Panama route, many of whom were destined for Oregon, ranged between 15,000 and 20,000 annually.

John H. Kemble, the historian of the Panama route, summarizes its significance in his concluding statement:

> For twenty years the steamers with their red paddle wheels and black-plumed smokestacks, the dug-out canoes, and later the screaming locomotives of the Panama Railroad connected California and the Pacific coast with the eastern United States. The trans-continental railroad eclipsed the Panama route in all its functions in 1869, but it is note-worthy that, throughout its formative years, the Pacific sea-board's communication with the nation and with the world was chiefly by the Panama route.[4]

No less important was the expansion of traffic via Cape Horn. This was the vital freight route to the Far West during the entire pioneer period, until the completion of the first transcontinental railroad to San Francisco in 1869. Here in 1849 ships of all descriptions moved toward San Francisco Bay where tons of merchandise and an estimated 20,000 gold seekers were unloaded after the long, arduous, six-month journey of some 20,000 miles. Many ships, upon reaching the Promised Land, were either dismantled or allowed to rot at their moorings in the bay.[5] Some were destined to sail again once their captains were fortunate enough to find crews. As mentioned above, some, selling at much less than cost, were placed in the Oregon-California coastal trade.

The graceful, streamlined California clipper ships, built especially for the California trade, provided one of the greatest sagas of the sea with their record-shattering runs during the early fifties. Captains raced to reap golden harvests while the demands of the California market held. The great clippers cut the sailing time for the Cape Horn voyage to San Francisco from six months to slightly more than three. Twenty-two passages of less than 100 days are recorded for the long voyage. In 1851 the famous clipper *Flying Cloud* on her maiden voyage stormed over the route from New York to San Francisco with a record-breaking run of just 89 days. During the height of the trade, freight at $60 per ton and $1.00-$1.50 per cubic foot plus the sale of merchandise at fantastic prices meant substantial profits above the cost of the ship and cargo for a single voyage. The San Francisco market, though temporarily overstocked by 1851, remained generally profitable for two years more. After 1853, the great boom in clipper ship construction subsided as it became apparent that the demands of the California trade would not justify further expansion.

After 1855, the Cape Horn route was used principally for heavy freight shipped in clippers and the slow ponderous sailing vessels of the earlier era. Freight rates fell from $60 per ton in 1850 to $30 by 1853. They declined to $13 per ton in 1855; to $10 per ton in 1857; and to $7.50 in 1858.[6]

Trans-shipment to Oregon required lighter craft, barks and brigs, owing to the dangers of navigating the bar at the mouth of the Columbia River. However, Oregon merchants frequently placed misleading advertisements to the effect that they had just received goods from New York via some famous clipper. For example, in the summer of 1853, George Abernethy and Company advertised a large invoice of clothing just received from New York "per clipper ship Staghound." This advertisement actually refers to the clipper's arrival at San Francisco. No record exists of the *Staghound* or any other large clipper ship clearing customs at Astoria during these years.[7]

The Pacific Mail Steamship Company established regular mail, freight and passenger service between San Francisco and Oregon in 1850. During 1849 the mail had been dispatched in sailing vessels and the service had been irregular. In June of 1850, the Pacific Mail steamship *Caroline* inaugurated regular monthly service to Oregon, and on her first trip went all the way upriver to Portland. For the rest of the year the company provided service only as far as Astoria, but early in 1851, its new ship *Columbia*, a 777-ton side-wheeler built especially for the Oregon route, began making the regular run to St. Helens, a new town on the Columbia a short distance downriver from the mouth of the Willamette. In the same year the company established a regular semi-monthly service for its entire system from Panama to the Columbia. Twice each month the sturdy *Columbia* made the connection at San Francisco with the Panama-bound steamships. The company now guaranteed to make the entire run between Panama and Astoria, including all the necessary intermediate stops, within twenty-five days. In return the government increased the mail subsidy to a yearly payment of $348,250.

The *Columbia* was destined for a long and successful career on the San Francisco-Oregon run. Though her service was supplemented occasionally by one of the company's other ships, she made 102 trips between Oregon and California and one to Panama during the first five years of her service. During this period she carried 10,000 passengers and 80,000 tons of freight over a total distance of 220,000 miles.[8]

Towns and River Navigation

In 1850 Oregon's area of settlement was small and sparsely populated. According to Governor Lane's census in 1849, the year so many of Oregon's pioneer farmers went to the gold fields, the territory's population was only 9,083. The official United States census takers enumerated 13,264 a year later. This number probably did not include the immigration of 1850 so the increase of over 4,000 in one year is attributed primarily to men returning from the California gold fields. It may also have included a good many newcomers who had arrived by sea.

The figures for the overland immigrations for 1850 and 1851 have been generally underestimated. F. G. Young, for example, repeats the figures of 2,000 for 1850 and 1,500 for 1851 given by Elwood Evans in 1877. The *Oregon Statesman,* April 25, 1854, however, shows an estimate of 6,000 for the overland immigration of 1850, and 7,000 for 1851. In November, 1850, the Rev. Ezra Fisher noted that the "Immigration is rapidly coming in by land and water," and a year later he observed that: "The overland immigration is large. . . . Its number is estimated at from four to five thousand souls. We are constantly receiving accessions by water, so that it is thought that our white population by the first of March [1852] will be at least 30,000." Thus the territory's population may have doubled between 1850 and the arrival of the large immigration of 11,000-15,000 in 1852.[9] The number arriving by sea was probably larger than has been generally assumed reflecting the greater population mobility resulting from the establishment of regular passenger service via steamship from San Francisco.

Oregon's population growth during the early 1850s was due principally to the enactment of the Donation Land Law in September, 1850, and not directly to the stimulus of gold. The federal government rewarded the pioneers of the 1840s for their important role in the expansion of the American empire by granting every married man who had come to the territory prior to December 1, 1850, 640 acres of land, 320 acres of which was to be held by his wife in her own right, if they agreed to occupy it for a period of four years. Single men could file for 320-acre plots. For those arriving in the territory between December, 1850 and December, 1853, 320-acre plots were to the granted with 160 acres for the wife in her own right. For most of the settlers located in the territory in 1850, the Donation Law simply confirmed claims for 640-acre units already made. These claims either had been taken upon faith that the provisions of Linn's unsuccessful bill of 1842 would eventually be enacted, or under the actual laws of the Provisional Government. The effect of the Donation Law is reflected in the large immigration of 1852 which resulted in the expansion of the settled area southward into the Willamette Valley and into southern Oregon.[10] Here was the expanding hinterland so important to the men of business, the innovators in commerce and industry, upon whom the pioneer farmers depended for markets and the supply of goods they could not produce for themselves.

Oregon had become more attractive to merchants. Few were established in 1850, and of the 164 listed by the census takers of that year, the majority seem to have arrived only recently. Ninety-five, considerably more than half of them, were either single men or men unaccompanied by their wives and families and quite likely were transients exploring business opportunities in Oregon at that time.* Most were

---

*An analysis of the schedules for the census of 1850 (microfilm of the original in the Oregon Historical Society Library), reveals that of the total of the 164 merchants listed, 137 were native Americans, 25 were foreign born and the place of birth for two was "unknown." In 1850, 70.1 per cent of the native born and 58.5 per cent of the total number of merchants in Oregon were from the Eastern Seaboard states. Eighty-one, or more than half of the native born, were from the Middle Atlantic and New England states with New York leading all the states with 26. Kentucky was second, however, with 17 of the 41 born in the Trans-Appalachian West. Pennsylvania followed with 15, Massachusetts with 12, and

seeking "a competence," and some like William S. Ladd, who arrived in Portland in 1851, preferred a location in an agricultural area. Ladd mistakenly believed the economy of California to be based permanently upon gold production. While noting the complementary nature of the economies of Oregon and California, he chose Oregon, the producing area, over California, the consuming area. Perhaps some of Oregon's new merchants had been discouraged in San Francisco where so many merchants were already scrambling for the mining trade.[11]

With Oregon's modest population growth and economic development came the rise of towns. Oregon City had been the only important town in the territory during the 1840s. Here land values had risen steadily and virtually boomed during the California gold rush period. Abernethy, Philip Foster, and other American merchants had participated in the speculation, but leading the list was Dr. John Mc-Loughlin, the town's original proprietor. In 1849, he is reported to have refused $350,000 for his holdings at Oregon City, and to have stated that he would not sell for less than

---

Virginia and Maine with 10 each. The sectional breakdown shows 43 from the Middle Atlantic states; 38 from New England; 15 from the Upper Seaboard South; and 41 from the Trans-Appalachian West. Of the foreign born merchants, 15 were from the British empire, six from Germany, and four from France.

Sixty-nine, or 42 per cent of Oregon's merchants listed by the census of 1850, were married, and most of these had participated in the overland march. In checking the states of nativity of wives and children, it appears that 21 of the merchants born in the Eastern Seaboard states and four of the foreign born made one or more stops in the western states before making the final leg of the journey to Oregon. Eighteen of the 24 married merchants born in the Trans-Appalachian states made at least one other stop in a western state before migrating to Oregon.

Only those listed in the census as merchants were used in this analysis. This excluded traders, millers, and sea captains, who in some instances were also merchants. McLoughlin gave his occupation as trader; Kilbourne, sea captain; and Peter Skene Ogden, chief factor. Walter Montieth, who with his brother Thomas Montieth was soon to become one of the most prominent merchants in Linn County, and founder of Albany, gave his occupation as a carpenter. There were 12 listed as traders and only one druggist. Of the 109 mariners in the official compilation, *Statistics for the Census of 1850*, p. 1,004, 11 were sea captains. There were 1,702 adult males listed as farmers.

The comprehensive analysis of Jesse S. Douglas, "Origins of the Population of Oregon in 1850," *Pacific Northwest Quarterly*, XLI, 1950, pp. 95-108, suggested the method used in the above analysis. Douglas' statistical analysis of Oregon's total population in 1850 corrects glaring errors in the *Compendium of the Seventh Census* on Oregon. He also clearly presents the pattern of the westward advance of families whose ultimate destination was Oregon by studying the place of birth of children. He found surprisingly enough that, though only 26.4 per cent of Oregon's total population was from the Atlantic states, 89.2 per cent of these were adults. The number of adults from the Atlantic states comprised 43.9 per cent of Oregon's total adult population and these, he concludes, migrated westward at a relatively early age.

$500,000.[12] This, of course, was before the fateful clause in the Donation Act deprived him of his claim.

Expectations at Oregon City were high. With a population of about 600 in 1849, many believed it would become the industrial and commercial center of Oregon because of its location at the falls of the Willamette. Since traffic on the upper and lower sections of the river had to converge at the portages in the vicinity of Oregon City, its townsmen confidently believed it held the key to the commerce of the Willamette Valley. The falls also made it the most promising industrial site in the territory. In 1849 the town boasted two saw mills, two flour mills, ten or twelve dry goods stores, several mechanics' shops, and five churches.[13]

As was typical of the American frontier, town builders had appeared in Oregon during the 1840s to locate and plat out townsites at choice locations in the Willamette Valley and the Tualatin Plains. Enterprising merchants, millers, or merchant-farmers sought out propitious landings, millsites, or other favorable features, and located their claims with townsites in mind. Usually it was one or two individuals, whether merchant, miller, postmaster, or simply speculator, who made the original claim, platted out the town, and as town proprietor, began to sell lots. Several founders probably combined all these enterprises and did some farming as well. The towns platted prior to 1849, except Oregon City and possibly Portland and Astoria, had little or no commercial importance. In 1850 the Rev. Ezra Fisher observed: "We now have several rising towns just beginning to spring up . . . which will not fail to become important business places." A year earlier he had noted that Oregon City was the only town in Oregon worthy of the designation.[14]

On the lower river, however, ocean-going ships could reach Oregon City only with great difficulty, if at all. Rapids and shoals at the mouth of the Clackamas River made navigation treacherous for a distance of four miles below the falls. Ocean-going vessels could navigate that far upriver only at certain times of the year and ship captains were reluctant to make the attempt. Oregon City merchants hoped that they could somehow entice ocean-going vessels to their docks, and thought that they could alleviate the problem by having steamers tow the vessels upriver.[15] But lack of direct access to the sea remained Oregon City's greatest handicap, a fact that enhanced the prospects and aspirations of the new towns on the lower river, each of which sought to become Oregon's principal commercial city.

Portland was one among several of Oregon City's challengers. As has been noted, its origins date back to 1845 when Francis W. Pettygrove and Amos L. Lovejoy, the original proprietors, surveyed their land claim on the west bank of the Willamette twelve miles from its mouth. The place had little importance until San Francisco bound ships began to load out cargoes of lumber and flour there. It seems to have had a bad reputation during the later 1840s as a place where the "ague" prevailed. At any rate, it became a convenient loading place for ocean-going sailing vessels, and by 1848 was recognized by many as the head of navigation on the Willamette.[16]

But the new town of Milwaukie also sought this recognition. It had been laid out in 1846 by Lot Whitcomb at a point on the east bank of the river at the foot of the rapids just four miles from Oregon City. Whitcomb followed the common pattern of combining town proprietorship with his shipping, lumber milling, and merchandising enterprises. During the gold rush his town became another important place for loading out lumber for San Francisco. The town was handicapped by its lack of direct access to the rich farming areas of the valley and to some extent by its proximity to the shoals in the river. Its aspirations were dealt a heavy blow when the lumber trade subsided in 1853, but for a time, from 1849 to 1853, Milwaukie was a formidable rival of the other little towns on the lower Willamette.[17]

There were three other aspirants, all downriver from Portland. In 1846, M. M. McCarver and Peter H. Burnett, veterans of the overland immigration of 1843, had platted out the town of Linnton on the west bank of the Willamette four miles from its mouth, and had been busily promoting its advantages. Linnton's prospects were good during the early gold rush years but it was destined to fade into insignificance with the rise of Portland.[18] So also with Milton City located near the mouth of the Willamette. St. Helens, located on the west bank of the Columbia a few miles downriver from the mouth of the Willamette, vigorously entered the contest for commercial supremacy during the gold rush years. All the lower river towns were handicapped, however, because of the low range of hills separating the river from the Tualatin Plains to the west.

In 1850 all of Oregon's towns having populations worth mentioning were located at or below the falls. Leading the list was Portland with a population of 821, followed by Oregon City with 697, Milton City with 264, Astoria with approximately 250, Milwaukie with 168, and Linn City with 125.[19] Most of this growth, it must be assumed, came during 1849 and 1850.

With settlement and the rise of towns came the development of commerce and navigation on the Willamette River. During the 1840s keel boats, rafts, river schooners, and other craft had served the sparse settlements of the upper valley as far inland as Salem, a hamlet which the census takers of 1850 could not classify as a town. There were also a few other stations along the river where wheat, flour, and produce were loaded out for shipment downriver to the falls. Short portages by road on either side of the river—at Oregon City on the east and at Linn City on the west—were used to transport cargoes around the falls. Goods destined for the new country stores appearing in the interior followed the same route upriver.[20]

Steam navigation of Oregon rivers began in 1850. The little *Columbia,* so designated to distinguish her from the Pacific Mail steamship of the same name, was the first river steamer built in the territory. After the installation of machinery brought up from San Francisco, she was launched at Astoria in July of 1850 by her owners and builders, James Frost and Customs Collector John Adair. An observer noted: "It . . . is a right pretty one, 90 feet long, & 14 ft. wide, nicely finished with white pine from the East! think of that in this wooden country. . . . I think it will prove a good speculation. . . ." She did, indeed, for beginning her twice-weekly schedule immediately, her owners collected $25 per passenger or per ton of freight. By 1856 she had made 100 trips to Portland and is said to have made over $500,000 for her owners. But she was small, slow, and actually dangerous, and soon was overshadowed by more stately river boats.

118

In 1853, the editor of the *Oregonian* referred to her as "not a great improvement upon Fulton's first production."[21]

Steam navigation on the river expanded rapidly. Lot Whitcomb, Berryman Jennings, and S. S. White launched the first steamboat built on the Willamette at Milwaukie on Christmas Day, 1850, and christened her the *Lot Whitcomb*. Her length was 160 feet and her beam 24 feet. She began to compete immediately with the little *Columbia* on a twice-weekly schedule to Astoria, and was used to tow vessels on the Willamette. Her captain, J. C. Ainsworth, experienced in steamboating on the Mississippi and destined to become one of Oregon's most famous river men, had been persuaded to leave his employment on the Sacramento River by the owners of the *Whitcomb*. Jacob Kamm, also headed for a long and profitable career in river navigation, installed the machinery. In 1851, Abernethy, Clark and Company bought out Jennings and Whitcomb after Ainsworth had obtained an interest in the boat. The *Whitcomb* operated on the river until she was sold in California in 1854.[22]

At about the same time as the *Whitcomb* appeared, the Pacific Mail Steamship Company decided to extend its line of operations up the Columbia to some point on the river closer to the settled area in response to the demands for better mail and freighting service. The river site for the northern terminus of the San Francisco-Oregon run then became another factor in the growing rivalry among the little river towns. The company passed over Oregon City, Portland, and Milwaukie, and selected the convenient deep water landing at St. Helens on the west bank of the Columbia, near the mouth of the Willamette, still some distance from the settled areas. Here in 1851 a wharf and warehouse were built and the ocean steamship began making its regular northern stop at this place. The *Lot Whitcomb* made the connection at St. Helens for the Willamette traffic, and for a time she proudly by-passed Portland. Town boosters at St. Helens were elated. As a part of the rivalry the town leaders of both Portland and St. Helens had projected roads and even railroads to connect their respective towns with the Tualatin Plains and ultimately with

Lafayette, a new town farther south on the Yamhill, a tributary of the Willamette.

Portland businessmen and the new town proprietors, Lownsdale, Coffin, and Chapman, were not idle. They had acquired part interest in the steamship *Gold Hunter,* which began to make runs between Portland and San Francisco. The effort was unsuccessful because the San Francisco partners duped the Portlanders by selling the steamship, ending an early effort at competition with the Pacific Mail Steamship Company on the Oregon run. However, the episode of the *Gold Hunter* proved that an ocean-going steamship could load at Portland's docks as easily and conveniently as sailing vessels.[23]

Portland's great advantage in the rivalry for commercial supremacy among the towns of the lower river was its proximity to the rich farming area of the Tualatin Plains, westward across the low range of hills that paralleled the river behind the town. Completion of the Canyon Road to this area in 1851 determined the issue. Although the rivalry continued, especially between Portland and Oregon City, the advantages for trade and commerce of the former were soon recognized and Portland became the entrepôt for Oregon. The Pacific Mail Steamship Company was virtually forced to move its northern terminus for the Oregon-California run to Portland. There residents proudly greeted the arrival of the *Columbia* when she tied up at the Portland dock for the first time on May 1, 1851.[24]

Several steamers were soon operating on the lower Willamette engaged in the transportation business between the towns from Oregon City to St. Helens. They were also useful in towing sailing vessels upriver from Portland. Steamer operations extended as far as Astoria on the coast and up the Columbia to the Cascades. A number of these river steamers were ready built and transported to the Willamette on board sailing vessels from San Francisco; some sailed up from San Francisco; and several were built locally and outfitted with imported machinery. Both George Abernethy and Company, and Allan, McKinlay and Company, the leading merchandising houses at Oregon City, either owned or employed river steamers to handle produce and merchandise to and from Portland and to provide transportation for passengers. There were eleven steamboats operating on the lower river system and three others building in September, 1853.[25]

By 1850 the villages of the upper Willamette Valley and the Tualatin Plains had attained some importance as the frontier expanded southward and westward. There were thirty-eight merchants in Marion, Polk, and Yamhill counties in 1850, but only three in Linn and one in Benton counties on the southward-moving frontier.[26] Their country stores in all probability were the nuclei from which the several valley towns emerged. Walter and Thomas Montieth, founders of Albany, and J. C. Avery, founder of Marysville (later Corvallis), are examples of the town proprietor who was also merchant and miller. A check of several of the locations cataloged in McArthur's *Oregon Geographic Names* suggests a similar pattern for the rise of the other interior towns, most of which boast founding dates in the late 1840s when the original land claims were made. Salem's origins date back to the founding of the Methodist Mission at that site, and Champoeg originated as a Hudson's Bay station and the community center for the early settlers on the French Prairie. Founding dates for other towns which were particularly important during the 1850s as markets for Portland and Oregon City wholesalers were Hillsboro, 1849; Lafayette, 1847; Dayton, 1848; Forest Grove, 1846; Independence, 1845; Corvallis, 1847; Albany, 1848; Eugene City, 1846; and Dallas, also in the late 1840s. Oregon's villages grew in order to accommodate expanding farm communities; their proprietors, even Portland's, hardly conceived of a great metropolis.[27]

The Willamette River was the essential line of transportation and communication connecting most of these towns with Oregon City, Portland, and the outside world. Dayton and Lafayette were located on the navigable portion of the Yamhill, a tributary of the Willamette; and the communities of Hillsboro and Forest Grove in the Tualatin Plains were served by the Tualatin River, another tributary. All the other towns mentioned here, except Dallas, were on the Willamette itself.

Oregon's towns remained small. Most of the new settlers, who came after the Donation Act was enacted, sought 320 or 640-acre plots of land and not town lots. In fact there was an exodus from the existing towns, and many heads of families who otherwise might have remained in towns or settlers who might have been attracted to them had to fulfill the four-year residence requirement on their land claims. Thus the act was both a stimulus and a deterrent to town growth.[28]

In 1851 steamboats appeared on the upper river in answer to the needs of an expanding commerce, while flatboats, keelboats and other river craft continued to transport grain and produce downriver. The portages at both sides of the river at the falls were well established. But with the advent of steam navigation, the new town of Canemah located just above the falls on the Oregon City side, alongside a natural harbor of relatively calm water, became important for the construction and launching of steamboats, and the point at which a great portion of the river's commerce was transferred. During the epoch of river transportation and communication Canemah and Linn City, on opposite sides of the falls, were the northern terminals for the commerce of the upper Willamette Valley. Regular steamboat service upriver from the falls to Salem and Corvallis was established by 1852.[29] Thus the development of river navigation and the rise of towns in Oregon are further manifestations of the stimulus of gold and the new tide of immigration.

Other effects of the California gold rush upon frontier Oregon are worth noting. A general recklessness resulting from the plethora of gold pervaded the Willamette community to the despair of ministers. Church attendance declined alarmingly and it seemed that the causes of religion and temperance were lost. But the Rev. G. H. Atkinson quickly rationalized the new importance of gold and saw it as the magnificent instrument of the Divine Will. He observed:

> Why was not this gold discovered until now? How will it affect the kingdom of Christ? Already we see a check on papal influence. By its wealth in this territory, it was holding men in bondage, but money has made them independent and free. Also we might have urged in vain for an Eastern population to counteract popery, but Providence by these mines, has brought it, a vast living stream. God stored it and kept it till it was needed for these purposes.

Less concerned with such mighty questions, George Gibbs, a lawyer from New York state, commented as follows:

> The general healthiness of this country will induce great numbers to come here in preference to California. Excepting in some of the low grounds on Columbia & Wahlamet, I doubt if there be a healthier country anywhere. If folks did not drink themselves to death occasionally I don't know what else they would die of. Somehow or other too a rough mountain & forest country like Oregon possesses strong attractions, especially to the roving class of our men . . . There is . . . a general recklessness pervading all men— money is of but little consideration to any but those who look forward to a return to civilized life. They therefore spend it as freely as they make it, gambling and drinking are the everyday vices of the country—though to do the people justice they are in great measure the only ones. . . . For myself I shall be contented when the possession of a competence takes me out of it. Where one has a wife and family around him it is a different thing, though it is a shame to bring a white woman into such a country.[30]

The Willamette Valley retained its role as one of the principal sources of flour and provisions for the mining frontier as it expanded from California northward into the Pacific Northwest during the 1850s and 1860s. As a producer of agricultural products, the Willamette Valley held a similar relationship to the mining frontier as that of the newer agricultural communities that sprang up in its wake in closer proximity to the mines. This valley of course had an older heritage of pioneering, but its economic prospects had been extremely unpromising during the 1840s.

Otherwise the cultural pattern in the Willamette Valley shows many striking similarities to that of the mid-region of the Mississippi Valley. In a somewhat different climate men who had come mainly from that region surveyed and laid out their farms on the rich virgin soil of another river valley. Here were the same Yankee and southern elements.[31] Here were the country stores, mills, churches, small towns, and hundreds of farmsteads. The familiar steamboat had appeared by 1850. Here were the farmer, housewife, preacher, mechanic, and merchant of the older west transplanted to a remote frontier. Instead of the Mississippi River, the life-line of commerce was the Pacific Ocean, and San Francisco was the New Orleans of the Far West.

Chapter VII

Front Street

"A first rate business down in Portland . . ."

By 1851 the Oregon frontier, the farthest outpost of America civilization, manifested a degree of stability and permanence. Its faltering pioneer economy of the 1840s had given way to one bolstered by gold during the exciting early years of the California gold rush. Oregon had an ample supply of hard money and gold dust and a market outlet at San Francisco for her flour, lumber, and provisions. New lines of transportation and communication by steamship and by sailing vessel assured regular mail, freight, and passenger service to and from San Francisco and the East. This was Oregon's vital life-line by sea.

With these and other advantages the prospects for Oregon's development in 1851 were more promising than ever before. Steamboats had appeared on her rivers and several aspiring villages were rising in the Willamette Valley. Oregon's small population had long been poorly supplied, but now a hinterland suitable for the development of wholesaling had appeared. Territorial government, instituted in 1849, assured law and order. The Donation Law of 1850 gave security for property rights, and its promise of free land would certainly attract thousands of new settlers to the remote territory.

Oregon was an underdeveloped frontier area, a pocket of civilization near the Pacific Ocean in the midst of the vast wildernesses of the Pacific Northwest. The conquest of this territory was to continue for many years as the frontier penetrated the valleys and plains of the interior, skirting the deserts and mountains that were unsuited for agriculture, grazing, or mining. Only 132,857 acres of land had been improved by 1850[1]—in the aggregate about 208 square miles, and the population during the early months of 1851 was probably less than twenty thousand.

Settlements outside the sparsely inhabited Willamette Valley had already appeared. The generally southward-moving Willamette frontier itself reached out toward the head of the valley, and farmers and prospectors were exploring the valleys of the Umpqua and the Rogue rivers further to the south. Settlements north of the Columbia in the Cowlitz Valley and the Puget Sound area had begun. A few cattle ranchers were established east of the Cascades in the vicinity of The Dalles.

The changing pattern of trade which now involved Oregon was a small part of the much broader picture in which the dynamics of American capitalism played a dominating role. America's maritime frontier in the Pacific had long excited the men of commerce in New York and New England. Now the greatest fruit of Manifest Destiny yet harvested, California gold, was flowing eastward in vast amounts. Gold and Manifest Destiny filled the minds of men as they talked of untapped sources of profit in the Far West and in the Asiatic trade. The China trade, long important in the thinking of American traders and men of the sea, had taken on new significance with the rise of San Francisco. Soon, in 1854, Commodore Perry would display his ominous American hardware and his flag at the gates of Japan.[2]

Oregon had attracted few merchants prior to 1850, but with reasonable assurance of a money supply and a growing market area, many now came to the new territory. Although they faced the uncertainties of the inflationary cycle accompanying the gold discoveries in California, a trend that would rule the economy of the Far West through 1853, these men saw in merchandising the surest means of accumulating capital and of gaining prestige in the frontier community. Those who took the role of middleman figured prominently in the rise and development of Portland as Oregon's principal emporium. Modest profits earned during the early 1850s became foundations for the substantial fortunes of a later day. Thus the merchant not only supplied the frontier community but also accumulated the capital needed for its further economic development.

By 1851 Portland had become Oregon's most important town, the place where ocean commerce and most of that coming down the Willamette River converged. Not long before it had been referred to as the "head of navigation" or that place "twelve miles below Oregon City."[3] As has been noted it had become a significant shipping point during the early years of the gold rush and by 1851 it had virtually established its commercial pre-eminence. Although Oregon City still commanded much of the upriver trade during the 1850s, it was gradually overshadowed by the growth and importance of that place "twelve miles below."

Portland was a mere village of 821 persons in 1850, yet it was the largest town and most important port north of San Francisco. Located on the left bank of the Willamette River mid-way between the falls at Oregon City and the river's mouth, it stretched out on the low lands along the river for half a mile. To the west at a distance of only 200 yards there rose the dense native forest. Front Street, its main thoroughfare, was a rough muddy dirt road parallel to the river. Along its wooden sidewalks there straggled a few store buildings and warehouses where in 1851 a half dozen mercantile establishments practically constituted the business district.[4]

Indeed it could be said that Oregon's business activity now focused on this little street. At the nearby docks lofty sailing vessels and steamships took on and discharged valuable cargoes. Portland merchants, and occasionally a few upriver merchants whose goods came directly from San Francisco, were eager to examine the condition of their consignments. After May, 1851, when the Pacific Mail Steamship Company's steamship began its regular schedule to Portland, each arrival of the steamship with mail, passengers, and goods from San Francisco and the outside world became a gala event for the villagers. Merchants eagerly received news of prices and market conditions from "below" (San Francisco), or "home" costs from New York. Goods destined for upriver points were transferred to river steamers or to the wagons that often congested the muddy little street. Here, during busy seasons, was bustling activity where merchants, farmers, and ship captains traded and discussed business.

Among the merchants who arrived in Portland during 1851 were Henry W. Corbett, Henry Failing, Cicero H. Lewis, and William S. Ladd, all four destined for long and distinguished business careers in the city on the Willamette.

All were under thirty—Failing was just seventeen—when they arrived in Portland. All but Ladd had come directly from New York, where they had gained training and experience in the ways of business and an intimate acquaintance with the New York business community.

Cicero H. Lewis arrived at Portland in the summer of 1851 and opened a small grocery business. He soon entered a partnership with his boyhood friend, L. H. Allen, who remained at San Francisco. This is an example of a rather common arrangement whereby firms maintained houses in both cities. Frequently the Portland business was merely a branch of a San Francisco house. Such was not to be the case, however, with the firm Allen and Lewis, which was to become one of the foremost wholesale houses not only in Portland but of the entire West Coast.[5]

William S. Ladd began his business career in Oregon. He had been a New Hampshire schoolmaster, later a railway freight clerk, and at the age of twenty-four he booked passage from Boston to San Francisco and thence to Portland, where he arrived in April, 1851. He started with no financial backing, but within a year, after working for other merchants as a clerk and after selling goods sent up from San Francisco by his boyhood friend, C. E. Tilton, he was able to establish a promising business.[6]

All of these young merchants were neighborly, each commanding the other's fullest respect while practicing the rules of competitive business in the tradition of *laissez faire*. They soon gained social pre-eminence in the town and ultimately became pillars of Portland's aristocracy. With their eastern backgrounds they helped to impress upon the young community the distinct New England cultural tone which pervaded the town from its inception.[7]

What motivated these and other merchants in their choice of Oregon's raw frontier? They were, first of all, seeking a "competence" for the purpose of launching business careers. The excitement caused by the California gold rush in New York's commercial community no doubt stirred the minds of the sharp, more adventuresome young men of the counting houses and made the Far West seem especially appealing. Everyone knew of the phenomenal profits of the California trade, but what about Oregon? Ladd had been influenced by pro-Oregon propaganda of the type which had circulated in the 1840s and which was still current in New England, and tales of the California hide and tallow trade. He also had been impressed by the experience of a man named Carr, a storekeeper in Ladd's home town of Sanbornton Bridge, New Hampshire, who went to San Francisco in 1850, purchased a stock of goods for $3,500, and went on to Portland to sell the entire lot for $10,000. Shortly after Carr returned to New Hampshire, and after an earnest conversation with the successful fortune hunter, Ladd himself was on his way to California. Probably others with similar experiences advertised Oregon as a place of opportunity. Ladd viewed the gold rush with suspicion but evinced confidence in a society based upon agriculture. These young men came to the Far West merely to explore business opportunities, but unlike others, they chose to remain in Oregon and to identify their careers and fortunes with the future prospects of the new community. Thus profit-seeking young businessmen from the East responded to the challenges of the frontiers of the Far West and went out to earn their fortunes as others had done earlier on the successive frontiers of America's westward advance.

Oregon's early merchants number among her less heralded pioneers, probably because so many of them did not arrive until after the rough days of the 1840s had passed. Few of them ever experienced the hazardous overland journey on the Oregon Trail. Because they came by sea, these men were never included in the hallowed ranks of overland pioneers, early explorers, mountain men, missionaries, or frontier politicians. Even such early pioneers and veterans of Cape Horn as Captain John H. Couch, F. W. Pettygrove, and George Abernethy received relatively little acclaim. But men like Ladd, Corbett, Failing, and Lewis came to exert powerful influences upon the economic, political, and cultural development of Oregon. It is asserted that Ladd, though he never held political office except a brief term as mayor of Portland in 1854, became the most influential and powerful man in Oregon through his business and financial wizardry. He started on the road to power and influence on Front Street, where early in his career, that thrifty young

New Englander worked out his taxes by pulling stumps from the street.[8]

Two Portland business firms, those of Henry W. Corbett and of Josiah and Henry Failing, merchant capitalists, have been chosen for this study to demonstrate the role and function of the entrepreneur in a frontier economy. This function, according to Schumpeter, is that of an innovator who effects new combinations in trade or industry by establishing his credit and one who gains entrepreneurial profits without having necessarily risked any capital at all.[9] The records of the Corbett and Failing enterprises also reveal the completion of new trade patterns and processes that had begun to develop after 1848 between Oregon and its sources of supply, and within Oregon itself. The trade pattern involving New York, San Francisco, and Portland became more clearly defined during the years 1851-54, and once established it remained essentially the same for the rest of Oregon's pioneer period—until the completion of the transcontinental railroad to San Francisco.

Henry W. Corbett launched his Oregon business under the auspices and guidance of the New York dry goods firm, Williams, Bradford and Company, his former employers. At New York in October 1850, he purchased a wide assortment of dry goods, boots and shoes, groceries, liquors, and miscellaneous articles, and shipped them direct to Portland on board the bark *Frances and Louisa*. The cost of the entire cargo was $24,621.57 of which $13,092.35 was paid for in cash and the rest on acceptance of Williams, Bradford and Company for ten months from November 1, 1850.[10] Corbett entered a partnership with Williams, Bradford and Company by which each party was to share the profits of the "Oregon concern" equally. Corbett was responsible for the goods and the conduct of the business in Oregon while his former employers provided the entire capital outlay.[11]

Corbett came by steamship via Panama to Astoria and arrived in Portland on the little river steamer *Columbia* in March 1851, shortly before the arrival of the *Frances and Louisa*. He rode through the Willamette Valley and acquainted himself as thoroughly as possible with the market conditions. After the arrival of his goods in April, he lost little time establishing himself in a wooden store at the corner of Oak and Front streets. He advertised confidently that his was "The largest and most complete assortment of Goods ever offered in this market." He assured country merchants that he would be "constantly receiving goods from New York" and that he intended to keep on hand a full assortment, which he would sell "at the lowest market prices, his motto being *'small profits and quick sales.'*" He opened for business on April 28, and sold at wholesale and retail. His day-book for the fourteen-month period from April 28, 1851, to the end of June, 1852, shows an array of customers from virtually every town, river station and cross-roads in the valley. By 1852 he had a stock of $10,000 on his own account. A major purpose of the venture was to give the young merchant a "competence" in business, for his patrons wrote revealingly in February 1852, that "We know you to be careful, active and prudent, otherwise we would never have tried to give you so good a start."

In the spring of 1851 when Corbett started his business in Portland the Oregon countryside was still inadequately supplied to meet the heavy demands for consumer goods that had prevailed during the preceding three years. He evidently arrived ahead of many of his future competitors for his sales for May totaled almost $14,000, exceeding that for any other of the fourteen months of his initial Oregon venture. But other merchants arrived, and before the end of the year a total of thirteen vessels with cargoes of goods from the East reached Portland. Competition served to force down prices, and the Willamette Valley seems to have been reasonably well supplied with a wide assortment of needed merchandise by that time. This flow of goods to the Portland market is partially explained by the temporary overstocking of the San Francisco market where in 1851 auctioneers rattled off bales of valuable goods, hardly worth storing, at nominal figures, and many shippers suffered tremendous losses.[12] No wonder Portland received goods and a flock of new merchants!

Wholesale price ranges in Oregon reflected the general trend as the more competitive situation arose, but prices did not fall to the disastrously low levels that prevailed for a time in San Francisco. In Oregon tobacco was as high as $1.00 per pound in the spring of 1851, ranged between 50 and 70 cents per pound during the remainder of the year, but fell to 42 and 52 cents per pound in the spring of 1852. Lucke's tobacco, a standard brand much in demand in Oregon, wholesaled at 24 cents per pound in New York during 1852. Coffee, selling at 18 and 22 cents per pound at Portland in May 1851, was down to $12\frac{1}{2}$ and $14\frac{1}{2}$ cents per pound a year later. Tea ranged at 50 and 55 cents per pound during most of 1851 and the spring of 1852, but was down to $42\frac{1}{2}$ and 45 cents per pound by June 1852. Between the summer of 1851 and the spring of 1852 the wholesale price of brandy fell from $2.50 to $1.25 per gallon; port wine from $3.00 per gallon to $1.50, and in the spring of 1852 the wholesale price of whiskey was from 65 cents to $1.00 per gallon. The average yearly wholesale price of Brazil coffee at New York was nine cents per pound in 1851 and 1852; of Java coffee, 12 cents per pound in 1851 and 11 cents per pound in 1852; of whiskey, 23 cents per gallon in 1851, and 22 cents per gallon in 1852; and of manufactured tobacco, 26 cents per pound in 1851 and 20 cents per pound in 1852.

Corbett dealt heavily in dry goods, and his sales of the regular run of the cheaper cloths like brown sheetings, shirting, muslins, drills and the ordinary grades of prints show an Oregon wholesale price ranging between 10 and 20 cents per yard with the greater proportion of them falling between the 10 to 15 cent price range. New York wholesale prices for the same variety of goods were from 5 to 10 cents per yard. Brown sheetings, for example, wholesaled in Portland at $12\frac{1}{2}$ cents per yard in May 1851, varied in price from $11\frac{1}{2}$ to 14 cents per yard during the summer, reached $10\frac{1}{2}$ cents per yard in November, and were still selling at $10\frac{1}{2}$ cents in May 1852. It could be purchased wholesale in New York at $6\frac{3}{4}$ to 7 cents per yard in the spring of 1852. Thus the advance on New York costs for this type of dry goods ranged between 50 and 100 per cent. A reverse trend, reflecting the rapid building in the area, may be observed in nails. The wholesale price of this item in Portland ranged from $7.00 to $9.00 per hundred pounds during 1851, but rose to $10 and $12.50 in the spring of 1852. Nails wholesaled in New York as low as $2.75 in the spring of 1852, and at $3.75 and $4.00 in November and December,

1852.[13] Thus wholesaling at Portland was profitable and goods now flowed into the valley with greater ease.

Corbett enjoyed a fairly brisk trade in the fall of 1851 and again in the spring of 1852. While laying the groundwork of his Portland business he frequently received advice from his New York patrons who evinced a genuine and understandable concern for his personal welfare as well as his success in business. They wrote in January 1852: "We hope you will find your spring trade good & that *cash* purchases and cash sales will come out right in the end. If you stick to that text you cannot fail, with your industry and tack [*sic*], to do well." They urged him not to risk too large a stock because of the fire hazard, and because "insurance is out of the question so far away." They advised him "to avoid such articles as suffered most from Jewish & other competition such as clothing &c & confine yourself strictly, as you were disposed to do, to cash sales and cash purchases."[14]

Corbett and his New York patrons appear at first to have considered the Oregon business a temporary, speculative venture, and in January, 1852, Williams, Bradford and Company urged him to return to New York. They had been advised that the best of the Oregon trade had been done and that "people begin to look sharp after their gold dust . . . and want credit." They were concerned about Corbett's health and thought that it might have been well to have closed the Portland store the previous fall. They noted that "The expenses of the Oregon Trade are enormous & will fast eat up the profits." Although they relied upon Corbett's own judgment in the matter they seemed to desire that he return to safety in the East, in spite of the fact that enthusiasm for the California trade had risen to fever heights in New York. "All the world is crazy about California now & every passage ticket taken up till April next. Extra boats & clippers *all full*," declared Corbett's former employers.[15]

In July Corbett left for New York on the first of his many eastward journeys via San Francisco and Panama. During slightly more than fourteen months in Oregon his total sales had exceeded $83,000. He had sent several remittances in gold dust to New York and the profits for the venture, some $20,000, were divided about equally between Corbett and Williams, Bradford and Company. His original stock had been replenished with goods bought in San Francisco. He left the Portland store in charge of R. N. and F. McLaren, and planned to keep up the assortment by buying and shipping the goods out from New York himself.[16]

As Corbett returned to his former employment with Williams, Bradford and Company he probably was uncertain about his future. He attempted to establish himself as a New York buyer for Oregon merchants. With reference to his experience in New York and Oregon, he urged Oregon merchants to avoid the large mark-ups frequently charged in San Francisco and the expenses of going there to make their purchases and to allow him to buy for them in New York with nominal charges for his services. Oregon appealed to his adventurous spirit, however, and after about a year in New York he surprised his Portland partners by returning unexpectedly in the summer of 1853 with his bride.[17]

J. Failing and Company, another Portland firm established in 1851, may be unique in that during its early years it was dominated by the New York partner. But it is an example of the process by which supplies flowed to Front Street from New York. C. W. Thomas, a New York capitalist, supplied the largest share, if not all of the capital for the enterprise,[18] and attempted to manage the business from New York. He was already widely engaged in merchandising and shipping enterprises, being a member of a New York wholesale firm and a part owner of the clipper ship *Hurricane,* which was used in the trade between New York, San Francisco, and the Orient. Josiah Failing and his son, Henry, the other partners, had charge of the business in Portland. The senior Failing had been a paper stainer, a drayman, and for several years the city superintendent of carts in New York, before he departed for Oregon at the age of 47. He had also been deep in the affairs of the Baptist church in New York and soon was actively promoting the interests of that denomination in Portland. By virtue of his age and responsible manner he became the dean of Portland's early business community. Henry Failing already had five years of valuable business experience for since the age of twelve he had worked as a clerk and accountant, first for a French importing house, and from 1848 to 1851 for Eno Mahony and Company, a leading New York importing and jobbing dry goods house.[19]

Thomas' main function in the business, along with his many other activities, was to keep the Portland house constantly supplied with the numerous items of general merchandise needed for the Oregon trade. He had a similar arrangement with Wycoff and Company, the San Francisco house.

Thus an Oregon firm with substantial New York capital backing was launched in October, 1851. Like Corbett's enterprise, established upon the credit and standing of Williams, Bradford and Company, the Failings had a somewhat similar relationship with C. W. Thomas. This was quite different from the earlier experience of George Abernethy who had first to build up his own capital resources in Oregon before he could obtain the necessary credit from New York firms. It was also quite different from the practice prevailing to a considerable extent at San Francisco during the early fifties when New York and foreign merchants dumped large quantities of goods in the market to be sold on commission or at auction on their own account and risk. There were examples of this practice at Portland, but the Failings, with their New York contact assured, planned a wholesale business which they hoped would grow as the country developed.[20]

Such a business involved risks, and many merchants on Front Street lacked sufficient experience in the Oregon trade to evaluate the market demands. Added to this were the difficulties caused by the great distance between Portland and its source of supply. It took more than a month to get a letter to New York and from six to nine months to get the goods out. Thus merchandise shipped out to meet a specific demand existing some six to nine months previously might find an entirely different market situation.

Thomas made every effort to surmount these difficulties. He urged his Oregon partners constantly to keep him informed with respect to the demand for all categories of goods. He required them to estimate the length of time their supplies would last and to inform him as to which goods sold well and which had not. He wrote in 1852:

> I agree with you in thinking there will be a first rate business down in Portland next fall & I believe that you will make first rate sales and first rate profits . . . if you only will keep me well informed I assure you that I will

134

send you the goods to keep up an assortment continually and it will not happen again that you will be out of an assortment as you were last spring, —but . . . if you keep me in the dark, I will not take it upon myself to do all the buying by *guess*. . . .[21]

Again he wrote in the same tenor:

There are several instances when you would have goods supplied you if you had given the required information for instance with regard to 'Planes' if you . . . had written that they would sell immediately and that the probability was that in 5 or 6 weeks after you had recd [*sic*] them they would be all sold you would have had on the way, say near to San Francisco now another lot and in about 6 weeks from now another lot and in about 6 weeks from now you would have had them in store . . . so it has been with other kinds of goods.

The Failings made some or all of their remittances to Thomas directly in gold dust. It could be purchased in Portland at around $17 per ounce varying as to its quality. The supply of gold dust, which originally came northward with Oregon miners returning from California or in exchange for Oregon products during the early years of the gold rush, was now increased or replenished by Oregon's own mines. It was possible to buy exchange from one of the two San Francisco banking and express companies with branches in Portland: Adams and Company, and Wells, Fargo and Company. But they, as well as Portland merchants themselves, sought to profit on their purchases of dust in the gold markets of San Francisco or New York. Thus gold that might have been used for greater development of the territory was exported in sizeable quantities. The Failings avoided shipping their dust through the express companies and sent it by steamship uninsured since the carriers were liable. In November of 1852. Thomas reported: "in each instance that you have sent there has been a profit on the remittances. . . . I have no doubt that if you can get *Good Clean Dust* even if you pay a higher price for it that we shall almost always have advance—on the cost and charges."[22]

But in January, 1853, J. Failing and Company lost sizeable shipments of supplies by shipwreck which drastically reduced their expected inventory for the spring trade. Three sailing vessels, each with consignments for them, were lost within a three-day period while attempting to cross the Columbia's treacherous bar. The bark *Vandalia* went down on January 9, and the barks *Mindora* and *J. Merrithew,* both on January 12. Several lives were lost in these disasters and groceries, liquors, and other goods as well as the bodies of the victims were strewn along the coast from Cape Disappointment to Gray's Harbor and beyond. These were among the many serious sea disasters on the North Pacific Coast that occurred during Oregon's pioneer era. A year earlier the unseaworthy steamship *General Warren* went down with the loss of forty-two lives. The editor of the *Oregonian* vigorously condemned the owners of this ship, who "enter into a sort of *barter* between the lives and property of our citizens and the profits to be derived to them by these old *tubs,* which have been condemned else where as unseaworthy of patronage or support." For the Failings the accidents of January, 1853, meant a setback from which they did not soon recover because the goods were uninsured. Thomas did not insure but reduced his costs by shipping relatively small consignments on board different ships on the Cape Horn route.[23]

Thomas continued to press his Oregon partners for information concerning the demands of the market and he made every effort possible to keep them in constant supply. He insisted that they become the "No. 1 house in Oregon." He demanded copies of their "account sales" so that he could compare them with the original invoices, and thus gauge the demands of the Oregon trade. He wanted to know whether he had sent too few or too many goods, in particular instances, for the market demands. He reminded his partners that he had no way of knowing when they were to need any one of a thousand items, and insisted that they keep a memorandum of every item when they saw it running short and not wait until the last minute to make up a list. The success of the business, as he saw it, depended upon attention to these details if they were to have the kind of goods that would meet a good demand at all times. He predicted that "the time will come when you will be noted as keeping up the best assortment of goods in all Oregon." Encouraged by the news of the emigration of 1852, Thomas expected the following year to "be a good one for sales," if only his partners would follow his directions. He was a strict task-master, indeed, as he insisted repeatedly that they observe these elementary lessons. This was the exacting school in which the young Henry Failing furthered his business training.

In February 1853, Thomas informed the Failings that he would have sent out twice as many goods for the spring trade as he did had he been better informed as to the condition of their stock. In anticipation of a possible short supply he instructed them to purchase in San Francisco, if necessary, to meet their spring demand. He urged them to keep in touch constantly with Wycoff and Company, of San Francisco, in order to receive specific items from them when the Portland market was more favorable than that of San Francisco, or to ship out goods they might have on hand to San Francisco when a better demand existed there. On one occasion, for instance, he noted that J. Failing and Company was selling white sugars for 15 cents per pound, when the price in San Francisco was 18 and 20 cents per pound and urged them to ship some of their white sugars to Wycoff and Company.

Portland merchants obviously had to be aware of the condition of the San Francisco market. Most of them made all of their purchases there, but those who shipped from New York had to be doubly cautious in order to avoid losses due to the fluctuations of the San Francisco market. Thomas wrote his Oregon partners in February 1853: "Hardware is as cheap there as here . . . Bar lead is now here 8 cts the lb it is quoted at San Francisco 7 cts of course you had better buy it there even if you have to pay 9 cts the lb . . . it would be foolish for me to buy here at 8 cts the lb."

At the same time Thomas suggested that the Failings corner the Portland nail market. He observed that while nails were selling in New York at six cents per pound they were quoted in San Francisco at 4½ to 10 cents per pound. He urged his partners to purchase all they could get at San Francisco at from five to seven cents per pound, and all they could find in the Portland market at not more than seven cents per pound. This, he reminded them, would automatically raise the price in Portland to 10 and 12½ cents per pound and "it would not be a bad hit."[24] There is no

137

record of the outcome of this suggestion, but such practices seem not to have been uncommon when the opportunities arose. For example, W. S. Ladd discovered early in 1852 that the supply of turpentine was low in San Francisco and shipped as much as he could get northward on board the *General Warren*. When he learned of the disaster that befell this ship and his cargo, he immediately bought up all the turpentine he could find in Portland, before his competitors realized what had happened. He easily recouped his loss. Bancroft, in his biographical sketch of Ladd, equates the quality of shrewdness evinced in this matter with such attributes of character as abstinence and regular church attendance.[25]

Thomas, on one occasion, attempted to monopolize the Oregon supply of a most popular item of hardware and resented the intrusion of another Oregon buyer. He wrote in November, 1852:

> When I first bought of Mr. Farr, I told him that he must not sell to any one from Oregon, as I would buy all the planes I wanted from him—His planes are considered here as being the best and no doubt that you will find it the case so with you that there will be a reputation for his 'planes' and this fact of this Oregonian trying to buy them prove it somewhat.

The Failings seem never to have been able to satisfy the shrewd Thomas. In April of 1853, another blast issued from Pearl Street, New York:

> You are letting me have light by degrees your last letter informs me that you could sell more goods if you had them, and that one single merchant from the Interior will buy as large an amt as you have had sent out to you. If you had given me information before, you should have had more goods but you seem to withhold your views & rely on me to make a guess as to the extent of your trade well of course you have only yourselves to blame but I really think it is foolish in you not to let me know all at once the State of affairs as regards business in Oregon.

How the Honorable Josiah Failing, just recently elected Portland's second mayor, responded to this criticism or how he could be expected to foresee the conditions of Oregon's changing market are not known. He was busy promoting various improvements to facilitate the city's commerce.[26]

The promising business situation in Oregon encouraged Thomas, however, and he shipped out goods with a total invoice value of more than $56,000 to J. Failing and Company during 1853. This was twice the amount he had shipped in 1852. He divided these consignments into small shipments valued at from $1,000 to $4,000 and placed them on board San Francisco-bound ships, often on board one of the great clippers. He sent out a relatively large shipment consigned to J. Failing and Company on board the clipper *Hurricane,* of which he was co-owner, in August of 1853.[27] From San Francisco these goods were trans-shipped on board one of the vessels in Abernethy's packet line, the regular steamship, or one of the other vessels engaged in the coastal trade.

During 1853 two barks, the *American* and *Culloma,* were loaded out with merchandise at New York and made the long voyage direct to Portland via Cape Horn. Either Abernethy or one of his associates owned both these ships and each had made the trip previously while in the service of Abernethy's shipping company. But they were among the few ships that had been "up for Oregon" at the New York docks for some time. Thomas had hoped to ship a large consignment on board the *American,* which was represented to him as a first-class ship, "½ clipper." But finding her to be "such an old tub of a vessel" and fearing that she would take eight or nine months to get to Portland, he refused to ship much by her. Actually the *American* made the trip in just over five months.[28] Thomas tried to get the entire consignment for the *Culloma,* but he was duped by those who controlled the ship. He reported the incident as follows:

> They talked with me about taking the Vessell to what firm I wished it to be consigned and after they got all out of me that they wanted then they said they had made arrangements with some one—They agreed to take freight at a Certain price & tell me when the Vessell was to be put up.— They afterwards had the Vessell nearly full & then informed me that I could ship but that the price would be at so and so an advance . . . it is my opinion that either the owner or the Ship merchant here is somewhat of an humbug . . . I was very greatly vexed that they should pump me and afterwards serve me a mean trick.

139

Thomas started making plans to send out a vessel to Portland in 1854, himself. He was determined to prevent "the ship merchants in the Oregon trade" from having it all their own way.[29]

During the early 1850s, George Abernethy's firm at Oregon City was still probably the largest mercantile house in Oregon.[30] From 1851 to 1855 he was in New York where he purchased merchandise and directed the affairs of the Oregon City and San Francisco branches of the business.[31] During this period he and his associates made their last attempts to ship direct from New York to Portland without a stop at San Francisco. This notable attempt of an Oregon pioneer to establish a line of ships from New York to Portland fell before the speed and efficiency of the great clippers. But Abernethy, Clark and Company continued in the coastwise trade between San Francisco and Portland which their packet line of sailing vessels dominated, for heavy freights at least, during most of the decade. This company functioned mainly in the commission and forwarding business and often employed ships owned by others, in addition to their own. Goods purchased in San Francisco by Portland and other Oregon merchants and those from New York that were trans-shipped at San Francisco often came to the Portland dock on board one of the ships of this line. Most Portland merchants purchased their goods in San Francisco, though several, like H. W. Corbett and J. Failing and Company, made or had most of their purchases made for them in New York.

A tremendous volume of merchandise flowed from New York to San Francisco during 1852 and the spring of 1853, during the period of the clipper ship's supremacy. In December 1852, Thomas reported about twenty-five ships up for California at New York and that a vast amount of goods had already been shipped. He observed that "if the Ships continue to leave as fast as they do now much longer you certainly will have too many goods." Again in February, 1853, he reported that in spite of the high rates of freight, 70 to 80 cents per cubic foot to San Francisco, the number of vessels that had sailed for California the previous six months was astonishing, and that some twenty more were up for California at New York and Boston. But he had to compete as best he could, and poured $40,000 worth of merchandise into Oregon for the Failings' fall trade.[32]

Of the thousands of common items of merchandise sent out for the Oregon market during the 1850s, many sound strange today. Included were such items as fancy de laines, stripe shirting, Kentucky jeans, four and five finger grain cradles, men's lined and browned brogans, brown sheeting, boiled oil, saleratus, butter tryers, cheese tasters, candles, varnished oak hames, low top hames, French glass, and men's calf boots, to name only a few. To get an idea of volume, Thomas shipped over 6,000 pounds of Lucke's tobacco on one occasion, and almost 15,000 yards of brown sheeting on another, the latter as a part of a large invoice of many kinds of goods. Also, the Failings frequently received relatively large shipments of iron.[33] The vast array of essential items of groceries, hardware, liquors, dry goods and other articles which this remote frontier area could not or would not produce for itself and the role of the merchant capitalist in supplying them at so great a distance is impressive, indeed.

All photographs in the following section are from Oregon Historical Society files.

The endpapers (*Jennie Clark* at the front and *Express* at the back) are detail views from the Kuchel and Dresel lithograph of Oregon City, 1858.

The *Jennie Clark* was the first sternwheeler built on the Willamette. Jacob Kamm and J. C. Ainsworth undertook her construction at Milwaukie, and were owners with George Abernethy and Ransom Clark. She began the run between Portland and Oregon City in February, 1855.

The second sternwheeler launched on the Willamette, the *Express,* ran on the lower river for some years, and was purchased by Portlanders who founded the O. S. N. Co. Popular Captain James Strang was master until the *Express* was broken up about 1864. Her engines were taken to Lake Pend Oreille and placed in the first steamer on the lake, the *Mary Moody.*

James Douglas

John McLoughlin

Peter Skene Ogden

John McLoughlin directed Hudson's Bay Company affairs in the Oregon Country for twenty years. When he retired from the Columbia Department to Oregon City in 1846 his old associates Peter Skene Ogden and James Douglas managed the fur empire. Douglas became first governor of the crown colony of British Columbia in 1859.

A rare 1851 Portland view looking south from the corner of Front and Stark. Some say the American brig *Henry* in the distance delivered new beaver hats worn by swells leaning against D. C. Coleman's general merchandise store.

At least five boats are tied up around the mills at Oregon City. Just below the Imperial Mills in this 1867 (?) view is McLoughlin's home. Controversial Abernethy Island shows to the left of the mill roof.

145

Energetic George Abernethy sailed from New York City to Oregon City in 1839-40. He had great impact on the political and economic life of Oregon in pre-statehood years as provisional governor and audacious entrepreneur.

Cicero H. Lewis left New Jersey and eventually opened a Portland store with Lucius Allen. Married to Captain Couch's daughter, Lewis invested in telegraph, railroad and water works ventures.

Jacob Kamm left Switzerland and worked on Mississippi and California steamboats. As engineer Kamm helped to build some of the first steamboats in the Pacific Northwest and became a founder of the O.S.N. Co.

Henry W. Corbett was photographed by Matthew Brady during his term as U. S. Senator (1867-73). Far from his Massachusetts birthplace, Corbett won fame and fortune as Oregon merchant, banker, stage owner, capitalist and political figure.

W. S. Ladd directed his complex business affairs from the first brick building in Portland. Ships, land, railroads and finance all engaged the interests of Portland's early mayor and merchant capitalist.

Josiah Failing and his son, Henry Failing (right), both Portland pioneers of 1851, were born in New York. Both became mayor of Portland. When Josiah retired from his mercantile career in 1864, sons Henry and Edward continued the merchandise business at Front and Oak. Henry married Emily Corbett, sister of Henry W.

Capt. John H. Couch, redoubtable promoter of Portland as head of ocean-going navigation, was born in Massachusetts. His first visit was on the brig *Maryland* in 1840. On his second voyage he located a Portland land claim where he conducted a mercantile business until 1847. An officer in the Provisional Government, Couch, like Abernethy, helped found the *Oregon Spectator*. He served as Portland port warden, pilot commissioner, county commissioner with Capt. John Gates (right), steamboat designer born in Maine who came to Portland in 1860. For twenty-seven years construction engineer for the O. S. N. Co., Gates also became mayor of Portland.

Simeon G. Reed (left), Captain John C. Ainsworth and R. R. Thompson appear in this remarkable portrait of the "Triumvirate" of the Oregon Steam Navigation Company. Reed first worked for W. S. Ladd (1852). Ainsworth piloted the *Lot Whitcomb* in 1851. Thompson through his river shipping ventures and donation claim at The Dalles, controlled the portage at that point.

CLIPPER SHIP "HURRICANE" OF NEW YORK.

The crack clipper *Hurricane* sailed between New York, San Francisco and the Orient. Part owner C. W. Thomas in early years supplied capital as senior partner in J. Failing and Company of Portland.

The *Sierra Nevada,* veteran of the Pacific coastal trade, was built in New York (1851). In 1862 she made a record run of seventy-two hours from San Francisco to Portland. Before sale to Ben Holladay she carried some $20,000,000 in northwestern gold to the San Francisco mint. (Original painting at OHS.)

Launched at Milwaukie Christmas Day, 1850, the *Lot Whitcomb* was named for the founder of the Willamette river town. With Ainsworth as captain and Kamm as engineer, she ran to Astoria twice weekly. She ended her career running between Sacramento and San Francisco.

Surveyed in 1863, Umatilla Landing emerged as a strategic Oregon site on the Columbia for transfer of eastbound miners and freight. 1864 view of the river bank.

Detail of Lewiston, Washington Territory, a year before Idaho Territory was created. Called "Ragtown" by Californians, the settlement located at the confluence of the Snake and Clearwater featured Hill Beachey's canvas-roofed Luna House (right).

151

A Portland view, looking north from Alder along First. The bank was organized in 1865 and opened in May, 1866. H. W. Corbett and Henry Failing gained control of the First National in 1869 and moved to the Corbett Building on First in 1871.

An unidentified Idaho mining town of the 1860s. Note barber pole and "Miner's Brewery and Bakery."

Running the turbulent Cascades of the Columbia was one of many hazards of water, rail and wagon transportation between Portland and the Idaho mines. This later view shows the *Hassalo* running the rapids.

Col. J. S. Ruckel built a quartz mill at the site of Baker, close to Blue Mountain mining centers, in 1864. The town, pictured here in 1865, was near the Oregon Trail and a crossroads for transportation routes to the mines. The post master of Auburn, site of eastern Oregon gold discoveries in 1861, is said to have moved office and baggage to Baker City about 1866; two years later the town took the county seat from Auburn as well.

Crack O.S.N. Co. steamboat *Oneonta* whistles departure for The Dalles. In 1870 Ainsworth brought the expensive

1867 view of The Dalles from north bank of Columbia River. Note steamers *Idaho* and *Iris* at the landing and Mt. Hood in the background. Strategic Fort Dalles was on the rise above the portage town. (Watkins photo.)

The hardworking "S. G. Reed" pulled the crowded cars of the Oregon Steam Navigation Company's Cascade railroad,

A close-up of the ornate locomotive named for a president of the O. S. N. Co. It was built by Danforth, Cooke & Co. and featured a wheel-driven pump which forced water from the tender into the steam boiler. (Watkins photo.)

A significant but ill-starred venture was the Oswego Iron Company, founded in 1865. This industrial complex of

Chapter VIII

Oregon's Emporium

"The town will be full of goods . . ."

By 1851 Portland had become Oregon's emporium. During the three-year period, 1851-53, its business grew with the expansion of the agricultural frontier in the Willamette Valley and southern Oregon and with the extension of the mining frontier to Oregon in 1852. It depended upon its position between an expanding hinterland and the sources of supply as well as the California market for Oregon lumber and provisions. Oregon's economy during these years continued to be subject to the inflationary trend accompanying the California gold rush. This cycle ran its course and ended with financial panic in San Francisco and Oregon in 1854.

Optimism prevailed among businessmen in the Far West in 1852. Large immigrations were expected to swell the populations of California and Oregon during the year. Gold would attract thousands more settlers to California and the promise of free land beckoned other thousands, though fewer, to the fertile valley of the Willamette. Immigration to Oregon, it was anticipated, would double the existing population.

The Willamette Valley itself faced shortages of wheat and flour during the spring and summer of 1852 since the 1851 crop proved inadequate to meet the existing demands. In June some Oregon flour mills had to shut down due to the scarcity of wheat, and ships were unable to get adequate cargoes. The price of flour rose, consequently, and by July speculators were buying up this and other scarce commodities. The editor of the *Oregonian* predicted that the supply of wheat on hand together with the new crop, which was expected to be short, would be scarcely sufficient during the next twelve-month period to supply the needs of the new immigrants, the existing local demand, and that of the new mining area in southern Oregon; and not a barrel would be left to export to California. Already too much money was leaving the territory because of insufficient local production.[1]

It seems strange that Oregon farmers failed to produce more wheat during 1851 and 1852. The price was $1.50 and $2.00 per bushel in the spring of 1851, and the California demand for flour had not diminished appreciably. Among the factors accounting for low production were: competition with Chilean flour in the California market; greater production of wheat in California itself; the limited capacity of Oregon farms in terms of improved lands and available labor; and farmers leaving the Willamette Valley for the new mines in southern Oregon.

The disadvantage of competing with Chilean flour in the California market seems to have been most discouraging. At times during 1851 it was quoted at Portland either at the same price as the Oregon product or at a lower rate. The Whig editor of the *Oregonian* advocated a tariff to protect the California market for Oregon producers against Chile's supply of cheap labor.[2] During the fall of 1851 and the winter of 1851-52, both Oregon and Chilean flour ranged consistently between $12 and $13 per barrel wholesale at San Francisco. In March, 1852 the price fell to $9.00 due to increased supplies from Chile following the winter harvest there. But Oregon's own supply was growing dangerously short by this time. In May Oregon flour was quoted at $8.00 and $9.00 per barrel at San Francisco and that from Chile at $10 per barrel. By July the price of Chilean flour rose to $17 and $18 per barrel with no Oregon flour quoted.[3]

California produced some of its own wheat. Some Californians boasted that they could produce all their own provisions although in 1852 most of her men were engaged in mining and relatively few in agriculture. The editor of the *Oregonian* labeled these boasts "presposterous" and called the Californians a "non-producing people." He proclaimed ironically that "those who have travelled over the parched hills and barren plains of California will be better convinced when they see those 'immense wheat fields groaning' than hear tell of them in prospect." Many more Californians did turn to agriculture, however, after they experienced the high price of provisions in the fall and winter of 1852-53.[4]

The productive capacity of the land under cultivation in the Willamette Valley was limited. Here probably fewer than 3,000 heads of families were engaged in farming. There is no way of determining the actual acreage, but it should be remembered that wheat farming in Oregon during the early 1850s was still handicapped by the laborious use of scythe and cradle in fields that in many cases had been prepared only recently for farming. A farmer, writing in January 1852, noted:

> Few of our farmers are yet prepared to cultivate the earth in such a way as to ensure the highest results which the land is susceptible of being made to Yield. Our emigrants often hurry in a crop after they arrive, with as little preparation as possible, in order to bread them the following year; others attempt nothing more than to raise a sufficiency for their own use—and the very facility with which grain is produced leads to habits of careless cultivation. Hence it often happens that two, and sometimes three crops of wheat, are harvested from one sowing. These volunteer crops, too, are often very good. . . . What are now called the best claims, . . . combining the three great elements of convenience, good land, timber, and water, are principally held by claimants under the present law. But the best land . . . in the very heart of the grazing portions, and what will one day be the great agricultural spots, I mean the central portions of the prairies, are yet as the Creator left them, uncultivated, unclaimed.[5]

Settlers in the upper Willamette Valley in 1852 were few, indeed; and Marysville, soon called Corvallis, was the southernmost trading center of any significance. This new town was then at the head of navigation on the Willamette and received goods from Portland via the river at the rate of $40 per ton. The town was well supplied in the spring of 1852 with goods which for the most part had been purchased in San Francisco. Bushrod Wilson, a Marysville resident, thought Abernethy's direct shipments from New York had little or no effect upon the general price levels in Oregon. He reported prices in the spring of 1852 to have reached relative stability and to have fallen considerably since the fall of 1851.* Practically all items of consumer's goods could

---

*Wilson attempted to give his brother, located at St. Anthony Falls, Minnesota Territory, a fair appraisal of the business opportunities in Oregon. Ready-made clothing, he noted, retailed at prices only slightly above 50 per cent advance on New York prices. Domestic unbleached cloths sold at 12¼ cents per yard; bleached, at 18 to 25 cents; and calicoes at 8 to 30 cents per yard. Coarse brown sugar sold at 12½ cents per pound; crushed sugar at 18, loaf sugar at 30, and coffee at 18 to 30 cents per pound.

be imported cheaper than they could be manufactured in Oregon, Wilson noted, owing principally to the high cost of labor.

The mining frontier advanced into southern Oregon, and by the spring of 1852 the territory felt the stimulus of gold from her own mines. "The mines are coming closer and closer to us every day," Bushrod Wilson wrote, and "new discoveries are being made continually further north [in northern California and southern Oregon]. We have good rich mines within 125 miles of us now."[6] Pack trains laden with flour and other provisions set out from Marysville through the rugged country to the south to reach the mining country. Marysville thus began to share the mining trade of southern Oregon.

Oregon's most notable gold rush had begun early in 1852. Throughout the previous year prospectors from California's Shasta area had descended the Siskiyous to probe for pay dirt in the gulches and crevices of the rugged Rogue River country. Two packers, in late December 1851, or early January, 1852, made the rich strike in the valley on Bear Creek. The town of Jacksonville, at first a tented mining camp, sprang into existence at the site of the mines.[7] In April the editor of the *Oregonian* reported that the miners were doing well, making from $16 to $100 per day, but he cautioned his readers to make "a liberal discount—as in all cases of news from the gold mines." In view of the expected immigration in the fall he advised emphatically: "Let others dig the gold from the mountains while the farmers of Oregon remain at home and raise food for those who prefer the uncertain chances of mining; and in the end the farmer will be possessed of far the greatest amount of wealth, obtained with less toil and hardships than that endured by the miner." In May it was reported that miners were averaging one ounce per day. In July an observer noted that "A few of the

Some of Wilson's remarks reflect other conditions of frontier society. He declared that he had not seen "any smart workers or smart anything else among the women in this part of the world . . . Any women [*sic*] who can make a Missouri saleratus buiscuit, boil potatoes with the hide on, and make dish water coffee is a finished house wife here . . . but things have improved some since I came here. We are nearly out of the Hoozier—and will soon begin to talk Boston. There will be a large emmigration this fall and I am in hopes of picking up a wife what is a wife or go along jogging the same old delightful, enchanting road of Old Bachelorism." (Punctuation and capitals supplied.)

162

gold claims are rich and pay well," but he did not think they were "generally so." By August the figures were down to $5.00 to $12 per day for those miners who had an adequate supply of water. But one man is reported to have made $50,000 during the first season, and one nugget worth $500 and others weighing from six to ten ounces are said to have been taken from the Jacksonville mines. A year later, as the mining area spread, nuggets weighing up to 73 ounces were taken from the headwaters of the Illinois River in the Siskiyous.[8]

No doubt the southern Oregon mines lured men away from Willamette Valley farms during 1852 despite the repeated pleas of the *Oregonian* for maximum production of agricultural products. But this was no general exodus such as had occurred during the early years of the California rush, though the *Oregonian* reported that many of the new immigrants arriving at Portland in August "manifest great haste to get off to the mines." According to estimates some 1,500 to 2,000 men, mainly Californians, were in the immediate vicinity of the new town of Jacksonville in the summer of 1852.

Jacksonville, the principal trading center of the mining country, was accessible by trails from northern California over the Siskiyous, from the Willamette Valley, from Scottsburg near the mouth of the Umpqua, and later in 1853 from Crescent City on the California coast 100 miles away. Long pack trains with mules heavily laden with provisions and merchandise were soon familiar sights as they filed into the little town. Demand for provisions grew during 1852, and local farmers were unable to reduce it appreciably because of the severe drought they suffered during the first season. At Jacksonville during the winter, after the trails were closed because of snow, flour sold at $1.00 and $1.25 per pound with other provisions in proportion. Tobacco brought $1.00 per ounce. It is doubtful that local production even under favorable conditions could have contributed very much to alleviate the shortage during the first year.

But some farmers had located their donation claims on the richer parts of the Rogue River Valley in 1851 and others came during 1852. In July, 1852, the *Oregonian* reported that "A considerable part of this lovely valley, is gravelly, poor land, affording some grass. . . . Other parts have a good black clay soil, and must produce well, though no crop has been perfected since the settlement commenced. I was told the claims are all taken—so rapid has the immigration been."[9]

Jacksonville itself had all the attributes of a reckless, rollicking mining town. Within a year it rose from a camp of tents into a substantial town with some 150 to 200 good frame buildings. Gambling was common and almost every place of business was a grog dispensary. Miners often lost their earnings of a week, month, or entire season in one night of drunken revelry, and were obliged to start out anew.

But the community grew in spite of its isolation and several interruptions in gold production. A saw mill or two soon provided for the local lumber demand, and farmers in the vicinity, many of whom were also miners, now cultivated the rich lands of the Rogue River Valley. After the successful harvest of 1853 the community was able to supply a considerable part of its own flour. But shortages of water in many of the diggings handicapped the miners during the dry summer and fall seasons.[10] Gold production was also interrupted by a short but severe Indian uprising that burst upon the Rogue River country during the fall of 1853. Indian resistance and general hostility toward the gold hunters and farmers culminated in the Indian war of 1855-56, when, as usual on the frontier, the Indians suffered from the white man's grim determination to exploit the land.[11]

In 1853 the mining area spread even to the beaches of the southern Oregon coast. Gold in substantial quantities was taken from deposits of black sand on the beaches at Port Orford, Gold Beach, and Coos Bay. Beach mining was a rewarding enterprise for many gold seekers that year, but many others were disappointed. Though the coastal rush fizzled in 1854, beach mining continued in a somewhat desultory fashion for some time thereafter.[12]

Portland and other Willamette Valley towns felt the stimulus of southern Oregon gold during the summer of 1852, soon after the rush began. In June pack trains came direct to Portland arriving "almost daily after provisions, goods, etc. for the mines on Rogue River." Since "the supplies at Marysville, Salem and other points up the valley" were limited, traders were "compelled to come to this place."[13] Thus Portland and the Willamette Valley towns held an initial advantage in supplying the mining country.

But the new town of Scottsburg near the mouth of the Umpqua held an almost equal advantage. Since the development of agriculture in the Umpqua Valley was just beginning it could do little toward supplying the mining country with provisions. Goods and provisions imported by sea from San Francisco flowed from Scottsburg to Jacksonville by pack train, however. Scottsburg immediately became a thriving port and rival of the Willamette Valley towns. In 1852 as many as 500 pack mules at Scottsburg awaited supplies for the mines in a single day.[14]

The expected tide of immigration had occurred in the fall of 1852, with the arrival of many new home-seekers to take advantage of the Donation Act before its time limitation ran out. In August the *Oregonian* reported that "the immigrants are now arriving in large numbers," and in November the two steamers operating up the Columbia as far as the Cascades were making three trips per week and returning each time "loaded to the guards" with immigrants and wagons. Portland strained to accommodate them as "every nook and corner" of its buildings became crowded and many had to camp out. In December an observer stated that "The suffering among the emigrants is very great, both from their want of preparation for the winter & the dearth & price of provisions—flour is worth 42$ per bbl, the usual price being 10 to 12$." Some 11,000 to 15,000 people, according to estimates, arrived in the territory this year and most of them sought new farm homes in the Willamette Valley.[15]

Thus the territory had to accommodate this new influx of population at the very time it faced shortages of provisions. To export flour to California where the demand was also mounting was soon out of the question. Immigration to the land of gold in 1852 doubled that for 1851, to swell the population there beyond the 200,000 mark. At San Francisco the price of flour rose from $16 and $19 per barrel in September to $32 per barrel in October, and to $38 and $43 by December.[16] It reached the same high level at Portland in December, as we have seen.

Importers such as Henry W. Corbett, George Abernethy and the Failings were of course vitally affected by the development of agriculture and mining in Oregon, for on the expansion of trade and settlement their futures depended. They were, however, involved in the great labyrinth of commerce extending from America's principal supply center, New York City. They had to be somewhat more cosmopolitan in their outlook and better informed generally than most of their Oregon compatriots. Their perspectives extended beyond the Willamette Valley to encompass the entire pattern of trade from New York to Portland, and from New York to Jacksonville and Puget Sound. They learned the risks and all the other problems of buying, shipping and selling in this lengthy line of commerce.

Due to the immigrant and mining demands trade was especially good on Front Street during the fall of 1852. W. H. Barnhart and Company, a Portland mercantile firm whose sales figures for this period are available, shows a jump in sales from $7,510.63 in August to $12,070.65 in September, and a total for the fall season, through December, of $44,511.30. By comparison, for the fall season of the previous year, 1851, W. H. Barnhart's sales had totaled $21,691.69 and H. W. Corbett's, $26,397.33. There was a seasonable increase in demand at this time of year as country merchants bought their winter supplies, but in 1852 the additional pressures of the new demands are reflected in a much greater volume of sales. The figures for J. Failing and Company are not available, but they reported a brisk trade during the season, which greatly pleased C. W. Thomas, their New York partner.[17]

By January 1853 the scarcity of flour in Oregon had become so severe that the commodity had to be imported to supply the local and mining markets. The editor of the *Oregonian* took this occasion to urge Oregon farmers again to "Look at the price of provisions, the quantity you can raise, the sure market at your doors and *stay away from the gold mines.*" He noted the risks of mining and questioned not only the productivity of the labor in mining but also the value of the gold resources of the mining region itself.

Portland merchants began importing Chilean flour in mid-January 1853. The first shipment to San Francisco, where there was also a severe shortage, was sold in lots off the ship at $32 and $32.50 per barrel. Immediately some $1,500 worth of flour, consigned to W. S. Ladd and Company, was reshipped on board the steamship *Fremont* to Portland, where the price was from $36 to $40 per barrel. In the same month the *Columbia* landed a much larger shipment. Flour from Chile and the East continued to flow into San Francisco, and the price there fell to $10 and $10.50 per barrel by the end of February. Throughout the spring months on the Oregon-bound run, the steamship regularly brought not only flour but quantities of other provisions to the Portland market. For example, the *Columbia* carried 1,267 sacks and 640 quarter sacks of flour, 27 casks of ham, 12 firkins of butter, 152 sacks of beans, and four barrels of pork from San Francisco in April. The price of flour at Portland dropped to $25 and $28 per barrel by April 1, and stood at $19 on April 6; but with the arrival of the *Columbia's* large cargo it fell to $15.[18]

Thus speculators sought to profit in the Oregon trade before the prices went down there, too. A large part of the *Columbia's* cargo of flour was consigned to W. H. Barnhart and Company whose San Francisco branch wrote: "We send 900 qr [quarter] sks flour . . . Hammer away on it as long as it will pay . . . Flour I think will not be lower than the present figure . . . This has been bit lower than that went up the str [steamer] previous and I'm mistaken if we don't make something on it." The market held with flour selling in Portland at $18 and $20 per barrel in May. On her two northward trips during that month the *Fremont* carried a total of 5,947 quarter sacks and 62 barrels of flour, 15 barrels of pork, 100 bags of oats, and 10 cases of lard. Flour and provisions continued to flow to Portland from San Francisco on board the steamship and sailing vessels through June.[19]

Prices at Jacksonville fell precipitously during the spring of 1853 from the extremely high winter levels noted above. Supplies deluged the little town after the trails had opened in February. Miners were doing unusually well, according to reports, with plenty of water for the dry diggings and with more reasonable prices for provisions. Prices quoted in February were: "Flour 50 cts, sugar 45, coffee 75, beef 25 cts per pound," and in April, flour, 18 cents, coffee, 30 cents, and salt 30 and 35 cents per pound. Twenty-five thousand pounds of flour arrived in one week in April. On June 7, a Jacksonville woman noted, "Another very large pack train yesterday loaded mostly with flower," and again on June 17, she observed, "This morning a large pack train passes of fifty mules." Provisions were "plenty and cheap" as Jacksonville's market, like those of the Willamette towns, had become overstocked by early summer. Portland tradesmen had enjoyed a "brisk" trade throughout the spring months, however, as imported provisions and merchandise had flowed to the "upper country." The process of supplying remote frontier communities was rapid, indeed.[20]

The extent and importance of the trade between the commercial centers of northern Oregon and the southern Oregon mining region is difficult to determine. No one knows the amount of gold produced in southern Oregon during 1852 and 1853, or the amount that flowed northward; nor the value of goods and provisions packed into the mining area from the Willamette Valley. By the middle 1850s it appears from the most reliable estimate that southern Oregon produced at least $1,250,000 in gold annually. The annual output for 1852 and 1853 must have been considerably less but it may have been as high as $1,000,000. During 1852 and the spring of 1853 the towns of the Willamette Valley benefitted considerably by the mining trade, though they were forced to share it with Scottsburg, and in 1853 with Crescent City, on the California coast, founded for the express purpose of tapping directly the mining trade of southern Oregon and northern California.[21]

But conditions in California ruled the economy of the Far West, and signs appearing in 1852 were none too promising for merchants. During that year vast quantities of merchandise flowed from New York and from foreign ports to San Francisco. Merchandise sold readily for high prices but as shipping continued during the early months of 1853, merchants began to realize the limitations of the San Francisco market. As the year advanced it became increasingly burdened with inventories far in excess of the demands. About 745,000 tons of goods valued at more than $35,000,000 flowed into San Francisco during the year. Prices fell as the market became gradually overstocked and many merchants, particularly those from New York or abroad, who had their cargoes sold at auction or on commission, suffered heavy losses.

As trade declined during 1853 California's economy seemed to be sustained only by speculation in real estate. At the end of the year the effect of the decline of trade was finally felt, and the speculation bubble burst. The financier no longer obtained returns of from 30 to 60 per cent on well-secured loans of capital. Owners of real estate who had previously realized huge profits from rents, ranging from $200 to $1,000 per month for stores and shops, and who were now erecting expensive brick buildings, had to accept greatly reduced rates. By the spring of 1854 the clipper ship *Bald Eagle* and others returned to New York with full cargoes of goods similar to those they had just recently brought out. This deflationary trend culminated in a severe financial panic on February 23, 1855, when the banking houses of Adams and Company and Page, Bacon and Company closed their doors. There were hundreds of business failures in 1855, after the banks closed; and land and all other forms of property became almost worthless overnight. Some disappointed men on board the Panama-bound steamship prophesied, "It'll be a ghost town," as the bay city passed from view.

But the plethora of goods at low prices was a boon to the growing population of California. Gold production was greater in 1854 than in any previous year. Gold dust valued at $54,947,830, a small part of which must have come from Oregon's mines, flowed eastward from San Francisco via the isthmus. It was estimated that the total amount exported exceeded $65,000,000.[22]

The effects of the over-supply of the San Francisco market were ultimately felt in Oregon, but during the first six months of 1853, the prospect for business seemed exceptionally favorable at Portland. As we have seen, the expanding market area for imported necessities promised profits to the men on Front Street, and speculators hoped to realize substantial gains on their imported provisions in the markets of the Willamette Valley and the mining area. Gold dust seems to have been plentiful as it flowed northward from the southern Oregon mines to add to the existing supply.

But Oregon's predominantly agricultural community was unable to share significantly in supplying the California market with provisions.

Throughout the gold rush years, however, Oregon lumber found a market at San Francisco in addition to the constant local demand. Although the California demand had subsided in 1850, it revived after the great fire in San Francisco on May 4, 1851, the most devastating of the series of fires, beginning in 1849, that had reduced large sections of the city to ashes. By the winter of 1851-52 the wholesale price of lumber at San Francisco reached $80-$90 per thousand board feet. It fell to $50-$60 per thousand in March 1852, when the Oregon wholesale price was $20-$25 per thousand. During the fall of 1852 there was a brisk demand for lumber in California due to the heavy immigration and to the fire that destroyed more than fifty-five blocks in Sacramento in November. Shortly after this disaster the price of lumber in California soared as high as $600 per thousand board feet, but by January 1853, it was quoted at $60-$70 per thousand at San Francisco.[23] Lumber production in California soon caught up with the demand, and by May 1853, the day of phenomenal profits in the Oregon-California lumber trade had ended.

Available shipping records show Oregon's export pattern for the first six months of 1853. Over five and one-half million board feet of lumber, most of which was placed on board the sailing vessels at from $28 to $40 per thousand, flowed to the San Francisco market during the six-month period. The steamships *Columbia* and *Fremont,* making the Pacific Mail Steamship Company's regular runs, frequently carried relatively large shipments of gold dust for Adams and Company and Wells, Fargo and Company. The largest monthly total, as compiled from the shipping manifests, shows $79,135.25 in gold dust shipped to San Francisco in April, to become a small part of the millions exported from that port. The only other important items of export were quantities of potatoes and onions which sold at San Francisco in April at 8 to 9 cents and 25 to 30 cents per pound respectively. The total value of Oregon's export to California from January 1 to April 1, 1853, reported in the *Journal of Commerce,* was $295,525.04.

In the total import picture vast quantities of merchandise destined for Front Street and other points in Oregon bulked large in volume and in value. New wholesale and retail outlets appeared on Front Street. In April Portland boasted "about forty merchants who are doing a good business" and "five river steamers [which] are constantly arriving and departing from our wharves; besides numerous sailing vessels and ocean steamers which run between this port and San Francisco." In June it was noted that "Business is evidently increasing in our city . . . Daily a large number of teams in our streets are loading with goods, while the steamer and pack trains are carrying a large amount of freight to the upper country." W. S. Ladd began construction of Portland's first brick store building in May and by the end of summer his and four others adorned the landscape of Front Street as the era of brick emerged.[24] Several new firms were just opening in June. R. N. and F. McLaren reported to H. W. Corbett, who was then in San Francisco, that:

> Our reputation for keeping fine & nice goods is dailey increasing. Some days we do a big retail trade. Last week we averaged about $500 pr Day Whole Sale & Retail . . . we can establish a good house if we are only kept supplied with desireable goods . . . We have, however, & always can do the heavyest trade in Portland.

But the town and its hinterland were becoming dangerously overstocked with goods. By mid-June the market was more abundantly stocked than one merchant had ever seen it before and trade was "dull."[25] There would be no improvement as long as the heavily laden clippers continued to stream round the Horn to San Francisco. From there goods flowed out to bulge the supplies of every market in the Far West, especially that of Portland.

By the fall of 1853 the overstocked San Francisco market was the dominating influence governing business in the Far West. With her exports declining Oregon had little defense against the deflationary forces set loose in San Francisco. With California producing its own lumber, the market for that product was in oversupply by May, and shipments from Oregon became increasingly less profitable.[26] In December the schooner *Spray* with about 165,000 board feet of lumber on board cleared Astoria for the new and untried Australian market. The harvest in the Willamette Valley in the summer of 1853 was good but hardly sufficient to provide for more than the local demand and that of the incoming immigration which brought 6,449 newcomers to Oregon.[27] Greater production of lumber and flour would have only met a diminishing demand in San Francisco. Despite the new immigration, inventories mounted in Portland's own stores and warehouses during the summer and fall.

San Francisco merchants sought every possible market outlet for their goods and urged Oregon merchants to take consignments on short term credit beyond the amounts justified by the Oregon demand. They also flooded the rising coastal towns, Scottsburg and Cresent City, with goods and provisions. In May 1853, a member of the San Francisco firm of Allan, Lowe and Company had taken a large consignment of goods to Scottsburg expecting to do a good business there. He noted that while "The Umpqua is now attracting a good deal of attention," that "in the present depressed state of the market the merchants are glad to send their goods anywhere they think they will sell rapidly." But as the season advanced Crescent City gradually shared more and more of the trade with the mining region of southern Oregon and northern California, and after 1853 Scottsburg lost out in the competition entirely.[28]

Portland and other Willamette Valley towns had already felt the impact of the competition with these towns and the diversion of the trade threatened to wipe out their share also. In June, W. H. Barnhart and Company reported that "Dust has become very scarce and trade unusually dull . . . We have been compelled to pay over seventeen dollars for dust this str [steamer] on act [account] of the scarcity." The McLarens reported that they had sold gold dust at $17.40 per ounce. They protested the action of Page, Bacon and Company, San Francisco, in raising the exchange rate from 3 to 4 per cent on their remittances to New York. By fall the flow of gold dust to northern Oregon had almost ceased. The editor of the *Spectator* commented: "Ruin is beginning to stare us in the face. . . . The shipments of dust from Southern Oregon and Northern California are almost entirely stopped. It nearly all goes south, immediately to the cities of California. So that there is no profit now arising to our people from that source."[29] Thus, the merchants and traders of northern Oregon had all but lost their share in the mining trade, a significant factor in the oncoming depression.

The editor of the *Oregonian* noted these efforts to divert the mining trade from Portland through Scottsburg, Crescent City and other coastal points, but pronounced their success "indifferent." He continued:

> Portland may sincerely wish success to all these places. The yearly increase in the population of the Willamette Valley will render her more and more independent of that fluctuating demand which the mines afford and furnish such a stimulus to the energy and enterprise of her merchants, as only a constant, vigorous and healthy trade with a farming and mechanical community can supply.

He saw San Francisco as the great commercial mart of the Pacific, and the "natural and unlimited" outlet for the produce and manufactures of Oregon. In his argument favoring the development of agriculture and manufacturing he ignored the fact that the San Francisco market itself rested upon that same "fluctuating demand which the mines afford."

But optimism prevailed in northern Oregon during the fall of 1853. Trade revived after a dull summer season and merchants prepared for a large fall trade. In late August Oregon City merchants were reported doing ten times as much business as they had at the same time a year before. Fireproof stores, new imported milling machinery, and river improvements were promising signs of economic growth. The editor of the *Oregonian* pointed proudly to over forty commercial houses, four steam saw mills, and other manufacturing establishments as evidence of Portland's progress. The city's merchants employed capital to the value of about one and a quarter million dollars. Fourteen river steamboats were now on the Willamette, where in 1850 there had been only the little *Columbia.* There was a good demand for flour at San Francisco in October where it was quoted at $13 to $16 per barrel, but Oregon could not supply more than her own local demand. The immigration, though only about half the size of that for 1852, no doubt contributed to the generally optimistic business outlook. The arrivals of the *Robert Burton, Culloma,* and the *American* direct from

New York during the year suggested that Oregon had attained greater significance in the wider avenues of trade. As merchandise continued to flow in, even the "full and complete assortment" of goods in the Portland market was considered a healthy sign by the indomitable editor of the *Oregonian*. "That they find ready sale at remunerative prices is plainly evident from the constant renewal of the supply," he proclaimed, and "So long as trade thrives, the people must be thrifty."[30] Other men on Front Street probably shared these views.

But as early as August Corbett's partners, the McLarens, in advising him to exercise extreme caution while buying at San Francisco, noted:

> We were obliged to scratch for freight money $1000. We managed to get Ladd & Co. to give us an order by paying $300 and a draft on ourselves at 6 days Sight. We however Discounted our paper and thereby keep up the *credit* of the *House*. We have sold about $2000 since you left. Trade is far better and is beginning to improve much . . . Be sure to buy a few Cigars and that 10 Gal Keg of _____ for Customers. . . . Do not buy any kind of goods that you are not sure will meet with ready sale. The town will be full of goods. And if we get a quantity of Unsale-able goods in Store we will have much difficulty in making remittances to New York.[31]

In September Wells, Fargo and Company called in some of their cash from their Portland agent, W. H. Barnhart, because of the difficulty of keeping it *"actively* and *profitably* employed" in purchasing gold dust or exchange. In December their agent at Oregon City reported: "There is no money here for love or drafts." At the same time the *Oregonian* insisted unrealistically that the course of commerce which had increased "more than a hundred fold the last year . . . is still onward."[32]

But depression had already struck. Gold once plentiful as a result of the supply from California and later from the southern Oregon mines had been drained from the region in large amounts. Not enough attention was given to replenishing the supply. Now, said the editor of the *Statesman,* there was a shortage, a tightening of the money market, and the existing gold supply was inadequately distributed. The roots of the difficulty lay not only with insufficient production but the inadequate and fluctuating market in California. Even if Oregon had produced more flour and lumber these products could not have been absorbed by the existing California market. A larger population and a more reliable export market were still Oregon's most pressing needs. The editor of the *Statesman* called for more production, more labor, and a greater accumulation of capital for use in productive enterprises. Why should Oregon, with the "best wheat growing soil in the world," have to import flour and numerous other articles, he asked. "To take a single illustration," he commented:

> The people of Oregon, as a rule, purchase their pickles and preserved fruits in New York and Boston. For these two articles alone, no small sum of money leaves the Territory annually. So of our wearing apparel. What of that is manufactured here? Everything is purchased, and nothing made. So of our tools; so of our utensils, and everything we use.[33]

Trade during the winter months was much slower than usual and in spite of expectations did not revive appreciably in the spring. Merchants were burdened with heavy inventories; more goods were on the way; and the glutted condition of the market was expected to continue indefinitely. Prices were "low." The number of stores and shops in Portland now numbered nearly one hundred. Money was tight and three per cent per month could be obtained readily on good securities. In February Corbett and McLarens reported:

> The trade is such now that we are obliged to give from 30 to 60 days credits . . . Our market is now very much over Stocked and in fact the territory is well supplied with all kinds of goods. Never in our Oregon History have we been compelled to record duller times than at present. owing in part to the over stocked market in San Francisco. And the new cost [coast] towns that have sprung into existance drawing off the mining custom.

But Jacksonville's market was also overstocked as goods flowed in from the coastal towns. Miners, who now had no fear of shortages, were making new strikes or returning to claims, abandoned during the summer because of the lack of water or Indian troubles. All necessaries of food and clothing, whiskey, and other merchandise were available at reasonable prices.[34]

In December one Douglas County merchant, after stocking up on credit with supplies from the Willamette Valley for the mining trade, reported the difficulties he faced in meeting his obligations. His flour and other goods had not moved, he explained to his Portland creditor, partly because of the mildness of the weather, but principally because of the competition of a San Francisco merchant who had established a branch store less than a mile away, where goods were sold at wholesale and retail at only slight advances over San Francisco prices.

> For instance, he wholesales a good article of coffee at 20 cents retail .23, Colgates family soap per box 1.50 single bar 25 cents and all his other goods in proportion how he can afford it is a *caution,* ain't it. Yet he seems to be determined to establish a permanent business having erected a large store 60 x 30 so you see our part of the country is drawing some attention.[35]

After finally overcoming his illusions of prosperity, the editor of the *Oregonian* advocated the curtailment of credit. He condemned the practice of San Francisco merchants who had urged consignments on short term credit upon Oregon merchants beyond their actual needs in 1853. Now with country merchants asking and receiving credit, wholesalers would soon be forced to apply for terms and thus prices for consumers would rise. Of course, those who bought in the East already enjoyed credit for the period required for the delivery of shipments from New York. But the editor observed that Portland merchants possessed enough capital to make all their purchases for cash. So country merchants were urged to cease granting credit to farmers and to make their own payments to Portland wholesalers in cash. The advice probably reflected the thinking of the Portland business community rather accurately. At least, it did not go unheeded, for in March, Corbett and McLarens were appealing to their valley customers in such terms as "money is close & goods cheap," and "We are 'Short' do what you can for us."[36]

But insufficient production, over-supply of goods, and loss of savings seemed to threaten the territory's very existence. The editor of the *Oregonian,* now agreeing with his Democratic rival in Salem, wrote:

Up this beautiful river . . . thousands of tons go annually to supply the population . . . what do we export to pay for this enormous amount of goods? We have to answer, with many regrets, comparatively nothing but gold; when we should be sending thousands of barrels of flour, and large quantities of rye, oats, barley, all kinds of vegetables, butter, cheese, eggs, pork and beef—the result of which would turn the trade in our favor—but as it is our commercial men see with alarm every steamer leaving with large amounts of specie, *not* as heretofore with gold dust, but that which shows *too* plainly that the bags of dust "salted down for a time," by our early settlers and adventurers to the mines, who reaped there a rich harvest for their labors, are now empty. The tables are turned, the times are changed, the gold is gathered from the surface, and we now, when almost too late, hear the farmer, mechanic, and merchant, all complain of hard times and scarcity of money; and which we fear will ere long prove fatal to the commercial interests of our City, and the Territory at large.[37]

Added to problems attending the depression the decision of the Pacific Mail Steamship Company late in 1853 to make St. Helens rather than Portland their northern terminus annoyed the men on Front Street. The company intended to use its crack river steamer *Multnomah* to connect between St. Helens and the lower Willamette towns. This had been the plan in 1851, and now it was to be carried out. Substantial warehouses, mills and a wharf were erected at St. Helens and in November the *Columbia* ceased coming to Portland. Portland businessmen were alarmed and some of their less responsible members hanged the company's agent in effigy on Front Street. He was labeled the "enemy of Portland" and one who intended to fill his "private purse" at the expense of the company and the public good. The editor of the *Oregonian* thought these protests foolish and announced Portland's position as the emporium of Oregon in glowing terms. "Let them go where they please; the city of Portland is entirely independent of them, or their favors. We can do far better without their aid, than they can without ours. If there is carrying to be done there will be carriers." In fact, an opposition steamship, the *Peytona* did appear. The leading merchants of Portland including the editor promptly drew up a set of resolutions in December by which they condemned the action of the Pacific Mail Steamship Company as "antagonistic to the best interests of

Portland," and agreed to give the *Peytona* all their freight and influence. No reason for the mail company's decision is given in the newspaper accounts, but after a few months the run to Portland was resumed.[38]

The depression is reflected by reduced volumes of sales and by somewhat lower prices. Corbett and McLarens probably like many others, had received goods to be sold on commissions of from 5 to 10 per cent for the account and risk of San Francisco or New York merchants. In April, 1854, they reported to one such merchant that "the market is over Stocked with clothing we cannot price it, at anything like the Invoice price but hope the market may improve." Thus prices in some lines of goods must have fallen below cost, but this was not true of most basic items of general merchandise. After resuming the personal direction of his business in May 1854, Corbett sold amazingly little during the remainder of the year. During this eight-month period the totals for each month except October were less than $3,000. The figure for May was only $1,199; those for June and December were under $2,000; and the high point, for October, was $4,295.82.

The business records of two different firms and occasional published lists provide the following pattern for the wholesale prices of certain basic items of general merchandise both at New York and Portland. Brown sheetings and drills which sold at Portland as low as 10½ cents per yard in 1852, and as high as 12 and 13 cents per yard in September, 1853, reached the low point of 10 cents in the summer of 1854. They had wholesaled at New York at 7½ and 8 cents in the fall of 1853. Denims costing 10 and 10½ cents in New York in 1853 sold at 11½ and 12½ cents per yard in 1854. Thus the advance of this kind of goods, which was bought in vast quantities, was never less than 1½ cents, and even when prices were lowest was seldom less than 20 per cent. The freight cost, even at the high rates prevailing in 1853, would be negligible on a yard of dry goods. Tobacco, to use another example, sold at 35-50 cents per pound in the spring of 1853, and for 25-50 cents per pound in 1854. Lucke's brand, which wholesaled in New York for 22 cents per pound throughout 1854, sold wholesale at Portland at 35 cents per pound in the summer and fall of 1854, an advance of more than 50 per cent. Tea, selling for 55-75 cents per pound, had not varied much from previous years. Coffee actually advanced from 12-15 cents per pound in 1853 to 19-23 cents per pound in the summer and fall of 1854. In February, 1854, the advance over New York costs on all kinds of hardware was reported at 20 to 30 per cent. But nails that cost $4.50 per hundredweight in New York were selling at $7.00 and $7.50 in Portland in the summer of 1854, an advance of more than 50 per cent. At the end of the year the price of nails rose to $6.00 in New York and to $9.00 and $11 per hundredweight in Portland.[39]

Shipping declined sharply during 1854, though sizeable cargoes of merchandise continued to arrive. Flour sold for $14 and $15 per barrel during the early part of the year and essentially supplied the local demand. Lumber was quoted at $15 to $18 per thousand in February but by fall cargoes were loaded on board sailing vessels at $8.00 and $10 per thousand. Most of the lumber exported went to San Francisco but foreign markets were also being sought. Four cargoes of lumber—one to Hong Kong, one to Honolulu, one to Callao, Peru, and one to either Honolulu or Australia—cleared Astoria during the year. In addition a considerable amount of treasure left the territory during the early part of the year and small consignments of provisions went to San Francisco occasionally. Imports, of course, declined also. Thomas shipped goods worth only $14,500 during the year compared to the $56,000 in merchandise shipped to the Failings in 1853. He failed to realize his great dream of shipping out an entire shipload of goods to his Portland partners. Freights declined on the New York-San Francisco run, as the great era of the clipper ship drew to a close, from 60 cents to $1.00 per cubic foot and $30 per ton in 1853, to as low as 25 cents per cubic foot and $15 per ton in 1854.[40]

The inflationary cycle caused initially by the California gold rush came to an abrupt end with the depression of 1854. Oregon had benefitted when the California market for her products appeared and as gold flowed northward. Not until after the California market was well supplied during 1850 and 1851 were merchants attracted to Oregon in significant numbers. Here favorable market conditions for merchandise existed with minor exceptions until the summer and fall of 1853, when the market, like that of San Francisco, became overstocked. Oregon's export trade had fluctuated according to the California demand for lumber and provisions. It dwindled and almost disappeared in 1853 because of an increasing local demand, and decreasing demands in California. The gold of southern Oregon stimulated business in Oregon in 1852, but it was hardly the sustaining element of northern Oregon's economy. Much of this gold, perhaps most of it, was drained out directly to San Francisco, going through Portland, Scottsburg and Crescent City and in like manner from San Francisco to New York. Perhaps southern Oregon gold helped to postpone the depression, but the forces that determined the cycle from inflation to deflation are to be found mainly in conditions in California. San Francisco held the economic hegemony of the Far West, and the southern Oregon mines were an extension of her own mining frontier. Oregon's economy from 1848 to 1854 was characterized by a single inflationary cycle caused by California gold.[41]

But in the process the Oregon merchant received his start because of the supply of gold and the unusual demands prevailing in the territory during this inflationary period. He began to accumulate capital that could be used to promote the territory's further economic development. But he could not prosper permanently without greater and more diversified production, a larger population, and a reliable export market.

PART III

Between Gold Rushes, 1855-61

Chapter IX

The Eastward Thrust of the Frontier

"The whole Indian race . . . will be exterminated."

The most serious Indian war in the history of the Pacific Northwest broke out in the fall of 1855 when tribes in several parts of the region went on the warpath simultaneously. Actually two major conflicts occurred, one east of the Cascades and one in southern Oregon, as well as skirmishes in the Puget Sound area, but all were parts of the same general problem and derived from the same basic cause. The Indian everywhere saw his means of subsistence threatened by the converging frontiers of settlement from east, west and south.

An effective Indian policy might have prevented the war but federal authorities did little to meet the Indian problem during the early territorial period. No attempt to extinguish Indian title to land was made until after the Donation Law became effective. The first treaties, made with the Willamette tribes in 1851, provided for reservations and subsistence, but they were never ratified by the Senate. The debilitated valley Indians had long faced the dire prospects of starvation and extinction and were now the victims of the white man's bad faith. The proud and warlike tribesmen of the interior, restless since the Cayuse War of 1848, continued to feel the effects of the declining influence and gradual withdrawal of the Hudson's Bay Company. In southern Oregon war and depredation had prevailed intermittently since the beginnings of settlement in 1851. The Indian department could do little to meet the problem, for it suffered from delayed federal appropriations and poor credit facilities. In 1853, when its payments were two quarters in arrears, merchants charged five per cent per month for goods purchased on the credit of the government.

Joel Palmer, Superintendent of Indian Affairs for Oregon Territory from 1853 to 1856, is noted for his humanitarianism and his efficient management of the Indian department. He inaugurated the reservation system in Oregon and sought

183

earnestly to promote and preserve peace between the races. After General Joseph Lane's month-long campaign in southern Oregon in August 1853, Palmer negotiated the Table Rock treaty with the Rogue River Indians. This, Palmer's first treaty, provided for a 100-square-mile reservation on the north side of the Rogue River, a total of $60,000 in annuities to run for a sixteen-year period, and additional amounts for agricultural implements, blankets, clothing, and other benefits. Both parties agreed to preserve the peace in this troubled area. The Senate promptly ratified the Table Rock treaty and one with the Cow Creeks in April 1854.[1]

Encouraged by this action, Palmer negotiated treaties with all the bands of the various Indian tribes of southern and western Oregon including the Willamette and coastal groups during 1854 and 1855. The Table Rock treaty served as a prototype for all the Palmer treaties, and in each case provisions were made for graduated annuities not to run longer than twenty years, and for the confederation of colonization of bands with similar habits and customs upon other reservations. Stipulations concerning schools, shops, and other services were included.

Before Palmer completed his work in western Oregon he and Governor Isaac I. Stevens of Washington Territory called together the leaders of the potentially hostile interior tribes, the Yakimas, Nez Perces, Walla Wallas, Cayuses, and Umatillas, at the Walla Walla council grounds in May 1855. The Indian agents sought a peaceful and permanent solution. They urged the acceptance of the reservation system and emphasized the futility of resistance. The Indian leaders were apprehensive, restive, and somewhat hostile, but after considerable persuasion they signed three separate treaties embracing the same general principles as Palmer's other treaties. The Indians agreed to cede the vast interior, to receive relatively large annuities and other benefits in return, and to retire to reservations. The Nez Perces retained a 5,000-square-mile tract and the Yakimas and the confederation of Walla Wallas, Cayuses, and Umatillas smaller reservations.[2]

During and after the Walla Walla council many tribesmen questioned the wisdom of signing the treaties, and several chiefs soon regretted their action. Perhaps Stevens and Palmer acted too hastily in the council without sufficient consideration of the vagaries of the Indian mind. Stevens, seeing the inevitability of settlement and the prospect of a transcontinental railroad, was somewhat impatient as he pushed for a prompt and final settlement of the Indian problem. Military men, dissatisfied with the way the negotiations were conducted, soon blamed the Walla Walla treaties for the outbreak of 1855.

But the appearance of settlers, especially miners en route to Fort Colvile, precipitated the war east of the Cascades. In July 1855, Palmer announced that the upper Columbia Valley was open for settlement and soon a few farmers moved into the area. After the discovery of gold in the Fort Colvile vicinity several small groups of prospectors crossed the Indian country to this distant post during the summer of 1855. Palmer's announcement was precipitous and illegal since the treaties had not been ratified. The Indians held that the whites had no rights in the area whatsoever until such time as the treaty stipulations concerning annuities were met. They determined to prevent travel and settlement in the interior and it was only a matter of a short time until a series of incidents set off a general war between the races.[3]

Citizens of southern Oregon it is alleged, deliberately started the war in that region in October, 1855. Although the Indians seem to have been willing to abide by the provisions of the Table Rock treaty, many of the settlers, probably a minority, had no respect for the treaty, nor did they regard the Indians as having any rights at all. The four-year record of spasmodic conflict had surcharged the atmosphere with hatred, distrust, and contempt for the entire Indian race. Irresponsible and inhumane actions on the part of the settlers caused new incidents which invited the horrible retaliation of the savage. Many citizens throughout the territory, and in southern Oregon particularly, advocated race extermination as the only feasible solution to the problem. The editor of the *Oregonian*, who urged this method consistently, wrote as follows:

> The whole Indian race in southern Oregon will be exterminated ... Self-styled philanthropists at a distance may prate

about the cruelty and wickedness of such a course; but were they in the situation of our citizens—subjected to the ruthless hand of savages—they too, would be in favor of exterminating the race. Treaty stipulations amount to nothing with these Indians, their most solemn pledges are disregarded whenever the opportunity to plunder presents itself.[4]

The prospect of an Indian war was especially appealing to the reckless miner and irresponsible merchant in southern Oregon in the summer of 1855. Business was dull, miners were inactive because of the dry season, and the claims for the war of 1853 amounting to $258,000 had just been paid in full by federal officials. Before hostilities began Palmer wrote: "There is perhaps no portion of the United States where the opinion prevails more generally among the people that the treasury of the United States is a proper and legitimate object of plunder than in portions of this territory." And again after the war had begun he repeated the charge and exonerated the Indians in the following language:

> The future will prove that this war has been forced upon those Indians against their will . . . by a set of reckless vagabonds for pecuniary and political objects, and sanctioned by a numerous population who regard the treasury of the United States a legitimate object of plunder. The Indians in that district have been driven to desperation by acts of cruelty against their people; treaties have been violated and acts of barbarity committed by those claiming to be citizens, that would disgrace the most barbarous nations of the earth.[5]

Others agreed with Palmer. Matthew P. Deady, a leading Oregon jurist and politician, believed there would have been no difficulty in the Rogue River country if Charles Drew, a citizen of southern Oregon, and his friends had not wanted it. Delazon Smith, another politician, stated that "the Rogue River war is gotten up by Ross, Drew, Henry & Co. for the purpose of swindling the government." Indian agent Ambrose saw it as a deep political plot and noted that the high prices paid by the government for the previous war had much to do with the origin of this one. It was Jesse Applegate's opinion that when mining became unprofitable in southern Oregon, the miners turned to the more lucrative business of killing Indians. William C. Hazlitt, the *London Times* correspondent at Victoria in 1858, wrote regarding them as follows: "One's blood boils with indignation at the conduct of wretches who pretend to respect the principles of equality, but who violate every principle of humanity. Their policy towards the Indian is simple *extermination.*"[6]

The prevailing public opinion, however, and that held by most responsible people was that war was inevitable. Settlers, therefore, resented the official reports of Palmer and General John E. Wool, commander of the Pacific Department, alleging speculative and political motives on the part of the settlers. These, as was later shown, served to prejudice Washington officials and Congressmen against the territorial cause. Local political pressure forced Palmer's removal in the fall of 1856. J. Ross Browne, a treasury department official sent out to investigate the charge that the war was started for speculation purposes, confirmed the opinion of the settlers. "The origin of the war," he asserted, "is not different from that of any other Indian war. It is the natural result of emigration and settlement."[7]

A volunteer army of 3,500 men from the territories of Oregon and Washington was in the field from the fall of 1855 until mid-summer, 1856. Altogether some 6,000 men served but the approximate number in service at any one time was 3,500. Few regular troops were immediately available and General Wool found cooperation with territorial officials difficult because of his public opposition to the war. Wool opposed Governor Curry's decision for a winter campaign and the independent prosecution of the war by the territories. Governor Curry would not allow regular officers to command Oregon volunteers. "We have no authority to call for volunteers . . . or to furnish them with supplies," Wool disgustedly told one of his subordinates, and "Therefore, the less you have to do with them, . . . the better it will be for the service."[8]

The exciting campaigns must be omitted here. The burden of the war in its early stages fell upon the volunteers, though a regiment of regulars was dispatched from San Francisco. The winter campaign of the volunteers east of the Cascades in 1855 and 1856 was indecisive. The regulars went into action against the interior tribes in the spring of 1856 and, by November, had defeated them. The southern campaign ended with the unconditional surrender of the Indians to the volunteers in the summer of 1856.[9]

The war taxed the strength of the two territories and diverted the energies of the settlers to unproductive enterprises. War against an elusive foe over a vast mountainous terrain created problems of considerable magnitude. To supply the men in the field, commissary and quartermaster's agencies were established in all the principal towns to purchase provisions, equipment, and other supplies. Hundreds of horses and mules had to be purchased to transport men and supplies to distant encampments.

Territorial officials made all such purchases on the credit of the United States government. Certificates called "scrip" were issued for the purchase price of goods, horses, mules, and provisions on the assumption that all debts so contracted would be paid by the United States. Scrip issued in Oregon during 1855 and 1856 totaled $3,040,344.80, and became a part of the circulating medium. Scrip certificates contained the clause that payment would be made "whenever the Congress of the United States shall, by appropriation, provide for the payment thereof." Since everyone expected at least a two-year delay in payment it soon depreciated by 50 per cent. With the growing uncertainty of payment after the war, scrip reached the low point of ten cents on the dollar, and much of it fell into the hands of speculators.[10]

During the war Portland merchants hesitated to sell on such uncertain terms. For this the editor of the *Oregonian* condemned them fiercely in the invective that he usually reserved for Democrats. Dryer declared:

> There are men in the community who . . . utterly refuse to sell the government officers those things absolutely necessary to fit out and sustain our gallant volunteers. . . . They refuse even to furnish, at exorbitant prices, articles which they have on hand for sale to the Commissary and Quartermaster's departments, without the cash in hand . . . they won't trust Uncle Sam when the territory is invaded by a hostile foe . . . These men are now engaged in figuring up how much they can make out of this war, by remaining at home behind their counters . . . until the battles are all fought and the victories all won . . . when they will step in and purchase the certificates for services rendered, supplies furnished, &c., &c., at nominal rates and thereby make a splendid fortune. . . . The more cautious speculators, (or in other words, the *simon* pure SHYLOCKS) already begin to inquire whether there is any reasonable doubt as to the United States government assuming responsibility of the

present war and of paying the expenses thereof, and how long it will be before the general government will pay up—what will the war warrants be worth—whether they will draw interest, &c., &c. . . . Money, goods, and merchandise is all they think or care about.

C. W. Thomas of New York refused to allow his Portland partners in the firm, J. Failing and Company, to sell goods to the government on credit for two years with interest at the rate of two per cent per month. He suggested that second grade goods might be sold at that rate, but "saleable" goods at not less than three per cent per month. Entries in H. W. Corbett's day-book for May 6, 1856 show that he charged exactly double the current wholesale price in Portland for goods sold to the territories.[11]

At least one merchant, Sigmund Rosenblatt, had no choice: he was forced to sell to the territorial authorities. Officers of the volunteer army requisitioned quantities of blankets and other staple goods from his store in Eugene early in the war. Although he received 10 to 12 dollars in scrip for blankets worth seven dollars, he had to sell the scrip at a discount of 50 per cent and suffered a considerable loss on the entire transaction.[12] There may have been other cases of this kind of conscription, but more likely it was an isolated case in which volunteer officers took advantage of a helpless Jewish merchant.

In general the Indian war of 1855 and 1856 had a retarding effect upon the region's development. The diversion of capital and manpower to a non-productive purpose strained the available resources of the pioneer communities. Matthew P. Deady wrote that "Portland I think was quite slow and dull until this Indian war concentrated a good deal of business here. There were a good many operations and of course a large portion of this scrip was concentrated here."[13] Although the war stimulated business to a certain extent, remuneration for goods and services was inadequate and unnecessarily delayed. Indian hostility was also a factor in the region's relatively slow population growth during the decade, as fewer immigrants risked the dangers of the emigrant roads.

The Indian problem east of the Cascades remained unresolved for two more years after the victory of 1856. In

August of that year General Wool ordered the interior except for the Colvile mining region closed to settlers, and the Indians were to retain full rights to their lands until such time as the Senate ratified the treaties. But ratification was delayed and the Yakimas and other northern tribes threatened the routes to Colvile and Fraser River in 1857 and 1858. General N. S. Clarke, Wool's successor, reversed his policy and ordered firm measures, and the campaigns of Col. George Wright and Col. E. J. Steptoe in 1858 curtailed Indian hostilities in the interior. The treaties were ratified the following year.[14]

Thus the Indian wars prepared the way for the eastward advance of the frontier. Hundreds of miners had already moved northward by the interior routes to Colvile and Fraser River, and 2,000 farmers moved into the Walla Walla and Umatilla valleys in the summer of 1858. General Harney officially re-opened the area for settlement in October, 1858. Thus volunteer, regular, miner and farmer each played his role in the eastward thrust of the frontier during the later 1850s.

Navigation of the Columbia developed to accommodate the increased traffic. Steamboats on the lower river carried supplies regularly from Portland to the Cascades and from the Cascades to The Dalles. In 1859 the steamboat *Colonel Wright* began a regular run from the Deschutes Landing above The Dalles to Fort Walla Walla.[15] Thus The Dalles, after 1855, became a bustling trading and outfitting center and one of the most important market outlets within Portland's expanding hinterland.

The Indians of western Oregon and Washington all came under the reservation system after the war of 1855 and 1856, and those of the interior after the ratification of the Walla Walla treaties in 1859. Joel Palmer, who was dismissed from his superintendency in 1856, had established the reservation system and extinguished the Indian title to about two-thirds of the present state of Oregon. During his three years as superintendent he had tried conscientiously to protect the Indians and to improve their status when such humanitarian purposes were not shared by most of the territory's population. His dismissal caused Oregon scrip to rise in value ten per cent in the East.[16]

190

The Indian departments of Oregon and Washington were combined in 1857 under J. W. Nesmith, the new superintendent. During 1857-58 when the department's business was largely confined to the western tribes, his administration is an interesting example of the handicap of slow communication and the uncertain policies of his superiors in Washington.

Payments on the department's indebtedness were in some cases four years in arrears and Nesmith had no choice but to continue the ruinous credit policies of his predecessors. During 1857 and 1858 the cost of operating the seven agencies and the central office of the superintendency varied between $100,000 and $160,000 per quarter exclusive of the old indebtedness and the annuities promised the Indians. The superintendent was constantly in arrears in making disbursements because of delayed appropriations or the tardiness of the Washington office. Some claims had to be sent directly to Washington and after going through a costly process of "red tape" several were denied. Because of the known delay and uncertainty of payment the superintendent and his agents had to purchase goods at exorbitant prices. Nesmith complained frequently and bitterly to the Commissioner of Indian Affairs concerning the government's impaired credit in the region.[17] The following exerpt is typical:

> There is no use in disguising the facts; the officers here are at the mercy of the community who supply what is bought, and no man furnishes supplies without taking the risk of being kept out of his pay for a year or two. To suppose that the laws which govern trade will make exceptions in favor of what is here a proverbial non-paying Indian department, is anticipating something not very likely to occur. When good and valid demands against the department for supplies furnished and labor performed from one to two years ago, are freely offered at from twenty to thirty per cent. discount. it can hardly be expected that purchases on credit can now be made as low as for cash; besides, after this non-paying policy has forced, and does daily force us to purchase on credit, and the supplies have been consumed by the Indians, it strikes me as a little too late to talk about "rigid economy."[18]

One attempt to defraud the Indian department is worth noting. A contractor agreed to provide a large quantity of the best quality flour for the Siletz Reservation at $20 per barrel. This price included $2.00 per barrel for transportation, but it was still more than twice the Portland price. After delivery it turned out to be more than half "sweeps and shorts." When apprehended the contractor stated that he had been defrauded unknowingly by the Abernethy milling company at Oregon City and he promised to make it right.[19] Fraud was the intent, however, and those responsible for it had the attitude that anything was good enough for the Indians. This may have been an isolated case or, perhaps, a more general practice.

In spite of the poor credit of the Indian superintendency its use of federal funds helped to bolster and stabilize the region's economy. Its expenditures were unusually heavy during 1859 as were those of the military department for improvements in the interior. Lieutenant John Mullan, then building his famous road across the Rocky Mountains to join the Columbia and Missouri river routes, purchased quantities of supplies at Portland and The Dalles. Portland merchants reported a scarcity of coin and a plethora of government drafts during the hard times of that year.[20]

Territorial Delegate Joseph Lane laid the problem of the Oregon and Washington war claims before Congress in the summer of 1856. The legislation which followed, unlike that for the 1853 claims, required the Secretary of War "to examine into the amount of expenses necessarily incurred in the suppression of hostilities in the late Indian war in Oregon and Washington." The act authorized the secretary to name a commission of three to conduct the examination required.

The commission, composed of two regular army officers and one civilian, began its work on the scene in October 1856. For a year they examined accounts, muster rolls, and vouchers on file in the several commissary and quartermasters' offices in the towns and posts of the two territories. They authenticated claims for merchandise, provisions, livestock, transportation charges, administrative costs, and wages for the civilian and military personnel involved in the war. Their report, submitted in October 1857, showed a total of $4,449,949.33 for Oregon and $1,481,474.45 for Washington.

A subsequent report added $80,032.52 for a grand total of $6,011,456.36, exclusive of Indian spoliation claims.

Congressmen, aware of the alleged speculative motives of the settlers, suspected the report. The House resolution of February 8, 1858 now required R. J. Atkinson, the third auditor of the treasury, to examine all the vouchers and other papers in his office relating to the Oregon and Washington war claims and to revise the accounts. According to his instructions he could not allow claims for the services of an individual in more than one capacity at the same time, nor allow the volunteers higher pay than that provided in the schedules for pay and allowances in the regular army. In revising the other accounts he had to consider the nature and peculiarities of the service and all other factors bearing on the cost of livestock, goods, and services. This required authentic information about local conditions including prices, wages, and other costs prevailing in each of the several communities that served the volunteer forces in 1855 to 1856.[21]

It was a tremendous task and two years elapsed before Atkinson completed the audit. He made a preliminary report in January of 1859, however, citing the high prices for goods and services and certain irregular practices. The prices allowed for the large number of horses bought for the government service ranged from $200 to $500 each. After the war government owned horses sold at auction at $35 to $80 apiece, and a smaller number at $100 to $300. Mules, however, sold at auction at $200 to $360. The actual cash price for best quality horses was $200 and upwards. Shoeing horses at Portland cost the government two and three dollars per shoe. During the war flour supplied to the volunteer army sold as high as $20 per barrel at Jacksonville and at $10 to $14 per barrel at Portland, or about double the actual cash value of the commodity. At first glance all prices seemed uniformly exorbitant, especially when compared to eastern prices, but this report failed to take the depreciation of scrip into account. Atkinson discovered several cases in which volunteers made claims for services in other capacities as well as for their military service.[22]

As mentioned above scrip depreciated by 50 per cent soon after the war began. Its average value after the war seems to have been between 25 and 37½ per cent. In some cases speculators purchased it as low as ten cents on the dollar. General John E. Wool reported that one speculator purchased $60,000 in scrip at 17 cents on the dollar. Wool, who remained convinced that speculation was a primary cause of the war, charged that:

> As usual, purchases were made by speculators and moneyed men . . . at much reduced rates. This cannot but be regarded as another species of speculation by which the government has been defrauded and honest men cheated of their just dues. . . . It is true the people have suffered, and what have they gained? Nothing but scrip, which has been sold from ten to twenty-five cents in the dollar.

Oregon's Governor John Whiteaker viewed the problem in a somewhat different light. In his letter to Atkinson in September 1859, he asserted that

> Scrip depreciated in the hands of holders according to the belief or disbelief that General Wool and others would be able to defeat or delay the payment. The claims are still largely held by the original owners, and they have no market value at this time; our people not being able to determine whether the government will ever pay, therefore there are no transactions in scrip.[23]

During the hard times of 1859 and 1860 the scrip problem became an issue of considerable importance in Oregon. A convention of businessmen met at Eugene in August 1859, and drew up a petition, which after citing the circumstances of the war, urged speedy government action on the war claims. They pronounced the war unavoidable and denied that it was the intent of anyone to rob the United States Treasury. The petition asserts that if the war was chargeable to any source save the intent of the Indians, it was due "to the inefficiency of the general government in not making earlier settlements with the Indians for their claim on the public domain."

The irascible editor of the *Oregonian* tried to make a political issue out of the problem. After condemning a proposal that a New York firm take up the entire debt at a discount of ten per cent he turned on the Democrats. It was their war in the first place, he asserted. They had contracted an indebtedness of $6,000,000 and now a Democratic administration and a Democratic Congress refused to pay the debt. Thus the scrip problem became one of many issues in the political campaign of 1860 in Oregon.

Atkinson completed his audit and made his report on February 10, 1860. As nearly as could be ascertained the actual cash prices prevailing in the territories during the war were allowed. In a few cases the revised rate fell below that prevailing in 1855 and 1856, but more often the opposite was true. Due consideration was given to the gradually higher price levels as one proceeded southward from Portland in Oregon. An advance of more than 100 per cent over Portland prices, for example, was allowed for merchandise sold at Jacksonville for the volunteer forces. The pay and allowance schedules of volunteers were revised to accord with those of the regular army for their actual time of service. By these means the total claims were reduced from $6,011,457.36 to $2,714,808.55, or by about 55 per cent.[24] Congress, in March 1861, after one more year of delay, accepted the third auditor's report and appropriated the sum he had recommended. During 1861 the claims were paid in bonds bearing six per cent interest from January 1, 1861. Thus Congress finally discharged the debt but failed to consider such important factors as scrip depreciation and the fact that citizens had been deprived of the use of their capital for almost six years.

Civil War inflation caused further losses to Oregon and Washington Indian war claimants. After Congress made the appropriation in March 1861, the third auditor's office issued the bonds as fast as the claims could be validated. Easterners or eastern representatives of far western firms processed their claims first and none of the new bonds reached the Pacific Coast until late in the year. Few were cashed before the New York banks went off specie payment in December 1861, or before the passage of the First Legal Tender Act a few months later.* After having been deprived of part of his

---

*After learning of the appropriation the Failings sent $6,000 in scrip to C. W. Thomas for collection. They expected to get from 40 to 60 per cent on their original claim. "As you are aware in selling the goods we charged such prices as would in our opinion remunerate us for waiting until the government made appropriatons supposing the debt to be paid in 2 years." A telegram, John A. Hatt to Failings and Hatt, c/o Ladd, Reed and Co., San Francisco, April 26, 1862 shows that Hatt sold some of the bonds issued to the Failings at 94 and 95 cents on the dollar. The average value of currency in terms of gold during 1862 was 88.3 cents.

capital for six years the businessman who wanted to recover it now had to accept payment in an inflated currency, since the government discharged all such obligations in greenbacks.[25]

To the Colvile and Fraser River Mines

In the meantime the mining frontier made its first thrust into the Inland Empire. The restless prospector from California and southern Oregon combed the Fort Colvile area and led the way to the Fraser and Thompson rivers to set off the region's first major gold rush in 1858. Gold led men into the interior and in great measure determined the direction of the eastward moving frontier. It continued to excite the minds of the settled farmers and the serious capitalists of the Willamette Valley. Except for the brief rush to Fraser River, this extension of the mining frontier northward was not spectacular and was essentially the prelude for the golden decade to follow. It will be discussed here in relation to the region's economic development prior to the depression of 1859-61.

In mid-decade southern Oregon was the only gold producing area in the region. Here, in spite of the Indian wars, the frontier communities began to take on a settled character with the development of mining, agriculture, flour and lumber milling. Two flour mills processed the abundant wheat crop of 1855, and the price of flour fell to 4 cents per pound, or $8.00 per barrel, from the exorbitant levels of 1852 and 1853. Other basic foods were now produced locally and sold at reasonable prices. Merchandise was expensive as it still had to be packed in by mule train from Crescent City on the California coast or from the towns of the Willamette Valley.[26]

Mining dominated the southern Oregon scene. In 1855 men using placer methods easily made from $3.00 to $5.00 per day on most any of the numerous streams in the area except during the dry season of late summer. By 1856 all the newest improvements in mining equipment were in use, although the unreliable water supply remained a serious handicap. No accurate figures for total production exist, and the estimates of Walling, author of the most substantial history of the region, seem high. He asserts that gold mining reached its maximum in 1856, and he estimates production for that year at $3,000,000. He estimated the average annual gold production of Jackson County alone, from 1856 to 1860, to be $1,250,000. He also asserts that this was the most wealthy and most populous county in Oregon in mid-decade. Available census data for 1854 and 1860 hardly bear out this assertion, but the possibility of a large floating population in the area cannot be ruled out.* When the Indian war ended in 1856, however, the exciting and dangerous earlier day of the miner gave way to peaceful and stable development in the mountainous, isolated Rogue River country.[27]

News of another strike reached the settlements in June 1855. Prospectors in the vicinity of the old Hudson's Bay post at Fort Colvile far in the interior of Washington Territory were reported making from $10 to $30 per day. Soon scores of adventurers from southern Oregon and elsewhere were in the Willamette towns on their way to the new eldorado. The *Oregon Argus* reported the excitement among packers, miners, and townsmen at Oregon City so great that the return of ex-Governor Abernethy went unnoticed and suggested that even if President Pierce had arrived his presence would have attracted little attention "unless he happened to bring 'news from the mines'."

This movement marks the beginning of the development of the region beyond the Cascades. Placers near Fort Colvile produced from $1.50 to $6.00 per day and some as high as $20 and $50 per day during August. The editor of the *Oregonian* offered his usual word of caution about the deceptive nature of gold rumors and noted that some men going to the mines were "better qualified for weeding onions, rocking cradles, or milking cows at home, than for penetrating an Indian country." But it was mainly experienced prospectors from California or southern Oregon who packed their quicksilver, tools and provisions and made the long trek northward. All they needed to know, they said, was that the new locations panned as much as 50 cents per

*An official census in 1854 of Jackson County listed a total population of only 1,881. Territorial Papers of Oregon (Microfilm, O. H. S.; originals at the Oregon State Archives, Salem). After careful investigation, J. Ross Browne, United States commissioner for the mining regions west of the Rocky Mountains, estimated the gold production of western Oregon for the entire mining period through 1867 at only $10,000,000.

day per man. With proper equipment and machinery built on the spot, they were confident that each of them could obtain from $30 to $50 per day in such places.[28]

Some Portland businessmen believed the region's survival depended upon the success of these mines. Business had not sufficiently recovered from the depressed conditions of 1854 and of the early months of 1855 to inspire confidence in the future of the isolated Willamette Valley. The panic in San Francisco that had doomed the banking and express business of Adams and Co., the largest financial house on the coast, in February 1855, and the failure of many other businesses with it was still fresh in men's minds. More gold, they thought, would somehow save them.[29]

The Indian war of 1855-56 interrupted the Colvile mining episode. A few miners stayed among the friendly Indians of the region and others returned to The Dalles but the interior route was no longer safe. After the war General Wool ordered the interior east of the Cascades closed to settlement, but this order, issued on August 2, 1856, specifically excepted Colvile miners from the general proscription, providing they refrained from inciting or molesting the Indians.

Mining activities in the area now resumed. A few men worked their claims during the fall and winter of 1856-57; and many newcomers arrived during the following spring and summer. Prospectors roamed about between the Spokane and Pend Oreille rivers and northward. Reports were generally favorable but the man with pan and rocker could make only $2.00 to $7.00 per day. Some now organized themselves into companies and using quicksilver did somewhat better.[30]

But there were no phenomenal strikes. Provisions were high and dry goods and clothing sold from 200 to 300 per cent above Portland prices. Some miners gave up and turned to farming for this was not the great bonanza dreamed of by miners and businessmen.[31] Other prospectors assiduously continued their search over an ever widening area. Gold was known to exist farther to the north and in August 1857, four men returned to Colvile with $1,200 for one month's work on the Thompson River far across the international border. Ten more returned in September with fine specimens of gold and with glowing reports about the rich new

198

mining country. Some of them had made as much as $50 per day.[32]

The news rioted throughout the Pacific area and in the spring and summer of 1858 a veritable rush was on. Thousands clamored for passage on board the steamships at San Francisco and other thousands left California by the inland routes via The Dalles or the Willamette Valley. Puget Sound promoters advertised a projected road from Bellingham Bay to the Fraser. This project was designed to make the little town of Whatcom on the bay the San Francisco of the north, but the rough terrain over which this short road was to pass soon proved the unfeasibility of the entire plan. Portland responded by advertising the Columbia River and either of two interior routes leading directly to the mines from The Dalles. It is estimated that 20,000 went by sea and probably another 10,000 by land during the spring and summer of 1858.

The steamships were loaded to the gunwales. In June the *Panama* carried 1,070 on one trip from San Francisco to Victoria, and the *Republic, Commodore,* and *Sierra Nevada* all carried more than 900 on trips made in June and July. At the height of the rush a total of 7,149 left San Francisco in June and 6,278 in July. With passenger rates at $30 for "roughs" and $60 for "nobs" and additional freights the coasting steamship business boomed. Sailing vessels also benefitted but they carried far fewer passengers.[33]

The rush was on. Almost overnight it transformed the quiet fur trading post of Victoria into a bustling growing city populated mainly by Californians. Here men scrambled for passage on board the few steamers destined for Fort Hope or Fort Yale. Here men cursed the tax and regulations imposed by Sir James Douglas, the governor of Vancouver Island and chief factor of the Hudson's Bay Company. Here were the high prices, the speculation, and the same procession of humanity that made the Fraser River rush so reminiscent of the exciting days in California almost a decade earlier. Here were the serious-minded and the reckless, the preacher and the prostitute, the shrewd gambler and the hard-working laborer or mechanic, and, everywhere, the experienced California miner. Here were numerous San Francisco merchants who had either brought their stocks of goods with them or who served as representatives of San Francisco houses. But here also was the stronger hand of the law which assured order and prevented maltreatment of the natives.[34]

After travel on a crowded steamboat or on the hazardous road into the interior the miner was on his own in the gold field that stretched northward from Fort Hope for 60 miles along the Fraser to the mouth of the Thompson, and from there for greater distances on the upper Fraser, the Thompson, and other tributaries. Gold was found in abundance as miners spread out on the bars along the rivers. Oldtimers said they had never seen such diggings. Returns reported in the spring, which stimulated the summer rush, ranged from $8.00 to $150 per day.[35] D. B. Sheets, who left the Northwest Boundary Survey to go to the mines, thought that the gold fields were practically inexhaustible. He wrote:

> Make no more inquiries about the mines. . . . I have a claim from which we take out $50 to $150 per day with three rockers. When I left the mines men were taking out from one to sixteen ounces in a day with one rocker. After the river falls which will be by the middle of June, every man that goes to the mines and works can make one ounce per day.

There were many other such reports. In August one claim near Fort Hope worked by six men yielded $600 in six hours. At that time there were 3,000 miners in the immediate vicinity. Some made fortunes; others had difficulty making ordinary wages at $3.00 per day.[36]

There were many handicaps. The country was extraordinarily rough and inhospitable. Miners could not work on the lower river because of high water during part of the summer. Provisions, transportation charges, and all other supplies were high and difficult to obtain. In July the price of flour at San Francisco was $12 per barrel; at Portland, $22 per barrel; at Victoria, $30 per barrel; and at the mines, $50 per barrel. By October it had reached $100 to $160 per barrel in the mining country. Lumber sold at $100 per thousand at Victoria and nails sold for $1.00 to $1.50 per pound at the mines in the summer. Freight by pack mule from Fort Hope to the Thompson River cost from 50 to 55 cents per pound during the summer of 1858.[37]

The rush to Fraser River subsided about as suddenly as it had begun. As early as July, while the movement was still at its height, Hazlitt, the London *Times* correspondent, reported the return of about 1,000 disappointed miners to San Francisco. In August the pressure for passage at San Francisco ended, although hundreds were still moving northward to the new mines via the interior routes. In October, miners, thwarted by high water and the scarcity of provisions, left the area by the hundreds and bitterly denounced the country and those who had written so favorably about gold. But the new mining area became one of the more important gold producing areas in the Far West, and the newly established British colony to the north with its predominantly American population and culture rested firmly upon its foundations of gold. By conservative estimates gold production in British Columbia in 1859 more than doubled that for 1858, and for the decade from 1858 through 1867, it totaled $26,110,000.[38]

Portland sought a share in the Fraser River trade. In April the editor of the *Oregonian* blasted the newspapers of Puget Sound for advocating the difficult Bellingham Bay route. Former Hudson's Bay men familiar with the entire region advised the superiority of routes via the Columbia River, The Dalles, and northward through the interior. In this way, they pointed out, all the hazards of navigating the lower Fraser could be avoided. Two interior routes via The Dalles were proclaimed equally feasible: one, northward through the Yakima Valley; and the other via the Columbia to Walla Walla and northward to the Okanogan. Portland businessmen met at Corbett's store in June and took up subscriptions to obtain the most reliable information concerning these routes and to publicize their advantages.[39]

Fraser River gold attracted many from Oregon and Washington. Lumber mills on Puget Sound closed down and sailors there deserted their ships in April. In Oregon no better proof of the excitement is needed than the threat it posed to the economy of the Willamette Valley, which preyed on the mind of the editor of the *Oregonian*. He wrote "A word to Oregonians! You who have a farm, shop, or business, you who can and are willing to labor, stay at home, and you will toil less, take more comfort, and obtain more gold in the end, than those who go now to the newly discovered gold mines on Fraser's river."[40]

The Fraser River excitement no doubt contributed to the prosperity enjoyed in Oregon in 1858. Flour and other provisions flowed northward from Portland via both steamship lines and on board a few sailing vessels. The rush to Fraser River created a market for Oregon beef and as a result large herds of cattle were driven to Puget Sound for the northern market. Merchandise and provisions flowed directly from San Francisco to Victoria, however, as the ships on the sea route often by-passed Portland entirely. Victoria was an outpost within San Francisco's growing hinterland, and Fraser River gold helped to make up deficits in California's declining exports of the precious metal.[41]

The Portland merchant had his eye on the interior. He could not hope to compete with San Francisco for the Victoria trade so he gave his attention to The Dalles and promoted the interior routes. Many parties of miners came through the Willamette Valley and other groups of California miners followed the route in the interior east of the Cascades to The Dalles. One group from the Sacramento Valley consisted of 500 armed and mounted Frenchmen divided into regular military companies. They came by way of the Willamette Valley, Portland, and The Dalles. The steamers *Mountain Buck* and *Hassalo* were crowded with men and animals en route to The Dalles from Portland during the height of the rush. Joel Palmer, Major Robertson, a Mr. Wolff, and David McLoughlin led large parties by the interior routes during 1858 and 1859.[42] Palmer was first to take wagons northward on the Okanogan route and the old Hudson's Bay brigade trail to Fort Hope. He had invested in a large outlay of mules, horses, wagons, provisions, and mining equipment in July 1858. Reports said he made $20,000 in his freighting and trading enterprises during the first season. He continued in the northern trade to the Fraser and later to the Similkameen through 1860.[43]

The rise of The Dalles trade was the principal benefit that Portland merchants derived from the gold rush. The *Oregonian* reported in August 1858 that "Trade is light with the exception of what goods are sold to go to The Dalles, and these are articles adapted principally for miner's uses." A week later trade at The Dalles and business of all kinds was pronounced "brisk." Everything betokened prosperity for the region for a brief season in 1858. While The Dalles trade continued to be important, it did not meet the expectations of the more optimistic Portland merchants as the number of people going to the northern mines declined. A Portland merchant, writing a few years later, pronounced the whole Fraser River episode, a great "humbug."[44]

Chapter X

Economic Development, 1855-61

"Importing all we consume ..."

The development of the Pacific Northwest during the later 1850s continued in the pattern of the American frontier of the pre-railroad era. Here was an underdeveloped agricultural economy dependent upon river and ocean transportation. Here industry was still in its primitive stages. Here as elsewhere men sought wealth from land, mines, and forests and converted a small part of the region's vast resources into valuable goods and improvements. The merchant continued to provide necessary goods from outside the region and to accumulate capital from the profits of trade. The period under consideration, 1855-61, was one of relative prosperity which began and ended with depression and falls between two booming gold rushes. But it is also one of relatively slow or retarded growth when compared with California and the rapidly developing agricultural and industrial economy of the Mississippi Valley. Due to its remote location, Indian hostilities, and the expiration of the Donation Act, the region had become less attractive to the emigrant.

The Willamette Valley

By 1855 the Willamette Valley had taken on a settled character. Farmsteads and small towns dotted the upper valley from Oregon City to Eugene and beyond. Value had been given to the land whether it was cultivated or not. After the expiration of the Donation Act in 1855, complaints arose against the high prices asked by farmers who held favorably located unused farm lands which were parts of original donation claims. It was believed that all or nearly all of the arable land in western Oregon had been appropriated by 1857, and the Willamette Valley seemed to have become crowded. Pressure existed in the mid-decade for opening the area east of the Cascades for settlement.[1] Due to the dangers of the interior, however, few settlers moved to the upper Columbia Valley prior to 1858. Of the 52,465 people in Oregon in 1860, 39,001 were concentrated in the counties drained by the Willamette and its navigable tributaries. Most of the others were located in the growing communities of southern Oregon. Of the 896,414 acres of improved farm land in Oregon in 1860, 766,928 acres were in the Willamette Valley.[2] Here wheat was the most important staple, and numerous mills provided the flour which flowed downriver to Portland to become the valley's most valuable export.

As was characteristic of newly settled areas, farmers and townsmen had an eye for speculation. Land in the Willamette Valley sold, as a general rule, for $5.00 to $10 per acre during 1857, while more favorably located sites near towns brought considerably more. Lands near Portland, for instance, were held at prices ranging from $25 to $50 per acre. A Tualatin Plains farmer reported that: "1 man has a claim joining Portland and he sold 4 acres at 50 dollars per acre on a hill side that is so steep that a cow can scarcely climb the mountain and his levil [sic] land brings him from 30 to 40 dollars per acre just for the timber and he keeps the land."[3]

The Willamette River was the essential artery of commerce. Steamboats plied its waters from Canemah and Linn City at the falls to the towns and boat landings of the upper valley. But it had to be improved at considerable expense to the government and individuals before it became safe throughout its navigable length. Prior to 1856 steamers went as far as Corvallis, and in that year the run was extended to Eugene, the natural head of navigation. Freight was high. Quotations for May 1855, were $16 per ton from Canemah to Salem; $22 per ton to Albany; and $24 per ton to Corvallis. The advance on staple merchandise at Eugene during 1855 and 1856 was from 25 to 100 per cent above Portland prices. Freight on wheat destined for John McLoughlin's mill at Oregon City cost 20 cents per bushel from Corvallis to Canemah in 1856. By 1859 the rates were one-half those for 1855, and freight from Canemah to Salem cost $6.00 per ton and to Corvallis $8.00 per ton during the hard times of 1860.[4] But during most of the decade the river rates were considerably higher than those from San Francisco to Portland by sea.

Steamboats were most active on the lower Willamette between Portland and Oregon City, where the merchants Allan, McKinlay and Company and George Abernethy and Company of Oregon City and others competed for the trade. Here Oregon's pioneer steamboat men, J. C. Ainsworth and Jacob Kamm, took leading roles in the development of river navigation as builders, engineers, and capitalists. In 1854 these men, in association with the coastal shipping firm of Abernethy, Clark and Company, built the fine new steamer *Jennie Clark* for the Oregon City trade. In 1858 the *Carrie Ladd* was built for the same route. Owned by Ainsworth, Kamm, Abernethy, Clark and Company, and W. S. Ladd, she was the queen of the river for a few years.

River men also developed steam navigation on the Columbia River. The Indian war of 1855 and 1856, mining activity, and the general eastward thrust of the frontier made The Dalles run, with portages at the Cascades, increasingly important during the decade. One portage built by Joseph S. Ruckel on the south side and another by D. F. Bradford and Company on the north side were completed at the Cascades in 1855 and 1856; and the Columbia River Navigation Company under the management of Benjamin Stark provided a tri-weekly service from Portland to the portages. Freight to The Dalles was $30 per ton, of which $7.50 went to Stark's company, $7.50 for each of two handlings at the Cascades, and $7.50 for the steamer from the Cascades to The Dalles. The merchants retired from the field of river transportation and Ainsworth, Kamm, the portage owners, and other river men developed Columbia River navigation during the later 1850s. Under Ainsworth's leadership they established the Oregon Steam Navigation Company in 1860 and were destined to monopolize Columbia River traffic and to collect millions in Idaho gold during the next decade.[5]

Better transportation facilities by land also appeared. By 1855 a tri-weekly stage ran from Oregon City to Corvallis. In the following year this service, except during the rainy months, was extended to Eugene and to Winchester on the Umpqua. From there to Jacksonville freight went by pack train and wagon. The road connecting Jacksonville with the towns of the Willamette Valley was favored over the hazardous but shorter route from Crescent City for the transportation of freight. Thus southern Oregon remained a part of Portland's commercial hinterland.

Roads and mail service were uniformly bad. Complaints against the mail service were constant during the decade. At best it took one month, but usually between 35 and 45 days, for mails from New York to reach Portland via the isthmus, and several more days passed before it arrived at the upper Willamette towns by steamboat or stage.[6] Roads were practically impassable during the winter. One farmer who had held his wheat crop for a higher price found that he could not move it when the price reached $2.00 per bushel during the winter of 1858 due to the condition of the road from his farm to the steamboat landing.[7]

The Export Market

The recovery of the San Francisco market for Oregon flour early in 1855 brought relief to the depressed conditions that had prevailed in the Willamette Valley the previous year. During the summer it became a drug on the market at San Francisco but in the fall it revived with the rise of an export demand for markets in Chile and Australia. Throughout the year and especially during the fall, quantities of flour, potatoes, eggs, butter, bacon, pork, and other provisions flowed southward on board the six sailing vessels active in the trade and the Pacific Mail steamship to San Francisco. The *Ocean Bird,* for example, carried 8,047 quarter sacks of flour, 2,597 sacks of wheat, nine barrels of salmon, and five kegs of butter in November 1855.[8]

Oregon's economy and its relative prosperity during the later 1850s depended largely upon the California demand for its products, chiefly upon the demand for flour. The price of wheat fluctuated on the Portland market between 80 cents and $1.50 per bushel, and at lower levels in the upper valley, from 1855 through 1857. Its price was susceptible to greater variations than the price of flour because of seasonal supply and marketing conditions.

The price of flour, which depended upon the San Francisco demand and fluctuated accordingly, provides a fair index to the region's prosperity during this period as shown in Table 1, p. 209. It ranged between five and seven dollars per barrel for the two grades throughout 1855.[9] During the fall, winter, and spring of 1855 and 1856 the Indian wars created a new demand for flour and provisions and the prices were inflated locally in terms of the scrip issued by the territorial government. But this had little bearing on the export price, which also rose. An extremely dry season threatened the California crop in the spring of 1856, causing considerable speculation in flour in San Francisco[10] and this brought the price from $8.00 to more than $10 per barrel in April. Flour at Portland rose, accordingly, to $8.00 and $9.00 per barrel during the spring, but as the speculation subsided and the Indian wars ended it fell to the $6.00 and $6.50 levels during the latter part of the year.

Early in 1857 the San Francisco market felt the effect of the crop shortage of the previous year and the price of flour rose to $15 and $16 per barrel in March. Now California had to depend upon Oregon for flour, at least through the spring months. An observer there noted "there is no wheat here, for the reason that but little was grown last year in any portion of the State, and none can be spared in the Atlantic States or Chile." Wheat sold as high at $4.50 per bushel in the interior of California. In May the same observer reported the imminence of another crop failure because of dry weather.[11]

Operators of grist mills in Oregon and Washington responded to the demand. Flour at Portland rose to $9.00 and $10 per barrel in April 1857, while wheat sold for $1.25 per bushel. Contrary to the pattern of the two preceding years, the price of flour held at the relatively high level of $8.00 to $9.50 per barrel during the rest of the year, and it skyrocketed to $12 and $16 per barrel in the spring of 1858 when California felt the effect of its second consecutive crop shortage.

All categories of Oregon produce met a ready demand in San Francisco during these years. Henry W. Corbett, viewing business conditions from Portland's Front Street in March 1857, noted the effect of the California demand as follows: "buisness [sic] good our products such as Pork, Lard, Bacon, Butter, Eggs, Flour, Onions, Potatoes &c find a ready market

TABLE 1

WHOLESALE PRICES OF FLOUR, PER BARREL, AT PORTLAND, OREGON, 1853-61

	1853	1854	1855	1856	1857	1858	1859	1860	1861
January.........	$36-40	....	....	$ 6.50	$6-6.50	$ 10-10.50	$ 7-8	$ 5-6	$3.25-4.50
February.........	....	$14-15	....	6-6.50	6-7	12-13	6-8	5-5.50	3.25-4
March.........	25-28	15-16	$6-7	6-6.50	8-8.25	12-16	6.50-8.25	5-6	3.25-4
April.........	15-19	15-16	6	9-10	9-10	13-16	7-8.25	5-6.50	3.25-4
May.........	18-20	15-16	5	8-8.50	8.50-9	10.50-13.50	7.25-8	4.50-5	3.25-4
June.........	....	12-16	....	8-9	8-8.50	11.50-14	5.50-8	4.50-5	3.50-4.25
July.........	....	11-14	7	6-7.50	....	16-22	5.50-7.50	4-5	3.75-4.50
August.........	....	10-12	5-6.50	6-7	....	10-14	6-8	4	3.50-4.50
September.........	....	6-8	5-6	6-6.50	....	9-10	....	4	3.50-4.50
October.........	....	6	6-7	....	8-8.50	8-10	5.50-7	3.25-4	3.50-4.50
November.........	....	....	....	5-6.50	8-8.50	8-10	5.50-7	3.50-3.75	3.75-5
December.........	....	6-7	6.50-7	6	9-9.50	7-7.50	5-6.50	3.50-4	....

(Source: the *Oregonian*, 1853-61)

in San Francisco they find that our produce is driving the States provisions out of the market and things never looked more prosperous in Oregon than at the present time."[12]

Flour fell briefly to $11 and $14 per barrel on the Portland market in May 1858, only to rise to the $16 and $22 levels in July because of the gold rush to Fraser River. Oregon's flour and other provisions now moved northward to the new markets either by sea to Victoria or up the Columbia to The Dalles and from there to the new gold fields by the interior routes. Wheat rose from 90 cents and $1.00 per bushel in the Willamette Valley in the spring of 1857, to $1.50 and $2.00 per bushel during the winter and spring of 1858. For a brief time in July when the gold excitement was highest, it reached $4.00 per bushel. As the Fraser River fever waned the price of flour fell precipitously to the $8.00 to $10 levels at Portland in the fall of 1858. The San Francisco demand also declined due to the rapid development of agriculture in California. The price held at $8.00 and $10 per barrel at Portland through the spring of 1859, but thereafter it declined steadily until it reached $3.50 and $4.00 per barrel in 1860, and a low of $3.25 per barrel in 1861. By 1859 depression conditions had fallen upon the Willamette Valley for the second time in a decade.

As mentioned above, pork, eggs, butter and other provisions found a ready market in San Francisco. Portland price ranges for bacon were 12 to 20 cents per pound; for eggs, 30 to 45 cents per dozen; and for butter, 20 to 50 cents per pound prior to 1858. Eggs followed a seasonal pattern, reaching $37\frac{1}{2}$ to 45 cents per dozen during the winter. Prices for all items rose briefly during the Fraser River rush in 1858 and declined thereafter. Cattle were plentiful in Oregon and California, and beef, produced only for the local market, was cheaper than pork. Cattle sold at $12 to $15 per head at Portland in November 1859.

Oregon butter met a good demand at San Francisco prior to 1857, but thereafter the market for it was all but lost because of its poor quality. Quantities of different grades of butter were often mixed indiscriminately at the boat landings and were poorly packed and handled in transit to the San Francisco market. One Oregon shipper had to sell 3,000 pounds of butter for which he had paid 20 cents per pound in the Willamette Valley for 15 cents per pound in San Francisco. He had earlier refused 40 cents per pound for it at the dock. As the condition and reputation of Oregon butter grew worse, Portland itself began to import butter. The editor of the *Oregonian* lashed out at Oregon farmers for losing an important part of the export market because of their want of industry and their carelessness. He wrote in April 1858:

> During the last ten years Oregon has produced and shipped to California wheat, flour, pork, potatoes, onions, butter, cheese, &c., to the amount of several million dollars. Now California speculators are shipping here, from San Francisco, butter, which costs there 42 cents, and selling it for $1 per pound.[13]

There seemed to be little excuse for this since Oregon farmers could easily produce dairy products and a good demand existed in California.

By 1859 apples had become an important export item. Although fruit culture had begun in a small way during Hudson's Bay days, its effective introduction dates back to 1847, when Henderson Luelling brought several hundred grafted trees and sprouts across the plains from Iowa. William Meek also had brought in a few grafted trees and apple seeds in the same year. The two men entered a partnership and established a nursery at Milwaukie in 1848 from which they were soon supplying Willamette Valley farmers with young fruit trees. When the trees first began to bear in 1852, Luelling sold a few apples, some at one dollar apiece and some for as much as five dollars apiece in the Portland market. He sold his first box of apples for a net profit of $75. By 1853, he and Meek had four branch nurseries in the Willamette Valley. With the high prices for apples at Portland and San Francisco Luelling was able to say that his load of trees brought overland to Oregon in 1847, returned "a dollar a drop for the sweat I lost in getting the necessary water to keep them alive while we crossed the desert; and their luscious fruit repaid me many times over for the jeers, ridicule and contentions of my comrades."

The apple export trade began in a small way in 1853, when Meek and Luelling received $500 for four bushels of apples at San Francisco. In 1854, 40 bushels brought $2,500 in the same market, according to Bancroft. In the following year 1,500 boxes, weighing from 55 to 60 pounds each, were exported to California where they sold for 50 cents to one dollar per pound. In 1856 young orchards throughout the valley were in full bearing and some 5,000 boxes were exported bringing from 25 to 50 cents per pound at San Francisco. Production steadily increased; 15,000 boxes were exported in 1857 and twice that amount in 1858 when the San Francisco price ranged between 12½ to 20 cents per pound.

During the fall and winter of 1859 and 1860, some 90,000 bushels of Oregon apples were shipped to San Francisco. They sold for 2 to 6 cents per pound at Portland and brought from 2½ to 17 cents at San Francisco. The value of apples exported this season including small shipments to Victoria and other North Pacific ports was estimated at not less than $300,000. The 1860-61 season was good, but thereafter the California market subsided owing to the rapid development of the fruit industry there.[14]

Ships and Shipping, 1855-61

The life line of the Pacific Coast during these years was still the Cape Horn route. Although the Panama railway was completed in 1855, most merchandise and all heavier materials still came by the longer route to San Francisco, that destined for Oregon being forwarded to Portland on board the small ships engaged in the coasting trade. As has been noted, many, probably most, of the merchants at Portland and Oregon City made all of their purchases in San Francisco. "Not a great many merchants in Oregon . . . purchase goods in N. Y.," H. W. Corbett noted, "and most of those that do have been on there and made their arrangements." Corbett, J. Failing and Company, George Abernethy and Company, and a few other wholesalers purchased in the East, except when it was necessary or profitable to purchase in San Francisco. Freights from New York to San Francisco, via Cape Horn, fell from $12.50 to $13.00 per ton and 30 to 50 cents per foot in 1855 to $10 per ton and 20 to 30 cents per foot during 1856 and 1857,[15] reflecting the new competition of the Panama route after 1855 and the waning clipper trade.

Wakeman, Dimon and Company of New York and W. S. Ladd of Portland revived the idea of direct shipping between New York and Portland in 1857. They built the bark *C. E. Tilton* especially for the route and consigned a large cargo to J. Failing and Company. She sailed from New York on February 5 and arrived at Portland on June 8, after a record trip of 116 days. She was pronounced one of the finest ships ever to grace the Willamette. Though the total value of her cargo is not known, one of the largest shipments C. W. Thomas ever sent to J. Failing and Co., valued at $26,509.77, came on board the *Tilton*. Freight charges were $14 per ton and 35 cents per foot with the usual 5 per cent of the freight charge added for primage. Thomas departed from his usual practice by taking out insurance on this large shipment at 4½ per cent on $20,000, thus adding $900 to the cost of the goods.[16] There was an actual saving on freight, but the risks involved must have been too great. The *Tilton* operated in the coasting trade for a time but did not continue in the business for which she was intended. Later, in 1859, Wakeman, Dimon and Company sent the *Industry* direct to Portland,[17] but this seems to have been a last effort.

Several sailing vessels and one steamship operated in the coastwise trade between Portland and San Francisco. Abernethy, Clark and Company's Oregon and California Packet Line kept one or two of their four barks, the *Ocean Bird*, the *Charles Devens*, the *J. B. Lunt,* and the *Nahumkeag*, running back and forth constantly during 1855, 1856 and 1857. Sometimes the Abernethy line chartered other vessels, and a few independents cleared from the San Francisco dock of Abernethy, Clark and Company. The bark *Metropolis* and the brig *Francisco,* owned or controlled by the Portland firms of Allen and Lewis and Leonard and Green, ran in opposition to the Abernethy line. The *Desdemona* ran in opposition occasionally until she was wrecked at the mouth of the Columbia in January 1857. The *Samuel Merritt* and the *Susan Abigail* were also among the oldtimers familiar to Portland residents. The steamship of the Pacific Mail line arrived at Portland at regular fortnightly intervals. "Steamer Day" at Portland was one of unusual and bustling activity when merchants and other residents received the "latest" news from New York and San Francisco.

Abernethy, Clark and Company purchased the fine new clipper bark *Jane A. Falkenberg* for $25,000 and added her to their line in 1857. Built in New Bedford in 1855, she had made the Cape Horn run to San Francisco on her maiden voyage in 115 days. Her graceful lines impressed the Portland townsfolk when in September 1857 she landed the largest cargo of merchandise ever brought from San Francisco to the Willamette. Owing to financial difficulties, the Abernethy firm soon sold the *Falkenberg* to Captain George Flavel, who made her famous in Pacific waters.[18]

Several Portland and Oregon City firms served as commission and forwarding merchants, usually in conjunction with their regular retail and wholesale businesses. Among the more important ones were those engaged directly in the shipping business—Abernethy, Clark and Company, Leonard and Green, and Allen and Lewis. Hiram Clark of the former and L. H. Allen of the latter managed the San Francisco branches of their respective firms. W. S. Ladd and Company also had a representative at San Francisco.* It was a common practice for Portland merchants to receive produce on the accounts of their upriver customers. H. W. Corbett, for example, either sold the produce sent down by his customers on the Portland market or forwarded it to San Francisco and applied the proceeds to their accounts for merchandise.[19] This seems to have been an accommodation rather than specialization in the commission and forwarding business, however.

Although trade improved considerably after Oregon products regained their place in the San Francisco market in 1855, there was still a paucity of exports. During the second half of 1856, 44 vessels entered the Columbia with a total tonnage of 14,772, and 40 vessels cleared with a total

---

*The following shipment from Allen and Lewis, Portland to L. H. Allen, San Francisco, Manifest, bark *Metropolis*, June 30, 1856, Astoria Customs House Records (Microfilm, O. H. S.) , provides an example of the process: 7,500 quarter sacks of flour valued at $15,000, 82 cases of bacon, 86 sacks of wheat, 40 firkins of butter, 150 sacks of oats, and 300 sacks of bran. Manifests of the brig *Francisco* for her four trips during 1856, *ibid.*, show a total of 20,064 quarter sacks of flour 1,226 sacks of flour, 606 sacks of wheat, 7,120 pounds and 13 half barrels of lard, 32 tons of bacon, 20 tons and 51 kegs of butter, 20 barrels of pork, 153,000 board feet of lumber, 20 sacks and 103,711 pounds of potatoes, 10,600 feet of laths, 60 barrels of whiskey, and 3 tons of iron.

tonnage of 13,426. While this represented an improvement, the tonnage figures alone suggest an adverse balance of trade.[20] The picture is made worse when one compares the greater value of the manufactured goods imported with that of the bulky produce and lumber exported.

Optimism about the development of trade with the Orient, the great dream since the time of Jefferson, persisted. David Logan, lawyer and Whig politician, wrote in 1857:

> There is to day a better prospect, than ever before, for the speedy growth both in wealth & numbers of the Pacific Coast and of Oregon in particular, rich in minerals, Grass, & Timber . . . Japan, Australia, the Islands of the Pacific, the coast of Mexico, China & South America lay at her door—to them our Commerce is extended & is rapidly increasing whilst labor & interprise [sic] can increase it to any extent.[21]

But Oregon's foreign trade remained insignificant. The Australian market for lumber had been tried in 1854, and a few shipments of Oregon produce went to Hong Kong and other Pacific ports during the decade. The *Metropolis* made several trips to Honolulu, but nothing resembling a regular trade developed between Oregon and the islands. Shipments to foreign ports from the lumber mills of Puget Sound provide a brighter picture, however.

Lumber production played an important role in the development of western Oregon and Washington. Lumber mills in the Willamette Valley and southern Oregon were numerous, a total of 126 for Oregon in 1860; but except for those on the lower Willamette and Columbia rivers, they produced essentially for a local market. Improvements of all kinds in the new towns and on the farms created a demand for lumber, nails, and all other building materials. The high freight rates on the Willamette and other costs prohibited production on the upper river for the export market. The price of lumber at Salem, for instance, was from $17 to $20 per thousand board feet in 1857, and from $18 to $25 in 1858, while the wholesale price for the export market at Portland, Oak Point, and other places on the lower river system was from $8.00 to $11 per thousand during the mid-decade.[22]

The Abernethy mill at Oak Point on the Washington side, some sixty miles from the mouth of the Columbia, produced most of the lumber that was exported through the port of Astoria during the 1850s. It was one of the most improved mills in the region. Here the ships that sailed in the Abernethy line, after unloading their cargoes of merchandise at Portland, would load out full or partial cargoes of lumber, provided the San Francisco demand warranted shipment. "Here is evidence," a visitor at Oak Point reported in 1855, "of the energy, enterprise, and ability of one of the most efficient and prominent Companies on our Pacific Coast, . . . Abernethy & Co. The lumber cut here is of the best quality, and by the fastest saw in Oregon." In the same year when three ships operated in the Abernethy line, lumber could not be carried away fast enough to keep up with the mill. Lumber put on board at Oak Point in that year at a cost of $8.00 per thousand board feet brought only $10 per thousand at San Francisco. In 1856 the market improved and lumber flowed from Oak Point and the Puget Sound mills even more freely. This business seems to have been profitable for the rest of the decade, in spite of the tremendous growth of the industry in California. The price of lumber placed on board the sailing vessels at Oak Point was $10 to $12 per thousand board feet during 1858 and 1859.[23]

But the lumber export business had shifted to the millsites and towns on the more accessible and less dangerous waters of Puget Sound. From here a regular fleet operated in the coasting trade between the Sound and San Francisco and several ships loaded out cargoes for Australia, Asia, and England during the decade. One mill alone provided 52 cargoes in 1856. In 1858, each of six Puget Sound mills produced from 4,000 to 5,000 board feet daily; eight others, from 10,000 to 15,000; and one had a daily capacity of 40,000 board feet. In the same year the ship *George Raynes* bound for Sydney carried out 800,000 board feet, the largest shipment of lumber to leave a port on the Pacific Coast up to that time. By 1860 lumber production in Washington Territory had almost doubled that of Oregon. For the year ending June 1, 1860, the total value of lumber produced in Washington Territory was $1,172,520; in Oregon, $690,008; and in California, $3,943,881.[24]

The coastwise trade between San Francisco and Portland became more competitive during the later 1850s with the steamships virtually driving the sailing vessels from the field. At first an independent steamship appeared in opposition to the Pacific Mail Steamship Company in 1857. This developed into the Merchant's Accommodation Line, running the *Brother Jonathan* and the *Pacific* in opposition to the *Panama* of the Pacific Mail Company early in 1858. Large quantities of Oregon produce went out on board the steamships and communication with San Francisco was now weekly or semi-weekly. The effect of opposition was to reduce freights on the mail steamship from $12.50 per ton in April 1857, to $6.00 per ton by February 1858. The sailing vessel rate continued at $5.00 per ton until the Fraser River rush in the spring and summer of 1858, when for a brief time all vessels enjoyed the boom, and rates rose to $10 per ton on the Portland run.[25] When the rush subsided, however, the steamships were supreme in the widened field of coastwise shipping from San Francisco to Victoria.

One by one the sailing vessels on the Portland-San Francisco run disappeared. Advertisements for the Oregon and California Packet Line ceased, and the old familiar Abernethy vessels were no longer seen on the river. During 1859 Abernethy, Clark and Company ran only the *Live Yankee* northward for cargoes of lumber at Oak Point and limited amounts of produce at Portland.[26] During 1860 scarcely a single sail was seen on the Columbia River. With the Idaho gold rush of the 1860s, however, the packet service by sailing vessels revived but not the old Abernethy line.

George Abernethy's Failure

As has been explained George Abernethy's entrepreneurial activity embraced practically every field of pioneer enterprise. With meagre financial resources he had developed flour and lumber milling, wholesale merchandising and ocean and river transportation. He was first among Oregon merchants to establish his credit in New York and Oregon's first wholesale merchant. Early in the decade he had attempted direct shipments from New York to Portland but this had proved impractical. His business associates by mid-decade included Hiram Clark, his first partner, Thomas

Pope, his brother-in-law, and his brother, A. S. Abernethy. From 1851 to 1855 Abernethy was in New York buying merchandise while his associates attended to the various aspects of the business in Oregon and California. He contracted a sizeable debt in New York, the amount unknown, some time prior to 1854, probably for the purpose of purchasing ships.

The Abernethy enterprises flourished during mid-decade. Shipments of lumber to California have been mentioned. George Abernethy and Company, the merchandising firm, enjoyed exceptionally good sales during 1855, and no doubt continued to do so until depression conditions again struck the valley in 1859. The shipping firm, Abernethy, Clark and Company, gave satisfactory service to Portland merchants, handled freights carefully, and if damage occurred, promptly rectified it. Corbett, for example, had complete confidence in the firm prior to 1857, when they failed to follow his instructions in making a remittance to an eastern firm. In complaining about over-measurement, Corbett wrote to Clark, with whom he was on especially good terms, as follows: "I have not claimed deductions unless I thought they were actually my due. Captain Wiggins [one of the pioneer ship captains in the coasting trade] has always made things right, but the Capt. of the Lunt and the Govr [Abernethy] was [sic] a little crusty." Such incidents seem to have increased after 1857 and Portland merchants evinced less confidence in the Abernethy line.[27]

Abernethy's grand plan ended in failure. From the few records available it seems to have been due to competition in the carrying trade, indebtedness, over-extension, and the depressed conditions from 1859 through 1861. On February 11, 1861 the *Oregon Statesman* announced: "The firm Abernethy & Clark, Oregon City and San Francisco, have failed; the deficit is reported at $120,000. It has been an enterprising firm, but we think an unfavorable opinion has prevailed in business circles as to its financial soundness for several years."

The final blow came when the disastrous flood of the Willamette in December, 1861, washed away Abernethy's mill and his pioneer brick store along with a considerable part of Oregon City. Thereafter Abernethy continued in business as a Portland commission merchant until his death in 1877, and his brother, A. S. Abernethy, prospered in the lumber business at Oak Point, where the mill by 1871 produced up to 4,000,000 board feet annually.[28] But the series of disasters that befell Abernethy's various enterprises between 1857 and 1862 mark the end of the promising dream of one of Oregon's earliest pioneer merchants. While Abernethy has been remembered chiefly for his work as Oregon's provisional governor from 1845 to 1849, and for his religious bias and identification with alleged Methodist duplicity in Oregon's early days, his achievement in business in spite of failure was an important contribution to the early economic development of the new commonwealth.

Limited Development and Depression

In spite of the favorable conditions of the mid-decade the Pacific Northwest suffered the effects of inadequate population and capital resources and an adverse balance of trade. Conditions which had impelled thousands of settlers to emigrate to Oregon from the Mississippi Valley between 1843 and 1853 no longer existed. As we have seen, the Donation Act had expired in 1855 and few lands in the western valleys of Oregon were left unappropriated. Prior to 1858 settlement of the interior had been blocked by military order and the Indian threat to the emigrant roads. Under these conditions this remote region, in spite of its salubrious climate, could not match the attractions of the newer states and territories of the Mississippi Valley where land was abundant and where the railroad was revolutionizing the older economy.

But emigration to Oregon and Washington resumed in a small way in 1858. Even before the Fraser River rush the *Oregonian* reported newcomers arriving on every steamer and suggested that the farmers sell idle acres from their 640-acre holdings. "There is entirely too many thousand broad acres of land lying idle and useless for the *upward* and *onward* progress of our country," the editor declared. The population of Portland rose from 1,280 in 1857 to 2,917 in 1860, and that of the state from 42,677 in 1858 to 52,465 in 1860. The number of native born in Oregon in 1860 was 16,564 showing the increase by immigration to have been

219

relatively slight since Oregon's population in 1853 was at least 35,000. Oregon's small population was one factor in the delay of statehood until February 14, 1859.[29]

Although Portland retained its village complex it went through a new phase of development in 1858 and 1859. Building improvements of all kinds appeared as the town prepared to accommodate the new population and to expand its business. Several new brick buildings appeared including Henry W. Corbett's two-story store, built in 1858 at a cost of $10,000, and that of Failings and Hatt, built in 1859 at about the same cost. Solid, more comfortable homes appeared in the residential area to the west.[30]

However, the growth of Oregon and the Pacific Northwest compares unfavorably with that of the frontier states and territories of the Mississippi Valley during this and later decades. The population of Oregon reached 52,465 and that of Washington Territory 11,594 in 1860. By comparison Kansas Territory surged from practically nothing in 1854 to 106,390 in 1860; Minnesota from 6,077 in 1850 to 172,023 in 1860; and Iowa from 192,214 in 1850 to 674,913 in 1860. In Table 2 the figures on improved farm acreage show the phenomenal growth of agriculture in the Mississippi Valley and California and its relatively slower growth in the Pacific Northwest during the decade of the 1850s.

TABLE 2

FARMS AND IMPROVED FARM ACREAGE IN THE FRONTIER
STATES AND TERRITORIES, 1850 AND 1860

	Number of Farms		Improved Farm Acreage	
	1850	1860	1850	1860
Oregon	1,164	5,806	132,857	896,414
Washington Territory	..	1,330	..	81,869
California	872	18,716	32,454	2,468,034
Nebraska Territory	..	2,789	..	118,789
Iowa	14,805	61,163	824,682	3,792,792
Minnesota	157	18,181	5,035	556,250
Kansas Territory	..	10,400	..	405,468
Illinois	76,208	143,310	5,039,545	13,096,374
Missouri	54,458	92,792	2,938,425	6,246,871

Although greatly overshadowed when compared with other parts of the United States the industrial growth of the Pacific Northwest during the decade of the 1850s was substantial when considered in terms of the region's small population. In addition to the lumber and flour mills already mentioned there were many small shops or factories producing implements, leather goods, wagons, liquors, and numerous other items of a basic nature. The value of the products of Oregon's lesser industries in 1860 was $1,108,-703, while that of flour alone was $1,178,050, and of lumber, $690,008. The aggregate value of all the products of Washington's industries in 1860 was $1,406,921; and of this, $1,172,520 represents the value of the lumber produced by her 32 saw mills.[31] The manufacture of woolens, the construction of ocean-going ships, and coal mining were among the new industries that appeared during the decade.

The woolen industry in Oregon was launched in 1858. In 1856 Joseph Watt, a sheep farmer who could find no market for raw wool, had joined a group of enterprising Salem men to form the Willamette Woolen Manufacturing Company. One of the directors of the new company had gone east and persuaded L. E. Pratt, an experienced factory man, to come to Oregon to build and manage the new plant. Pratt, Oregon's pioneer woolen manufacturer, designed the factory at Salem, installed the new machinery he had purchased in the East, and had the new plant in production by January, 1858. By March, 450 spindles and 15 looms were in operation. Although the company subscribed a considerable amount of capital, it had a heavy indebtedness during its early years. There was, however, a ready market in the region for the blankets, flannels, and cassimeres produced by the factory, and in 1859 the Indian department purchased part of its annual supply of blankets at Salem.

Pratt developed a system whereby the merchants who distributed his goods accepted raw wool from customers, when possible, in exchange for blankets, cloth, and other merchandise. He exchanged finished products for the wool and thus assured himself of a supply of raw materials as well as outlets for his goods. H. W. Corbett, one of his Portland distributors, sold large quantities of this woolen cloth on a commission basis. Figures for the year ending June 1, 1860, show that the factory employed 27 males and 13 females for an annual labor cost of $16,200. The company was capitalized at $70,000 and the value of the product for that year was $85,000. Soon the supply of raw material was greater than the factory demand and Pratt made his first sale of raw wool in the eastern market in 1862. Civil War demands stimulated the production of raw wool, which soon became an important Oregon export.[32]

In addition to steamboat construction on the Willamette, ship building developed on the coast at Coos Bay where excellent timbers for this purpose existed in abundance. A. M. and R. W. Simpson, at North Bend, built schooners, brigs, and barkentines during the latter part of the decade. In 1861, H. H. Luse began production of the same kind of ships at nearby Empire City. The industry retained its importance as long as the demand for the small sailing vessel held during the next three decades. The lumber industry at Coos Bay developed simultaneously.

Nelson Northrup of the Portland firm of Northrup and Simonds pioneered in the coal mining and lumber industries at Coos Bay in 1855. Shipments from the Newport mine began on a regular basis in 1855 and 1856, when Coos Bay coal brought $40 per ton at San Francisco. At about the same time the coal mining industry was in its initial stages of development at Bellingham Bay and other points on Puget Sound.[33]

Since the beginnings of settlement the salmon fishery had some importance but it developed slowly. The tin can had not yet replaced the barrel in preserving and shipping fish nor had markets of any importance outside the region developed. The value of the salmon produced in Oregon in 1860 was only $13,450 and in Washington, only $18,900. Washington also produced cod and halibut. But strange as it may seem in a country whose rivers were laden with salmon in season, the oyster fishery in 1860 was more valuable than all others combined. It was pioneered by a group of fishermen in 1854 at Willapa Bay, then known as Shoalwater Bay, in Washington Territory a short distance north of Astoria. Here the town of Oysterville appeared and by 1857 three schooners were making regular runs to supply the San Francisco oyster market. The value of the oyster fishery, which employed 100 men, was only $44,597 in 1860, but it grew rapidly during the next two decades only to decline even more rapidly when a series of disasters struck the industry during the 1880s. Oysterville then became a ghost town.[34]

Wages were high in Oregon during the 1850s. Laborers received from $2.00 to $3.00; carpenters, from $3.00 to $7.00; and other skilled workmen from $4.00 to $6.00 per day in 1857 and 1858. Skilled workers and clerks had charged the government as high as $10 per day during the Indian wars. With reference to the high cost of living, a member of the constitutional convention remarked in 1857 that $400 was "more money" in Rhode Island than $1,500 was in Oregon.[35]

Oregonians distrusted banks and corporations. Without a dissenting vote Democrats and the Whig minority in Oregon's constitutional convention, which met at Salem in 1857, prohibited banks of issue in the new instrument of government. The constitution makers also inserted the principle of limited liability after considerable debate on the subject of corporations, and restricted the spending power of the legislature in order to secure maximum economy in state government. The document evinces the principles of Jeffersonian and Jacksonian democracy throughout and the influence of the constitutions of Mississipi Valley states which were taken as models. Reuben P. Boise, speaking in the convention, declared that there was nothing new in this constitution and that intelligent men of the territory would see nothing in it they had not seen before.[36]

Distrust of corporations, especially those for internal improvements, derived partly from the direct experience of several Oregonians in unsound ventures during the territorial period. In 1851 the Portland and Valley Plank Road Company had been incorporated to build a plank road via the old Canyon Road westward from Portland into Yamhill County. After completion of a ten-mile stretch the venture had ended in financial failure. The Tualatin Valley Plank Road Company had completed the work in 1856, but it was always a poor road and this company also failed. A telegraph company had been incorporated to build a line from Portland to Corvallis, but after considerable expense and waste of materials, Californians, it was alleged, made off with the money subscribed by Willamette Valley residents. John

223

Waymire, speaking in favor of limited liability in the constitutional convention, asserted:

> Let us bring this thing right home and apply it to things we have seen. We have here a plank road. How was that got up? . . . They got honest, responsible men to subscribe, and they made them pay to the last dollar. And who had benefited by this plank road? Nobody but these fancy stock gentlemen who never paid anything. The road was a humbug and a curse and . . . a base swindle which had cost the yeomanry of the country their hard-earned thousands—all the stock they subscribed. Would gentlemen now hold these stockholders to the amount of all the property they had? . . . We also had a telegraph here, and the history of that was the same as that of the plank road. The public had been swindled, and the telegraph was not only useless but a nuisance to the country.[37]

Oregon suffered for want of capital. Industry and internal improvements could not be developed sufficiently when millions flowed out each year to pay for necessities and there was little prospect that capital would flow in from outside sources.[38] The merchant, as we have seen, enhanced his capital resources from the profits of trade, but these were needed to secure and to expand his merchandising business. He had little disposition in the late fifties to risk his capital in new or untried enterprises. In his message to the state legislature on May 10, 1859, Governor John Whiteaker decried the conditions which required the export of capital as follows:

> The continual draughts upon the capital of the people, for many of the necessaries of life which are shipped to this country, is being felt by all classes of citizens. It is true there is no capital brought to the country, except what comes from the mines of our own and neighboring States. And it is equally true that this source fails to keep up the supply for business transactions under our present system of importing all we consume. That there is a sufficient amount of gold produced in the country to answer all the reasonable demands of our people cannot be denied; but that it is scarcer now than it has been for the past several years is conceded by all. If we were to receive twice the amount we now receive from the mines, and the same system of economy should continue, the same results would nevertheless be realized. . . . Oregon has the elements to produce her own supply of leather, hats, salt, iron &c., all of which enter largely into our consumption, . . .

To say some of these articles can be shipped to Oregon cheaper than they can be produced here is no argument . . . for if the capital that annually finds its way from Oregon was saved . . . we would be able to pay a much higher price for an article of domestic or home production than we now pay for the imported article.[39]

When the San Francisco market for Oregon produce all but collapsed in 1859 depression struck the Willamette Valley. Trade at Portland did not revive in the spring according to the normal pattern and was off by at least 50 per cent during the summer. Only the fall apple trade and the prospect that the Indian war claims might be paid held any immediate hope for the Portland merchant.[40]

Except for apples the California market for Oregon products had practically disappeared by the summer of 1859. "Hard times," with no prospect for improvement, was the cry in the fall after a disappointing summer season. Some 90,040 tons of valuable imports as against 16,579 tons of less valuable exports were recorded at the custom-house at Astoria between January 1 and November 1, 1859, showing clearly the adverse balance of trade. Specie and gold dust badly needed for the area's improvement had to make up the difference. The editor of the *Oregonian,* after calling for more production and less consumption of "foreign" goods, blamed the Democrats for the troublesome times as a matter of course. No one could get a government contract, he declared, "unless he is a regular full-blooded Lane, Smith, Chapman, and Geary Democrat." A farm group blamed the "rich" transportation men for charging exorbitant freight rates during the shipping season, and made an unsuccessful attempt to organize their own transportation company.[41]

Pessimism and panic gripped Portland's business community as 1860 dawned. Trade was dull and money scarce owing to the low prices of all kinds of produce. The wreck of the Pacific Mail steamship *Northerner* off the the Oregon coast with the loss of more than thirty lives, some of whom were Portland businessmen, added to the gloom. Conditions grew worse during the year as the price of flour continued to fall. The depression in agriculture became extremely severe.

While Oregon suffered, prospects for California wheat growers improved considerably. California agriculture was moving rapidly toward a position of ascendancy over mining, and with more than 30,000 farmers and farm laborers the Golden State produced 5,928,470 bushels of wheat in 1860, compared with Oregon's 826,776 bushels in the same year. California, ranking twelfth in the production of wheat and first in barley among the states in 1860, could easily supply her own foodstuffs and have an exportable surplus as well. California wheat and flour began to flow to New York and abroad.[42] This did not immediately benefit the Pacific Northwest, but it did inaugurate a new export pattern for the Far West which was to develop significantly with the demand created by the Civil War and by the accelerated industrial development of Europe and the East during the 1860s.

Oregon prices for breadstuffs had declined steadily during 1859 and remained low during 1860 and 1861. The price of wheat was 55 and 60 cents per bushel in the Willamette Valley and flour sold for $3.50 to $4.00 per barrel at Portland during the summer and fall of 1860. Farmers were discouraged and reluctant to sell. They were advised to ship even at low prices and perhaps share in the California export market. *"There are times when we must make present sacrifices for future good. You have to come down to the low prices till you get out of the woods. It is, do that, or do worse,"* a dealer in Oregon produce explained.[43]

Trade with the upper Columbia was more promising. New settlers in the interior valleys, the numerous miners prospecting the northern country deep into British Columbia, and Lieutenant John Mullan's crew of engineers building the famous Mullan Road across the Rocky Mountains all depended in some measure upon Portland for supplies. The Similkameen gold mines, discovered in the fall of 1859, caused a brief flurry of excitement during the spring of 1860. "If the mines prove productive, we shall have a market for our produce," Henry Failing declared hopefully. Prospectors were active in the interior, but there was little gold and the extent and richness of the gold country were matters of rumor and conjecture during the year.

Discoveries on the Clearwater in the fall of 1860 launched the region's golden decade. The rush to Idaho began in 1861, and at last Henry Failing could report in October that "The mines are no longer a supposition but a reality."

During 1861, his trade was almost entirely with the upper Columbia while previously it had been almost exclusively with the Willamette Valley.

Gold did not immediately alleviate depression in the Willamette Valley. Rather, conditions grew worse in 1861. Flour reached the low level of $3.25 per barrel early in the year and all produce and stock were so low that many farmers were tempted to sell their property and leave the country. Increasing numbers of valley merchants were unable to pay their Portland creditors, and real estate values depreciated to the extent that it was not profitable for merchants to attach the real property of their delinquent customers in the courts. By the fall of 1861 the Willamette Valley was virtually impoverished, and gold seemed to be the only hope. Gold dust flowing down the Columbia at the rate of $50,000 per week from the Idaho mines in the fall of 1861 did not immediately increase the amount of money in circulation in the Willamette Valley, since the demands for Oregon produce in the mining country at that time were not great enough to relieve the surpluses appreciably.[44]

The disastrous flood on the Willamette in December 1861 added to the distress. The angry river rose suddenly and laid havoc to towns and farms as it overflowed its banks for a 150-mile stretch. Linn City and Champoeg disappeared and Oregon City and Portland were inundated. Flour mills at Oregon City and Linn City were destroyed, and hundreds of farmers and townsmen suffered heavy losses. Now, according to one observer, the prospect of having a considerable population in the mining country as a market for produce was the only factor giving any value to property.[45]

There were, however, some signs of improvement. California's excessive exports of wheat had caused a flow of low-priced flour from Portland to San Francisco during the fall and winter of 1860 and 1861. This along with exports to Victoria and an increasing demand for provisions in the new mining region helped to relieve the surpluses in the Willamette Valley. By the fall of 1861 flour had reached $3.75 to $5.00 per barrel, though the price of wheat had remained at 55 to 60 cents per bushel throughout the year.

Except for 1858 the agricultural depression in Oregon coincided generally with that prevailing in the nation after the panic of 1857,[46] but it seems still to have been an isolated phenomenon. It was closely related to Oregon's remote location, small population, and underdeveloped condition, but a principal cause was the declining demand for Oregon's exportable surpluses. Relief came with the Idaho gold rush when the mining country became sufficiently populated to absorb the surplus farm products of the Willamette Valley.

Chapter XI

Wholesale Merchants:
Henry W. Corbett and Henry Failing

"Times are good here—no banks to brake."

The Portland wholesale merchant benefitted by the broadened market as the hinterland grew larger during the later 1850s, but he still functioned primarily within the agricultural economy of the Willamette Valley. As we have seen, the fluctuating export demand for flour provides a fair index to the region's prosperity during the later 1850s. Prices of merchandise were not subject to such extreme fluctuations, however, and volume varied in terms of the purchasing power of the farmers. Sources of supply had become more regular and dependable and merchandising more competitive. When the market recovered in 1855 the day of extreme shortage or excessive supply had ended. The merchant who could capture and maintain a reasonable share of the market was assured his profits, and competition made him alert to every legitimate advantage to be gained in trade.

Wholesaling, except in drugs and medicines, had not reached the specialized stage. Portland's leading merchants, many of whom sold at wholesale and retail, dealt in all categories of general merchandise. They sold everything from notions to farm machinery, though their stocks could generally be classified as hardware, dry goods, and groceries. W. T. A. Davis had nearly complete control of the wholesale drug business of Oregon, however, and he sold drugs and medicines at 50 to 100 per cent advance on New York cost.

Since Henry W. Corbett and J. Failing and Company were among Oregon's larger wholesale merchants, an analysis of their activities exemplifies an important business process as well as the problems of the businessman in this remote frontier area during the later 1850s.[1]

Corbett was an individualist. Having rid himself of the annoying partnership with R. N. and F. McLaren in June 1854, he operated and controlled his entire business as a single proprietorship from 1854 to 1871, a somewhat unique circumstance, since all of his major competitors were organized in partnerships.[2] He poured his profits back into the business each year. He scrupulously avoided speculative ventures, but sought every means to improve and expand his business. His early career reflects sound business judgment, resolute character, and the ambition to make a fortune and to promote the arts of civilization. He made his own decisions in meeting the daily challenges of competitive business.

Corbett was one of the few Oregon merchants who purchased in New York. He operated within the established pattern of trade between New York, San Francisco, and Portland, but he devised and developed his own system, which may or may not have been typical. He depended upon favorable credit facilities in New York, which he always carefully safeguarded and sought to extend. By maintaining his earlier friendships and business contacts in New York and by always remitting promptly, his reputation as a responsible businessman grew in the New York community itself. He utilized the best of references whenever necessary. During the mid and later 1850s most of his New York business was conducted through a single firm, the dry goods house of Hopkins, Hayes, Palmer and Company, and after their failure in 1858, through the hardware house of Samuel Roosevelt and Company. In filling his orders the New York house purchased from the commission houses in that city and in Boston, received the consignments ordered directly from other firms, and attended to all his shipments to San Francisco.

As soon as Corbett received the bills or invoices by mail, he would sign and return notes payable to each of the firms where purchases had been made. These, dated as of the date of the bill or invoice, were for eight to ten months and included interest for two to four months at the rate of 5 to 10 per cent per annum. Thus he was not charged interest for the six months required for shipment. He did not, however, receive the same discounts on his purchases as those nearer New York who purchased on 60 to 90 days time. By controlling his orders and staggering his notes, he avoided having an excessive number of obligations falling due within the same month. To do this he sometimes took the liberty to extend the note to twelve months with a few firms like Samuel Roosevelt and Company with whom he did a large business.

He dispatched drafts shortly after the arrival of the goods and usually about two months before his notes fell due, since the mail required from 30 to 40 days to reach New York via Panama. During 1857 and 1858, two of his most prosperous years, he seldom remitted more than $5,000 at one time, and usually not less than $3,000 nor more than $8,000 per month including the small remittances for freight and purchases in San Francisco. For his New York remittances prior to 1859 he usually purchased drafts at Portland or San Francisco on the Assistant Treasurer of the United States at New York. Government drafts were more reliable and at times paid a premium of 2 to $2\frac{1}{2}$ per cent. He also sent drafts on Wells, Fargo and Company or other banking houses doing business in New York and San Francisco in spite of his distinct distrust of banks. These funds, in effect, were deposits with the firm representing him in New York and were used to take up his notes as they became due. His earlier notes simply read, "payable at Hopkins, Hayes, Palmer and Company, 14 Cortlandt Street, New York." Later he sent drafts on the firm representing him against his own deposit to pay his notes.[3]

Corbett had regular business relationships with San Francisco firms and often went there to make financial arrangements or to purchase goods. His orders there were mainly to fill out his assortment or to meet shortages he had not anticipated. Occasionally a large supply of items or a decline in prices made it profitable to purchase at San Francisco. He wrote to Samuel Roosevelt and Company in January: "Competition is getting strong in our hardware line and I find I can buy from Wm. Alvord & Co. [San Francisco] . . . about as cheap as I can buy of you and land them or sometimes a little cheeper. I must buy cheep or those that buy in Cala will outsell me they can keep their stock better assorted and replenish easier and quicker. study your own interest I desire to patronize you as far as possible."

Prior to 1859 Abernethy, Clark and Company served as Corbett's San Francisco agent. This firm attended to his shipments arriving from New York, paid his freights, received his produce from Portland, and forwarded his goods. He made remittances to them to cover his freights and other obligations. His drafts sent to San Francisco were on Abernethy, Clark and Company, Wells, Fargo and Company, and the banking house of Garrison, Morgan, Fritz, and Ralston. After 1858 William Alvord and Company represented him in San Francisco.[4]

Corbett exercised constant vigilance in his relations with eastern firms. He would not be cheated, and if shipments did not conform to his orders and instructions, he fired a complaint east immediately. He was not without his own means of retaliation as the following complaint shows:

> I have added no interest for the 2 months as I think some of the goods high, and some of the Ribbons Old Styles, *not fresh,* instead of new styles . . . some of these goods looked as though they were put in thinking they would do for Oregon . . . I gave your house cr [sic] for better taste. I would now say our trade requires fresh goods no others need be sent.

Inferior or old-fashioned merchandise dumped in the market at an earlier time had a way of hanging on, however. For five years Corbett had shoes on hand from a consignment sent out to be sold on commission. When he finally settled the account there were still "8 or 10 pr Lyte Kid Buskins" which he said would "take 5 or 6 years more to sell," but that in the meantime he had them "on Exhibition as a sample of the early efforts of New England shoe makers." He always tried to buy quality goods as cheaply as possible, and to avoid a reputation for selling shoddy merchandise. After condemning a shoe jobber for sending a "very poor thin & slazey" shipment of "Boy's Brogans," Corbett reminded him that the better quality of boots and shoes sent the more he would sell and the more both would gain in reputation. He advised another shipper as follows: "don't pack any more goods in Heavy Boxes or fill up with Black Wadding at 20 to 25c per lb on a Heavy Box & Black Wadding is rather poor speculation, as we get nothing for Boxes and but a small price for

Wadding. Therefore remember to pack in Trunks and fill with something valuable say a piece of Black Alapaca."[5]

News of the financial panic in New York reached Oregon in November 1857, and Corbett took every possible step to protect his credit in the East and to assert his solvency. "Awful crashing in N. Y. I see with good times in Oregon I am glad to say," he wrote. He had the misfortune of having one of his drafts for around $1,200 protested right at the time he learned of the eastern crisis. He complained bitterly, asserted that he was "affraid" of bankers and was deeply chagrined that any of his paper should be protested in New York. Abernethy, Clark and Company had disregarded his instructions and instead of sending the $1,200 draft on Wells, Fargo and Company had sent it on Robb, Hallet and Company. Even before he knew it had been protested he wrote to his San Francisco agents that he did not have "mutch" confidence in Robb, Hallet and Company and "if it is protested I shall look to you for the collection of it. . . . I advise you to be into them for about that amount." He dispatched eastward all the money necessary to meet his immediate obligations and to make good the protested paper. During the previous few months he had remitted over $12,000 of which $9,980 was on the Assistant Treasurer of the United States, New York, and "if that Busts up," he declared, "I will be bad off."[6]

As soon as he learned that Hopkins, Hayes, Palmer and Company were likely to fail along with many of the other better houses, Corbett requested Samuel Roosevelt and Company to become his New York representative and to look after his remittances, paper, and shipments. Roosevelt accepted his proposition, but to persuade him Corbett wrote a long, revealing letter concerning his financial status at the end of 1857, with the following inventory as evidence of the compact nature of his business and his general solvency:

Merchandise	$ 47,288.14
Real Estate, at Cost (Including the entire block on which his residence was located, his Store and lot, and ¾ of a block unimproved)	8,095.13
Bills Receivable	17,742.81
Total	$ 73,126.08
Debts	22,362.78
Total "worth"	$ 50,763.30

He assured the New York firm that he had few bad debts, that his real estate was worth more than $10,000, and that he was worth at least $50,000, "all made in my legitimate business . . . after 7 years in Oregon." To another correspondent he stated that he was worth at least $60,000 and that he would not sell out for $65,000. He assured Roosevelt and Company that his orders would never exceed the amount he could meet easily, and that his remittances would be made so that funds would be available in New York all the time, except in rare instances when they might run short $200 or $300.[7]

Corbett thought Oregon's prosperity and its lack of banks might prevent the crisis from reaching the Far West. "We experience the benefit now of having no Banks on the Pacific," he wrote to a Boston firm, and "Buisness [sic] this year has been remarkably good." To another eastern firm he wrote optimistically: "We have no banks of Discount here, I therefore depend entirely on recpts [sic] from my own business."[8] Banks of issue, as has been mentioned, were prohibited in the proposed new state constitution made in convention at Salem in 1857 prior to the eastern crisis.

Corbett used every argument at his command to convince his eastern creditors of his solvency. He usually gave a list of references along with forceful, self-confident, but somewhat frantic assertions like the following: "if you want to know whether I am good or not ask Mr Charles Williams formerly Williams Bradford & Co. I *say I am!* times look squally on the Atlantic and you will probably want to know who you sell to. I am good for all I order. times are good here no banks to Brake." To others he wrote, "I know I am as good and safe as anyone," and, "I know I *am* responsible, which is more than every New York jobber can say."[9]

With stronger competition on Front Street during the later 1850s Corbett tried to gain greater advantages in purchasing. He sought the same terms as those enjoyed by the best New York jobbers. He emphasized that the better he was able to compete, the greater his trade would be, and this to the mutual advantage of both himself and his creditors. When, on one occasion, he learned that a Boston firm had given one of his competitors a 40 per cent discount while he received a 30 per cent discount for the same item he protested vigorously. He also discovered that some of his competitors purchased direct from manufacturers. Although the usual manufacturer's time was only six months he tried to purchase direct from them through his New York representative, and by 1859, he was making a few such purchases giving his note at six months dated at New York and payable there.[10]

The 1850s were profitable years for Corbett. Existing records for his business during these years, though incomplete, give an indication of its extent. His sales totaled $44,521.67 for 1855, $46,876.44 for 1856, and $31,529.03 for the first half of 1857.[11] The interest rate in Oregon during these years was from 2 to 5 per cent per month, which, it is assumed, was roughly equivalent to the average profits from trade.[12] But the average interest rate during these years came nearer 2½ per cent per month, so by using this figure, or 30 per cent per annum, Corbett's profits must have exceeded $14,000 during each of these years. This is corroborated by one of his own rare statements on the subject of profits where he says he grossed $10,000, but due to extra expenses, netted between $7,000 and $7,500 during the first half of 1858.[13]

Corbett's day-book for the period, January, 1855 through June, 1857, reveals a steady and growing business. The number of orders was seldom more than thirty per month, and more than half of these were for sums less than $100, but there were many substantial sales ranging from $100 to $2,000. Table 3, p. 236, reveals the volume of his business by months and seasons for the two and one-half year period.

Staple items of general merchandise sold at Portland at advances of from 30 to 100 per cent over New York costs and in some cases higher. Some items such as salt fell far below this range, but merchants kept them on hand to attract other trade. The wide variety of particular items and classes of goods makes restoration of exact price patterns almost impossible. Of the business records examined for this study, those of H. W. Corbett and J. Failing and Company seldom provide both the Portland price and the New York cost. Further, there were many varieties of the same class of dry goods, different grades and brands of tobacco, groceries,

TABLE 3

H. W. CORBETT'S SALES, 1855-57

Year	Mon.	Total Sales by Months	Sea-son	Total Sales by Seasons	Average Monthly Sales by Seasons	Total Sales by Years	Average Monthly Sales by Years
1855	Jan.	....$2,622.79		$	$	$	$
	Feb.	.... 3,256.70					
	Mar.	.... 3,233.34					
	Apr.	.... 3,008.26	Spr.				
	May	.... 3,616.13	1855	9,857.73	3,285.58		
	June	.... 5,269.90					
	July	.... 3,718.14	Sum.				
	Aug.	.... 5,807.07	1855	14,795.11	4,931.70		
	Sept.	.... 3,307.69					
	Oct.	..... 4,625.18	Fall				
	Nov.	.... 2,716.83	1855	10,649.70	3,539.90		
	Dec.	.... 3,339.28					
						44,521.67	3,710.14
1856	Jan.	.... 6,869.91	Win.				
	Feb.	.... 4,395.62	55-6	14,604.81	4,866.27		
	Mar.	.... 2,473.11					
	Apr.	.... 3,338.41	Spr.				
	May	.... 4,130.08	1856	9,941.60	3,310.53		
	June	.... 2,939.05					
	July	.... 6,723.74	Sum.				
	Aug.	.... 2,944.23	1856	12,607.02	4,202.34		
	Sept.	.... 3,492.77					
	Oct.	.... 2,480.37	Fall				
	Nov.	.... 4,824.54	1856	10,797.68	3,599.23		
	Dec.	.... 2,264.61					
						46,876.44	3,906.37
1857	Jan.	.... 3,307.68	Win.				
	Feb.	.... 3,753.88	56-7	9,326.17	3,108.72		
	Mar.	.... 4,073.54					
	Apr.	.... 7,584.50	Spr.				
	May	.... 6,735.42	1857	18,393.46	6,131.15		
	June	.... 6,072.01					
						31,529.03*	5,304.84*

*First half of 1857

boots and shoes, and hundreds of hardware items. Price quotations in the *Oregonian* help fill out the picture for certain categories of goods. Table 4 gives the yearly averages for the New York cost of certain staple articles of general merchandise taken from the *Aldrich Report,* and the yearly range of Portland wholesale prices as derived from business records and newspaper quotations.[14]

TABLE 4

COMPARATIVE WHOLESALE PRICES OF SELECTED MANUFACTURED STAPLES, NEW YORK AND PORTLAND, 1855-60

	Nails Dollars Per 100 Lb. Keg		Brown Sheeting Cents Per Yd.		New Orleans Sugar Cents Per Lb.		Rio Coffee Cents Per Lb.		Tobacco Cents Per Lb.		Candles Cents Per Lb.	
	N.Y.	Ptld.	N.Y.	Ptld.	N.Y.	Ptld.	N.Y.	Ptld.	N.Y.	Ptld.	N.Y.	Ptld.
1855	4.10	7.00-9.50	7.29	10.5-12.5	6	....	10	15-20	20	27.5-42.5	15	31-40
1856	3.92	6.25-7.50	7.05	11	8	12-12.5	11	14-15	22	25-42.5	14	35-37.5
1857	3.72	....	8	11-13	9	14-17	11	14-17	28	....	14	....
1858	3.53	5.50-6.50	8	11-14	6	13.5-17.5	11	14-16.5	24	....	19	30-32
1859	3.86	....	7.75	12.5-15	7	11-13	11	12.5-22.5	23	....	20	20-35
1860	3.13	5.25-6.00	8	10.5-12	7	13.5-14.5	14	17-25	20	....	18	....

237

Although farm machinery had been introduced in Oregon during the 1840s, it was not until the middle and later 1850s that a modest but important market for it arose. As early as 1841 Wilkes had observed a neglected threshing machine at the Willamette Mission, and George Abernethy advertised two threshing machines for sale in 1849. Bancroft states that the first McCormick reaper was introduced in Oregon in 1852. In the mid-years of the decade George Abernethy and Company and Hull, Knapp and Company appear to have been the largest dealers in reapers, combined mowers and reapers, and threshing machines, but Corbett also sold in the limited market.[15]

The manufacture of reapers in the United States grew steadily after 1855 with the development of new farm lands in the Mid-West. Among the leading reaper models were the Buckeye, Manny, Hussey, Ketchum, and the famous McCormick manufactured at Chicago. Some of all these models found their way to Oregon. The number of McCormick reapers sold in the United States rose from 2,500 in 1855 to 4,000 in 1856. Most of the 125,000 reapers in use in the United States in 1860 were produced during the preceding five years.[16]

Corbett placed his first orders for farm machinery early in 1856 for the harvest of that year. He obtained five McCormick combined mowers and reapers, and three Pitts eight-horse threshing machines from the Boston firm of Ruggles, Nourse, Mason and Company. The Chicago price for a combined mower and reaper was $155, but with the freight charges it cost $275 to land one at Portland. The total cost per thresher landed at Portland was $600. Corbett expected to sell the McCormick machine for $500 and the thresher for $900 for clear profits of 80 and 50 per cent respectively. He tried to sell all the machines before they arrived by accepting a $100 down payment on each. But he had to meet competition. George Abernethy and Company advertised reapers at $400, the two-horse thresher at $400, and the eight-horse thresher at $850. Corbett actually sold his reapers for $375 and his threshers for $700 for a profit margin much less than he had expected.[17] But he continued to purchase farm machinery and greatly increased his sales during the following decade.

It was difficult for Pacific Coast dealers to get the popular McCormick reaper. The manufacturer purposely designed the Far West as an outlet for his surplus and out-dated machines, while he concentrated upon the growing midwestern market with his improved models. When Corbett attempted to purchase direct from the McCormick factory in 1858 he was unsuccessful. It was not until the development of wheat production in eastern Oregon and Washington during the 1870s that the market for farm machinery in the Pacific Northwest came into its own. Then this region became one of the best outlets for the McCormick reaper.[18]

Earlier, however, the Hussey Company welcomed an opportunity to introduce their machine in the Oregon market. They shipped one combined mower and reaper to Samuel Roosevelt and Company for Corbett at the regular home price of $130.50 less 10 per cent, fully equipped and with several extra parts because it was going so "far off." The manufacturer wrote that: "if it does not give better satisfaction as a Reaper and Mower than any machine of the kind ever before introduced in that or any other section of the country we shall be very much mistaken hoping that the introduction of this machine may make sales of many more of the same sort."[19]

With rare exceptions Corbett experienced cordial relationships with his valley customers. He naturally sought their business and treated them according to the prevailing standards of business ethics. He bought or forwarded produce shipped downriver by them and applied the proceeds on their accounts. He granted them credit and accommodated them in various other ways. Most often his credit terms were from 30 to 90 days but in some cases longer. He accepted notes to run at interest at from $1\frac{1}{2}$ to 3 per cent per month after the stipulated period of time had expired. Some ran for a year or more. He seems to have had little difficulty in circumventing the legal rate of interest of 10 per cent per annum and rarely allowed it except as an accommodation to a good customer.[20] At times when he felt the pressure of his eastern obligations he issued friendly duns or toured the valley making his collections. He spared no effort in making collections in 1857 and 1858 when, alarmed by the eastern crisis, he sought to command all of his financial resources. "We dont often call . . . for money," he wrote one of his best customers, "but we have to once in awhile *when* a *pinch comes*." He had customers from all the valley towns as well as Vancouver and The Dalles on the Columbia. Among the larger accounts were those of D. Beach, J. G. Burkhart, J. M. McConnell, all of Albany; Cook and Burbank, Independence; J. Holman, Salem; and Worth and Bro., of Corvallis.

Relations between Corbett and his customers were sometimes strained. He answered an accusation from one of them as follows: "As to your insinuation of my desire to double the debt, I will pass over as unworthy of notice by any high minded man, and please you to reconcile such insinuations as best you can with your own conscience."

On another occasion he pursued a bad debt with relentless vigor. He instructed his Oregon City attorneys to garnishee the defaulter, a man named Prescott, and to *"Wake up* the *Sheriff."* He told his attorneys:

> You must get hold of everything you can even the Watch that was garnasheed in the hands of the Watch Maker in Town must be looked after. I have no confidence in Prescott leaving off drinking, as I am told he drank while down here three times before breakfast. therefore I desire you to keep every thing snug and in propper train and get hold of every thing you can. Make the sheriff do his duty.

Corbett wrote, concerning the delinquency of another careless customer, that "he can pay it if he is amind to, but he is a great 'humbug'."[21] But he actually had few bad debts to contend with during the decade.

Oregon's first bank appeared in 1859. W. S. Ladd, the first example of an Oregon merchant turned banker, and C. E. Tilton, Ladd's old friend and associate in San Francisco, opened the Ladd and Tilton Bank on June 1, 1859, in the newly added second story of W. S. Ladd's Portland store. The capital stock of $50,000 represented accumulated profits derived from the respective merchandising enterprises of the two men following the California gold rush.

The Ladd and Tilton was essentially a commercial bank. It received deposits and made short-term loans at 1½ to 5 per cent per month during its early years. Although its functions were strictly limited by the constitutional provision prohibiting banks of issue, the new bank provided facilities for exchange on San Francisco and New York, and, in general, the means for the better utilization of the community's capital. Deposits increased from $10,000 in June 1859, to $113,344.36 at the end of 1861. The capital stock was increased to $150,000 when Stephen Mead of New York entered the firm in 1861. The bank maintained a relationship with the New York firm of A. E. and C. E. Tilton to facilitate the business of exchange.[22] With these beginnings it grew into a sound and prosperous institution during the next decade when millions of dollars poured into Portland from the Idaho gold fields. The only bank in Oregon prior to 1865 (excluding such financial houses as Beekman's in Jacksonville), the Ladd and Tilton was destined for a long and enviable career as one of the region's leading financial institutions.

The records for the business of J. Failing and Company during the 1850s are scanty but from those available it seems that their business was somewhat more extensive than Corbett's. C. W. Thomas, the New York partner, shipped goods having a total invoice value of $63,198.94 during 1855, $67,378.20 during 1856, and $85,685.61 between January and September, 1857. Shipments were made on board some of the more famous ships in the San Francisco trade, among them the *Hurricane,* owned by Hunt, Thomas, and Company, a firm in which C. W. Thomas was a major partner. Invoices show that J. Failing and Company imported large quantities of the same kind of goods as Corbett. They also imported large quantities of iron and seem to have made this a kind of specialty. Their relations with their valley customers were similar to those of Corbett. Appended to an order from John Waymire was the following note: "By filling the above order at a *cheep rate* you will receive another *big order* ere long accompanied by lots of *cash;* otherwise you may bob & bob and catch any thing if you can."[23]

A financial statement made on January 1, 1859, when the firm was reorganized, shows the profits for the half-year from July 1, 1857 to January 15, 1858 at $14,157.03, and for the entire year of 1858 at $15,760.21. It also reveals a business organization that was probably different from that of any other Oregon firm. The exact relationship between the partners prior to 1857 is not known, but C. W. Thomas had provided most if not all of the initial investment. In 1857 Thomas' interest in the firm was three-fifths and that of Josiah Failing and Henry Failing, one-fifth each. From January 15, 1858 to December 30, 1858, Thomas owned one-half of the firm and each of the Failings, one-fourth. On the first of January 1859, the firm was organized under the name of Failings and Hatt. John A. Hatt was an employee or associate of Thomas in the New York firm of Hunt, Thomas and Company. His function in the new company was that of buyer in New York, and the extent of his investment is not disclosed. Thomas remained as a "special" partner in the new firm with an investment of $20,000, but at the time of the reorganization he withdrew assets amounting to slightly more than $48,000. The capital stock of Henry and Josiah Failing in the new firm was $10,696.13 each.[24]

Prior to the reorganization in 1859, Thomas held the business of the firm under his control. The Failings were more the Oregon agents of Thomas rather than partners. They remitted the invoice amounts directly to him and had little or no knowledge of the credit terms he obtained. They never knew the amounts or due dates of notes payable in the East. But with Thomas conducting the eastern end of the business they enjoyed the same buying advantages as eastern firms, and this no doubt gave them a distinct competitive advantage in the Oregon market.

After January 1, 1859, Thomas continued to direct much of the affairs of the firm in the East, though he no longer had the responsibility for buying. Part of the new agreement was that he would contribute additional capital to the firm if it ever became necessary. But in 1861 he placed a severe strain upon the company by withdrawing part of the firm's capital without giving the Failings proper warning. This necessitated the transfer of the company's indebtedness to Portland, where they borrowed money from the Ladd and Tilton Bank either at no interest or at nominal rates. Henry Failing, writing in 1861, stated: "Our competitors have in their business the accumulated profits of years and have the facilities for doing business which we do not possess. This is not due to any lack of money making in our business but to the withdrawal of capital."[25]

By 1859 Henry Failing had taken over the active management of the Portland store, while his father investigated politics and followed a more leisurely way of life. Henry Failing now corresponded regularly with John A. Hatt, the New York partner. In addition to orders he wrote long, deliberate analyses of the state of the Oregon market and the economic conditions of the region. He wanted Hatt completely informed so the purchasing could be done intelligently and efficiently. "Trash," he said on one occasion, would no longer do for the Oregon market as the store was already too full of "refuse."

As the depression set in during 1859, the Failings granted extensive credits in order to hold their customers. Now there was less assurance of payment, and collections even from their best customers became difficult and in some cases impossible. Henry Failing felt that Portland merchants would do well just "to wade through this year without loss," and that his firm was doing as well as any other under the circumstances. With a few "bad debts" threatening them, both Corbett and the Failings began to deny credit to some of their customers. "I shall be obliged to borrow money and pay 2 to 2½% per month," Corbett complained to one upriver merchant in August, "unless my customers pay me. I have given you all the indulgence I can without injuring myself." In September he summarized the entire situation in his characteristic style by writing, "Times quiet, money tight, pleanty [sic] goods on hand, Customers scarce."[26]

During the depression years Failing was most concerned about keeping down his orders and making enough money in business to keep up his remittances. He kept his New York partner informed about everything that had a bearing upon the business. In November 1859, he observed pessimistically:

> with the present state of the San Fco market we cannot compete with those purchasing in Cala. & make any money. The most we can do is to keep our trade and be in hand for better times. We could sell more goods if we [were] willing to wait for our pay, and take losses, but we do not think it prudent. We have now too much, and if we can only collect

even if we make nothing we shall be doing better than most others.

In December he continued his analysis of business conditions in the following report to Hatt:

> It is almost an impossibility to collect money and until the prices of produce advance it can be no better . . . I can see no symptoms of any change in the San Francisco market . . ., and if trade does brighten up here so that we can sell more goods than we have ordered, we can supply ourselves in San Fco while if we ordered largely we could at best make no money on them, while we would only occasion you a great deal of trouble . . . and run the risk of being embarrassed.

Although the business of Failings and Hatt showed a profit of $14,000 for 1859, the firm did not have the use of all the profits because of the many accounts outstanding. Henry Failing thought the rate of profit on the goods actually sold during 1859 was greater than that of any other Portland firm and was certain "that no house importing their goods has done so well." He also reported: "It is almost impossible for those who are in debt to cancel their obligations owing to the low prices of all kinds of produce—flour is offering @ 4.50/5 pr barrel & no sale—we have in store a considerable quantity of flour taken on accounts which we cannot realize the money from."[27]

Soon, however, the gold discoveries in Idaho, Montana, eastern Oregon, and the Kootenai district of British Columbia of the early 1860s were to stimulate the development of the entire region. The frontiers of settlement were to converge decisively upon the Inland Empire. New towns, new transportation facilities and other improvements were to appear. All branches of frontier enterprise were to expand and the surpluses of the Willamette Valley were to find a ready market. As Portland's hinterland expanded she enjoyed her first great boom during the Idaho rush. Her leading merchant capitalists, with their accumulated profits, were to rise to greater stature and wealth and to expand their various capitalistic enterprises.

PART IV

Gold Down the Columbia, 1861-69

Chapter XII

Gold from Idaho and Montana

"Half rival to San Francisco itself . . ."

The early 1860s saw the decisive advance of the mining frontier eastward into eastern Oregon and Washington and the areas that shortly became Idaho and Montana territories. Here thousands sought out the rich creeks and gulches for pay dirt. Here rose a succession of new el dorados in a vast region which a short time earlier was virtually an unknown wilderness. The Columbia River, the gateway to this Inland Empire from the west, suddenly developed into a great route of travel and commerce. Portland, already established as the terminus for ocean-going ships, was advantageously situated to command the trade of the Columbia and to take her share of the gold pouring from the Idaho and Oregon mines. Her merchants and other capitalists built up their city and expanded the facilities of trade and commerce as they supplied the new hinterland. With the stimulus of gold capitalistic enterprises and improvements of greater magnitude appeared, as western Oregon and Washington settled into a post-frontier era. Elsewhere in the region new mining and agricultural communities rose from the raw conditions of the frontier.

Idaho Gold and the Growth of Portland

In the summer of 1860 E. D. Pierce and a party of prospectors, who had been combing the interior for several years, made the first discoveries of gold in Idaho, then a part of Washington Territory. The Pierce party found gold on Orofino Creek, a tributary of the Clearwater, some forty miles east of the site where the town of Lewiston was soon to rise at the confluence of the Clearwater and the Snake. News of the discovery shortly reached Walla Walla, The Dalles, the Willamette Valley and California, and by the following spring the rush was on. Many depression-ridden Willamette Valley farmers left for the mines despite the protests and fears expressed in Portland newspapers. Twenty-five hundred miners and four or five thousand other people—packers, businessmen, farmers and men of other occupations needed to sustain the new effort—were in the mining country by late summer. Here in the Clearwater area, or the Nez Perce district, rose the towns of Orofino and Pierce City on the Orofino and, farther to the south, Elk City on the south fork of the Clearwater. Lewiston, at the head of navigation on the Snake, sprang into existence as a supply center for the mines.

Prospectors probed relentlessly in the mountainous region to the south and in September, 1861, a phenomenal strike was made near the Salmon River 140 miles southeast of Lewiston. A new rush occurred as many of the miners in the Nez Perce area pulled stakes and stampeded for the new diggings. By October, 1861, miners were making an average of $100 per day on 140 claims.[1] Portlanders were astounded by the fabulous reports. Henry Failing wrote in November:

> We have seen parties with whom we are well acquainted who say they have taken out $100 to $300 per day and others claim to have made as high as $1000 pr day. As yet but few miners have been in there, the weather excessively cold, provisions high and miners afraid to remain for fear of starvation as pack animals can hardly be got through now. As yet there has been no sluicing and the mining has been done with rockers.

He reported again in December:

> . . . miners are leaving claims which pay $50 to $75 per day. Miners have to pack provisions on their backs through the snows and can only work with rocker 4 to 5 hours per day. It is said that as high as *400 ounces* has been taken out by one party in a day. [Probably Weiser who took out $6,600 in one day.] The whole country is wild with excitement and men are constantly going in over the mountains which are now covered with snow. Flour and bacon are worth 75 cts pr lb at Lewiston and $1.25 in the mines.[2]

The severity of the winter of 1861-62 when snow and sub-zero weather prevailed throughout the Columbia Basin was without precedent. The few miners who wintered on the Salmon River at the 6,000-foot level suffered severely and some fell victim to disease and cold. Others en route overland to the mining region from The Dalles were later found frozen to death in the snow. One victim, I. E. Jagger, was a young Portland merchant who had just established a promising mercantile firm at Lewiston.[3]

The rush to Salmon River resumed in the spring of 1862. Thousands converged on the Idaho mining country from all directions. Californians came by land and sea. Northward bound ships of the two steamship lines from San Francisco were heavily laden with passengers, and the *Brother Jonathan* of the California Steam Navigation Company carried 1,000 on one trip. Men from all walks of life left their homes in western Oregon and Washington. Passenger traffic taxed the boats of the Oregon Steam Navigation Company on the Columbia to Wallula and Lewiston, providing a lucrative source of revenue for the company.[4] "The stream of miners is still kept up, moving on its way to the mines," the *Oregonian* reported in April. Although the editor had abandoned his earlier skepticism about the development of trade on the upper Columbia, he held consistently to the theme, "agriculture is our chief reliance," and noted in March 1862, that: "Among the numerous miners that throng our wayfares, we see many hale and hearty farmers, advanced beyond the middle age of life. We regret to see them leaving for the mines." An emigration, estimated at 30,000, of whom "nearly all were going to Washington Territory," was en route from Omaha via the Oregon Trail. Smaller parties from Minnesota were bound for the mining country via Forts Union and Benton on the northern route.[5]

The diggings in the Salmon River district were rich, particularly at Baboon Gulch, but the easy pickings in the vicinity were soon exhausted. In the summer a new excitement caused a stampede to Buffalo Hump, forty miles northeast of Florence, the new mining town serving the district, which quickly subsided because miners had no means for mining the quartz found there. Warren's diggings, across the Salmon River to the southeast some twenty-seven miles, for years proved profitable for several hundred hard-working miners. Packing goods and provisions into Florence was extremely difficult, and as the mining fever there subsided, thousands of miners, packers, and others moved on to more profitable fields before the year ended. But the foundations for permanent mining and agricultural communities in northern Idaho had been laid. Lewiston, the principal depot for the Nez Perce and Salmon River districts, had become a thriving commercial center, where goods and provisions from San Francisco, Portland and the Willamette Valley sold for fabulous prices.[6]

Eastern Oregon was also the scene of various mining activities. Here discoveries on the Powder, John Day, and Burnt rivers were made in 1861 and 1862. A large mining community developed on the Powder River, with the town of Auburn as its center. Miners were handicapped by lack of water but capitalists of the Oregon Steam Navigation Company promptly came to the rescue by investing heavily in the famous Auburn Ditch built in 1862-63. Millions in gold came from this and other areas in eastern Oregon during the 1860s, but not in the same proportions as from Idaho and Montana. Auburn, a flourishing town with an estimated population of 5,000 to 6,000 in 1863, declined rapidly during 1864 and 1865, as the diggings gave out. After Chinese miners finished the clean-up, the town itself disappeared. As elsewhere, however, mining stimulated permanent settlement and agricultural communities now appeared in the valleys of eastern Oregon. Many of the new emigrants were attracted to the Grande Ronde Valley where the town of La Grande soon became another important trading center.[7]

The main trunk line of transportation and communication to the Idaho mines from the west was the Columbia and Snake River system. As mentioned earlier, the Oregon Steam Navigation Company, a combination of the several Columbia River navigation interests, was established in 1860 in time to take full advantage of the Idaho rush. The original capital, $172,000 divided into 345 shares, represented the over-appraised value of the steamboats and improvements pooled by the several members of the company. The first board of directors were Captain J. C. Ainsworth, the company's leading figure and its president during its entire history except for one year, Simeon G. Reed, Lawrence Coe, Daniel Bradford and Joseph Ruckel. Coe represented the interests of R. R. Thompson, who was the owner of The Dalles portage and the first to develop steam navigation on the upper river with the *Colonel Wright*. Reed represented the interests of Benjamin Stark and the earlier Columbia River Navigation Company. Bradford and Ruckel, owners of the portages at the Cascades, had formerly competed on the middle river between the Cascades and The Dalles.[8]

By June, 1861, six months after it was organized, the Oregon Steam Navigation Company could have declared a six per cent dividend. Instead, it increased its capitalization to $690,000. Separate dividends of two and two and one-half per cent were declared on the new capitalization in August, 1861. In September the capital stock was increased to $996,000, and another two per cent dividend was declared. Before the year ended the company paid two more dividends, one for two and the other for one per cent, making a total return of forty-eight per cent on the original investment in one year. The company had been incorporated in Washington Territory but at the end of 1862 it was chartered under the laws of Oregon with a capital stock of $2,000,000 divided into shares of $100 each.

During 1862 and 1863 the company paid no dividends but made heavy expenditures on improvements. Since its formation Ainsworth had been annoyed with Ruckel and Bradford, important figures in the company, for two reasons: they had retained ownership of the portages at the Cascades, and they refused to share in the cost of damages to goods in transit. Control of the portages was the key to the monopoly of the river and by clever manipulation Ainsworth acquired them for the company from these two competitors within the company's ranks. Thompson also sold his portage at The Dalles to the company and soon a 15-mile railroad costing almost $1,000,000 was in operation from The Dalles to Celilo Falls. There was also a six-mile railroad at the Cascades. Other improvements were the necessary buildings and wharves at every station on the route from Portland to Lewiston, including a new $50,000 wharf at Portland. In addition several costly steamers were added to the three sections of the river. The company's earnings of $1,300,000 for 1863 were used to defray expenses, but between May and December, 1864, the company paid dividends totaling 12 per cent.[9]

Freight and passenger rates on the Columbia were extremely high. This was due in part to the nature of the river, which required the use of three different steamboats and two portages for the through trip. The company derived its profits from upriver freights and passenger fares rather than from the large shipments of treasure downriver. During the spring rush of 1862, the *Okanogan* on the upper river cleared $15,000 on each trip. Receipts for the *Tenino's* passenger load on one trip upriver from Celilo to Lewiston totaled $10,945, and on another, $18,000 for freight, passengers, meals, and berths. Fares between Portland and Lewiston and between Portland and other points on the river varied during the gold rush period, ranging up to $68 in gold one-way to Lewiston. In the spring of 1862, the freight rate from Portland to The Dalles was $25 per ton, to Wallula $80, and to Lewiston $125.[10]

An "O. S. N. ton," except for heavy articles such as nails, was determined by ship's measurement, or 40 cubic feet. "In measuring a wagon or any piece of freight the full length, height and thickness were taken and carried out full size, the largest way of the piece." In the case of a wagon, the tongue was extended to get the full length, then raised to get the full height. According to one story this practice was jokingly challenged by Capt. T. W. Lyles, a stockholder in the Oregon Steam Navigation Company, at a board of directors meeting in Portland. It is reported by P. W. Gillette as follows:

> 'Mr. Chairman, I move that Eph Day, a purser on one of our boats be discharged from the service of the company.' Now Eph was one of the favorite pursers, and everybody sprang up to know what was the matter with Eph Day. After quiet had been restored Captain Lyles said: 'I see, gentlemen, that Eph Day is purser on a boat of only 150 tons register, yet I find that he comes in at the end of every trip with a report of having carried from 250 to 300 tons of freight, and, gentlemen, he substantiates his reports by bringing in cash for those amounts of freight. Now while I do not claim to be much of a steamboat man, yet I can see, gentlemen, that if we allow our boats to be overladen in this manner and made to carry twice as much as they were designed to carry, they will soon be worn out and we will have no boats.'

The meeting, according to the story, was adjourned amid roars of laughter.[11]

Following are the figures for the traffic via Oregon Steam Navigation Company boats during the period of the Idaho gold rush:

Year	Number of Passengers	Tons of Freight
1861	10,500	6,290
1862	24,500	14,550
1863	22,000	17,646
1864	36,000	21,834[12]

When the Idaho trade first opened some Portlanders feared that shipments might go directly up the Columbia, by-passing the Willamette city entirely.[13] "Our greatest fear is that the influx of population will be so great, that we shall be unable to keep a great portion of the trade here, and that the trade will go direct to San Francisco," Henry Failing declared in the fall of 1861. Early in 1862 the California Steam Navigation Company, one of the two ocean steamship lines serving the Columbia, threatened to run steamboats directly up the river from Astoria. "Should the Oregon Co. not buy them out," Henry Failing reported, "and should they succeed in thus diverting the trade from here it would be very disastrous to Portland." But he thought there was sufficient capital at Portland to prevent the diversion, "unless the Emigration to the new mines should be very large."[14]

Although the Oregon Steam Navigation Company had gained an initial advantage on the Columbia it faced the most formidable opposition of its history during 1862 and 1863, not from California interests, but from rival companies in Oregon. The People's Transportation Company, which involved almost all the steamboat men not directly connected with Oregon Steam Navigation Company, turned to the lower Columbia after eliminating all rivals on the Willamette. H. W. Corbett, Captain A. P. Ankeny and others formed the Merchants Line, also known as the Independent, and placed the steamer *Spray* on the upper river to run from the mouth of the Deschutes to Lewiston. For five months the *Spray* did a highly profitable business while the People's Transportation Company ran in opposition to the Oregon Steam Navigation Company on the lower river as far as the Cascades. Without control of the portages the opposition had little chance for success, but it did force a drastic reduction of rates. Freights were cut from $25 to $5.00 per ton to The Dalles, and from $125 to $25 per ton to Lewiston, bringing about a flood of business on the river. The opposition ended in the spring and summer of 1863 when the Oregon Steam Navigation Company purchased the *Spray* and came to an agreement with the People's Company. By this agreement the People's Company would retain the Willamette trade and the Oregon Steam Navigation Company that of the Columbia with each pledging not to trespass on the other's territory. With the "Opposition Settled," as Simeon G. Reed put it, the freight rate to Lewiston immediately rose from $25 to $95 per ton in June, 1863.[15]

The merchants at Lewiston had, of course, suffered because of the sudden reduction in freight rates. Merchants lost more than fifty per cent on goods shipped in before the rates fell. One merchant who had gone into business at Lewiston with a capital of between $9,000 and $10,000 found himself in debt for $24,000 for goods purchased at Portland and transported to Lewiston at the high rates. The selling price of flour which had cost him $24 per barrel to land at Lewiston suddenly fell to $9.00 per barrel in the spring of 1863.[16]

As if by magic when the prospects for mining and trade in northern Idaho were somewhat dim, the rush to the newly discovered and more extensive gold fields of southern Idaho began in 1863. In August 1862, a party led by George Grimes and Moses Splawn had discovered the rich mines of Boise Basin, thirty-five miles northeast of the present city of Boise. They had prospected on their journey from the northern mines south via Powder River to southern Idaho. While he was in the Nez Perce district Splawn had been informed by an Indian friend that the glittering metal existed in abundance in the mountains far to the south. From the Indian's description Splawn had a fixed mental picture of the topographic features of the area he sought and was thus led to the new el dorado. Immediately, mining of the rich placers of Boise Basin began in the fall of 1862.

The news spread and in March, 1863, the great rush from Oregon, California and other parts of the mining country began. Most Californians came overland through the interior, although many also came by sea to Portland to crowd the upriver boats of the Oregon Steam Navigation Company. The road from the Umatilla steamboat landing to Boise Basin was lined with people on horseback or on foot, and long pack trains loaded with merchandise and provisions.[17] The editor of the *Oregonian,* while trying to explain to Oregon farmers that their farms were their mines, expected "that more than half the voting population of the Willamette valley" would be absent from their homes after the first of April, 1863. Other thousands of adventurers and war-weary farmers were en route from Omaha to the mining and farm lands of Colorado and the Far West.[18]

In Boise Basin new saw mills working day and night produced lumber at from $100 to $200 per thousand board feet, to build rockers, sluice boxes, houses, stores and various other improvements. Mining camps were transformed into the towns of Centreville, Placerville, Pioneer City, and Idaho City, while down in the Boise River Valley, Boise City appeared in the summer of 1863, soon becoming the depot for the entire mining region of southern Idaho. By mid-summer the population of the basin had grown to 10,000 or 15,000 according to estimates, and by the end of the season the population of southern Idaho was probably not less than 20,000. Estimates place gold production during parts of 1863 and 1864 as high as $1,000,000 per month.

Regular freight and passenger service developed on the routes overland from Walla Walla and Umatilla to the Boise Basin. In addition to their freighting service by pack train the firm, Hailey and Ish, provided a passenger service on saddle trains from Walla Walla. This firm furnished each passenger a horse, saddle, and provisions for the trip and allowed him to carry a small amount of baggage for a fare of $50, paid in advance. Packing provisions and merchandise over the 300-mile route was very profitable, according to Hailey, with freights at 16 to 25 cents per pound. Freights, in 1864, varied between 10 and 30 cents per pound according to the conditions of the roads. Regular stagecoach and wagon freighting services over these routes also developed. The Oregon Steam Navigation Company offered through freighting service by steamboat and wagon, and there were several competing stagecoach companies including the firms, Hailey and Ish and Greathouse and Company. After these two companies combined in 1865, the new firm practically controlled the staging business serving southern Idaho.[19]

Portland was the principal supply center for the Idaho mining country during the early rush period. The rise of Lewiston and the development of the Salmon River mines finally relieved Portland's depressed flour market as large quantities of this and other provisions flowed upriver in the spring of 1862. The wholesale price of flour at Portland rose from $4.00 to $5.00 per barrel in January to $8.00 and $9.00 in March.[20]

The provisions market remained good during the Boise rush from 1863 through 1865, as the mining country continued to rely upon the Willamette Valley as its principal source for supplies of flour, bacon, butter, eggs, and other basic items. Flour wholesaled at Portland at $6.00 to $8.00 per barrel during the fall, winter, and spring of 1862-63. After falling temporarily to $4.25 and $5.50 in the winter of 1863-64, it rose steadily until it reached the $8.00 and $14 levels during the winter and spring of 1864-65. In June 1864, the *Oregonian,* noting the unusual receipts of flour from the upper Willamette, commented: "The most of this flour is immediately trans-shipped to the mining region, . . . and while our exports do not show much by Oregon vessels, it is easily accounted for from the fact of having a better market nearer home."[21] Thus the supply seems to have been sufficient for the demands of the mining country in spite of the diminution of the farming population of western Oregon.

It should be noted, however, that some of the immigration of the 1860s came directly to the Willamette Valley. "We are rejoiced," the editor of the *Oregonian* declared in September, 1862, "to see so many of the newcomers to Oregon settling in the Willamette Valley." Again, in October, 1865, he reported that, "The immigrants from the plains are pouring into the valley by every possible avenue. Every arrival of the upriver boat brings a vast throng of these fatigued and travel-worn pilgrims."[22]

In addition to flour, bacon, and other provisions, large herds of cattle were shipped or driven into the interior from

256

the Willamette Valley. Since the early days of settlement cattle herds had been growing ever larger in western Oregon for virtually no outside market existed prior to the Fraser River gold rush of 1858. These herds originated in part from the California cattle driven northward to supply the Hudson's Bay Company and the earliest settlers. More important, however, were the large herds from the improved strains of the Mississippi Valley, driven overland during the 1840s. C. S. Kingston gives 10,000 as a conservative estimate for the total number of cattle driven across the plains during that decade. By 1860 the number of cattle in Oregon and the Territory of Washington was 182,382. Thus the Willamette Valley became the "cattle nursery of the Pacific Northwest" as its surplus cattle moved inland to new grazing lands during the mining period to become the foundations for the large scale cattle ranching industry of the 1870s and 1880s in eastern Oregon and Washington.[23]

Portland merchants had to evaluate carefully all the reports concerning new mines, the extent of the gold fields and the probable size of the incoming population in order to gauge their own buying. Most of them correctly anticipated the 1862 rush and laid in heavy supplies of merchandise the preceding fall, when returnees confirmed the richness of the Salmon River mines earlier at Portland than in San Francisco. But they had to be prepared to extend credit and take extraordinary risks as the new hinterland opened. "It must . . . be a long winded business," Henry Failing explained, "as it takes a long time to get goods in the mines and freight is so high that the traders cannot pay for their goods in short time without a large capital."[24]

Unlike many of its competitors, the Portland firm of Failings and Hatt did not lay in extra quantities of goods and thus failed to share largely in the fall trade of 1861. While the suddenness of the Salmon River demand caught them somewhat unprepared, the main problem was the withdrawal of some of the firm's capital by C. W. Thomas, a New York partner. The ever-conservative Henry Failing became even more cautious in purchasing in New York. The firm enjoyed a larger trade than usual during the fall of 1861, but the stock, though well assorted, was low. The unexpectedly heavy fall trade broke the assortment and wholly depleted the store of goods most in demand in the mining country. Although given the preference over other houses, Henry Failing found himself unable to supply some of the largest dealers from the upper country, and thus missed sales of $5,000 on up to $15,000.[25] This firm, and the Portland mercantile community generally, had to adjust quickly if it were to meet the demands of the new trade.

This it seems to have done, for in 1862 during the Salmon River excitement, Failings and Hatt enjoyed an extensive and very profitable trade,[26] and Portland experienced a business boom such as it had never known. According to Gillette:

> the rush of freight to the docks was so great that drays and trucks had to form and stand in line to get their turn in delivering their goods. Their lines were kept unbroken day and night for weeks and months. . . . Often a merchant would place a large truck in line early in the morning, then fill it by dray loads during the day. The great rush continued for months. A San Francisco merchant established a store at Lewiston and shipped via Portland a large stock of goods, which arrived in Portland in the spring, but they did not reach Lewiston until late in the summer, because he had no one here to get them in line to take their turn.[27]

During the year Portland was crowded. New businesses of all kinds appeared. The town grew in population from 2,917 in 1860 to 4,057 in 1862, and strained to accommodate the new and transient population.[28] Buildings, wharfs, warehouses, graded streets and other improvements appeared in response to the stimulus of gold. The editor of the *Oregonian* boasted about the solid and permanent nature of Portland's growth, and observed:

> Eighteen months ago, and any number of vacant houses could be found in the city, but to-day scarcely a shell can be found sufficient to shelter a small family. . . . Rents are up at an exorbitant figure, and before a house is half completed, at least a half dozen applications are made to rent the whole building or parts of it. . . . There are a large number of hotels, restaurants, and boarding houses in the city every one of which is crowded almost to overflowing . . . the town is full of people and more coming in. . . .[29]

The heavy fall trade for the winter supply of the upper Columbia towns continued through December, 1862, but the expected revival did not occur during the spring of 1863. As the excitement in northern Idaho waned and before

Portlanders learned the importance of the Boise Basin, business on Front Street declined alarmingly. In 1862 Portland merchants could gauge the demands of the interior trade, somewhat, by the size of the constant stream of people coming through the city en route to the mines. During the spring of 1863, however, the immigration from California largely went overland direct to the Boise mines. In March Henry Failing noted that money was scarce, collections hard to make, and no demand. "Most houses here have made preparations for a large trade, have good stocks," he explained, "and are very much disappointed, . . . a buyer for cash or who is good can buy goods cheap."[30]

With business at Portland dull, the editor of the *Oregonian*, having lost his optimism, gave the following analysis of the problem:

> Faces are growing long, and money is becoming scarce. . . . No one will doubt that the chief cause of the trouble is the over anxiety to engage in trade. Every one who has a little money thinks he can make more most easily by some sort of traffic and he therefore puts all that he has, and all that he can borrow by mortgage of his homestead, into a stock of goods, a band of cattle, or a steamboat. Thus he embarks in speculations for which he has no experience or fitness, and is speedily astonished to discover that his profits do not pay his expenses. . . . There is to-day more trading done, or attempted to be done in this city, and more capital embarked in that and kindred pursuits, than should be thus employed if our population was five times what it is at present. There is a store for almost every dwelling, and there is not adjacent country sufficient to need what the trade can supply . . . if it is expected to be profitable. . . . For these reasons, we are always sorry to see a man who might do well in his shop or on his farm, throw away the certainty of success for the uncertainties of trade and speculation. Instead of being a thrifty producer, he becomes an unprofitable consumer, and thus contributes to the constant stream of waste that flows from a country where trade is overdone, and where more in value is imported and sold than is produced by intelligent industry. . . .[31]

But trade revived by June 1863, and vast quantities of merchandise and provisions, now destined for the Boise Basin, again flowed upriver. To Henry Failing the risks of the trade had become much greater since he had to extend credit to the Boise traders on the then uncertain prospects of the mines, or not sell at all. He took pride in the fact that his trade had been with "the best type of customers buying in the Portland market," but now he had to sell to parties in whom he had less confidence or to "keep our goods." Among the merchants who had gone to Lewiston were several trusted young Portland men, often times former employees of Portland merchants, who readily received the necessary credit for their initial ventures. Henry Failing either did not know the Boise traders or he was skeptical about them and this in his mind made the Boise trade far more hazardous than that of Lewiston. "The profits we are getting are satisfactory," he wrote, "but we shall no doubt lose a good many debts." It was a business in which the risk had to be taken for "had we refused to sell those who embarked in business this year, if successful would lose the chance of the business next year and as profits were good . . . we have sold the goods, and at worst will come out even."[32]

Goods sold at high retail prices at the Boise mines in 1863. This was due more to high freight costs for packing goods overland and the high profit mark-ups of the Boise merchants than to the high transportation rates levied by the Oregon Steam Navigation Company as has often been believed. By examining wholesale prices at Portland, freight rates to the mines, and the retail prices in the Boise area for the early stage of the rush, Professor Johansen has shown that in most instances the highest percentage of the retail prices went to the Boise merchants or to the packers. Flour, for instance, which wholesaled at Portland for \$8.00 per barrel, or 4 cents per pound, was transported to Wallula for 7 cents per pound, from Wallula to Walla Walla for 2 cents per pound, and Walla Walla to Boise for 25 cents per pound. Thus the total freight cost was 38 cents of which the packers received 25. The minimum retail price at the mines was 60 cents per pound, or \$120 per barrel, of which the Boise merchants received 22 cents per pound or $36\frac{2}{3}$ per cent of the retail price. The Oregon Steam Navigation Company received $11\frac{2}{3}$ per cent and the Walla Walla-Boise freighters, $41\frac{2}{3}$ per cent. By similar calculations, Professor Johansen discovered that the Boise merchants received $49\frac{1}{3}$ per cent of the retail price of molasses, the Oregon Steam Navigation Company, $4\frac{1}{3}$ per cent and the packers, $33\frac{1}{3}$ per cent. For beans costing 3 cents per pound at Portland and selling for 75 cents per pound at Boise, the merchants at the latter place took $57\frac{1}{3}$ per cent of the retail price.[33]

While San Francisco was still the grand emporium for the ever-widening mining hinterland of the Far West, Portland became increasingly important as a secondary supply center for the northern mining region during the 1860s. Portland merchants who bought most of their supplies in New York had to purchase some goods, especially mining tools, in San Francisco. When necessary, they also purchased other goods there depending upon the urgency of the demand or the price advantage. Other Portland merchants and some from the upper Columbia continued to make all their purchases at San Francisco. As the Idaho trade grew larger Henry Failing feared that it would all go direct to San Francisco unless the profit margins at Portland were cut drastically. "We have thus far sold that trade, because we have credited largely and time has been a great object with dealers there," he explained in the summer of 1863. To meet the San Francisco threat and to profit from the trade, merchants, like Corbett and Failing, who had sufficient capital and credit facilities to do so, continued to purchase in New York. By 1863 other Portland merchants, who now had abundant capital and had formerly purchased only in San Francisco, had begun to purchase in New York or were making arrangements to do so. Portland merchants realized they could not be dependent upon San Francisco and keep the trade.[34]

Mining tools had to be purchased at San Francisco, however. Failings and Hatt bought large quantities of mining hardware including picks, shovels, gold pans, sluice forks and sluice brushes there in 1863. The picks had to be of California manufacture as no other kind would sell. This was also true of all placer implements and of mining machinery. Failing reported to his New York partner in June, 1863: "The class of goods we have ordered from San Fco do not pay much profit but we must have them in order to sell other Hardware and we should not dare to order such goods in this quantity from you as the mining trade is too uncertain. As it is we think they are sending too much mining hardware up the river."[35]

During the spring of 1864 large quantities of goods purchased in San Francisco were landed at Portland for trans-shipment upriver. Although they shared largely in the Idaho trade, Portland merchants became increasingly alarmed, especially in September 1864, when obstructions in the Willamette prevented its navigation by ocean-going ships. Now San Francisco goods went directly up the Columbia, and Portland's merchants hurriedly subscribed $10,000 to open a temporary channel until such time as they could get a dredge.[36] Meanwhile direct trade overland between San Francisco and Idaho had begun. In May 1864, the Idaho and California Wagon Road Company sent its first train over the new route from Sacramento via Red Bluff and the Pitt and Malheur valleys to Boise. This became a flourishing trade as the long wagon trains lumbered over this and other new routes as well as the old Sacramento-Fort Hall immigrant road on their forty-day trips. In October 1865, the *Idaho World* reported that three-fourths of trains coming into Idaho were from California.[37] Thus, Portland failed to command the trade of southern Idaho while it maintained a somewhat dependent relationship with San Francisco.

Portland could hardly compete with the great mart at San Francisco. Some Idaho and upper Columbia merchants, who purchased in ever growing quantities, by-passed Portland largely because they found it inadequate for their buying needs. In December 1865 the editor of the *Oregonian* observed that when an Idaho merchant came down with the intention of buying $50,000 worth of goods, and upon finding the Portland market out of a few of the most important items, he was likely to go on to San Francisco and purchase his entire lot there. As an example of inadequate supply the editor noted that only twenty-three kegs of eight-penny nails were on hand in the entire Portland market. He thought that it was now time for Portland merchants to specialize in the various lines of merchandising, increase their supplies, and thus share the market to a greater degree than had been possible earlier.[38]

Samuel Bowles, editor of the Springfield, Massachusetts, *Republican,* on his visit in the summer of 1865, noted the growth and commercial importance of Portland. He termed it "half rival to San Francisco itself," and the only other prominent town on the Pacific Coast showing signs of "steady, uninterrupted prosperity." He wrote:

> The population of Portland is about seven thousand; they keep Sunday as we do in New England, and as no other population this side of the Missouri now does; and real estate . . . is quite high,—four hundred dollars a front foot for best lots one hundred feet deep on the main street, without the buildings . . . and altogether Portland has the air and fact of a prosperous, energetic town, with a good deal of eastern leadership and tone to business and society and morals.[39]

At Boise, meanwhile, the market had become overstocked except for flour and a few items of groceries in the fall of 1863, and with an ample supply, prices were considerably lower during 1864 than in 1863. The trade, generally, continued profitable through 1864, but the process of supplying the new mining region was rapid indeed, as goods sought the higher price levels. Many Boise merchants suffered severe losses because of heavy inventories and declining prices during 1864 and 1865, and found their obligations at The Dalles, Portland or San Francisco increasingly difficult to meet. In 1865 there were many failures, due partly to the fire that wiped out Idaho City in May of that year. This incident, in turn, stimulated business, especially for nails and other building materials, and within a few months the town was restored more substantially than ever, although much of it was to burn down again in 1867.[40]

A visitor to the southern Idaho mines in 1865 reported that many men who had gone there in "indigent circumstances" had succeeded remarkably. One Boise merchant who had suffered from fire, depression, flood, and bankruptcy in the Willamette Valley, had become, by 1865, "joint owner in four stores . . ., a fast freight and passenger stage line near 400 miles long, a large hotel, and much other property."

Idaho City in the center of the Boise Basin was a typical mining town. It mushroomed into existence in 1863 and, although it was Idaho's largest town during the gold period, the extent of its business was far out of proportion to its size. A contemporary observer gives the following account of life and society in Idaho City in September, 1865:

> The town is situated in what is termed the 'Boise Basin', . . .
> and is the largest town in the Territory. It is in the midst
> of an important placer district, and contains from five to
> seven thousand inhabitants, on week days, and from ten to
> fifteen thousand on Sundays. For Sunday is a populous and
> profitable day with a mining town. On that day all the
> miners for miles around visit the town to purchase supplies,
> exchange greetings, gamble, guzzle, and indulge in the dis-
> sipations of mining metropolitan life. Idaho City, seen on
> Sunday, is a very different town from the Idaho City of any
> other day. It is altogether the busiest of the week with shop-
> keepers, victualers, gamblers and whiskey dispensers.
>
> Idaho City is built in and over the mines, and one-third
> to one-half of the buildings in the place have been already
> mined under; nearly all undoubtedly will be. In a mining
> country the miner is king, and his will is the law. If he finds
> 'pay dirt' under a house, he locates and records his claim,
> and commences to undermine it, without saying 'by your
> leave' to owner or occupant. Of course, as he digs, he props
> up the building . . . When a claim is worked out, he leaves
> it without filling under or further propping up the house . . .
> The city or territorial authorities have enacted laws for-
> bidding the undermining of buildings without making them
> secure from fall. But the miners elect the officers and com-
> pose the juries that administer the law; it is unnecessary
> to add, the miner wins the suit.

The same visitor also noted that:

> A leading clergyman of a popular denomination built a
> church at Idaho City, and occasionally preached at it on
> Sunday; and being engaged in merchandising, it was said his
> clerks kept the store open the while. At the time we were
> there, preaching had been suspended and the church rented
> to the United States for a courtroom; and the only time we
> visited it, Chief Justice McBride was trying a murder
> therein.[41]

In the meantime development of the Owyhee mining
district, about sixty miles southwest of Boise, had begun in
the summer of 1863, with the usual placer methods. Soon
rich quartz lodes were found and although returns from the
placers were remunerative during the first two years, the
transition to quartz mining was relatively rapid in this
district. Many claims were made, and here, unique in the
story of Idaho mining thus far, promoters appealed for outside capital. Although primitive arrastra quartz mills were
used in Boise Basin in 1864, stamp mills were sent into the

Owyhee district the same year. Two groups competed for the rich vein on War Eagle Mountain. One group obtained capital and support from J. C. Ainsworth and the Oregon Steam Navigation Company, while New York capitalists came to the aid of the other with subscriptions to the New York and Owyhee Company. After coming to an agreement on their conflicting claims to the vein, both developed quartz mining in the Owyhee district for several years thereafter. In spite of the bad reputation of some of the early promotional schemes quartz mining in the Owyhee district returned substantial profits over initial costs in a remarkably short time. Production declined in all Idaho mining districts as the output of the placers decreased in the later 1860s, and like California's earlier experience, this stage of mining gave way to more stable quartz production, financed to a considerable extent by British capital, in the 1870s and 1880s.

But the transition had already occurred in the Owyhee district, where as noted above, stamp mills were in operation by 1864. Quartz mining not only required capital but a more highly developed technology. Stamp mills crushed the ore into pieces weighing from one-half to two pounds. The quartz, now powdered or crushed, was roasted in a furnace. Next the ore was placed in tubs of water and stirred, and after an hour quicksilver was added to effect amalgamation and separation of the bullion from the rock. The bullion was then separated from the quicksilver by a process of squeezing.[42]

Much speculation occurred with the development of the Owyhee mines. One man who had once been willing to sell a claim for $12,500, later sold it to New York capitalists for $175,000.[43] Several Idaho and Oregon men had gone to New York to promote various mining schemes, among them, the successful New York and Owyhee Company. Some of these men had requested Henry Failing and other Portland men to give them letters of introduction and recommendation. Failing thought there were entirely too many men with "Quartz on the Brain" sponsoring wildcat mining schemes and refused to make any assertions as to the validity of any such scheme. Before going to New York a man named

Robbins, who seems to have been successful in his Owyhee promotional effort, requested a recommendation from Failing, who reported the incident as follows:

> I declined giving him any letters, telling him I would not recommend or endorse mining shares of which I knew nothing & I had never invested a dollar in them. That parties were constantly going East and to Cala. selling wildcat Stock, that I would not encourage it by giving letters to anyone. That there were undoubtedly good mines in Idaho, and they would probably some of them be successfully worked, but he was as liable to be mistaken in their value as any one else . . . but I positively refused to endorse him or any ground which he owned. This nettled him, and I heard of his denouncing Portland people for their want of enterprise in not encouraging his mission East. . . . Robbins failed here a few years ago. Was generally reputed as rich and made a bad failure. . . . He is a passionate, violent tempered man, and has no control over his tongue. He owes a large amount of money here. . . . I understand he has succeeded in organizing some mining companies and has made some money in N. Y. If New Yorkers suffer to the same extent, as those who have had business with him here, they will wish he had stayed at home. Bradford, Wes Ladd [O. S. N. men, then in New York] and others write that Robbins, McCarver & other Oregonians are forming large companies in New York to work silver mines and state that a man who will go East—tell a plausible lie and stick to it, can get along. . . . He [Robbins] has little reason to speak ill of people here, and had better pay his debts before abusing them.

This probably was George C. Robbins who helped to effect the consolidation of the two contending Owyhee companies. He had formerly been an assayer in Portland.[44]

Meanwhile discoveries on the Quesnelle River far to the north in British Columbia in 1860 set off a rush during 1862 and 1863 paralleling that to Idaho. These rich diggings stimulated trade at Victoria, which drew most of its supplies from San Francisco and Great Britain. Although Oregon supplied Victoria provisions, horses and cattle in considerable amounts, this trade had little direct effect upon the development of Portland. The value of exports from Portland to Victoria during 1864, for example, was $160,531, and of imports from Victoria to Portland, $55,771. New Westminster appeared as an entrepôt for the Fraser River hinterland, and other towns rose and boomed as gold stimulated the development of the British colony. In 1863, the Kootenai mines in the extreme southeastern part of British Columbia, some fifty miles north of the international border, were discovered. Here mining developed on a large scale during 1864 and 1865, but declined rapidly in 1866. Here, in spite of tariffs to protect Victoria and New Westminster traders, a large portion of the supplies needed by the miners came from Portland via Walla Walla or Lewiston.[45] Thus Portland, except for the Kootenai trade, profited very little from the new gold strikes in British Columbia.

Portland's Struggle for the Montana Trade

The Montana trade, however, was another matter. Reports of gold were current among the few residents of Montana prior to 1858, when James and Granville Stuart panned a little of the precious metal on Gold Creek in the Deer Lodge Valley on the west slope of the Rocky Mountains. Development did not begin until 1862, when several parties, including the Stuarts, started mining in the creeks and gulches of the Deer Lodge area and across the Continental Divide to the south. Most phenomenal were the rich gold fields discovered in Grasshopper Creek in 1862, in Alder Gulch in 1863, and Last Chance Gulch the following year. Population grew rapidly as millions in gold poured from the Montana mines, and the towns of Bannack, Virginia City, and Helena rose in quick succession. By 1865 miners from Idaho, British Columbia, and from all parts of the United States were in the Montana gold fields. The new territory's population was nearly 20,000 by the end of that year.[46]

From 1864 through 1868, San Francisco, Portland, Salt Lake City, St. Louis, and even Chicago competed on a grand scale for the mining trade of Montana and Idaho. Merchants of San Francisco struggled for this trade by every possible route: via the Columbia River, various overland routes, and finally the Central Pacific Railroad. St. Louis merchants, using the Missouri River and overland routes, however, were the principal victors in the contest for the Montana trade during the middle and later 1860s. But capitalists in Portland, chiefly the men of the Oregon Steam Navigation

Company, led a valiant struggle from 1865 to 1867 to retain the Idaho trade and to capture that of Montana and the Kootenai district. This struggle provides an interesting and important episode in the annals of trade and transportation in the Pacific Northwest.

The Mullan Road from Fort Benton to Walla Walla, completed in 1860, crossed through or near the future mining country, and was of primary importance in Portland's effort to get its share of the Montana trade. The prospect of a northern emigrant route, or possibly a transcontinental railroad, had stimulated some interest in the commercial development of Montana during the later 1850s. Although commissioned to build a military road across the Rocky Mountains to join the Columbia and Missouri rivers, Lieutenant John Mullan also had an emigrant route in mind. Some Oregonians thought the road would bring a new stream of emigrants to increase the region's population. While building the road eastward from Walla Walla, Mullan received supplies from Portland which were brought in by wagon or pack train from Walla Walla. In 1859, a year before the completion of the 624-mile road, the *Chippewa,* the first steamboat to navigate the Missouri River much farther than Fort Union, arrived at Fort Benton, the eastern terminus of the Mullan Road, some 300 miles upriver from Fort Union. Now, it was believed, the new emigrant route had appeared which would also provide opportunities for trade and settlement. The route immediately achieved a limited commercial importance as military and Indian annuity goods and supplies for the trappers flowed into Montana from both east and west.[47]

Frank L. Worden, one of Montana's earliest pioneer merchants, established a store at Hell Gate, near the present site of Missoula, in 1860, with goods purchased in Portland. He is an example of a pioneer who drifted eastward with the new frontier from California to the Oregon coast, the Walla Walla Valley, and Montana. He and his partner, C. P. Higgins, went into business at Walla Walla in 1858 and after a failure due to mismanagement, Worden made his way to Hell Gate with seventy-five horses laden with merchandise. In 1861 he went to St. Louis to purchase goods, but lost $9,000 worth of insured merchandise when the *Chippewa* blew up just short of her destination on the northward journey. Worden then went to Portland where after considerable persuasion he succeeded in getting credit from Failings and Hatt for $7,000 worth of goods.[48]

With the gold rush, freight and people came into Montana from three directions: by the overland route from St. Louis and Omaha; by the overland route from San Francisco and Salt Lake City; and by the Columbia River-Mullan Road route from Portland and Walla Walla. Of these the first, from St. Louis, was most important in supplying the Montana frontier through 1865. A fourth route, mainly an emigrant trail, came across Dakota from St. Paul to the Montana mines.

Traffic by steamboat on the Missouri River from St. Louis developed with the rise and growth of the Helena mining area in 1864 and after. During the six year period prior to 1865, only 2,010 tons of freight had reached Fort Benton via the river, with four boats arriving in 1862, three in 1863, and four in 1864. Thereafter the river became the most important freight route to the Montana mines.[49]

The Mullan Road, although designed for wagons, was mainly a pack trail. Mullan had stayed in the field until 1862 making improvements on the road, but even so wagons could get through only with great difficulty during a short season. Pack trains, however, could use it during the greater part of the year. During the 1865 season, 100 pack trains averaging 50 animals per train with each animal loaded with about 300 pounds carried 750 tons of freight from the Columbia River to Montana. The total value of these goods laid down at Helena was $1,440,000, at a freight cost of $240,000. Even so the *Oregonian* reported at the end of the year that the "goods now in the Montana market, have for the most part been brought from St. Louis."[50]

Goods and freights were extremely high. In 1863, Granville Stuart paid $4.00 per pound for tobacco, 40 cents per pound for bacon, and 60 cents per pound for sugar packed in over the Mullan Road. In 1865, freights were 15-16 cents per pound from Walla Walla, 25 cents from Omaha overland, 15-20 cents per pound from San Francisco, and 15-20 cents per pound by river from St. Louis to Fort Benton with an additional 5 cents per pound from Fort Benton to Helena via the eastern end of the Mullan Road. Since the Columbia River rates are not included in those given for the western route and as the St. Louis rates seem to have been in currency, freight charges from the three principal supply centers, St. Louis, San Francisco, and Portland, appear to have been within the same competitive range.[51]

In the fall of 1865, after a somewhat poor business year, Portland capitalists determined to capture as much of the Montana trade as possible. In July, Simeon G. Reed, vice-president of the Oregon Steam Navigation Company, had declared that, "we must leave 'no stone unturned' to divert all the Boise and Owyhee trade this way." In September he made similar declarations concerning the Montana trade. It was observed that only a few of the boats that had set out from St. Louis in 1865 went farther than Fort Union, that freights were high, and that the Missouri River route was extremely hazardous. At best boats could reach Fort Benton only in June or July when the river was high. H. D. Sanborn, a Montana merchant, looked to the west and urged Portland merchants to develop the Lake Pend Oreille route. Here all that was required was a good road built over a small segment of the route, a project that would cost much less than the improvements necessary to make the Mullan Road suitable for wagons. In any case, others argued, the routes from the west would be open from April to October, and Portland goods would have the advantage of a depleted market before the arrival of the Missouri River boats at Fort Benton. Since only eight of the twenty boats that left St. Louis went beyond Fort Union in 1865, it was thought that the river route might prove unfeasible. If so the over-land route from Walla Walla to Helena via the Mullan Road would be no more disadvantageous than the land route from Fort Union, through dangerous Indian country.[52]

These arguments stirred the minds of Portland men who were anxious to tap Montana's golden stream. The *Oregonian* urged Portland businessmen to spare no effort in gaining the Montana trade, and exaggerated the advantages of the proposed new route.[53] Portland and San Francisco merchants responded to the plea by contributing $11,225 to build the proposed new road along Clark's Fork of the Columbia. Now the *Oregonian* gleefully announced that

Montana merchants could visit Portland and San Francisco in winter as easily as those from Idaho. Throughout the fall and winter of 1865-66, the problem of the Montana trade was uppermost in the minds of Portland businessmen. In March Simeon G. Reed wrote to Ainsworth from Washington as follows:

> *Again* let me impress upon you and the people of Portland the importance [of] closely watching that Montana trade and divert it to the Columbia river—it can be done, but the people of Portland are altogether too slow—St. Louis is wide awake no lack of enterprise or capital there.[54]

The most important result of this agitation was the decision of the Oregon Steam Navigaton Company to place boats on Lake Pend Oreille and Clark's Fork of the Columbia.

For some time the principal owners of the Oregon Steam Navigation Company, W. S. Ladd, J. C. Ainsworth, Simeon G. Reed, R. R. Thompson, D. Bradford, H. Olmstead, Jacob Kamm, and Joseph Ruckel, had contended among themselves concerning the problem of expanding the company's facilities and its zone of operations. Ainsworth, Ladd, Reed, and Thompson hoped to place an expensive steamship on the San Francisco-Portland run and to broaden the company's activities in the interior. Bradford, then in New York, opposed all these plans and favored what he called the eastern method of making more dividends through stock manipulation. He urged his colleagues to get in tune with the times. But the Ainsworth faction, following the suggestion of its opponent, set about to achieve its own purposes by getting control of the company through stock manipulation. This group created rumors, put stock up for sale at a low price, purchased all they could get at the low figure, and then raised the price again. Thus these four, Ainsworth, Reed, Ladd, and Thompson, whose names are identified with the history of the Oregon Steam Navigation Company, gained complete control in 1867. In December of that year they rewarded themselves with a handsome dividend of 36.84 per cent, and then raised the capitalization to $5,000,000. In the meantime, in 1866, they had placed the steamer *Forty-Nine* on the Columbia to run north of the boundary to Arrow Lake in order to facilitate the Kootenai trade, and the *Shoshone* on the Snake above Olds Ferry in a somewhat unsuccessful attempt to compete with the overland route from the Columbia to Boise.[55]

To tap the Montana trade the Oregon and Montana Transportation Company had been formed as a subsidiary of the Oregon Steam Navigation Company in the fall of 1865. At first this company put a pack train on the Mullan Road, but on April 30, the steamer *Mary Moody* was launched on Lake Pend Oreille to run some 85 miles on the lake and up Clark's Fork to Cabinet Rapids. Here a short portage connected with the steamer *Cabinet,* built by the same company later in the year, which ran 56 miles on Clark's Fork to Thompson Falls. After making another portage there, connections were to be made with a steamer which would run to the mouth of the Jocko, but it was not until 1868 that the steamer *Missoula* was placed on this section of the river. The *Mary Moody* had been built on the lake with lumber whipsawed on the spot and her engines, those of an old Columbia River steamer, were hauled in and installed in the winter and spring of 1866. In June the *Oregonian* proudly announced that the *Mary Moody* was making daily trips to Cabinet Rapids with freight at one cent per pound and passage at $5.00.[56]

In March, 1866, several Montana merchants purchased supplies at Portland. Henry Failing did an active business selling mining goods and boots and shoes for Montana. He was glad to get rid of some cavalry boots for which there had been no market after the army left. He noted that freights to Montana were 35-40 cents per pound, but flour dealers thought they could soon ship their product to Helena as low as $13\frac{1}{4}$ cents per pound.[57]

But the expected large trade with Montana later in the spring did not develop, and gloom fell on the Portland business community. In May the *Oregonian* reported that merchants "doubtfully shake their heads with apprehension . . . concerning . . . business in general. They consider it extremely doubtful whether their sales for the markets of Montana will ever be on a large scale." While the trade revived during the summer and fall of 1866, this prediction was essentially correct as far as the later years were concerned.

Although the extent of the Columbia River trade with Montana is difficult to determine, 1866 was undoubtedly the peak year. When Portland merchants learned that the goods sold in March had reached the Helena market via the Lake Pend Oreille route before the arrival of Missouri River boats their confidence was restored. Several Montana merchants visited Portland during the summer and fall, and the *Oregonian* reported in August that a greater amount of freight was going to Montana than ever before.[58] At Walla Walla between January 1 and November 15, 1866, some 2,000 miners obtained horses and outfits for Montana. During the same period traders took 5,000 head of cattle and some 6,000 mules loaded with freight from Walla Walla and other Columbia River points. In 1866 Salt Lake City shipped more than a million dollars worth of flour to the Montana market at freight rates ranging from $1.10 to $1.25 per pound.[59]

The agitation for Portland to capture the Montana trade continued during 1867. A Deer Lodge merchant noted the advantages of the western route, the principal one being that a merchant making his purchases at Portland could sell in a depleted market early in the season while St. Louis goods met a glutted market. But he noted an essential difference, that goods sold for gold at Portland at about the same price as for currency at St. Louis, even though both places were supplied from New York. He also noted that the cost of freight from New York to St. Louis and from New York to Portland was about the same.[60]

Freights from New York to St. Louis by rail in 1867 ranged between $20 per ton for heavy goods like nails to $52.40 for dry goods and boots and shoes. Freight rates from New York to San Francisco via Cape Horn were also $20 per ton for heavy goods and up to 70 cents per cubic foot in 1865; and $15 and $16 per ton in 1866. The rate via Panama slow freight was $1.68 per one hundred pounds in 1866, whereas in 1861 and 1862 it had been $1.75 per cubic foot. Due to the competition of a new steamship line, freights on the San Francisco-Portland run fell from $10 to $3.00 per ton in 1866, and ranged between $5.00 and $7.00 per ton in April, 1867.[61] The St. Louis rates were in currency, and while not stated specifically in the sources, the other rates were probably in gold. Even considering the gold value of currency, which averaged 71 cents in 1866 and 72.4

cents in 1867, it seems that many categories of goods could have been transported by sea to Portland as cheaply or cheaper than to St. Louis by rail.

But the development of the Missouri River route destroyed Portland's hope for the Montana trade. In spite of hazardous navigation, thirty-one steamers landed 4,441 tons of freight at Fort Benton in 1866 at an average rate of 11 cents per pound, currency, from St. Louis. The additional levy from Fort Benton to Helena was four cents per pound in gold. At the end of the year it was estimated that about half the freight entering Montana had come by way of the Missouri River. In 1867 the river trade reached its peak when 5,000 tons of freight with an estimated value of upwards of $7,500,000 arrived on board thirty-nine boats. It is estimated that freight charges alone reached $1,000,000, and boats often paid for themselves in a single season.

In 1868, after the completion of the Sioux City and Pacific Railway to the Missouri at Sioux City, Chicago entered competition with St. Louis for the Montana trade and soon won the contest. The freight rate by rail and river boat to Fort Benton from Chicago was six cents per pound. The St. Louis rates also fell but Chicago merchants had the advantage.[62]

The Oregon-Montana trade declined, but retained some importance through 1868. In May of that year the *Montana Post* commented upon the early arrival of pack trains from Oregon as follows:

> We thus early in the season experienced the benefit of having communication with the outside; by means of which we can receive goods from one to two months in advance of the river route, and though the present rates of freight from Oregon here are about three times as great as from St. Louis, yet the price of many descriptions of goods will be materially cheapened by the arrival of these trains, even at freight ranging from 20 to 25 cents in gold, and the difference in prices caused thereby will be for the benefit of the people. As the season advances freight by pack trains will be reduced, but we are of the opinion that except early in the season, when our market is nearly bare of everything it will not pay to ships goods from Oregon here, and that in ordinary season it will be impossible to compete with goods from the States shipped by river. We notice the arrival of between one and two hundred animals thus far, loaded with

dry goods, clothing, groceries, etc., and other trains will soon be in, amply supplying our market with the goods which are scarce, and which have been commanding an unusually high price.

Later in the year a Montana visitor observed that

the trade of Montana with the Pacific coast . . . has now dwindled to insignificant proportions, and in place of the long trains of pack animals, loaded with clothing, and merchandise of every description, there is now received almost nothing save a few sacks of flour and boxes of apples.[63]

After the completion of the transcontinental railroad in 1869, it became cheaper to supply Montana from either east or west by rail to Corrine, Utah, and from there northward by wagon. Thus the river route declined in importance as a new pattern of transportation developed and as the day of gold began to give way to a new succession of frontier enterprises in the mountains, plains, and valleys of the Far West.[64]

The amount of gold produced in the Pacific Northwest during the 1860s is difficult to determine. Much treasure slipped out in the private possession of individuals and never became part of official records. Profits from production are likewise impossible to determine. Following are the somewhat conservative estimates for gold production in the region including Montana through 1867, as compiled by J. Ross Browne, U. S. commissioner for the mining regions west of the Rocky Mountains. George M. Dawson's figures for British Columbia are added:

Montana	$65,000,000
Idaho	45,000,000
British Columbia	26,110,000
Oregon	20,000,000
Washington	10,000,000[65]

A recent study shows the total output of the Idaho mines, for the same period, including the silver bullion of the Owyhee district, at $51,770,000. As early as 1863, it may be noted, $90,000 in silver bullion was shipped out of Portland on board the *Sierra Nevada* on one trip to San Francisco. Following are reasonably accurate estimates for the gold and silver output of the Idaho mines during the decade:

275

1862	$ 5,000,000
1863	7,450,000
1864	9,020,000
1865	12,910,000
1866	10,000,000
1867	7,390,000
1868	3,030,000
1869	1,610,000[66]

According to Trimble's calculations the region, including British Columbia and Montana, contributed about 40 per cent of the nation's bullion supply during the period 1861-67. If gold alone were considered this percentage would be much higher, since the total bullion supply included the silver output of the Nevada mines.

Gold was the region's principal surplus commodity and as such it flowed out in a continuous stream. But in spite of the high cost of production, it was used to create various forms of permanent capital. Gold production from 1861 through 1867 provided the region an annual average surplus of some $15,000,000, which was immediately available for development. This fact, according to Trimble, accounts for the relatively greater and more intense development of commerce and transportation in the Pacific Northwest during the mining period, than was true of newly settled agricultural regions with a much greater population.[67] The Oregon Steam Navigation Company is a case in point as is the development of ocean navigation and the stagecoach and express businesses. But gold also provided the impulse for the development of agriculture and numerous other branches of capitalistic enterprise.

Chapter XIII

Henry Failing
and the Greenback Problem

"Payable in U. S. Gold Coin."

Although the Civil War had little direct impact upon the Pacific Northwest, the Portland merchant had to meet new problems caused by the inflation of the currency, rising costs, and supply shortages. Confederate cruisers threatened his life-line of supply by sea, but still the staple goods, groceries, and hardware flowed in to supply the eastward moving frontier. Portland merchants fulfilled this important social function by their enterprise and skill. The career of Henry Failing from 1861 through 1866 demonstrates the problems involved and how he met them.

During the early 1860s Henry Failing gradually gained control of the firm, Failings and Hatt. In 1861, C. W. Thomas, the special New York partner and original sponsor of the Failings in their Portland venture, had withdrawn capital in violation of the terms of the partnership. He was to have contributed up to a maximum of $40,000, if needed. Withdrawal of capital, however, threatened if it did not actually impair, the credit of the New York branch of the business when the Idaho trade demanded maximum use of the firm's capital resources. Failing suspected that Thomas also helped himself to a part of the firm's regular remittances. He complained bitterly and wrote that "A curtailment of capital will curtail profits more than in proportion to the curtailment of capital."[1] His first step in getting the business under his personal control was to require John A. Hatt, the New York buyer and partner, to furnish complete information on notes payable and all discounts processed by Failings and Hatt, New York.[2] Next, he accepted Thomas' unexpected offer to sell his interest in the firm. Although the details of this arrangement are not known, Failing paid the Thomas notes during 1863, and thus ended a relationship that had grown unpleasant and actually dangerous to the business. Early in 1864 Failing purchased the respective interests of his father and Hatt, the other partners.[3]

Hatt continued as purchaser and shipper, but instead of being a partner in the firm, he was now the agent and employee of Henry Failing at a stipulated salary. The success of the business depended in great measure upon the sound business judgment of Hatt who did the purchasing at the distant source of supply. Although he was held strictly accountable as to prices paid and the quality of goods purchased, he still exercised considerable discretion on these matters. Failing appreciated Hatt's services and held him in high esteem.[4] Since 1861, Samuel T. House served as Corbett's New York agent with similar responsibilities to those now assumed by Hatt.

During the Idaho rush Failing had expanded his business to meet the demands of the trade using his credit facilities to the fullest advantage. He purchased greater quantities of goods in New York on credit, for six to nine months, and thus increased his indebtedness in the East. At Portland he enjoyed excellent credit facilities at the Ladd and Tilton Bank where at times he obtained loans at considerably less than the current interest rate. For a time during 1861, he obtained loans from Ladd at no interest and with no security. He utilized every possible resource to keep remittances constantly flowing to Hatt for the purpose of discounting his eastern paper, and in some cases, for making cash purchases. One such source was gold dust sent down by parties in Lewiston for deposit which he used to his own advantage until such time as payments were due. He thus acted in the capacity of a banker.[5]

When conditions in the Willamette Valley improved in 1862, Failing collected most of his old accounts including some that he had considered doubtful. He charged interest at two per cent per month and found at the end of the year that these charges almost balanced his own interest account at the bank. Many valley merchants paid their accounts in flour from which he also derived a profit. He paid interest at two per cent per month on some of his indebtedness at Ladd and Tilton's, while he continued to borrow some at no interest. At the end of the year he reported that he owed nothing in Portland on which he had to pay interest.[6]

The inflation of the currency enabled Failing to gain profits on inventory especially during 1862 and 1863. Prices advanced rapidly in the fall of 1862, and with large stocks purchased at low prices, either on hand or in transit, he enjoyed wider profit margins at the time of sale. By considering the six months time required for delivery a glance at Table 5, page 283, will show that brown sheetings and drills costing 13 and 12 cents per yard in gold sold for 30 and 32 cents at Portland in the fall of 1862 for margins of 130.8 and 166.7 per cent. The more normal margins as shown by the prices for 1861 before the currency became inflated, was 62.5 per cent. A yard of brown sheeting purchased in April, 1862 for 13 cents and sold for 30 cents in October shows a margin of 17 cents, most of which was profit to the merchant, while in 1861 and the early parts of 1862 the margin for the same merchandise was between three and five cents. This was true for merchandise like cotton goods and tobacco which rose rapidly because of scarcity in the East and to a lesser extent for other staples. Tobacco at Portland ranged from 25 to 60 cents per pound during the first half of 1862 and from $1.00 to $1.50 per pound in 1863.[7]

A small quantity of greenbacks appeared on the Pacific Coast through disbursements of the federal government after the passage of the Legal Tender Act of February 25, 1862. Although the Portland business community was apprehensive and uncertain, citizens at first were generally disposed to accept them at par as a matter of patriotic duty. To do otherwise, they feared, would show a lack of confidence in the government and the war effort, and might have an adverse effect upon government credit. The *Oregonian* urged loyal citizens "to sustain the credit of the government by receiving cheerfully the United States notes as the currency of the land." Resolutions passed by a group of citizens at The Dalles stated that "any person who shall attempt to depreciate the established currency of our government is considered by us an enemy of his country" and "That we, the laboring and producing citizens of The Dalles and vicinity, pledge ourselves to trade only with persons who are patriotic enough to take *the faith of the government at par.*"[8]

Businessmen, however, were in doubt. They held a distinct aversion toward paper money and lacked experience in its use. Many believed that the region's prosperity rested upon gold and the continued use of specie. During the fall of 1862 the few greenbacks that had arrived during the year circulated at 90 cents on the dollar. More greenbacks came in, early in 1863, and it was feared that if they were to circulate in large quantities, they would drive out the metallic currency altogether and thus reduce gold to a commodity status.[9] W. S. Ladd, writing to Benjamin Stark, owner of considerable holdings in Portland, stated:

> no one is loaning fearing to put out Gold and take the chances of taking in paper. . . . The great depreciation of Exchange on New York and the introduction of Greenbacks and the passage of the Usury bill has proved quite hard for us particular [sic] in Consequence of the former . . . one or two of your tennants [sic] paid their rent in Greenbacks which for gold is 10 to 15% off. we notified if repeated they must vacate—or pay in gold. . . . We are somewhat disinharted [sic] and have written to our Mr. T if agreeable to him we will close business to loan money at 10% 3% for income tax will not leave sufficient to pay our expenses and to put out gold in this Community at any such rate and take the chances of being paid in a Currency that is not equivalent to that you loan Can not do it.[10]

West Coast merchants soon took steps to protect gold and to deny greenbacks the status of money. In November 1862, San Francisco merchants agreed not to receive or pay out greenbacks except at their market value and to maintain gold as the standard. Portland merchants followed with a similar agreement on January 15, 1863, partly because San Francisco speculators had begun to dump greenbacks in the Portland market to take advantage of 90 cents exchange value when greenbacks were selling for considerably less in San Francisco. The Portland agreement stated that greenbacks were to be received "at rates current in San Francisco, as published from time to time in the daily papers of Portland, Oregon, by Ladd and Tilton Bankers."

Failing noted that "At present rates all importation of greenbacks will be stopped and if there is a concert of action on the Coast we shall be able to keep our gold here instead of paper circulation." The *Oregonian* urged the community to "keep the price of currency here a fraction below that of New York and it will unfailingly flow to that place." The editor thought that greenbacks should have had the force of government behind them and non-acceptance have been made a felony. "But it was deemed best to pay the capitalist holding national bonds his interest in gold," he asserted, "while the soldier receives his dues in depreciated currency." From April through August, 1863, the price of greenbacks at Portland was kept slightly lower than the New York rates. This may have been in part a safeguard against sudden fluctuations in the East, but its main purpose was to drive greenbacks out of circulation.[11]

During 1863, merchants feared that the legal tender notes would be forced upon them and that debtors would take advantage of their fear. They, therefore, took further measures to safeguard gold. Any debtor guilty of "greenbacking" would lose his credit standing in Portland's entire mercantile community immediately, and would have to purchase for cash at the regular gold rates or not at all. At first, this practice developed as a somewhat informal though highly effective system of "blacklisting," and later, regular notices were published in the newspapers by those who were victims of the practice. One such notice read: "H. I. Day, of Corvallis, has this day paid me $603 in greenbacks at par, in payment of his account for goods purchased at gold prices. C. H. Humiston, Portland, January 11, 1865." G. W. Vaughn, a Portland merchant, accepted greenbacks from Jacob Mayer under protest for payment of rent for a store on the corner of Morrison and Front streets and accused Mayer of "legal swindling" for having taken undue advantage of a lease made before the depreciated currency arrived on the coast. Merchants also took the precaution of placing the phrase "Payable in U. S. gold coin" on all bills. By following California's example this practice was given legal sanction by a specific contracts law passed by the Oregon legislature in October 1864, which simply made all contract obligations payable in coin. At the same time the legislature passed an act requiring "that all taxes levied by state, counties, or municipal corporations therein, shall be collected and paid in gold and silver coin of the United States and not otherwise." Thus legislators legally safeguarded the hard money standard, which already had the sanction of public opinion.

Greenbacks were at most an auxiliary currency circulating at their fluctuating gold values. On the West Coast they were always quoted in terms of their gold value, whereas in the East where they had all but driven gold out of circulation, gold was quoted in terms of a premium percentage on the greenback standard or at its actual value in terms of greenbacks. With the gold standard firmly established on the coast the effort to drive greenbacks out of circulation was abandoned. Throughout most of the war period after August 1863, greenback quotations at San Francisco and Portland were higher than in New York and bankers and brokers added five per cent to the New York quotations as a regular practice.[12]

It has been alleged that Oregon merchants made excessive profits by purchasing with greenbacks and by selling for gold.[13] This was true while large inventory profits were possible, but only as competition and the law of supply and demand permitted. Table 6 shows that the selling price and actual margin on crushed sugars were relatively stable during the war years, ranging between six and nine cents while the percentage of margin ranged between 50 and 100 per cent, or about the same as it had been before the war. As long as the currency price of gold increased, the general price level of goods, except for cottons and tobacco, increased proportionately. After gold began to fall, late in 1864, however, its currency value declined faster than the wholesale price index.[14]

Rising costs, of course, were reflected in the Portland prices. Henry Failing noted, however, that gold prices could not be advanced solely because of the inflation of the currency, and he would have preferred a speedy resumption of specie payments in spite of inventory profits.[15] This, doubtless, was the attitude of most businessmen, especially those in the Golden West.

Tables 5 and 6 compare the New York cost, using the currency cost converted to its gold equivalent, and the Portland selling price in gold for two basic items of cotton goods and two of groceries. These four are among the few

TABLE 5

COMPARISON OF NEW YORK AND PORTLAND WHOLESALE PRICES OF TWO ITEMS OF DRY GOODS AND TWO OF GROCERIES IN GOLD (TO THE NEAREST WHOLE CENT)

	Brown Sheeting Per Yd.		Brown Drills Per Yd.		Rio Coffee Per Lb.		Crushed Sugar Per Lb.	
	N. Y.	Ptld.	N. Y.	Ptld.	N. Y.	Ptld.	N. Y.	Ptld.
1861 April	08	13	08	11	12	20	08	16
July	08	13	08	13	12	20	08	17
Oct.	11	14	10	14	16	24	11	17
1862 Jan.	13	17	12	14	18	25	11	17
April	13	18	12	18	20	30	10	18
July	13	..	12	..	18	28	09	18
Oct.	18	30	19	32	18	27	10	18
1863 Jan.	20	27	18	26	19	33	09	18
April	24	27	22	25	20	33	10	16
July	25	..	20	..	22	..	11	..
Oct.	24	27	23	..	21	32	10	..
1864 Jan.	26	27	24	27	22	28	11	20
April	22	31	22	29	23	26	10	18
July	26	32	23	29	17	26	12	20
Oct.	26	35	30	30	18	29	12	19
1865 Jan.	26	38	26	38	20	25	13	19
April	25	35	19	32	19	24	12	20
July	22	35	20	34	20	24	14	19
Oct.	38	38	24	36	20	27	14	18
1866 Jan.	22	36	22	35	19	29	13	18
April	19	30	18	28	18	25	13	17
July	14	26	15	27	15	24	11	15
Oct.	14	23	15	24	18	25	11	15
1867 Jan.	16	22	16	23	16	27	11	14
April	14	20	15	22	18	24	11	15
July	12	20	12	21	16	21	12	15
Oct.	11	18	12	18	15	22	12	17

for whch almost continuous listings are given in the *Oregonian*. The Portland prices are the highest given for each of the months selected and represent fairly accurately the average price for the month for the best quality of the particular item quoted. Cheaper grades of the same kind of goods usually ranged only a cent or two lower. The New York prices are averages for the particular months given. The New York dry goods prices used here are for brown sheeting, 4-4 Atlantic A's, and 30-inch Pepperell drilling.[16]

Although he had made substantial profits on inventory during the later months of 1862, Failing realized the risks involved if gold were to suddenly decline while he had a large currency indebtedness in the East. He wrote:

We have thought it extremely hazardous to buy largely on time at such extreme rates, fearing that gold might fall, prices tumble and we should then lose heavily on our goods. It is of course smooth enough while prices are advancing and we can get a large premium on gold, but when prices fall it will be necessary to stand from under. So long as we are getting gold if we had sufficient capital to purchase for Cash and realize the premium on gold sufficient to cover the inflation of prices caused by the currency we would be safe enough. . . . We do not think it to our interest to avail ourselves of credit to any greater extent than we are compelled to in order to keep our trade and would prefer to buy entirely for cash . . . . our profits have been greatly enlarged by the advance in gold and before the collapse comes we hope by using caution to be able to incur the ordinary hazard of business.[17]

Thus purchasing in the New York market involved risks on the behavior of the price of gold. Portland merchants

TABLE 6

ADVANCE OF PORTLAND PRICES OVER
NEW YORK COSTS IN GOLD

	Brown Sheeting		Brown Drills		Rio Coffee		Crushed Sugar	
	Amt. in Cents	Per Cent	Amt. in Cents	Per Cent	Amt. in Cents	Per Cent	Amt. in Cents	Per Cent
1861 April	5	62.5	3	37.5	8	66.7	8	100.0
July	5	62.5	5	62.5	8	66.7	9	112.0
Oct.	3	27.2	4	40.0	8	50.0	6	54.5
1862 Jan.	4	30.7	2	16.7	8	38.9	6	54.5
April	5	38.4	6	50.0	10	50.0	8	80.0
July		..		..	10	55.6	9	100.0
Oct. 12		66.6	11	68.4	9	50.0	8	80.0
1863 Jan.	7	35.0	8	44.4	14	73.7	9	100.0
April	3	25.0	3	13.6	13	65.0	6	60.0
July		..		..	..	..	..	..
Oct.	3	25.0		..	11	52.4		..
1864 Jan.	1	3.8	3	25.0	6	27.3	9	81.8
April	9	40.9	7	31.8	3	30.4	8	80.0
July	6	23.1	6	26.1	9	52.9	8	66.7
Oct.	9	34.6	0	00.0	11	61.1	7	58.3
1865 Jan. 12		46.1	12	46.1	5	25.0	6	46.2
April 10		40.0	13	68.4	5	26.3	8	66.7
July 13		59.0	14	70.0	4	20.0	5	35.7
Oct.	0	00.0	12	50.0	7	35.0	4	28.5
1866 Jan. 14		16.4	13	59.1	10	52.6	5	38.5
April 11		57.9	10	55.6	7	38.9	4	30.8
July 12		85.7	12	80.0	9	60.0	4	36.4
Oct.	9	64.3	9	60.0	7	38.9	4	36.4
1867 Jan.	6	37.5	7	43.7	7	68.8	3	27.3
April	6	42.8	7	46.6	6	33.3	4	36.4
July	8	66.7	9	75.0	5	31.3	3	25.0
Oct.	7	63.6	6	50.0	7	46.6	5	41.6

anxiously awaited gold quotations, some four or five days late, by stage from Yreka, the terminus of telegraphic communication prior to March 5, 1864. Thereafter, with the completion of the telegraph to Portland, businessmen enjoyed direct communication with New York.[18] Table 7 shows the average monthly currency value of gold at New York for the war years after January 1, 1862.

During the war years greenbacks fluctuated violently and gold commanded a high average premium. Fluctuations corresponded with the reverses and successes of the Union army and such additional factors as the quantity of greenbacks issued and the general financial condition of the government. From January to April 1862, when the hope of ending the war was high, the premium on gold was relatively small and steady. From April 1862 through February 1863 it advanced steadily because of McClellan's failure, Burnside's disastrous defeat at Fredericksburg, the second issue of greenbacks, the Third Legal Tender Act, and the administration's financial and political difficulties. From March through August, 1863, the premium fell considerably, though it remained higher generally than the

TABLE 7

THE AVERAGE MONTHLY CURRENCY VALUE OF GOLD
AT NEW YORK, 1862-65

Month	1862	1863	1864	1865
January	102.5	145.1	155.5	216.2
February	103.5	160.5	158.6	203.5
March	101.8	154.5	162.9	173.8
April	101.5	151.5	172.7	148.5
May	103.3	148.9	176.3	135.6
June	106.5	144.5	210.7	140.1
July	115.5	130.6	258.1	142.1
August	114.5	125.8	254.1	143.5
September	118.5	134.2	222.5	143.9
October	128.5	147.7	207.2	145.5
November	131.1	148.0	233.5	147.0
December	132.3	151.1	227.5	146.2
Yearly Average	113.3	145.2	203.2	157.3

(From G. F. Warren and F. A. Pearson, *Wholesale Prices for 213 Years, 1720-1932*, Cornell University Agricultural Experiment Station, Memoir 142, 1932, part 1, p. 76. Tables for both the currency value of gold and the gold value of the currency are given here by months for the period, 1862-79.)

1862 levels, due to Jay Cooke's success in selling bonds and the victories at Vicksburg and Gettysburg. From September 1863 to July 1864, the premium rose again because of Lee's escape, lack of military success, congressional delay in voting taxes, the treasury's unsuccessful campaign against gold speculators, and the difficulty of selling bonds. From August 1864 through May 1865 the premium fell because of the circumstances leading to the end of the war. Thereafter, although the premium remained relatively high from 1865 through 1869, there were no extreme fluctuations. From 1869 until the resumption of specie payments in 1879, gold declined gradually.[19]

Throughout 1863 Failing sold at prices in gold above the cost in currency on most descriptions of merchandise, and his profits, especially during the spring and summer, were exceptionally good. He refers constantly, in his correspondence, to profits derived from the premium on gold, but it is difficult to determine exactly what he means by such "profits" since his gold was converted into its currency equivalent and used to purchase goods. Perhaps Hatt speculated a bit on the gold market, though the remittances were converted to currency either immediately or very soon after they were received. Most likely Failing confused the term "profits from the premium on gold" with profits on inventory caused by the inflation of the currency, since West Coast resistance to greenbacks prevented arbitrage. When the price of gold was 150 in the spring of 1863, every $1,000 in gold he remitted would have purchased goods having a currency value of $1,500. These he would have sold for considerably more than $1,500 in gold for an average profit margin well in excess of 50 per cent. This margin derived from the normal processes of trade and the premium on gold in the East seems to have had little to do with it, except as a factor in the rising cost of goods. With reference to the mining trade he observed that profits had to be large for such "a long winded business," because he had to wait from the time the goods were sold in the fall until such time as they were sold in the upper country during the following year.[20]

In the fall of 1863, he noted that his profits on certain categories of hardware, boots and shoes, and dry goods were slight and that he had lost money on some dry goods purchased at excessively high rates. In November, however, he reported that:

> We are not selling many goods lower than original costs in N. Y. currency—our rates being gold—& on many goods are getting cost and charges gold and on many small wares more—Early in the year we were making money fast as some goods on the way had advanced and we were making more than the difference between gold and currency. Now however we are making money slowly as our old goods which cost low are pretty nearly cleaned out except old stock of Common Boots, some shoes and Hats & hardware rubbish—[21]

From this evidence it seems that Failing's principal additional sources of gain, other than the fact that his business had expanded, were inventory profits. Since gold averaged 145.2 in 1863, and since he sold few goods at less than the currency prices in gold, it may be stated with certainty that his margin on the sale of goods averaged at least 45 per cent.

During 1864 as the greenback value of gold advanced rapidly from an average of 155.5 in January, to 176.3 in June, and to a high of 258.1 in July, Henry Failing continued to collect the premium on gold and to purchase on credit. But he became increasingly wary about contracting a large indebtedness in currency at New York. As long as gold was rising he increased his gold indebtedness at Portland, while using the premium from his remittances to make more cash purchases and to discount his paper. In June, when gold paid a premium of more than 100 per cent, he determined to pay his recent purchases made at high currency rates as rapidly as possible. He also noted that, "It may be that gold will continue to advance as it has in the past and it would be better to let the payments mature and save interest and perhaps get a larger premium, but I think it best to send all I can and be on the safe side."[22]

He thus hesitated to move too far in the direction of making cash purchases. Perhaps he could not afford to do so although there seems to have been no particular limit upon his credit at Portland. He reported in July that his gold indebtedness at Ladd and Tilton's, at two per cent per month, was as large as he cared to make it. The main reason, however, was that he continued to make money by purchasing on time while the currency depreciated further. His profits on dry goods were due to these factors alone, and he could sell boots and shoes at ten per cent less than New York currency cost and still make money. He could have purchased many goods, particularly hardware, almost as cheaply in San Francisco as in New York, and would have done so, "If it were not for the profits made by purchasing these goods on time and the depreciation of the currency . . . before payments matured . . ." In September 1864, he reported that his profits had been fair, even large on some goods purchased the previous winter and paid for when the premium on gold was high. But the rise in the price of cotton goods, as well as other dry goods and boots and shoes continued greater proportionately than the advance of gold and thus narrowed the profit margin.[23]

The tables turned when gold fell from the average of 254.1 in August to 225.5 in September, and 207.2 in October. Failing, learning with alarm that it had fallen suddenly to 193 on September 27, wrote as follows:

> The decline of gold has been more sudden that I anticipated, and though I have anticipated loss in purchasing on credit when gold should fall, I did not mean to get caught to such an extent on dry goods. I could not expect however to get through without losing at least some of what has been made by paying for credit purchases at high rates of gold. I could have avoided this by borrowing heavily in gold and purchasing nearly all for cash . . .[24]

He realized that even if gold remained above 200, which it did through February 1865, that he would lose money on dry goods and that the profit margin on all goods purchased when gold was high would be small. He reported heavy losses on the dry goods that had been purchased after gold had reached 200. He therefore determined to increase his gold indebtedness at Portland, convert all his available funds into currency, and authorized Hatt to make cash purchases and to discount notes in the East as rapidly as possible. His fall purchases were at extremely high rates, and he saw little chance to make any money on the greater portion of them even though gold still held above 200.

As the end of the war approached gold fell precipitously from an average of 205.5 in February, 1865, to 173.8 in March, 148.5 in April, and 135.6 in May. Failing continued to borrow and to make cash purchases for orders that he had to make while the profit margins narrowed or disappeared entirely. In March he reported heavy losses on many goods, especially boots. He also lost a large consignment of uninsured goods on board the bark *Industry,* wrecked at the mouth of the Columbia on March 15. In addition to losses due to the decline of gold and shipwreck, he had a large interest account to pay and expected to lose sizeable accounts in bad debts because of several failures at Boise and elsewhere in the interior. In April he was letting his stock run down, ordering very few goods, taking his chances in the San Francisco market in purchasing merchandise he had to have on hand, while taking losses on boots and shoes and cotton goods. Cotton goods had fallen so rapidly in the East that Portland dealers became frightened and lowered their prices drastically.[25] Failing determined now to convert all his indebtedness to gold and regretted not having done so some sixty days earlier. He reflected upon his situation as follows:

> It is not very pleasant . . . to lose such an amount as I have by the advance of the currency, but I have not fretted over it much, as I have always thought that peace and a return to a solid basis would amply compensate us for any loss— Latterly trade has been to a great extent a lottery.[26]

During the remaining months of 1865 and throughout 1866 Failing found business difficult. The days of extreme fluctuations of the currency were over, but the prices of goods had the tendency to remain high, and did not decline in the same proportion as gold. He ran up his gold indebtedness to $50,000 by July, 1865, and continued to borrow thereafter. He was fortunate in being able to borrow $20,000 from Multnomah County at the legal rate of 10 per cent per annum, and the rest from the Ladd and Tilton Bank at 1½ per cent per month. He had to refuse credit to some of his best customers. In November 1865 he reported that there were scarcely any goods that would bring more than a very small profit over the cost of importation, and in July 1866, that on some goods there was no profit at all. His profits for 1865 were only $2,900.[27]

A business slump struck Portland and the entire West Coast immediately after the war. This coincided with the waning of the Idaho rush, and Portland's failure to capture much of the Montana trade, and marks the beginning of the period of relatively slower development following the mining boom. The editor of the *Oregonian* again observed, as he had done in 1860, that the region's capital had been largely accumulated from the profits of trade, that insufficient amounts had been invested in home manufactures, and that the available money was controlled by a small group of men.[28]

Some people thought that the dull times were due, possibly, to the far western resistance to greenbacks. Bowles, on his visit in the summer of 1865, observed that this was the liveliest question being debated on the coast. While at San Francisco in August after completing his Oregon tour, he wrote:

> Our national currency of greenbacks are [*sic*] seen here simply as merchandise; you buy and sell them at the brokers, for about seventy-five cents in coin to the dollar. Of course being made a 'legal tender' by United States law it is competent to pay a debt here with them; but no man who shall do this once, without the sum being made proportionately larger of course, could henceforth have any credit or standing in this mercantile community. . . . But since only activity and prosperity are seen to have resulted in the eastern States,—while depression and dullness have been creeping over affairs in these States,—there has been a gradual change in public sentiment on the subject. Out of San Francisco, and especially in Oregon and Nevada, there is evidently a preponderating feeling now in favor of introducing the national currency.[29]

During the war years Failing had met the problems of competition by purchasing as advantageously as possible. In 1863 he required Hatt to make more purchases direct from the manufacturers and to rely less upon the New York jobbers. His competitors, he noted, purchased boots and shoes and hardware almost exclusively from the manufacturers, and he was forced to do so if he were to compete. The jobbers had been careless in many instances, while the manufacturers always shipped the merchandise in good condition. Since some manufacturers required cash purchases, Failing tried to keep a sufficient supply of ready cash in Hatt's hands for this purpose.[30]

The tastes of the Portland market, according to Failing, were rapidly changing. He no longer could work off poor or damaged goods, and reported that he did not dare offer his customers some of the "trash" he had on hand. This "is no market to sell trash because it is cheap," he declared. With reference to an inferior brand of hammer, he reported that "to show them to a man is to be laughed at and people would hardly take them as a gift. During the past 10 years we have sold an immense amount of trash, but it will do no longer."[31]

He had kept an inferior line of boots and shoes, while specializing in better grades of other goods, and certain small dealers who did not have credit elsewhere had to purchase boots and shoes from him almost of necessity. This practice had to be abandoned and Hatt succeeded in making arrangements with B. D. Godfrey and other New England shoe manufacturers for quality merchandise. Godfrey, himself, visited the Willamette Valley, and in 1866 was manufacturing the "Willamette Valley boot" expressly for Failing and Hatt. Boots and shoes did not pay well during the latter part of the war and even lost money for Failing, but this was the kind of merchandise that had to be kept on hand to attract customers and thus aid in the sale of other more profitable goods.[32]

Miners used only one kind of gold pan and a San Francisco house tried to monopolize its sale. Both Failing and Corbett tried to purchase them from the eastern manufacturer who made them, but failed. Corbett then supplied a sample to another eastern manufacturer and began receiving a supply in 1863. He even took the precaution of requiring them to be packed in square boxes surrounded by other goods so the San Francisco dealers would not suspect that he was importing them. Failing informed Hatt repeatedly that the gold pan had to be made of Russian iron without a seam and to exact specifications; a 16-inch diameter at the top, 10 inches across the bottom, and two and one-half inches deep.

The Portland wholesaler had to give special attention to brand names. The "Eureka" pick handle, manufactured exclusively by Turner and Day for William Alvord and Company of San Francisco was most popular. Failing purchased some from Alvord, and not knowing that "Eureka" was the special brand of Alvord, had Hatt searching for that brand in the East. He finally requested Turner and Day to send him pick handles precisely the same as those sent to Alvord, and to have them marked "Failing" if possible. It was a common practice of the manufacturer of spades and shovels to use the distributor's name as the brand and thus Failing received different kinds of shovels marked "Failing and Hatt," "Hatt," or "Henry Failing."[33] The following argument written in December 1864, must have impressed Hatt decidedly on the importance of a particular brand:

> I do not think I can do anything with any other make of axes than Hunts. You must understand that while competition is great and prices cut down to the lowest point . . . they want certain makes of goods and no substitute will answer. . . . If Hunts axes instead of being $18 were $24 [per dozen] & could be had no lower, it would be idle to offer another make though as good for $12. . . . You will see some reason for this when I tell you that most of these goods are carried by water 200 to 250 miles at an expense of $45 to $60 pr ton ships measurement and then packed or wagoned 350 to 500 miles at from 10 to 30 cts pr lb. according to the condition of the roads. You will see how little it matters whether the trader gets his axes @ $1 or $10 pr doz less if he does not get what he wants. . . .[34]

Henry W. Corbett, Failing's friend and competitor, met similar problems in purchasing, but seems to have been able to overcome them more easily. He expanded his capital resources at a fairly rapid pace during the early 1860s. In 1862 he had money to loan and made this fact known to his customers, and also received money from his customers for the same purpose. Thus, like Failing, he was trusted to fulfill a banking function. He frequently made small loans to Failing himself and on one occasion offered to endorse Failing's notes in the East to help his competitor meet his obligations. Corbett kept accounts at two New York banks, and though he seldom had occasion to do so, he could obtain loans in New York at any time.[35] As he became more active in other entrepreneurial activities, and in politics,* the later

---

*Corbett had been chairman of the Republican State Central Committee and was elected United States Senator in 1866. When Oregon unexpectedly voted for the Union ticket, he wrote as follows to Capt. John Mullan, June 5, 1862, CFOHS:

records of his firm reveal less about his finances. He undoubtedly capitalized upon the mining demand and throughout the 1860s merchandising continued to be his principal effort.

Failing made the following observation about Corbett's financial condition in June, 1863:

> Corbett has a large capital and though he has never made money as fast as we have yet he has kept his capital all in his business and has no one to divide with, has now a large capital in his business and a great deal outside which he can call in at any moment. His stock is not now and has not been as large as ours, nor has he sold as many goods in our opinion —but as he has purchased chiefly for cash for the year past, he is probably very easy . . .

Corbett correctly anticipated the rising prices of 1864, laid in a heavy stock the previous fall, and no doubt did well during 1864 as the mining demand held. Failing, however, felt that he could not take the risk of wintering a large stock of goods and of waiting until they were sold in the mining country. Corbett's stock was twice the size of Failing's in the fall of 1863.[36]

Thus, while Failing's mercantile career paralleled Corbett's, he accumulated capital at a slower pace. He seems to have been less venturesome and perhaps less shrewd than his neighbor. As noted above he did not become sole proprietor of his firm until 1864, while Corbett had rid himself of all partnership restrictions ten years earlier. By 1866, when Corbett's business was largely conducted by subordinates and when he was preparing to take his seat in the United States Senate, Failing was so bound to his counter that he almost failed to manage a trip to New York, his first chance since coming to Oregon in 1851, to be with his ailing wife. He wrote: "I have been accustomed to selling nearly all the goods, keep my own books, and unless I am here all the time my business suffers, and with the large amount of credit we extend, failures or embarrassments

---

"Glorious Union triumph . . . this is beyond the most sanguine expectations of any Union men we did not know "Secesh" was quite so dead. I don't think the Dixie party have elected a single man to the Legislature. The Union must be preserved so say you so say we all, without it our government is a failure, with it we are all powerful and defy all other nations under the sun. What say you—."

are likely at any time to occur, and my presence here is necessary."[37]

He did manage the trip and returned to Portland, where in the latter part of the decade he, in close association with Corbett, became one of the city's leading financiers.

Chapter XIV

The Passing of the Frontier

Gold flowing from the mines of Idaho, Montana, and eastern Oregon during the early 1860s provided a vital stimulus for the development of the Pacific Northwest. Numerous new towns with flourishing business enterprises sprang into existence in the Inland Empire, and interior valleys that might have remained untouched for years saw the rise of new agricultural communities. Monopolistic companies, the Oregon Steam Navigation Company, Wells, Fargo and Company and Ben Holladay's stage and steamship companies developed and dominated the new lines of transportation and communication. Stagecoaches provided better mail, passenger and express service, and the telegraph brought almost instantaneous communication with the East to penetrate the barriers that had isolated the distant region. For Portland the Columbia River trade with an expanding inland hinterland assured greater stability and permanence as it grew from village to city. Capital accumulated from the profits of trade and transportation became the foundation of the Willamette Valley's industrial development in the latter part of the century. From 1860 to 1870 the region, including Montana, grew in population from 64,059 to 150,462, an actual growth that was small in comparison to the Middle West, but still a gain of 135 per cent, and with Montana excluded, of slightly more than 100 per cent.[1]

Improved Communications

The stagecoach and express businesses developed rapidly as the mining frontier advanced into all parts of the Far West. The California Stage Company extended stage and overland mail service to the Willamette Valley in 1860, when it received the government mail subsidy for service on the new route from Sacramento to Portland. Stages left each point daily on seven-day runs from April to December and twelve-day runs during the remaining months of the year. Although the steamships made the trip from San

Francisco to Portland in less than five days on fortnightly schedules, the daily mail service by stage was a considerable improvement. The California Stage Company made connections with the Butterfield stages to give transcontinental passenger service to Portlanders. But more important was the mail connection with the Pony Express which had been inaugurated by the Central Overland California and Pike's Peak Express Company in April, 1860.

The most notable figure in the development of the stage-coach business in the Far West during the 1860s was Ben Holladay who, in 1862, gained control of the Central Overland and Pike's Peak Express Company, formerly the firm of Russell, Majors, and Waddell. Holladay had been engaged in transportation from Atchison to Salt Lake City and, by 1862, had a sizeable interest in the Central Overland and Pike's Peak Express Company. When this company failed, Holladay, to protect his own investment, took over all its assets for $100,000. Immediately he found himself in a commanding position due, first, to the expansion of mining in the Far West, and, second, to the disruption of Butterfield's southern route to California caused by the Civil War.

Holladay rapidly reorganized the company, now called the Overland Stage Company, and expanded its services from Atchison to Salt Lake City. In 1864, after securing mail contracts, he extended lines to Virginia City, Montana and to Walla Walla, Umatilla, and The Dalles to connect with the steamers of the Oregon Steam Navigation Company. Holladay let a sub-contract for the Boise City-The Dalles run, first to Thomas and Company, who after operating the line for a time, sold out to Hailey and Greathouse in 1866. Through passenger and mail service from Portland to Salt Lake City, established in 1867, reduced the time of communication with the East to six days less than that required via Sacramento.[2] Thus, a figure who has been variously but inadequately interpreted, controlled a giant monopoly that dominated the stage and mail services of the Pacific Northwest as well as a vital segment of the transcontinental route.

In 1865 the California Stage Company disintegrated after its failure to get a favorable mail contract for its northern route to Portland from Sacramento. The mail subsidy had been $220,000. Louis McLane, president of the Overland

Mail Company and general agent for Wells, Fargo and Company, assumed control of the Oregon line. In 1866 McLane sold the line to H. W. Corbett, who intended to make it "a permanent Oregon Institution. . . ." Corbett obtained the mail contract for $179,000 on a bid some $44,000 below that of any other "responsible" person, and paid $94,000 for the stock, barns, and other equipment of the route. This was one of Corbett's several investments at this stage of his career and one of the most unpromising.

Corbett tried to make the best of a bad bargain. He thoroughly reorganized the line, now known as the Oregon Stage Company, and urged every conceivable economy in its operation. "Through in Six Days to Portland," he advertised. In September 1866, shortly after he took control of the route, he reported that "Staging is very good this and last month quite as good as I expected." But he requested the post office department to allow him to suspend Sunday service and to dispatch the cumbersome loads of government documents by sea rather than by stage. "I dont [sic] desire to complain if I have a hard contract," Corbett wrote, "as I intend to carry it through as faithfully as I know how, if I dont loose [sic] over $10,000 a year on it, I can stand it." Corbett actively managed the stage company during 1866 and 1867, but after taking his seat in the United States Senate in the latter year he gave up his contract owing to a law against his holding it and possibly to his desire to rid himself of a "bad bargain" as alleged by a Chico resident. A group of capitalists, including Corbett's brother, Elijah, of Portland, purchased the route and obtained a new subsidy. In 1870 a new group, referred to as monopolists in the *Oregonian,* purchased the Oregon and California Stage Company. Operations along this line between the rail termini continued until the completion of the railroad route between Portland and Sacramento in 1887.[3]

From 1855, when Adams and Company failed, Wells, Fargo and Company dominated the express business of the Far West and to a considerable extent the banking business as well. Their agents handled most of the gold dust in transit from Idaho and Montana, via steamboat, ocean steamer, and stage coach to the mint in San Francisco. No new community of any importance was without its Wells, Fargo office, which in every town was as universal an institution as the saloon. The *Oregonian* gave the following tribute to this company for its many services and efficiency:

> The people of all new sections are indebted a great deal to Wells, Fargo & Co., for the facilities afforded by their express to hear from the outside world. Before any mail facilities can be established in the regions that become suddenly peopled through the discovery of gold, and opened up to commercial and mercantile communities, Wells, Fargo & Co. send their messengers on ahead and become the medium through which business to the amount of millions is transacted. Even after mails are established, this express continues to be the most reliable means of communication for years. Their rates of carrying are greater, but there is no uncertainty about the matter. Just now, Wells, Fargo & Co. are all we have to depend upon for obtaining our exchanges, letters, etc., in this valley. We could not hear from the Capital, or any interior town on the overland route, were it not for them, and we are greatly indebted to them for favors. A community like this can appreciate Wells Fargo & Co., even at the expense of a Government, which they have contributed, and are still contributing daily, to support.[4]

Wells, Fargo and Company had difficulties with Ben Holladay concerning the shipment of express over his stage line, and in 1866 threatened to establish a competing line between Salt Lake City and Denver. Holladay, realizing the effect that the completion of the transcontinental railroad would have upon the stage line, sold the entire Holladay Overland Mail and express system to Wells, Fargo and Company on November 1, 1866. Holladay received $1,500,000 in cash, $300,000 in Wells, Fargo stock, and a directorship in the company. Earlier, in 1864, Wells, Fargo and Company had absorbed the stage lines of the Overland Mail and the Pioneer Stage Line, operating between Salt Lake City and Sacramento. Thus the powerful express company came to monopolize the stagecoach and express business of the transcontinental route.

In 1869, the Central Pacific Railroad virtually forced Wells, Fargo and Company to pay $5,000,000 for the Pacific Union Express Company, a subsidiary of Central Pacific, or go out of business. The Pacific Union Express Company had few real assets, but had the all-important and exclusive express contract with Central Pacific. Wells, Fargo made the deal and continued in the express business on the expanding Central and Southern Pacific Railroad system until it merged into the American Express Company in 1918.

Most important in reducing the time of communication was the telegraph. An east-west telegraph line to San Francisco supplanted the short-lived Pony Express in 1861. A local line already existed between Sacramento and Yreka, so Portland, after 1861, received telegraphic communications in four and one-half days via the California stages from Yreka. Oregon capitalists incorporated the Oregon Telegraph Company at Portland on March 26, 1862, with a capital stock of $75,000, to connect Portland and Yreka. W. S. Ladd was president, Simeon G. Reed, secretary, and H. W. Corbett, treasurer. The line was in operation between Portland and Salem by April, 1863, but the loss of wire by shipwreck prevented its completion until March 5, 1864, when Portland received its first through message from San Francisco. Portland had a public celebration, the *Oregonian* came out with an extra edition with news in 20 hours from New York, and on March 8, 1864 the mayors of Portland, Maine, and Portland, Oregon, exchanged greetings by telegraph. The network soon was extended to Puget Sound towns and New Westminster in 1864 and 1865, and inland to Boise in 1868.[6] Although direct communication was delayed until 1864, the few days required for news via Yreka was a vast improvement over the month-long wait via Panama which had prevailed prior to 1861. Throughout the Civil War years Portland businessmen received news of the conflict and the indispensable New York price quotations relatively soon.

Oregon's Ocean Commerce, 1861-69

Throughout the 1860s Oregon's external trade was still largely coastwise between Portland and San Francisco and between Portland and Victoria. An attempt was made during mid-decade to establish a regular packet service to Honolulu, but trade between Oregon and the islands remained intermittent.[7] Manufactured goods purchased by Oregon merchants in New York continued to flow via the Cape Horn or Panama routes to San Francisco, where they were trans-shipped on board the steamships or sailing vessels

299

on the San Francisco-Portland-Victoria run. A steamship and various small craft made regular trips from Portland to Victoria and Puget Sound, while the large ships in the Puget Sound lumber trade avoided the Columbia River.

Gold was the region's most important commodity during the decade. From 1861 through 1867 large sums of gold dust came down the Columbia River on the boats of the Oregon Steam Navigation Company in the custody of Wells, Fargo agents or in the hands of passengers. On single trips to San Francisco the ocean steamships carried consignments of gold dust ranging in value from a few thousand up to $300,000, and on one occasion, $750,000, plus unknown quantities in the private possession of passengers. Wells, Fargo and Company had charge of by far the largest treasure shipments, although Tracy and King, Ladd and Tilton's Bank, and individual businessmen shipped small quantities on occasion. The total amount of gold dust assayed at Portland in 1863 was $4,505,731, and Wells, Fargo shipped $6,200,000 from Portland in 1865, $5,400,000 in 1866, and $4,001,000 in 1867.[8] Very little Montana gold came to Portland, and much of the gold from the Boise mines went overland to San Francisco via the Humboldt route.[9]

Other aspects of Oregon's export trade during the early 1860s can be told briefly. In 1861 considerable quantities of low priced flour flowed to San Francisco to relieve the surpluses of the Willamette Valley. But throughout the new gold rush period Oregon flour found its principal markets in the mining regions and flowed inland to Idaho, eastern Oregon and Washington, and coastwise to Victoria. Consequently little Oregon flour was shipped to San Francisco during this period, when, as shown by Table 8, the wholesale price at Portland fluctuated at relatively high levels. Oregon's most valuable exports other than gold, which flowed to San Francisco or Victoria, were apples, bacon, butter, lumber and raw wool. Small quantities of hides, leather, fruit trees, and other produce also were shipped to these markets.[10] As mentioned earlier, Oregon wool first reached the eastern markets in 1862, to inaugurate a trade that became increasingly important during the decade. Professor Lomax's statistics[11] for Oregon's wool exports for the decade are as follows:

300

1862	410,200 pounds	1866	758,200 pounds
1863	342,800 "	1867	662,000 "
1864	430,200 "	1868	421,460 "
1865	791,600 "	1869	1,039,400 "

There was ample business for the sailing vessels on the San Francisco-Portland route during the Idaho rush period. In 1859 and 1860 only the bark *Live Yankee* had made the run with any semblance of regularity, but in 1861, the Oregon-Calfornia packet service was revived and reached its height during 1862 and 1863. The barks *Jane A. Falkenberg, Almatia, Live Yankee, Samuel Merritt, Industry,* and *Helen W. Almy* sailed the route regularly during the first half of the decade. In the aggregate these ships entered the Columbia thirty-two times during 1862, and twenty-two during 1863. The bar at the mouth of the Columbia was always hazardous for the sailing vessel, and here on March 15, 1865 the bark *Industry* and her cargo were smashed to bits with the loss of seventeen lives. She was succeeded by the bark *W. B. Scranton* which met the same fate but with no loss of life at approximately the same place in 1866.[12]

Declining freights and competition greatly reduced the business of the sailing vessels during 1865 and 1866. In 1865 merchants curtailed their purchases due to the high costs and it became difficult to load out the sailing vessels with full cargoes at San Francisco. In January the *Falkenberg* sailed northward in ballast. Later in the year Captain Wiggins placed the brig *Sunny South* in opposition to the Oregon-California packets to reduce the freights from $5.00 to $4.00 per ton. In September the barks *Samuel Merritt* and *Live Yankee* carried freights from San Francisco to Portland at only $1.50 per ton. In 1866, with the rise of intensive competition between the steamship lines, captains and agents of sailing vessels had difficulty getting any freights at all.[13]

From 1861 to 1866 two steamship lines, those of Holladay and Flint, and the California Steam Navigation Company, served Portland. In 1861 Holladay and Flint had taken over the northern route after purchasing six steamships from the Pacific Mail Steamship Company for $250,000, or the value of any one of them in good order. Ben Holladay, it should be noted, was just beginning his phenomenal rise to power in the overland transportation business at this time. The Holladay steamship line ran one ship, usually the *Sierra Nevada,* and the California Steam Navigation Company continued to employ their two old steamships *Pacific* and *Brother Jonathan* on the San Francisco-Portland-Victoria route.[14]

The two companies shared the trade and by mutual agreement kept the rates uniform. Portlanders considered the steamship service inadequate and resented its monopoly by California interests. The old and frequently over-burdened ships were commanded by arrogant officers and the rates for freight at $10 per ton, and passage at $45 for cabin and $25 for steerage, were considered outrageously high. In spite of complaints about the service, two of the "old tubs" of the companies, the *Sierra Nevada* and the *Brother Jonathan,* made record runs of 72 and 69 hours, respectively, from San Francisco to Portland during the rush year of 1862.[15] Except for a few extra trips occasionally the steamship companies, between them, provided regular fortnightly service.[16]

On July 30, 1865, one of the worst marine disasters in the history of the North Pacific occurred when the *Brother Jonathan* struck a submerged rock and sank off Crescent City. She went down with all but nineteen of nearly 200 passengers, many of whom were businessmen and their families from Portland and other towns in the Pacific North-west. This was a severe blow and feeling against the steam-ship service intensified. The *Jonathan* had been overloaded at San Francisco in spite of the advice of her captain, and many believed that she would have completed the trip successfully if this had not been the case. The *Orizaba,* another of the California Steam Navigation Company's old ships, replaced the ill-fated *Jonathan,* much to the conster-nation of Portlanders.[17]

For some time the Oregon Steam Navigation Company had considered placing a first class steamship on the San Francisco-Portland route. The company, in 1865, faced the competition of the overland routes from Sacramento to Boise, and saw in the sea route from San Francisco to Port-land the weakest link in the transportation system serving the Idaho frontier because of high rates and poor service.

The *Oregonian* repeatedly urged Oregon capitalists to place a home-owned ship on the sea route. Simeon G. Reed in pressing the matter with the Oregon Steam Navigation Company noted that neither Holladay nor the California Steam Navigation Company would place new ships on the run as long as they could monopolize the trade with their "old tubs." It was rumored that Holladay intended to place two new ships on the Oregon run, but D. F. Bradford, writing from New York in August 1865, warned Reed not to "believe anything of the kind . . . I see Holliday [*sic*] often but he is a regular blower & my opinion is he will run the ships he has for all they are worth & then he is done . . ."[18]

Consequently the Oregon Steam Navigation Company contracted with the New York shipbuilding firm of Lawrence and Foulkes in the fall of 1865 for the construction of a new, well-appointed steamship to be named the *Oregonian*. The ship was built in secrecy, in order to prevent possible retaliation from Holladay, and launched in April 1866. She sailed to San Francisco but was never placed on the route for which she was intended because other new ships were already there.

The Anchor Line, an enterprise of G. Y. and J. Patton of Maine, placed the fine new steamship *Montana* on the San Francisco-Portland run in competition with the old lines in 1866. Holladay's new California, Oregon and Mexico Steamship Company, capitalized at $2,000,000, brought the new steamship *Oriflamme* from the China coast to meet the challenge of the Anchor Line. The Pattons planned to have two steamships on the route and while the *Idaho* was under construction in 1866, only the *Montana* ran in competition with the ships of Holladay and the California Steam Navigation Company.[19]

Competition brought drastic rate reductions in 1866, as the older companies met the competition of the Anchor Line. Freight rates fell to $3.00 per ton, and passenger rates to $20 for cabin and $10 for steerage. The *Orizaba* carried passengers at $10 and $3.00. Business was hardly profitable for any of the three lines as their ships raced back and forth between San Francisco and Portland. The *Montana* made eighteen trips; the ships of Holladay's company, nineteen;

and those of the California Steam Navigation Company, twenty-one, for an unprecedented total of fifty-eight trips by steamship for the route during 1866. Once rid of the disadvantage of having only one ship on the route, the Anchor Line was expected to win the contest when the *Idaho* appeared, since many shippers were disposed to give their preference to the new line.

The *Idaho* made only one trip under the Anchor banner early in 1867, and her appearance was the signal for Holladay to act. He organized the new North Pacific Transportation Company by consolidating the California, Oregon and Mexico Steamship Company, the Anchor Line, and the maritime interests of the California Steam Navigation Company. The Oregon Steam Navigation Company sold its new ship, the *Oregonian,* to the North American Steamship Company with the understanding that she would not compete against the Holladay line. The Holladay fleet now numbered some sixteen or seventeen steamships. The *Oriflamme,* Holladay's flagship, because famous, or notorious, as the scene of one of the stagecoach king's most lavish parties on her excursion to Victoria in 1869.[20]

By April 1867, rates for passage between Portland and San Francisco rose to $35 and $20, freights from Portland to San Francisco to $5.00 and $6.00 per ton; and from San Francisco to Portland to $6.00 and $7.00 per ton. The editor of the *Oregonian* now resumed his criticisms of monopoly and condemned San Francisco's stranglehold upon Portland's commerce. He also complained that Portland capitalists had failed to give the Anchor Line adequate support and had not given the owners of the steamship *Oregonian* sufficient encouragement.[21]

Entrance into the world market for wheat and flour was a most significant factor in the commercial development of the Far West during the 1860s. Before the Civil War California flour and wheat had found limited markets in China, Australia, and other parts of the Pacific, and in 1860 it began to flow to New York. The Chinese market improved during the early part of the decade, but, most important, California now shared in supplying the growing market in Great Britain to augment American wheat exports, which increased nine-fold during the Civil War. British ships came through the Golden Gate in increasing numbers to load out large cargoes for the English and European markets. Grain exports now sustained the Cape Horn trade to reverse the previous emphasis upon imports to the Pacific. The world demand, caused primarily by the accelerated industrialization of Europe, stimulated wheat production in all parts of the world, and California, in spite of severe drouth in 1863, kept pace with the other principal grain producing states in the United States.[22]

Oregon had little or no exportable surpluses of flour or wheat as long as the mining demand held, however. Production seems not to have increased much during this period and actual shortages existed during 1865. Flour destined for Idaho and Montana wholesaled at from $7.00 to $14 per barrel on the Portland market during the first half of 1865, and from $6.50 to $8.00 per barrel through the spring of 1866.

The Willamette Valley offered an attractive field for the expansion of agriculture as the world demand for breadstuffs increased. Here, it was estimated, less than one-tenth of the land was under cultivation. The average yield was 25 bushels per acre, but with careful cultivation the land would produce 50 bushels per acre easily, and in contrast with California, crop failures were unknown. Jesse Applegate observed in 1865 that the incentive for real cultivation was lacking among the Missourians, Tennesseeans, and Kentuckians who composed much of the farming population of the valley, because labor was dear, the markets distant, and the grain grew so easily. Land values ranged between $5.00 and $25 per acre depending upon improvements and nearness to rivers and towns, and some of the best farms were valued at $50 to $100 per acre.[23]

In 1866, as the mining demand waned, flour resumed its first rank position among Oregon's produce exports. As California wheat flowed to Europe and New York, Oregon flour helped to make up the deficit in the San Francisco market. During 1867, California wheat and flour reached the New York market via the Cape Horn route at cheaper freight rates than western wheat could be shipped by rail from Chicago. Some Oregon flour now found its way to the New York market where it sold at $15-$16 per barrel, currency, in the spring and summer of 1867. Although it was well received, there was a tendency to confuse it with California flour.

Flour fell to $4.00-$5.50 per barrel at Portland in the spring of 1867, but rose suddenly to the $6.00-$7.50 levels in the fall in response to demands in the East and abroad. Now, virtually for the first time, the world demand for breadstuffs determined the Oregon price. In October wheat hauled in by wagon at the rate of 30,000 bushels per week averaged $1.12 per bushel.[24]

Portland's produce exports increased substantially while the exportation of gold decreased during the later years of the decade. According to the estimates of S. J. McCormick, publisher of the *Portland City Directory*, based upon published shipping manifests, Portland's total exports for these years were as follows:

	Produce	Gold
1866	$ 555,457.00	$8,076,600.00
1867	2,462,793.75	4,001,000.00
1868	2,780,408.00	3,677,850.00
1869	1,066,502.00	3,018,657.00[25]

Portland's exports flowed principally to San Francisco, where, as mentioned above, the wool and now some of the wheat and flour were re-exported to markets in the East. McCormick's estimates of the value of the leading produce exports from Portland in 1867 and 1868 are given in Table 8.

As Portland's produce exports increased merchants experienced less difficulty meeting the demands for money on "steamer days" than formerly. In November 1867, the editor of the *Oregonian* commented optimistically:

> Of late the produce shipments have so nearly cancelled the New York bills for merchandise, that steamer days come and go with scarcely a ripple in the financial current. It used to be said that the constant drain of money to pay for imported goods was the great curse of this coast. Happily the revolution now going on in the breadstuffs trade is rapidly removing the curse and turning the treasure flows in our favor.

Oregon, however, had not reached the happy state of affairs when the value of her exports equalled the value of her imports.[26]

TABLE 8
ESTIMATES OF THE VALUE OF PRODUCE EXPORTS
FROM PORTLAND, 1867-68

	1867	1868
Flour	$ 727,680	$ 630,305
Wheat	68,715	67,142
Apples	33,596	29,625
Dried Apples	59,496	74,770
Oats	. . . .	91,496
Bacon	62,227	50,556
Salmon	29,708	24,740
Beef	15,300	27,795
Butter	33,808	28,810
Eggs	17,640	22,695
Wool	132,360	91,520
Horses	29,800	21,600
Pork and Lard	20,043	38,258

(Taken from *Portland City Directory,* 1868, p. 26; 1869, p. 15.)

Downriver commerce on the Columbia began in the mid-decade. During the rush years the freight traffic was almost exclusively upriver, but as the interior made the transition from mining to agriculture and stock raising the pattern changed. In 1865 wool, vegetables, hides and a few other items began to flow downriver, and the first shipments of flour from the Walla Walla mills were made in 1867. The Oregon Steam Navigation Company reduced the downriver freight rate from $17.50 to $6.00 per ton, and soon enlarged their boats to accommodate bulk shipments. The downriver freight increased steadily during the next decade, and by 1878 the Oregon Steam Navigation Company's annual shipments of wheat from the upper Columbia to Portland exceeded 20,000 tons.[27]

The emerging export pattern helped to reduce Portland's dependence upon San Francisco. Resentment intensified during the later 1860s as Portland newspapers denounced the San Francisco servitude at every opportunity and advocated direct trade with New York. There seemed to be enough capital at Portland to establish a line of packets from New York and sufficient trade to make such a venture profitable. Why should Portland merchants humble themselves before the arrogant magnates of the emporium of the Pacific by paying extra freight and commission charges? Freights via

307

the Cape Horn route from New York to Portland would cost but $1.00 per ton more than from New York to San Francisco, and Portland now had the means to rid itself of the annoying relationship. Finally in 1869, Mercer and Company established the long hoped for line of packets, but the experiment met with indifferent success.[28]

Far more important in freeing Portland from its dependence upon San Francisco was the foreign grain trade which began in 1868 or 1869. As mentioned above grain from the Far West was already important in the markets of Europe as California wheat flowed outward in increasing quantities in the 1860s. In 1868, 193 grain-laden ships sailed through the Golden Gate on voyages via Cape Horn to Liverpool and other English or European ports, and in 1869 the number leaving San Francisco reached a total of 240. The first grain ship clearing Portland for a foreign port to join the procession around Cape Horn sailed either in 1868 or 1869. While some writers insist that a ship loaded with wheat sailed from the Columbia River in the former year, it is a matter of record that the *Helen Angier* left Portland bound for Liverpool on April 24, 1869 with a cargo of 22,166 centals of wheat valued at $31,000. During the 1870-71 season twelve vessels cleared Portland for Great Britain with 198,780 centals (100-pound sacks) of wheat worth $399,519. The principal Portland shippers were the firms, Allen and Lewis and Corbitt and Macleay. Wheat exports from Portland increased during the 1870s as production in the Inland Empire and the Willamette Valley expanded rapidly. During the 1877-78 season 2,201,957 centals valued at $4,621,595 flowed outward from Portland. By the early eighties the Portland grain fleet numbered about 100 ships, while the number sailing from San Francisco during the 1881-82 season was 559. Wheat had become the great staple of the developing farm lands of the Pacific Northwest, and throughout the rest of the century and on into the next the grain export trade was vital to the region's economy.[29]

The trade pattern had begun to change in 1869, and it appeared that Portland would soon become independent of San Francisco. The editor of the *Oregonian,* writing in August of 1869, commented as follows:

It cannot be doubted that San Francisco is gradually losing her hold upon the trade of Oregon. Once she commanded it absolutely. Nearly all the goods sold or consumed in Oregon were purchased there or came through that mart, paying a large profit to her business men. But now we receive direct shipments from New York, from the Islands and from China . . . , and for the rest San Francisco . . . is gradually becoming a forwarding point through which our supplies are received. . . . In many lines of goods the merchants of Portland are now able to offer as favorable inducements to the buyer as can be had in San Francisco. Our interior merchants cannot now in general make it pay to pass by Portland and go to San Francisco to make their purchases.[30]

Portland's new measure of independence and the changing pattern of trade are among the several factors marking the emergence of a more mature society in the Pacific Northwest. The day of the pioneer, when Oregon farmers and merchants appreciated the great mart at San Francisco as a market for their produce and as a source of supply, had come to an end.

Industrial Beginnings

The industrial growth of the Pacific Northwest during the 1860s, while substantial for a remote frontier area, was relatively slight when compared with California and the middle western states. Oregon's principal industries, lumber and flour milling, were well established and were to develop on a greater scale later in the century as market and transportation facilities improved. The annual value of the products of Oregon's sixty-four flour mills in 1870 was $1,972,444, and of her 173 lumber mills, $1,072,061. The total value of the products of Oregon's industries in 1870 was $6,877,387; of Washington's, $2,851,052; of Idaho's, $1,047,624; and of Montana's, $2,494,511. The total value of California's industries in 1870, by contrast, was $66,594,-556, of which over nine million represented the products of her flour mills, and six million, her lumber mills.[31]

The later 1860s, however, was a period of industrial beginnings in the Willamette Valley reflecting the stimulus of gold, better market conditions, and in general, the emergence of a mature society. Here capitalists who had accumulated wealth from their merchandising, milling, transportation, and other pioneer enterprises now sought sound investments in land and promising new enterprises.

309

The woolens industry grew. The Oregon City Woolens Manufacturing Company, established in 1865 with Joel Palmer as president, soon rivaled the older mill of the Willamette Woolen Manufacturing Company at Salem. By the end of the decade there were new mills located at Dallas, Brownsville, The Dalles, and Ashland. In 1870 the total capitalization of Oregon's six woolen mills was $380,500 and the total value of the product was $492,857. In the 1870s W. S. Ladd was an officer in both the Salem and the Oregon City companies.[32]

George W. Hume, William Hume, and Andrew S. Hapgood established the region's first salmon cannery at Eagle Cliff on the Washington side of the lower Columbia in 1866. Two years earlier they had pioneered this industry, the first in the United States, on the Sacramento River. The fish run there had declined steadily after the introduction of hydraulic mining on the river in 1853, so the Humes and Hapgood moved their machinery to a new location beside the salmon-laden Columbia. During 1867, their first year of operation, Hapgood, Hume, and Company produced 4,000 cases, 48 cans to the case, which they sold to San Francisco distributors at $16 per case. Three average sized salmon, which cost 15 cents per fish, filled four dozen cans. In 1869, John West and associates established the first salmon cannery on the Oregon side of the Columbia (opposite Eagle Cliff) at Westport, where West already had a large lumber mill. H. W. Corbett and Company shipped salmon from the West cannery to Samuel T. House, Corbett's agent in New York, for distribution in the eastern market. The salmon fishing and canning industry expanded rapidly during the 1870s with thirteen canneries on the lower Columbia by 1874. By 1881 it had become a $2,000,000 industry and William Hume at that time was the leading packer with a $150,000 investment.[33]

The notable effort of Oregon capitalists to manufacture iron from Oregon's native ores at Oswego, near Portland, began in 1865 with the incorporation of the Oregon Iron Company. W. S. Ladd became president and H. C. Leonard, vice-president. Henry Failing, who had imported vast quantities of iron from the East, was among the twenty stockholders. Mining and smelting of the ore, which according to reports tested 60 per cent pure iron, began in 1866, with production in full swing the following years. Optimists labeled Oswego the "future Pittsburg" of the West. by October 1867, 224 long tons had been produced at a basic cost of $29 per ton and placed on the market at $50 per ton. At that rate, however, foundries could import iron costing $35-$37.50 at San Francisco plus $8.54 for freight, primage, and wharfage, cheaper than the selling price of Oswego iron on the Portland market. The costs of operation were high but the plant continued in production until 1869, when the furnace was blown out, after 2,395 tons of iron had been produced during the three-year period. The supply of ore, much of which was later proved to be of poor grade, was considered "inexhaustible." Production resumed in 1878 and continued intermittently until 1894, first by the Oswego Iron Company formed in 1877, and after 1882, by the Oregon Iron and Steel Company, a $1,500,000 corporation. A new and more extensive plant was built in 1887, and production reached its peak with 12,305 tons in 1890. But due to high costs of production without an ample supply of coal and of mining the low grade ore, the furnaces were blown out for the last time in 1894. Simeon G. Reed, W. S. Ladd, W. M. Ladd, E. W. Crichton, and L. B. Seeley, leading figures in the enterprise, had earnestly sought to make the industry a success.[34]

More important, at long range at least, was the paper industry launched at Oregon City in 1866 by a company headed by W. W. Buck and capitalized at $50,000. The plant opened with a rousing celebration and by 1867 had brown straw wrapping paper and manila paper on the market at $1.50 and $3.20 per ream, respectively. Raw materials used were straw and all the rags, old rope, worn out sails, and burlap that could be collected. The plant closed down in September, 1867, because of indebtedness and a sheriff's sale, but Buck and H. L. Pittock, the editor of the *Oregonian*, entered a partnership and soon had a new mill in operation on the Clackamas River. In 1871 Pittock bought out his partner and established the Clackamas Paper Manufacturing Company with a capitalization of $20,000. Pittock in 1884, along with J. K. Gill, formed the Columbia River Paper Company and built a large plant at La Camas on the Colum-

311

bia in Washington Territory.[35] From these beginnings has grown the giant paper industry of the Pacific Northwest, which today is dominated by the Crown-Zellerbach Corporation.

Henry W. Corbett, like Ladd, invested in various new and promising enterprises, while Henry Failing seems to have been more conservative and cautious. The careers of all three, however, evince a common pattern. As noted above, Corbett invested in the telegraph, river navigation, and a stagecoach line, while Ladd, one of the magnates of the Oregon Steam Navigation Company, promoted practically every new enterprise. Corbett, Failing, and Ainsworth were among the original incorporators of the Northern Pacific Railroad in 1864.[36] Corbett, also, was one of the incorporators of the ill-fated Oregon Central Railroad or as it was later known, the Oregon and California Railroad, and promoted its interests in the Senate. The complicated story of the two Oregon and California railroads and Holladay's victory over Portland capitalists in gaining the land grant for the "East Side" road is outside the limits of this study. Corbett, however, was identified with the "West Side" group and was a leading opponent of Holladay. In 1872 he purchased a controlling interest in the *Oregonian* to check the influence of Holladay's *Bulletin,* and after this task was accomplished, he retired from the newspaper business.[37]

In 1871 Corbett and Failing joined their merchandising firms into the wholesale hardware house of Corbett, Failing and Company. The day of the pioneer wholesaler in general merchandise at Portland had passed as the leading houses now specialized in particular categories of goods. Corbett and Failing were the senior members of the firm. Other members, the active managers, included Failing's younger brothers, James and Edward, Samuel T. House and for a time John A. Hatt in New York.[38]

Common to all frontiers were the businessmen who made the transition from merchant to banker and financier. As noted earlier both Corbett and Failing had begun to fulfill the functions of a banker more or less informally during the early 1860s. By 1869 they gained control of the First National Bank, established four years earlier, and increased its capital stock from $100,000 to $250,000. Failing became president, and Corbett, vice-president. Failing, while retaining an active interest in merchandising, gave his primary attention to the bank and retained the position of president for the rest of his life. C. H. Lewis of the firm Allen and Lewis and another of Portland's pioneer merchants was a stockholder in the First National and while he did his banking there he continued to accept the spare money of his customers on deposit, or to loan his surplus funds to them.[39]

W. S. Ladd, as has been noted, made the transition from pioneer merchant to banker ten years earlier than Corbett and Failing. Although the Ladd and Tilton Bank was organied as a partnership, it was managed much like a single proprietorship by Ladd himself. It had no board of directors nor loan committee and Ladd acted solely as his own judgment dictated. Ladd's attitude, according to the friendly biographer of his son, was that "the money in the bank he had made and it was his," and that "depositors had never lost through him and never would." The same writer gives the following characterization: "W. S. Ladd was an adventurous trader and speculator, he had imagination and a shrewd understanding of the strength and frailties of other men and a somewhat ruthless way of dealing with them. As was natural for a self-made man and a pioneer, he had a weakness for his own judgment and was dogmatic and dictatorial."[40]

As Portland grew from village to city with a population of 9,565 in 1870, its financial leaders also invested in lands and improvements. In 1865 Simeon G. Reed wrote as follows: "Real estate is changing hands quite lively here, and prices are advancing. The purchasers are not new comers, but in nearly every instance are old residents."[41] Portland's business leaders enjoyed good returns from such investments as land values increased and as their city experienced a series of building booms later in the century. Until recently the substantial old buildings that Ladd, Failing, and Corbett built between 1868 and 1880, as well as the tall Failing and Corbett buildings of a more recent date, have stood witness to each phase of Portland's growth and to the enterprise of its founders.

A role common to the successful businessman is that of patron of the arts of civilization. No attempt will be made here to catalog the many instances in which Corbett, Failing, and Ladd contributed to the development of religious, educational and charitable institutions, but some deserve mention. From the beginning of their careers in Portland they supported the churches. Corbett and Ladd contributed liberally to the First Presbyterian Church, the one which for many years attracted Portland's most fashionable congregation. In 1864, Corbett actively supported a struggling "Colledge [*sic*] called Tualatin Academy and Pacific University" located at Forest Grove. All three were members of the Portland Library Association which sponsored Portland's second library after 1864. Failing, who was very much interested in the success of this project, selected papers and periodicals, while a Judge Nelson was asked to select the books in New York. Most notable late in the century was the endowment of the Portland Art Museum by Corbett, Failing, and the trustees of the Ladd estate.[42]

By 1869, however, new patterns of trade and transportation affecting the Pacific Northwest had emerged to mark the end of a distinct frontier period. Portland now reached out to the markets of the world by sea and shared to some extent the benefits of the completion of the first transcontinental railroad to San Francisco. The new route by rail soon eclipsed the Panama route and further reduced traffic via the Cape Horn route, which had been for years the life-line of the coast.

The Pacific Northwest experienced its first railroad boom in the later 1860s as men of capital contended in one or the other of the Oregon and California companies. Railroad building in the Willamette Valley began seriously in 1868 as the Holladay line stretched southward from East Portland to reach Eugene in 1870 and Roseburg in 1872. Now merchants and farmers were no longer dependent upon the river as the new system of internal commerce emerged. After long delays the entire north-south route to Sacramento was completed in 1887.

Corbett, Failing and Company continued to ship heavy hardware via Cape Horn and their lighter shipments via Panama or by rail to San Francisco. They thus depended upon the sea until the Northern Pacific reached Portland in 1883 to complete the process of revolutionizing the old system of transportation. It then became necessary to close their New York office. A member of the firm noted the change in a letter to Samuel T. House, as follows:

> The Opening of direct rail communication has made a material change in our relations with the Eastern markets, and it is very doubtful whether the advantages of having a permanent office in New York, are as great as when all our goods had to go to the seaboard for shipment—We have from the beginning recognized this fact and our last year's experience confirms our judgment—. . . In the first place, our seniors said, they should hesitate about placing in the hands of a new and untried man, the powers in financial matters that they have without any question put in your own—More over the experience you have had as a buyer for our market could not be acquired without a long course of work—But in addition to this, we are much nearer our market of supply now many of our goods are bought in Western towns whom [sic] we can reach as readily and nearly as quickly as you—and it is therefore our determination as soon as can be conveniently arranged to close the New York office.[43]

During the latter part of the century railroads commanded the attention of magnates with outside capital, revolutionized the transportation and trade within the region, and prepared the way for its large scale industrial development. The system of river navigation on the Willamette and Columbia established by the pioneers of course did not disappear and actually went through a new stage of development before the revolution was completed. The Oregon Steam Navigation Company was not absorbed by the Northern Pacific until 1880.[44] But the advent of railroad building and the rise of foreign commerce in 1869 so altered the old system as to mark the end of a distinct period of pioneering that had stretched across three decades of the history of the Oregon Country from 1839 to 1869.

Notes

The following abbreviations are used for the periodicals most frequently cited in this study:

AHR   *American Historical Review.*
MVHR   *Mississippi Valley Historical Review.*
OHQ   *Oregon Historical Quarterly.*
PHR   *Pacific Historical Review.*
PNQ   *Pacific Northwest Quarterly*
RCB   *Reed College Bulletin.*
WHQ   *Washington Historical Quarterly.*

Introduction

(pp. 4-13)

1 This theme is fully developed in John S. Galbraith's new and authoritative study, *The Hudson's Bay Company As An Imperial Factor, 1821-1869* (1957). See Chap 5 particularly.

2 Frederick Merk, ed., *Fur Trade and Empire: George Simpson's Journal, 1824-1825,* pp. 73-74, 343, *passim.* W. K. Lamb's introduction in E. E. Rich, ed., *The Letters of John McLoughlin from Fort Vancouver to the Governor and Committee,* First Series, 1825-1838, *The Publications of the Hudson's Bay Record Society* (or H. B. S.), IV, pp. cxxiv-cxxv. Galbraith, *Hudson's Bay Company,* pp. 223-224 *passim.* O. O. Winther, *The Old Oregon Country,* Chaps. I-VII, provides a useful survey of Oregon's fur trade period.

The diplomacy of the Oregon Question from 1804 through 1826 can be traced in *American State Papers, Foreign Relations,* III-VI, and for the entire period through 1846, ed., William R. Manning, ed., *Diplomatic Correspondence of the United States, Canadian Relations, 1784-1860,* 3 vols., and in Hunter Miller, ed., *Treaties and Other International Acts of the United States,* II, III, and especially V. For important interpretative accounts of this question in relation to the fur trade, politics and settlement see Galbraith, *Hudson's Bay Company;* Frederick Merk, *Albert Gallatin and the Oregon Problem;* the following articles by Merk, "British Government Propaganda and the Oregon Treaty," *AHR,* XL, 1934, pp. 38-63; "British Party Politics and the Oregon Treaty," *AHR,* XXXVII, 1932, pp. 653-677; "The British Corn Crisis and the Oregon Treaty," *Agricultural History,* VIII, 1934, pp. 95-134; "The Genesis of the Oregon Question," *MVHR,* XXXVI, 1950, pp. 593-612; "The Ghost River Caledonia in the Oregon Negotiation of 1818," *AHR,* LV, 1950, pp. 530-551; "Oregon Pioneers and the Boundary," *AHR,* XXIX, 1924, pp. 681-699; and "The Oregon Question in the Webster-Ashburton Negotiations," *MVHR,* XLIII, 1956, pp. 374-404; Richard W. Van Alstyne, "International Rivalries in Pacific Northwest," *OHQ,* XLVI, 1945, pp. 185-218; Melvin C. Jacobs, *Winning Oregon: A Study of an Expansionist Movement;* Norman A. Graebner, *Empire On the Pacific;* and Leslie M. Scott, "Influence of American Settlement Upon The Oregon Boundary Treaty of 1846," *OHQ,* XXIX, 1928, pp. 1-19. The present author's Oregon Boundary Controversy, 1818-1846 (unpublished Master's thesis, University of North Carolina, 1947) also treats of the politics and diplomacy of the Oregon Question.

3 Galbraith, *Hudson's Bay Company,* pp. 82-98; Merk, ed., *Fur Trade And Empire,* pp. 44-46, 294n, *passim;* E. E. Rich, ed., *Simpson's 1828 Journey to the Columbia,* H.B.S., X, pp. xli-xliv, 47-56, 62-65; E. E. Rich, ed., *Peter Skene Ogden's Snake Country Journals,* H.B.S., XIII; T. C. Elliott, ed., "Journal of John Work, Covering Snake Country Expedition of 1830-31," *OHQ,* XIII, 1912. Other accounts of the Snake River trade include: W. T. Atkin, "Snake River Fur Trade, 1816-24," *OHQ,* XXXV, 1934, pp. 295-312 (for the pioneering efforts of the North West Company) ; Frederick Merk, "Snake Country Expedi-

tion, 1824-25," *OHQ*, XXXV, 1934, pp. 93-122; and Francis D. Haines, Jr., "The Relations of the Hudson's Bay Company with the American Fur Traders in the Pacific Northwest," *PNQ*, XL, 1949, pp. 273-294.

4 Sources for the Wyeth expeditions are F. G. Young, ed., *The Correspondence and Journals of Captain Nathaniel J. Wyeth*, in vol. I of *Sources of Oregon History*; "Mr. Wyeth's Memoir," Feb. 4, 1839, Appendix 1. *House Report No. 101*. 25th Cong. 3rd Sess., pp. 6-22; John B. Wyeth, "Wyeth's Oregon, Or a Short History of a Long Journey," in Reuben Gold Thwaites, ed., *Early Western Travels*, XXI, pp. 19-106; and Account Books for the Columbia River Fishing and Trading Company, Oregon Historical Society.

5 See Galbraith, *Hudson's Bay Company*, pp. 95-110.

6 For the British. American and Russian rivalry on the Northwest Coast, see *ibid.*, Chaps. 6-8; Simpson to the Governor of the Russian-American Company, March 21, 1829, and J. H. Pelly to Lords of the Privy Council for Trade, Feb. 7, 1838, in Merk, ed., *Fur Trade and Empire*, pp. 311-312, 343; Simpson to Governor and Committee, Mar. 1, 1829, *Simpson's 1828 Journey to the Columbia*, pp. 74-91; *McLoughlin's Fort Vancouver Letters*, First Series, pp. xviii, xxvi, xc-xci, ciii-civ; Report of Chief Trader P. S. Ogden of transactions at Stikine, 1834, *ibid.*, pp. 317-322; McLoughlin to Governor and Committee, March 14, 1835, *ibid.*, pp. 134-135; Duncan Finlayson to McLoughlin, Sept. 29, 1836, *ibid.*, pp. 323-335, *McLoughlin's Fort Vancouver Letters*, Second Series, H.B.S., VI, p. xix. Burt Brown Barker, ed., *The Letters of John McLoughlin Written at Fort Vancouver*, 1829-1832, contains many letters dealing with the intricacies of the coastal trade.

For the Dominis competition see Samuel Eliot Morison, "New England and the Opening of the Columbia River Salmon Trade." *OHQ*, XXVIII, 1927. pp. 111-132; Galbraith, *Hudson's Bay Company*. pp. 99-100; F. W. Howay. "The Brig Owyhee in the Columbia, 1829-30." *OHQ*, XXXV, 1934, pp. 10-21; and Helen Bowers, "Trade and Administrative Policies and Practices of McLoughlin," *RCB*, XXI (November, 1942), pp. 5-16.

7 Galbraith, *Hudson's Bay Company*, pp. 150-155; *McLoughlin's Fort Vancouver Letters*, Third Series, 1844-46, H.B.S., VII, pp. xi-xii. Extensive and valuable introductions by W. Kaye Lamb also accompany each of these two later series of McLoughlin letters.

8 Galbraith, *Hudson's Bay Company*, Chap. 10, and the same author's "The Early History of the Puget Sound Agricultural Company 1838-43," *OHQ*, LV, 1954, pp. 234-256. See also *McLoughlin's Fort Vancouver Letters*, Third Series, pp. xiii-xvii. Occasional references to the affairs of the Puget Sound Company are included in McLoughlin's correspondence in this and the preceding volume of his Fort Vancouver letters.

9 Galbraith, "Early History of the Puget Sound Agricultural Company," *OHQ*, LV, 1954, p. 253.

10 Samuel Eliot Morison, *The Maritime History of Massachusetts*, pp. 261-266; Alfred L. Lomax, "Hawaii-Columbia River Trade in Early Days," *OHQ*, XLIII, 1942, pp. 328-334. McLoughlin makes many references to the Hawaiian trade. See letters of McLoughlin to Governor and Committee, Nov. 15, 1836, and Oct. 31, 1837, *McLoughlin's Fort Vancouver Letters*, First Series, pp. 142, 204; and Oct. 24, 1839, *McLoughlin's Fort Vancouver Letters*, Second Series, p. 4. Also Merk, ed., *Fur Trade and Empire*, p. 319n.

11 *Ibid.*, p. 50.

12 Galbraith, "Early History of the Puget Sound Agricultural Company," *OHQ*, LV, 1954, pp. 237, 242. *McLoughlin's Fort Vancouver Letters*, Second Series, pp. xi-xii. See Merk, ed., *Fur Trade and Empire*, pp. 50-177, for Simpson's reorganization plans for the Columbia Department in 1824-1825, and *ibid.*, pp. xiii-xvii for the organization of the Hudson's Bay Company after its merger with the North West Company in 1821.

13 The Bureau of Labor Statistics, *Bulletin No. 367, Wholesale Prices 1890 to 1923*, p. 245; Governor and Committee to McLoughlin, Sept. 27, 1843, *McLough-*

lin's *Fort Vancouver Letters,* Second Series, p. 306. Also *ibid.,* p. 387; Edward
Roberts to Sir George Simpson, Feb. 3, 1846, quoted in E. E. Rich, ed., *London
Correspondence Inward From Eden Colvile, 1849-1852,* H.B.S., XIX, p. 161n;
the dividend percentages are taken from Galbraith's list for the entire period,
1821-1863, in *Hudson's Bay Company,* pp. 432-433. Governor and Committee
to Simpson, June 1, 1843, quoted in *McLoughlin's Fort Vancouver Letters,*
Third Series, pp. lvi-lvii.

14 Galbraith, *Hudson's Bay Company,* p. 12, quoting Douglas and Ogden, pp.
107-110, *passim.*

Chapter I

(pp. 14-30)

1 Charles Wilkes, *Narrative of the United States Exploring Expedition, During
the Years 1838, 1840, 1841, 1842,* IV, p. 308; Governor and Committee to James
Douglas, Nov. 15, 1837, quoted by Arthur S. Morton, *Sir George Simpson:
Overseas Governor of the Hudson's Bay Company.* p. 212. McLoughlin to
Governor and Committee, Nov. 16, 1836, *McLoughlin's Fort Vancouver Letters,*
First Series, p. 158, says 100 per cent is charged to missionaries and 150 per cent
to their servants. Later when Jason Lee reported to the Mission Board in New
York, July 1, 1844, Cornelius J. Brosnan *(Jason Lee; Prophet of the New
Oregon,* p. 251) , says that the company charged 70 per cent. Douglas to Governor
and Committee, Oct. 18, 1838, *McLoughlin's Fort Vancouver Letters,* First
Series, p. 240.

2 *Ibid.,* p. 242.

3 See *ibid.,* pp. 240-244 for Douglas' complete report on the Protestant missions.
For the origins of the Methodist missionary effort in Oregon, see Brosnan, *Jason
Lee,* Chaps. I-III, and "Methodist Annual Reports Relating to the Willamette
Mission, 1834-1848," Charles H. Carey, ed., *OHQ,* XXIII, 1922, pp. 304-307.
For Lee's overland journey in 1834 and his return journey in 1838, see his
"Diary," *OHQ,* XVII, 1916, pp. 117-146, 240-266, 397-430. For Lee's purpose
in locating the mission in the Willamette Valley see Daniel Lee and J. H.
Frost, *Ten Years in Oregon,* p. 127, and Brosnan, *Jason Lee,* pp. 70-72.
McLoughlin was favorably impressed by the Methodist missionaries and their
early work. See McLoughlin, "Copy of a Document," *Transactions of the
Oregon Pioneer Association,* 1880, p. 50. He was warned, however, by the
Governor and Committee, Dec. 31, 1839, *McLoughlin's Fort Vancouver Let-
ters,* Second Series, pp. 18n-19n, against the political motives of the Methodists
"not withstanding their high eulogiums [*sic*] upon us for hospitality and kind
offices . . ." "The Oregon Mission Record Book," C. H. Carey, ed., *OHQ,*
XXIII, 1922, pp. 230-236, reveals the privations, suffering and handicaps at the
Willamette Mission in its early years.

For the ABCFM effort see C. M. Drury's biographies of Whitman and Spalding,
and Bancroft, *History of Oregon,* I, Chap. V. The letter of H. K. W. Perkins
to Miss Jane Prentiss. Oct. 19, 1849, in Drury, *Marcus Whitman, M. D.* Appendix 6. pp. 458-459, questions the qualifications of the Whitmans for missionary
life. For references to mission drafts see letters of McLoughlin to Governor
and Committee, Nov. 15, 16, 1836, and Nov. 15, 1843, in *McLoughlin's Fort
Vancouver Letters,* First Series, pp. 163, 174-175, and Second Series, p. 142.

4 For the work and observations of the four Catholic missionaries mentioned, see
the edition of their reports and letters, now available in English, entitled
Notices & Voyages of the Famed Quebec Mission to the Pacific Northwest . . . ,
Carl Landerholm, editor and translator. See especially pp. 33-35, 45, 53-56, and
108-110 for comments of Blanchet and Demers about the Methodist mission-
aries. See Galbraith. "The Early History of the Puget Sound Agricultural
Company," *OHQ,* LV, 1954, p. 248, for the relationship of the Catholic mission
to the colonization plan. Priscilla Knuth's "Nativism in Oregon," *RCB,*
XXIV (January, 1946) , is an excellent study of that sentiment. W. H. Gray's
History of Oregon is an extremely pro-Protestant, anti-Catholic and anti-
Hudson's Bay Company contemporary account of early Oregon history by one

who was active in missionary work. For an excellent explanation of the adaptability of Catholic missionaries to wilderness conditions and the attitude of the Hudson's Bay Company toward them see Eden Colvile to Sir George Simpson, July 14, 1851, *London Correspondence Inward From Eden Colvile, 1849-1852,* E. E. Rich, ed., pp. 225-226.

5 J. Orin Oliphant, "George Simpson and Oregon Missions," *PHR,* VI, 1937, pp. 222-223; Merk, ed., *Fur Trade and Empire,* p. 108.

6 Bancroft, *History of Oregon,* I, p. 166; Alexis de Tocqueville, *Democracy in America* (Phillips Bradley edition), I, pp. 306-307; Brosnan, *Jason Lee,* p. 277; Lee to the secretary of Mission Board, Oct. 13, 1843, quoted in *ibid.,* pp. 211-212; and his defense before the Mission Board, July 1, 1844, quoted in *ibid.,* pp. 247-248.

7 Douglas to Governor and Committee, Oct. 18, 1838, *McLoughlin's Fort Vancouver Letters,* First Series, pp. 242-243.

8 *House Report No. 101,* 25th Cong., 3rd Sess., Jan. 4, 1839, Supplement, Feb. 16, 1839. Lee's petition is pp. 4-6 of the Supplement and pp. 1-3 of *Senate Executive Document No. 134,* 25th Cong., 3rd Sess. See also Brosnan, *Jason Lee,* pp. 97-107, 219-224; "Methodist Annual Reports," Carey, ed., *OHQ,* XXIII, 1922, pp. 307-315, 344; and Throckmorton, Oregon Boundary Controversy, pp. 55-67. For the many petitions and memorials on the Oregon subject that flowed to Congress from the states of the Mississippi Valley and Oregon, see *ibid.,* pp. 41-44 and C. J. Pike, "Petitions of Oregon Settlers," *OHQ,* XXXIV, 1933, pp. 216-235.

9 Norman A. Graebner, *Empire on the Pacific,* develops the thesis that American mercantile interests in the Pacific "determined the course of empire," and that the consistent aim of American policy regarding the Pacific Coast was to acquire the harbors of Puget Sound, San Francisco Bay, and San Diego.

10 Fred Wilbur Powell, *Hall Jackson Kelley, Prophet of Oregon,* Chaps. II-IV, VIII and IX. For the writings of Kelley see *Hall J. Kelley On Oregon,* Fred Wilbur Powell, ed. For a good evaluation of Kelley see Verne Bright, "The Folklore and History of the 'Oregon Fever'," *OHQ,* LII, 1951, pp. 247-248. McLoughlin's observations on Kelley may be found in his letter to the Governor and Committee, Nov. 18, 1834, *McLoughlin's Fort Vancouver Letters,* First Series, pp. 127-128; and in his Remarks on the Cushing Report, *McLoughlin's Fort Vancouver Letters,* Third Series, pp. 276-282.

11 F. P. Tracy to the Principal Officer of the Hudson's Bay Company, March 4, 1839, quoted in *McLoughlin's Fort Vancouver Letters,* Third Series, p. 14n; William Smith to F. P. Tracy, June 13, 1839, quoted in *ibid.,* p. 15n; and F. P. Tracy to Caleb Cushing, Jan. 6, 1839, *House Report No. 101,* 25th Cong., 3rd Sess.

12 For Lee's Great Reinforcement, see Lee and Frost, *Ten Years in Oregon,* pp. 216-240, and Brosnan, *Jason Lee,* Chaps. IX and X. The instructions of the Mission Board, including those to Abernethy, are in "A Document of Mission History, 1833, 1843," Robert Moulton Gatke, ed., *OHQ,* XXXVI, 1935, pp. 84-85. Abernethy's business career, discussed in this and subsequent chapters, also appears in the present author's "George Abernethy, Pioneer Merchant," *PNQ,* XLVIII, 1957, pp. 76-88.

Bancroft, *History of Oregon,* I, p. 171, states that the total cost of the *Lausanne's* voyage, including the cost of the goods, was $42,000. Brosnan, *Jason Lee,* p. 104, cites records showing an appropriation of $40,000 by the Mission Board in 1839. The actual cost of the goods, as estimated by Lee in his report to the Mission Board in 1844, *ibid.,* p. 262, was from $13,000 to $14,000. The assertion that the mission received a substantial subsidy from the government secret fund is now discredited. See *ibid.,* pp. 316-318.

For references to the colonization aims of the Methodists, see Governor and Committee to McLoughlin, Dec. 31, 1839, *McLoughlin's Fort Vancouver Letters,* Second Series, p. 19n, which states that "It is quite evident that they have promoted the present mania for emigration to the Columbia. . . ." For other comments see McLoughlin to Governor and Committee, Nov. 20, 1844, *Mc-*

Loughlin's Fort Vancouver Letters, Third Series, p. 35; Wilkes, *Narrative,* IV, pp. 344, 352; "Letters of Sir George Simpson, 1841-1843," Joseph Schafer, ed., *AHR,* XIV, 1908, pp. 79-80. Under an entry for April 15, 1839, in "A Document of Mission History," Gatke, ed., *OHQ,* XXXVI, 1935, p. 79, the idea that colonization was the aim of the Methodist Missionary Society is categorically denied.

13 *Ibid.,* pp. 81-83, 88-89; "Methodist Annual Reports," *OHQ,* XXIII, 1922, pp. 344-345; Nellie B. Pipes, ed., "Journal of John H. Frost, 1840-43," *OHQ,* XXXV, 1934, pp. 70, 155-156, 354-359, 364-366.

14 George Abernethy to the Rev. A. F. Waller, July 8, 1841, Abernethy Mss., Oregon Historical Society (hereafter cited O.H.S.); Lee to the Secretary of the Mission Board, Oct. 13, 1843, quoted in Brosnan, *Jason Lee,* p. 207; Lee's defense before the Mission Board, July 1-10, 1844, in *ibid.,* pp. 246-264. Wesley's views on economic theory are referred to in Marquis W. Childs and Douglas Cater, *Ethics in a Business Society,* pp. 55-56; Resolutions of the Missionary Society in "A Document of Mission History," Gatke, ed., *OHQ,* XXXVI, 1935, p. 79.

15 McLoughlin to Governor and Committee, Aug. 12, 1844, *McLoughlin's Fort Vancouver Letters,* Third Series, p. 3 and L. W. Hastings to McLoughlin, April 8, 1843, in *ibid.,* pp. 251-253. McLoughlin refers to mission drafts but not the amounts in McLoughlin to Governor and Committee, Nov. 15, 1843, *McLoughlin's Fort Vancouver Letters,* Second Series, p. 142. For one example of the care Abernethy took to avoid injury to the secular relations between the mission and the Hudson's Bay Company, see the discussion of the Shortess petition, circulated in the Willamette Valley in March, 1843, in C. J. Pike, "Petitions of Oregon Settlers," *OHQ,* XXXIV, 1933, pp. 224-225. This petition was allegedly inspired by the missionaries and was very hostile to the Hudson's Bay Company. Shortess is responsible for its content, but Abernethy wrote it in its proper form from Shortess' notes. Abernethy refused to sign it and would not permit its circulation in his handwriting.

16 Letters of Governor and Committee to McLoughlin, Dec. 31, 1839, and of McLoughlin to Governor and Committee, Nov. 4, 1842 and July 19, 1845, *McLoughlin's Fort Vancouver Letters,* Second Series, pp. 19n, 97, Third Series, p. 88; Wilkes, *Narrative,* IV, p. 328.

17 Wilkes, *Narrative,* IV, pp. 343-344; Brosnan, *Jason Lee,* pp. 176-180, 268; *McLoughlin's Fort Vancouver Letters,* Third Series, xl-xlii, where excerpts from Simpson's letter to Governor and Committee, Nov. 25, 1841, and his letter to McLoughlin, March 1, 1842, are quoted.

18 Morison, *Maritime History of Massachusetts,* p. 66, for the significance of the Cushing company. See Dan E. Clark, "Manifest Destiny and the Pacific," *PHR,* I, 1932, p. 7, for comments on Caleb Cushing's mission to China in 1843. He, the statesman of the family, said that he went to the Orient "in behalf of civilization."

19 For a short biography of Couch, see *Transactions of the Oregon Pioneer Association,* 1886, pp. 59-62. For other references to Couch and the establishment of the Cushing business in Oregon, see Marie Lazenby, "Down-Easters Out West," *RCB,* XXV (April, 1947), p. 12; Matthew P. Deady, "Annual Address," *Transactions of the Oregon Pioneer Association,* 1875, pp. 33-34; Edmund Sylvester, "Edmund Sylvester's Narrative of the Founding of Olympia," *PNQ,* XXXVI, 1945, p. 333; Bancroft, *History of Oregon,* I, p. 245n, and II, pp. 15-16n; letters of John McLoughlin to Governor and Committee, June 22, 1842 and Nov. 15, 1843, *McLoughlin's Fort Vancouver Letters,* Second Series, pp. 58, 130-131.

Chapter II

(pp. 31-52)

1 Ellen Churchill Semple, *American History and its Geographic Conditions,* pp. 210-211; Bancroft, *History of Oregon,* I, pp. 391-392; Dorothy O. Johansen and Charles M. Gates, *Empire of the Columbia: a History of the Pacific Northwest,* p. 255; Helen B. Kroll, "The Books That Enlightened the Emigrants," *OHQ,*

XLV, 1944, pp. 105, 113-118; Melvin C. Jacobs, *Winning Oregon: A Study of An Expansionist Movement*, pp. 34-36; letters of McLoughlin to Governor and Committee, Nov. 20, 1844 and Dec. 12, 1845, *McLoughlin's Fort Vancouver Letters*, Third Series, pp. 34, 152; John Minto, "Antecedents of the Oregon Pioneers and the Light These Throw on Their Motives," *OHQ*, V, 1904, pp. 38-53.

2 Lt. Peel to Capt. Gordon, Sept. 27, 1845, "Report of Lieut. Peel, 1845-46, "Leslie M. Scott, ed., *OHQ*, XXIX, 1928, p. 62.

3 Avery Sylvester, "Voyages of the Pallas and Chenamus," *OHQ*, XXXIV, 1933, p. 267. This citation is from the published part of Captain Sylvester's journal which records his trips between Hawaii and the Columbia from 1843 to 1845.

4 For a lucid analysis of the meaning of Manifest Destiny, see Dan E. Clark, "Manifest Destiny and the Pacific," *PHR*, I, 1932, pp. 1-17.

5 Estimates of the size of the immigrations from 1842 through 1845 and other comments about them may be found in *McLoughlin's Fort Vancouver Letters*, Second Series, pp. 75-77, 148; Third Series, pp. li, 34, 289.

6 See "The Oregon Archives, 1841-1843," David C. Duniway and Neil R. Riggs, eds., *OHQ*, LX, 1959, pp. 211-280, for documents on the formation of the Provisional Government. The organic laws are in *ibid.*, pp. 273-280. See also Russell B. Thomas, "Truth and Fiction of the Champoeg Meeting," *OHQ*, XXX, 1929, pp. 218-237; *McLoughlin's Fort Vancouver Letters*, Third Series, pp. xxxv-xxxix, and McLoughlin to Governor and Committee, Nov. 20, 1844, *ibid.*, pp. 33-34. Documents for the later history of the Provisional Government may be found in J. Henry Brown, *Brown's Political History of Oregon*.

7 Sylvester, "Voyages of the Pallas and Chenamus," *OHQ*, XXXIV, 1933, p. 268.

8 McLoughlin to Governor and Committee, May 29, 1843, *McLoughlin's Fort Vancouver Letters*, Second Series, p. 107; Bancroft, *History of Oregon*, I, pp. 422-423; Francis W. Pettygrove, Oregon in 1843, Pacific Manuscripts, Bancroft Library, University of California (Microfilm, O.H.S.).

9 Frederick V. Holman, quoting Burnett in *Dr. John McLoughlin: The Father of Oregon*, p. 77.

10 Letters of McLoughlin to Governor and Committee, Nov. 15, 1843, *McLoughlin's Fort Vancouver Letters*, Second Series, p. 127; and July 19, 1845, Third Series, p. 89. See *ibid.*, pp. liii-lv, 299-308, for a discussion of protecting British interests in Oregon and documents relating thereto.

11 McLoughlin to Governor and Committee, Nov. 20, 1845, *McLoughlin's Fort Vancouver Letters*, Third Series, pp. 125-127; *ibid.*, pp. lii-liii.

12 *McLoughlin's Fort Vancouver Letters*, Third Series, contains excerpts from the letters of Simpson to Governor and Committee, June 20, 1844, pp. 125-126n; Barclay to McLoughlin, Nov. 20, 1844, p. lii; and Douglas to Simpson, Nov. 16, 1843, p. xlv. For McLoughlin's problems with the settlers, see Lamb's summary in *ibid.*, pp. xl-lxiii, and McLoughlin to Governor and Committee, Nov. 20, 1845, *ibid.*, pp. 99-110. For the land claim problem, see *ibid.*, pp. 118-123; for American competition and quotes from McLoughlin's instructions of Aug. 28, 1835 and Sept. 27, 1843, as well as the defense of his credit policy, see *ibid.*, pp. 126-128. For the order to charge settlers 100 per cent, see *ibid.*, p. 141, and for the discontinuance of credit, see his letter to Governor and Committee, July 1, 1846, *ibid.*, p. 160. The "Report of Lieutenant Neil M. Howison On Oregon, 1846," (reprinted from *House Miscellaneous Document No. 29*, 30th Cong., 1st Sess.), *OHQ*, XIV, p. 87 states that the Hudson's Bay Company sold goods invariably at 100 per cent advance upon London cost.

13 Florence E. Baker, ed., "Letters of Tallmadge B. Wood," about April 1844, *OHQ*, III, 1902, pp. 395-398, and Feb. 19, 1846, *OHQ*, IV, pp. 80-85; John Minto, "From Youth to Age as an American," *OHQ*, IX, 1908, p. 128; Avery Sylvester, "Voyages of the Pallas and Chenamus, 1843-45," *OHQ*, XXXIV, 1933, pp. 259, 359, *passim;* letters of Douglas to Simpson, March 5 and April 4, 1845, *McLoughlin's Fort Vancouver Letters*, Third Series, pp. 182-183, 189-190.

14 Sylvester, "Voyages of the Pallas and Chenamus," *OHQ,* XXXIV, 1933, pp. 367-368.

15 *Ibid.,* pp. 360-361, *passim;* Edmond S. Meany, Jr., The History of the Lumber Industry in the Pacific Northwest to 1917 (Ph.D. thesis, Harvard University, 1935), p. 68; McLoughlin to Governor and Committee, July 19, 1845, *McLoughlin's Fort Vancouver Letters,* Third Series, p. 85.

16 F. W. Pettygrove, Oregon in 1843, Pacific Manuscripts, Bancroft Library, University of California. (Microfilm, O.H.S.)

17 Governor and Committee to McLoughlin, Sept. 27, 1843, *McLoughlin's Fort Vancouver Letters,* Second Series, p. 306; Governor and Committee to Simpson, June 1, 1843, excerpt quoted in *McLoughlin's Fort Vancouver Letters,* Third Series, pp. lvi-lvii; Simpson to McLoughlin, Ogden and Douglas, June 16, 1845, quoted in McLoughlin to Governor and Committee, Nov. 20, 1845, *ibid.,* pp. 135-136. Also *ibid.,* pp. lvi-lxi, and Galbraith, *Hudson's Bay Company,* p. 249.

18 These matters are treated thoroughly by W. Kaye Lamb in his introductions to *McLoughlin's Fort Vancouver Letters,* Second and Third Series.

19 W. Kaye Lamb's introduction to *McLoughlin's Fort Vancouver Letters,* Third Series, pp. xl-li, lxi-lxiii, gives the best analysis of this long controversy, showing the weaknesses of McLoughlin's position from the legal standpoint. McLoughlin's correspondence from 1844 to 1846, contained in the Third Series, abounds with references to the problem. See particularly, letters of McLoughlin to Governor and Committee, Nov. 20, 1845 and July 1, 1846, *ibid.,* pp. 119-123, 154-155. Other pertinent documents on this land controversy are contained in Brosnan, *Jason Lee,* pp. 291-315; and "Lee, Waller, and McLoughlin," Charles H. Carey, ed., *OHQ,* XXXIII, 1932, pp. 187-213.

20 McLoughlin to Simpson, March 20, 1843, quoted in McLoughlin to Governor and Committee, Nov. 20, 1845, *McLoughlin's Fort Vancouver Letters,* Third Series, p. 121; *ibid.,* pp. xliii-xliv; McLoughlin to Governor and Committee, Nov. 18, 1843, and the text of Thom's opinion, *McLoughlin's Fort Vancouver Letters,* Second Series, pp. 165 and 165n.

21 *McLoughlin's Fort Vancouver Letters,* Second Series, p. xviii; letters of Douglas to Simpson, March 5, 1845 and Nov. 16, 1845, *McLoughlin's Fort Vancouver Letters,* Third Series, pp. 185, xlv; McLoughlin to Governor and Committee, Nov. 20, 1845, *ibid.,* pp. 123, 140.

22 McLoughlin's ambiguous letter to Simpson, March 20, 1845 is quoted in *McLoughlin's Fort Vancouver Letters,* Third Series, pp. xlviii-xlix, and Simpson's letters to McLoughlin accepting the drafts is quoted in *ibid.,* p. xlix. Also, letters of McLoughlin to Governor and Committee, Nov. 20, 1845 and July 1, 1846, *ibid.,* pp. 114-119, 141-143, 153-154.

23 See Bancroft, *Oregon,* II, pp. 112-138, *passim.*

24 Simpson's orders for curtailment of operations at Oregon City in his letter to McLoughlin, Ogden, and Douglas of June 16, 1845, are quoted in McLoughlin to Governor and Committee, Nov. 20, 1845, *McLoughlin's Fort Vancouver Letters,* Third Series, pp. 137-140. McLoughlin's defense of his administration and the Oregon City project is in *ibid.,* pp. 140-143, 148-150; and in letters of McLoughlin to Governor and Committee, July 1, 1846 and to Sir J. H. Pelly, July 12, 1846, *ibid.,* pp. 154-165.

25 McLoughlin to Governor and Committee, Nov. 20, 1845, *McLoughlin's Fort Vancouver Letters,* Third Series, p. 143; David H. Coyner to a friend in Virginia, Booneville, Missouri, May 20, 1846, quoted by Verne Bright, "The Folklore and History of the 'Oregon Fever'," *OHQ,* LII, 1951, pp. 246-247. Father Demers, in his report to M.C., Dec. 20, 1845, *Notices and Voyages of the Quebec Mission,* Carl Landerholm, ed., pp. 235-236, states that the immigration of 1845 included a number of wealthy families.

26 McLoughlin to Governor and Committee, Nov. 20, 1845, *McLoughlin's Fort Vancouver Letters,* Third Series, p. 126; Lee's Report to the Mission Board, July 1844, Brosnan, *Jason Lee,* pp. 246-264; "Methodist Annual Reports," Carey,

ed., *OHQ*, XXIII, 1922, pp. 319-350, 359-361; W. H. Gray, *Oregon*, p. 213; "Diary of Reverend George H. Gary," Charles H. Carey, ed., *OHQ*, XXIV, 1923, pp. 155-156.

27 *Ibid.*, p. 176.

28 *Ibid.*, p. 103; "Methodist Annual Reports," Carey, ed., *OHQ*, XXIII, 1922, p. 361; *Oregon Spectator*, Oregon City, Nov. 12, 1846; Abernethy to C. L. Ross, Feb. 20, 1846, George Abernethy, letter press copy book, O.H.S. Abernethy's business correspondence, 1847-50, hereafter cited Abernethy Mss. O.H.S., is in this letter press copy book.

29 *McLoughlin's Fort Vancouver Letters*, Third Series, pp. xlvi-xlvii; McLoughlin to Governor and Committee, Nov. 20, 1845, *ibid.*, pp. 121-122; McLoughlin's statement, *ibid.*, p. 218.

30 *Ibid.*, pp. lv-lxiii; "McLoughlin's Proprietory Account With Hudson's Bay Company," Burt Brown Barker, ed., *OHQ*, XLV, 1944, pp. 1-41; Barker's "The Estate of Dr. John McLoughlin: The Papers Discovered," *OHQ*, L, 1949, pp. 155-185. Of the erroneous accounts, Gilbert, *Trade and Currency in Early Oregon*, cites an estimate that McLoughlin had extended credits totaling $100,000. Pettygrove, "Oregon in 1843," says McLoughlin loaned $80,000; that he paid this amount to the Company prior to his resignation, and that a large percentage was never repaid. Barker shows that the Company never deducted the amount of these debts from McLoughlin's personal account. It is doubtful that the debts owed the Hudson's Bay Company by the settlers ever reached such totals as given by Gilbert and Pettygrove and even more doubtful that there were any appreciable losses to the Company owing to the debts of the settlers. The text of the 11th clause of the Donation Act may be found in *U. S. Statutes at Large*, IX, p. 499.

31 McLoughlin to Governor and Committee, Nov. 20, 1844, *McLoughlin's Fort Vancouver Letters*, Third Series, pp. 32-33. Wilkes, *Narrative*, IV, p. 330, notes that on one occasion McLoughlin had purchased an entire consignment of liquor from an American trader and stored it at Fort Vancouver in order to prevent its distribution among the coastal Indian tribes.

32 Bancroft, *History of Oregon*, I, p. 471.

Chapter III

(pp. 53-69)

1 Galbraith, *Hudson's Bay Company*, p. 108.

2 "Howison's Report," *OHQ*, XIV, 1913, p. 37.

3 *Oregon Spectator*, April 1, 1847.

4 "Howison's Report," *OHQ*, XIV, 1913, pp. 39-40.

5 Letters of M. M. McCarver, *Oregon Spectator*, July 9, Oct. 15, 1846.

6 *Palmer's Journal of Travels over the Rocky Mountains, 1845-1846* (vol. XXX of *Early Western Travels, 1748-1846*, Reuben Gold Thwaites, ed.), pp. 216-218; "Howison's Report," *OHQ*, XIV, 1913, p. 38.

7 *Palmer's Journal*, p. 161; J. M. Bacon, Mercantile Life at Oregon City, Pacific Manuscripts, Bancroft Library, University of California. (Microfilm, Oregon State Archives, State Library, Salem Oregon.)

8 *Palmer's Journal*, pp. 217-218; "Howison's Report," *OHQ*, XIV, 1913, p. 39; Tallmadge B. Wood to his brother, Feb. 19, 1846, *OHQ*, IV, 1903, pp. 83-84; Bancroft, *Oregon*, II, p. 20.

9 *Palmer's Journal*, p. 218; Tallmadge B. Wood to his brother, Feb. 19, 1846, "Documents" *OHQ*, IV, 1903, p. 81.

10 Gilbert, *Trade and Currency in Early Oregon*, pp. 72-73; Bancroft, *Oregon*, I, pp. 211, 264-265, 414n; II, pp. 1-6, 27; Bacon, Mercantile Life at Oregon City; *Palmer's Journal*, pp. 159-161, 219.

11 "Howison's Report," *OHQ*, XIV, 1913, p. 8.

12 Bancroft, *Oregon*, II, pp. 15-17n, 22n.

13 Pettygrove, Oregon in 1843; *Oregon Spectator*, Dec. 10, 1846; "Howison's Report," *OHQ*, XIV, 1913, p. 42.

14 Pettygrove, Oregon in 1843; "Howison's Report," OHQ, XIV, 1913, p. 42; *Palmer's Journal*, pp. 223-224; "Lovejoy's Pioneer Narrative," *OHQ*, XXXI, 1930, p. 253; "Diary of Rev. George H. Atkinson, D.D., 1847-1858," E. Ruth Rockwood, ed., *OHQ*, XL, 1939, p. 185.

15 M. M. McCarver letters, *Oregon Spectator*, July 9, 23, 1846; Abernethy to A. F. Waller, Oct. 13, 1846, Abernethy Mss., O.H.S.; *Polynesian*, June 13, 1846, quoted in *Oregon Spectator*, Aug. 20, 1846; Bancroft, *Oregon*, II, p. 18.

16 *Ibid.*, p. 19.

17 M. M. McCarver letter, *Oregon Spectator*, July 23, 1846; Peel to Gordon, Sept. 27, 1845, "Report of Lieutenant Peel, 1845-46," Scott, ed., *OHQ*, XXIX, 1928, p. 64; *Palmer's Journal*, p. 219; Gilbert,*Trade and Currency*, pp. 47-52; *Oregon Spectator*, Aug. 19, 1847.

18 "Reminiscences of Clement Adams Bradbury, 1846," H. S. Lyman, ed., *OHQ*, II, 1901, p. 315; Bacon, Mercantile Life at Oregon City; "Lovejoy's Pioneer Narrative, 1842-48," *OHQ*, XXXI, 1930, p. 257; Stephen H. Bibler, "Specimen of Abernethy Rock: A Medium of Exchange," *OHQ*, XLIV, 1943, p. 250.

19 *Ibid.*, pp. 249-251; "A Pocket Full of Rocks," *Oregon Native Son*, I, 1899, p. 90.

20 "Howison's Report," *OHQ*, XIV, 1913, p. 10; Gilbert, *Trade and Currency*, p. 56.

21 *Ibid.*, p. 53; M. M. McCarver letter, *Oregon Spectator*, July 23, 1846; *Oregon Spectator*, Dec. 10, 1846.

22 *Oregon Spectator*, Dec. 10, 1846; April 1, 29, 1847.

23 *Oregon Spectator*, April 29, 1847.

24 Lewis E. Atherton, "The Pioneer Merchant in Mid America," *The University of Missouri Studies*, XIV, p. 94.

25 C. E. Pickett to Gen. McCarver, P. H. Burnett, Col. Ford, and D. Waldo, *Oregon Spectator*, June 10, 1847; Bancroft, *Oregon*, II, pp. 17-18.

26 *Oregon Spectator*, May 13, July 8, July 22, Sept. 30, Dec. 24, 1847, and July 13, 1848; Bancroft, *Oregon*, II, pp. 16-17n, 48.

27 *McLoughlin's Fort Vancouver Letters*, Third Series, pp. xviii-xxix; Morison, *Maritime History of Massachusetts*, pp. 266-268; Helen Bowers, "Trade and Administrative Policies and Practices of McLoughlin," *RCB*, XXI (November, 1942), pp. 12-13.

28 W. J. Ghent, *The Road to Oregon: A Chronicle of the Great Emigrant Trail*, p. 91; Bancroft, *Oregon*, I, p. 623; letters of George Abernethy to Edward F. Folger and to Capt. Roland Gelston, Nov. 8, 1847, Abernethy Mss., O.H.S.: W. M. Roberts to Pitman, Dec. 20, 1847, "Letters of the Rev. William M. Roberts, Third Superintendent of the Oregon Mission," Robert Moulton Gatke, ed., *OHQ*, XXI, 1920, p. 42.

29 Gilbert, *Trade and Currency*, p. 62.

30 *Oregon Spectator*, March 27, 1847; James Athey, Workshops at Oregon City, Pacific Manuscripts, Bancroft Library, University of California. (Microfilm, Oregon State Archives, State Library, Salem, Oregon.) Roberts to Pitman, Dec. 20, 1847, "Letters of the Rev. William M. Roberts," Third Superintendent of the Oregon Mission," Gatke, ed., *OHQ*, XXI, 1920, pp. 40-42.

31 See Kathryn Troxel, "Food of the Overland Emigrants," *OHQ*, LXI, 1955, p. 14ff for the advice given on the amount and kind of rations needed for the overland trip. Abernethy to Edward F. Folger, Nov. 8, 1847, Abernethy Mss., O.H.S.

32 Bancroft, *Oregon*, I, pp. 629-630. Thomas Cox, day book (microfilm at O.H.S.). Abernethy to Edward F. Folger, Nov. 8, 1847, Abernethy Mss., O.H.S.

33 Letters of George Abernethy to Edward F. Folger, March 11, 1848, and to Capt. Roland Gelston, Oct. 4, 1847 and April 28, 1848, Abernethy Mss., O.H.S. The

Rev. William M. Roberts to Pitman, March 18, 1848, "The Letters of the Rev. William M. Roberts, Third Superintendent of the Oregon Mission," Gatke, ed., *OHQ, XXII, 1921, p. 227.*

34 Bancroft, *Oregon,* II, pp. 17-18n, 23; Thornton's Memorial in *Senate Miscellaneous Document 143,* 30th Cong., 1st Sess., pp. 11-12, quoted by Gilbert, *Trade and Currency,* p. 63; "Correspondence of the Reverend Ezra Fisher," Sarah Fisher Henderson, Nellie Edith Latourette, and Kenneth Scott Latourette, eds., *OHQ,* XVII, 1916, p. 154. (Hereafter cited, "Fisher Correspondence," *OHQ,* XVII, 1916.)

35 Roberts to Pitman, March 18, 1848, "Roberts Letters," Gatke, ed., *OHQ,* XXII, 1921, p. 227; letters of George Abernethy to James B. McClurg, San Francisco, and to C. L. Ross, San Francisco, March 10, 1848, Abernethy Mss., O.H.S.

36 Abernethy to Capt. Roland Gelston, New York, April 28, 1848, Abernethy Mss., O.H.S.

37 William McBean to the Board of Managers, Nov. 30, 1847, in *Brown's Political History of Oregon: Provisional Government,* pp. 323-324, is the first written though somewhat inaccurate, account of the massacre; James Douglas to George Abernethy, Dec. 7, 1847, in *ibid.,* pp. 322-323. For McLoughlin's comment see his testimony at the trial of the Cayuse murderers, May 21, 1850, *ibid.,* p. 430. See Drury, *Whitman,* pp. 390-428, for the details of the massacre and its consequences, and Frances Fuller Victor, *The Early Indian Wars of Oregon,* Chaps. I-V, for an older but thorough analysis of the causes of the Cayuse War. Abernethy to Ogden, Jan. 19, 1848, in *ibid.,* pp. 124-126, expresses the gratitude of the community.

38 *Ibid.,* Chaps. VI-IX, for the Cayuse War, and pp. 248-251, for the trial of the Cayuse murderers. Also *Brown's Political History,* pp. 428-431.

39 *Brown's Political History,* pp. 424-427; see Victor, *Early Indian Wars,* pp. 503-520, for the rosters and muster rolls of the men serving in the Cayuse War.

40 Applegate, Lovejoy and Curry to James Douglas, Dec. 11, 1847; Douglas to Applegate, Lovejoy and Curry, Dec. 11, 1847; Proclamation of Governor Abernethy, Dec. 25, 1847; Hugh Burns to the Legislative Assembly, Feb. 8, 1849 in Victor, *Early Indian Wars,* pp. 135-137, 144-145, 253-255. Also *ibid.,* pp. 45-47. Stanley S. Spaid, Joel Palmer and Indian Affairs in Oregon (Ph.D. thesis, University of Oregon, 1950), pp. 43-45.

41 Victor, *Early Indian Wars,* pp. 253-255; Gilbert, *Trade and Currency,* p. 61.

42 For Abernethy's correspondence and official acts relating to the Cayuse War, see *Brown's Political History of Oregon,* pp. 322-432. Historians offer little or no criticism of Abernethy's conduct of the war nor of his governorship in general, but Bancroft, in *Oregon,* I, pp. 612-613, 782-783, condemns him severely, mainly because he was identified with the mission faction and anti-Catholic. Bancroft's adverse opinion was based partly on Bacon Interview, Mercantile Life at Oregon City, where Abernethy is called "a hypocrite" by a man who simply did not like Abernethy's cultured ways. Many other westerners probably reacted in a similar manner. The best biographical sketch, one which gives a scholarly appraisal of Abernethy's role, is Joseph Schafer's in the *Dictionary of American Biography,* I, pp. 29-30. Abernethy is one of the few Oregonians recognized in this compendium of noted Americans.

43 For pro-Meek and anti-missionary accounts of the controversy as to whether Meek or Thornton had the greater influence in Washington see Victor, *Early Indian Wars,* pp. 132-135 *passim,* and Bancroft, *Oregon,* I, pp. 620-621; and for a defense of Abernethy and Thornton, see Medorem Crawford, "Governor George Abernethy," *Transactions of the Oregon Pioneer Association,* 1886, pp. 39-40. See L. B. Shippee, "Federal Relations of Oregon," *OHQ,* XX, 1919, p. 349 for the political significance of the Cayuse War.

Chapter IV

(pp. 70-81)

1 Hunter Miller, *Treaties and Other International Acts of the United States of America,* V, pp. 3-5.

2 Galbraith, *Hudson's Bay Company*, pp. 108, 222-224, 242, 248-249, 255; letters of Simpson to McLoughlin, March 1, 1842, *McLoughlin's Fort Vancouver Letters, Second Series*, p. 263, and Jan. 1, 1845, Third Series, pp. 87-88n; Governor and Committee to McLoughlin, Dec. 21, 1842 and Sept. 27, 1843, *McLoughlin's Fort Vancouver Letters*, Second Series, pp. 297, 315; Aberdeen to Peel, Oct. 17, 1845, quoted by Frederick Merk, "The Oregon Pioneers and the Boundary," *AHR*, XXIX, 1924, pp. 698-699.

3 Galbraith, *Hudson's Bay Company*, pp. 248-249; letters of Eden Colvile to Sir J. H. Pelly, Nov. 22, 1849, to Sir George Simpson, Nov. 24, 1849, to Governor and Committee, July 21, 1852, *London Correspondence Inward From Eden Colvile, 1849-1852*, E. E. Rich, ed., H.B.S. XIX, pp. 9-10, 139, 185; Governor and Committee to Colvile, April 7, 1852, *ibid.*, p. 137n; Oscar O. Winther, *The Old Oregon Country*, pp. 58-59.

4 See Introduction, note 2 for sources and authorities on the diplomacy of the Oregon Question. Galbraith's interpretation in *Hudson's Bay Company* seems most satisfactory to the writer. That Oregon's "Pioneer homebuilders finally won Oregon for the United States" is the theme of Leslie M. Scott's "Influence of American Settlement Upon the Oregon Boundary Treaty of 1846," *OHQ*, XXIX, 1928, pp. 1-19. Frederick Merk's several articles trace the influence of particular factors having a bearing on the boundary negotiations. His earliest article, "Oregon Pioneers and the Boundary," *AHR*, XXIX, 1924, pp. 681-699, develops the idea that the pressure of American settlement convinced the Hudson's Bay Company to establish its main depot at Fort Victoria and that this in turn was decisive in Aberdeen's decision to sacrifice the disputed territory. Richard W. Van Alstyne in "International Rivalries in Pacific Northwest," *OHQ*, XLVI, 1945, pp. 185-218, and Melvin C. Jacobs in *Winning Oregon* find American settlement of major importance, while Norman A. Graebner's *Empire of the Pacific* discounts it and Manifest Destiny entirely as factors in the diplomacy of the boundary question.

The debates on the Oregon Question can be traced in the *Congressional Globe*, 27th Cong., 3rd Sess., 28th Cong., 1st and 2nd Sessions, and 29th Cong., 1st Sess., and are summarized in Throckmorton, Oregon Boundary Controversy, pp. 54-75, 170-204. For Polk's statements regarding Oregon up to 54° 40′ see Richardson, *A Compilation of the Messages and Papers of the Presidents, 1789-1897*, IV, pp. 373-382, 398-399.

5 Throckmorton, Oregon Boundary Controversy, pp. 143-153, 167-170; Galbraith, *Hudson's Bay Company*, pp. 233-250.

6 Douglas and Ogden to Governor and Committee, Sept. 20, 1847, Hudson's Bay Archives, quoted in Galbraith, *Hudson's Bay Company*, p. 255.

7 *Ibid.*, pp. 252-253; Bancroft, *Oregon*, II, pp. 73, 113-130, 260-281; McLoughlin to Governor and Committee, Nov. 20, 1845, *McLoughlin's Fort Vancouver Letters*, Third Series, p. 107. See U. S. *Statutes at Large*, IX, pp. 323-331, 496-500 for the Oregon territorial bill and the Donation Act.

8 Galbraith, *Hudson's Bay Company*, pp. 109, 248-249, 462n. For the effects of the gold rush at Fort Vancouver see letters of Eden Colvile to Sir J. H. Pelly, Oct. 26, Nov. 22, 1849, Jan. 14, March 5, 1850, *London Correspondence*, pp. 7-10, 15-16, 20; to Sir George Simpson, Oct. 15, 26, Nov. 24, and Dec. 7, 1849, *ibid.*, pp. 181-185, 189-190; John Work to Colvile, Nov. 26, 1849, quoted in Colvile to Pelly, Dec. 8, 1849, *ibid.*, pp. 12-13.

9 Colvile to Governor and Committee, July 21, 1852, *London Correspondence*, pp. 139-140; *British and American Joint Commission for the Settlement of the Hudson's Bay and the Puget Sound Agricultural Companies*, III, p. 180. (Hereafter cited *HBC vs US*.)

10 Frank E. Ross, "The Retreat of the Hudson's Bay Company in the Pacific Northwest," *Canadian Historical Review*, XVIII, 1937, pp. 268-270.

11 Ralph Richard Martig, "Hudson's Bay Company Claims, 1846-69," *OHQ*, XXXVI, 1935, p. 64; *HBS vs US*, III, p. 202; Astoria Custom-House Records, 1848-1869 (microfilm, O.H.S.); Colvile to Governor and Committee, July 21, 1852, *London Correspondence*, pp. 135-138; Douglas and Ogden to Governor and Committee, Sept. 20, 1847, Hudson's Bay Archives, quoted by Galbraith, *Hudson's Bay Company*, p. 255; and *ibid.*, pp. 265-267.

12 *Ibid.*, pp. 269-273; John S. Galbraith, "George N. Sanders, 'Influence Man' for the Hudson's Bay Company," *OHQ,* LIII, 1952, pp. 159-176. The diplomacy regarding the Hudson's Bay claims may be traced in Hunter Miller, *Treaties,* VIII, pp. 949-1065.

13 Galbraith, *Hudson's Bay Company,* pp. 263-275; *HBC vs US,* III, pp. 189-204; John A. Hussey, *The History of Fort Vancouver and Its Physical Structure,* pp. 91-114; Walter N. Sage, "The Place of Ft. Vancouver in the History of the Northwest," *PNQ,* XXXIX, 1948, pp. 101-102.

14 Galbraith, *Hudson's Bay Company,* pp. 275-281.

15 Herman J. Deutsch, in "Economic Imperialism in the Pacific Northwest," *PHR,* IX, 1940, pp. 385, 387-388, distinguishes between "imperialism" or the type of capitalism that was exploitive with the profits derived from the region being used elsewhere, and "pioneering" which was attended by the type of capitalism in which profits were used for the permanent development of the region.

Chapter V

(pp. 85-106)

1 President Polk's Fourth Annual Message, Dec. 5, 1848, in J. D. Richardson, *Messages and Papers of the Presidents,* IV, p. 2486.

2 *Californian,* Sept. 26, 1848, quoted in *Oregon Spectator,* Oct. 12, 1848.

3 This was especially true of the forty-niners who came via Cape Horn. Raymond A. Rydell, *Cape Horn to the Pacific: The Rise and Decline of an Ocean Highway,* pp. 125-126.

4 Rodman W. Paul, *California Gold,* pp. 24-25. The official figure for California's population by the census of 1850 was 92,597. Paul states that this figure was at least 19,000 short of the true figure, since returns for San Francisco and two other counties were lost. He gives the following summary, based upon considerable population data: "California's population jumped from 14,000 in 1848 to something less than 100,000 at the close of 1849, and . . . advanced to 223,000 by the latter part of 1852."

5 *Ibid.,* pp. 187-188; John W. Caughey, *California,* p. 258.

6 Paul, *California Gold,* pp. 20-21; John W. Caughey, *Gold is the Cornerstone,* pp. 46-47, 294-295. For the Australian gold rushes see W. P. Morrell, *The Gold Rushes,* Chaps. VII and VIII.

7 Galbraith, *Hudson's Bay Company,* p. 462n, citing Ogden to Simpson, Sept. 15, 1849, Hudson's Bay Archives; F. G. Young, "The Oregon Trail," *OHQ,* I, 1900, p. 370.

8 Bancroft, *Oregon,* II, pp. 42-47; Winther, *The Old Oregon Country,* p. 120.

9 *Biography of Rev. G. H. Atkinson, D. D., Journal of Sea Voyage to Oregon in 1848, and Selected Addresses and Printed Articles, and a Particular Account of his Churchwork in the Pacific Northwest,* Nancy B. Atkinson, compiler, p. 441. (Hereafter cited Atkinson, *Biography.*)

10 Letters of George Abernethy to Major Jas. A. Hardie, Oct. 10, 1848, and to Edward F. Folger, Feb. 16, 1849, Abernethy Mss., O.H.S. Bancroft, *Oregon,* II, p. 43n; James Taylor to William Taylor, April 16, 1849, "Oregon Territory in 1849-50," Priscilla Knuth and Charles M. Gates, eds., *PNQ,* XL, 1949, pp. 18-19; the Rev. Ezra Fisher to the Rev. Benjamin M. Hill, Sept. 20, Oct. 19, 1848, Feb. 2, 3, March 1, 1849, "Fisher Correspondence," *OHQ,* XVII, 1916, pp. 160, 164, 167, 169, 276.

11 George Abernethy to the Rev. Gustavus Hines, Feb. 19, 1849, Abernethy Mss., O.H.S.; Hezekiah Johnson to the editor of the *Western Christian Journal,* Jan. 25, 1849, "Letters of Hezekiah Johnson," J. Orin Oliphant, ed., *PNQ,* XXXVII, 1946, pp. 28-30; R. C. Clark, *History of the Willamette Valley,* I, p. 450; John Burkhart to David E. Blair, Dec. 5, 1849, "John Burkhart and Oregon Territory, 1849," Robert W. Johannsen, ed., *OHQ,* LIII, 1952, p. 202.

12 *Oregon Spectator,* Oct. 12, Nov. 9, and Dec. 28, 1848; James Taylor to William Taylor, April 16, 1849, "Oregon Territory in 1849-50," Knuth and Gates, eds., *PNQ,* XL, 1949, p. 19; C. H. Carey, *History of Oregon,* I, pp. 509-510.

13 George H. Atkinson to Josiah Little, Feb. 7, 1849, "Oregon Territory in 1849-50," Knuth and Gates, eds., *PNQ,* XL, 1949, p. 17; Bancroft, *Oregon,* II, p. 48n; letters of George Abernethy to Edward F. Folger, Feb. 16, 1849, and to C. L. Ross, April 20, 1849, Abernethy Mss., O.H.S.

14 Captain John H. Couch, Journal, Mss., O.H.S.; biographical sketch of John H. Couch in *Oregon Pioneer Transactions,* 1886, pp. 64-65; *Lewis and Dryden's Marine History of the Pacific Northwest,* E. W. Wright, ed., p. 26. (Hereafter cited *Lewis and Dryden's Marine History.*)

15 Letters of Abernethy to C. L. Ross, San Francisco, March 10, 1848; to Edward F. Folger, New York, March 11, July 13, 1848; to Captain Roland Gelston, New York, April 28, 1848, Abernethy Mss., O.H.S.

16 *Oregon Spectator,* Jan. 20, Oct. 26, 1848; Flora Belle Ludington, "Oregon Newspapers, 1846-70," *OHQ,* XXVI, 1925, p. 246; letters of George Abernethy to C. L. Ross, Jan. 9, 1849, and to Hiram Clark, Feb. 20, 1849, Abernethy Mss., O.H.S.

17 Letters of George Abernethy to Edward F. Folger, Feb. 16; to the Rev. Gustavus Hines, Feb. 19; to Charles Pope, Feb. 19; to C. L. Ross, Feb. 20; and to S. & S. Halsted, June 19, 1849, Abernethy Mss., O.H.S. J. Quinn Thorton, in *Oregon and California in 1848,* I, p. 330, refers to the number of mills in the territory.

18 *Oregon Spectator,* Oct. 12, 1848.

19 Letters of George Abernethy to C. E. Pickett, Nov. 8, 1848; to C. L. Ross, Nov. 8, 1848 and Feb. 20, 1849; and to Edward F. Folger, Feb. 16, 1849, Abernethy Mss., O.H.S.; the Rev. G. H. Atkinson to Josiah Little, Feb. 7, 1849, "Oregon Territory in 1849-50," Knuth and Gates, eds., *PNQ,* XL, 1949, p. 17. For similar comments, see the Rev. Ezra Fisher to the Rev. B. M. Hill, March 1, 1849, "Fisher Correspondence," *OHQ,* XVII, 1916, p. 276. For the loss of the *Vancouver,* see Bancroft, *Oregon,* II, p. 23.

20 The Rev. W. M. Roberts to Pitman, Feb. 14, 1849, "Roberts Letters," Gatke, ed., *OHQ,* XXII, 1921, p. 248.

21 C. L. Ross, Experiences of a Pioneer of 1847 in California, 1878, Pacific Manuscripts, Bancroft Library, University of California. Letters of George Abernethy to Edward F. Folger, Aug. 17, 1848; to C. L. Ross, Nov. 8, 1848, Jan. 9, 20, 1849; to Capt. Roland Gelston, April 9, 1849, Abernethy Mss., O.H.S. Bancroft, *Oregon,* II, p. 50; Gilbert, *Trade and Currency,* pp. 74-75; *Oregon Spectator,* Dec. 28, 1848; Rev. G. H. Atkinson to Josiah Little, Feb. 7, 1849, "Oregon Territory in 1849-50," Knuth and Gates, eds., *PNQ,* XL, 1949, p. 17; John Burkhart to David E. Blair, Dec. 5, 1849, "John Burkhart and Oregon Territory, 1849," Robert W. Johannsen, ed., *OHQ,* LIII, 1952, pp. 201-203.

22 Caughey, *Gold Is the Cornerstone,* pp. 212-213; H. H. Bancroft, *History of California,* VII, pp. 76-77.

23 Letters of George Abernethy to C. E. Pickett, Nov. 8, 1848; to E. H. Grimes, Nov. 9, 1848; to C. L. Ross, Feb. 20, 1849; to Ross, Benton & Co., July 2, 25, 1849; to Capt. Roland Gelston, April 9, Aug. 29, 1849; to Edward F. Folger, July 2, 1849; and to Hiram Clark, Sept. 19, 1849, Abernethy Mss., O.H.S.; George H. Atkinson to Josiah Little, Feb. 7, 1849, "Oregon Territory in 1849-50," Knuth and Gates, eds., *PNQ,* XL, 1949, p. 17; *Oregon Spectator,* Nov. 1, 1849; Gilbert, *Trade and Currency,* p. 76.

24 Letters of George Abernethy to Capt. Roland Gelston, May 18, 1849; to Ross, Benton & Co., July 2, 1849; to Hiram Clark, Feb. 13, 1850, Abernethy Mss., O.H.S.; H. H. Bancroft, *History of Washington, Idaho, and Montana,* p. 205n.

25 Edmond S. Meany, Jr., History of the Lumber Industry in the Pacific Northwest to 1917, (Ph.D. thesis, Harvard University, 1935, microfilm), p. 81. Gilbert, *Trade and Currency,* p. 75; H. W. Scott, *History of Portland, Oregon* (1890), p. 112; letters of George Abernethy to Edward F. Folger, July 26; to H. Clark Feb. 20; and to Ross, Benton & Co., July 2, 1849, Abernethy Mss., O.H.S. Letters

of E. Colvile to Sir J. H. Pelly, Oct. 26, Dec. 8, 1849, *London Correspondence,* pp. 7-8, 12-13. The Abernethy letters cited here reveal that in February the price of Oregon lumber delivered on board ship was $20 and $25 per M, and freights to San Francisco were $40 per ton and $5.00 per barrel. In July lumber put on board at $60 per M was transported to California at the rate of $60 per M.

26 Gilbert, *Trade and Currency,* p. 74; letters of George Abernethy to Capt. Roland Gelston and to Ross, Benton & Co., Aug. 29, 1849, Abernethy Mss., O.H.S.; *Oregon Spectator,* Nov. 1, 1849.

27 C. L. Ross, Experiences of a Pioneer of 1847 in California, 1878, Pacific Manuscripts, Bancroft Library, University of California. George Gibbs to his mother, June 26, 1850, "Pacific Northwest Letters of George Gibbs," Vernon Carstensen, ed., *OHQ,* LIV, 1953, p. 201; *Oregon Spectator,* Oct. 18, Nov. 1, Dec. 13, 1849; Gilbert, *Trade and Currency,* p. 76.

28 *Ibid.,* pp. 79-81, 86-87. In his letter to C. L. Ross, Jan. 9, 1849, Abernethy Mss., O.H.S., Abernethy complains of having received gold dust at $16 per ounce, which he paid out for wages at $11-$12 per ounce, and is grateful for Ross's offer to send him a supply of cash.

29 Gilbert, *Trade and Currency,* pp. 78-88.

30 *Oregon Spectator,* Nov. 1, Dec. 13, 1849; *Oregon Statesman* (Oregon City), March 26, 1851; George Abernethy to Charles Pope, Feb. 13, 1850, Abernethy Mss., O.H.S.

31 Gilbert, *Trade and Currency,* p. 74; Abernethy's correspondence often refers to the plethora of gold and the paucity of goods during the early part of 1849. Letters of Abernethy to Edward F. Folger, Feb. 16, 1849, to Ross Benton & Co. and to Capt. Roland Gelston, Aug. 29, 1849, Abernethy Mss., O.H.S.

32 Letters of George Abernethy to James Bishop, Feb. 13, 1849; to Munson S. Peet, Feb. 19, 1849; to Capt. Roland Gelston, April 9, June 30, Aug. 29, Sept. 7, 1849 and Feb. 13, 1850; to S. & S. Halsted, June 8, 19, Aug. 29, 1849, and Jan. 1, 8, 1850; to Haynes Lord & Co., to John Falconer, to de Gray and Stiles, April 9, 1849; to Hiram Clark, Feb. 20, Sept. 8, 18, 1849, Jan. 1, 8, 19 and Feb. 13, 1850; to C. L. Ross, Feb. 20, 1849, to Edward F. Folger, July 2, 26, 1849; to Charles Pope, Aug. 29, 1849 and Feb. 13, 1850; to Rev. William Roberts, Aug. 1, 1849, Abernethy Mss., O.H.S.; John H. Kemble, *The Panama Route, 1848-1869,* pp. 7, 32-37. For the condition of the San Francisco market from 1851 to 1853 see Rydell, *Cape Horn,* p. 134.

33 *Oregon Spectator,* Nov. 14, 28, 1850, July 3, 1851.

34 George Abernethy to Governor Joseph Lane, Dec. 9, 1851, Abernethy Mss., O.H.S.; C. W. Thomas to J. Failing & Co., Nov. 19, 1852, Feb. 5, 22, 1853, Corbett and Failing Mss., Special Collections, University of Oregon Library (hereafter cited CFUO) ; Bancroft, *Oregon,* II, p. 258.

35 Joseph Schafer, "The Western Ocean as a Determinant in Oregon History," H. Morse Stephens and Herbert E. Bolton, eds., *The Pacific Ocean in History,* pp. 295-296.

Chapter VI

(pp. 107-123)

1 *Lewis and Dryden's Marine History,* pp. 26, 53; *Oregon Spectator,* Nov. 28, 1850 (adv.); *Oregonian* (Portland), March 22, 1851 (adv.) .

2 Corbett and McLarens to Bingham and Reynolds, Oct. 10, 1853, CFUO (See Chap. VII, fn. 10) . References to Abernethy's shipping enterprise are widely scattered, but it is evident from the letter cited that the line was well established in 1853 with more than one ship in operation and with a warehouse in San Francisco. Many of Corbett's shipping manifests carry the heading, "Cleared by Abernethy, Clark & Co., San Francisco." The Oregon and California Packet Line is advertised in the *Oregon Statesman,* Nov. 18, 1856, *et seq.* For other references to Abernethy's line and its ships see *Lewis and Dryden's Marine History,* pp. 26, 47, 66-67, 130.

3   Kemble, *The Panama Route*, pp. 7-31, 36-38, 174-175, 185-196, 206-208, 308; *Oregonian*, July 12, 1851, *et seq.* (adv.); Gerstle Mack, *The Land Divided: A History of the Panama Canal and Other Isthmian Projects*, p. 156; Rydell, *Cape Horn*, p. 139.

4   Kemble, *The Panama Route*, pp. 46-56, *passim*, 147-148, 206, 209. See *ibid.*, Chap. III for the Aspinwall-Vanderbilt competition, and the *Oregonian*, July 12, 1851, *et seq.* for the advertisement of the Pacific Mail Co.

5   Rydell, *Cape Horn*, p. 125.

6   Morison, *Maritime History of Massachusetts*, pp. 341-344; Arthur H. Clark, *The Clipper Ship Era*, p. 104, Chap. VII; Rydell, *Cape Horn*, pp. 134-140.

7   *Oregonian*, July 25, 1853, *et seq.* (adv.); catalog for the Astoria Custom-House Records, 1848-68, O.H.S.

8   Kemble, *The Panama Route*, pp. 41-45; Bancroft, *Oregon*, II, p. 188; the Rev. Ezra Fisher to the Rev. Benj. M. Hill, July 10, 1850, "Fisher Correspondence," *OHQ*, XVII, 1916, pp. 318-319; *Lewis and Dryden's Marine History*, p. 35n.

9   *Oregon Statesman*, April 25, 1854; C. H. Carey, *History of Oregon*, I, pp. 508-510; F. G. Young, "The Oregon Trail," *OHQ*, I, 1900, p. 370; Fisher to the Rev. B. M. Hill, Nov. 16, 1850 and Oct. 1, 1851, "Fisher Correspondence," *OHQ*, XVII, 1916, pp. 332, 443. The *Oregon Spectator*, Nov. 4, 1851, estimates the 1851 immigration at from 7,000 to 9,000; and the *Oregonian*, March 23, 1852, gives it at from 6,000 to 10,000. The *Oregon Statesman*, April 25, 1854, estimates the immigration of 1852 at 11,000 to 12,000.

10 *U. S. Statutes at Large*, IX, pp. 496-500; Carey, *History of Oregon*, I, pp. 391, 399, 435, 509-510.

11 Copy of Original Schedules of the Census of 1850 for Oregon, O.H.S.; H. H. Bancroft, *Chronicles of the Builders of the Commonwealth*, I, p. 602; H. W. Scott, *History of Portland*, p. 105.

12 Eden Colville to Sir George Simpson, Nov. 24, 1849, *London Correspondence*, H.B.S. XIX, p. 185.

13 The Rev. Ezra Fisher to the Rev. Benj. M. Hill, Nov. 14, 1849, "Fisher Correspondence," *OHQ*, XVII, 1916, p. 285.

14 For the general topic of the rise of towns in Oregon see Lewis A. McArthur's convenient compendium, *Oregon Geographic Names*; Howard McKinley Corning, *Williamette Landings: Ghost Towns of the River;* and Johansen and Gates, *Empire of the Columbia*, Chap. 13. Important contemporary observations are found in the Rev. Ezra Fisher's letters to the Rev. B. M. Hill, Nov. 11, 1849, Jan 26, 1850, Jan. 30, May 25 and Sept. 6, 1852, "Fisher Correspondence," *OHQ*, XVII, 1916, pp. 285-300, 446-470.

15 *Oregon Spectator*, Nov. 14, 1850; Corning, *Williamette Landings*, p. 19.

16 Joseph Gaston, *Portland*, I, Chaps. X and XI; Atkinson, *Biography*, p. 119.

17 Corning, *Williamette Landings*, pp. 19, 27, 33, 62; Randall V. Mills, "A History of Transportation in the Pacific Northwest," *OHQ*, XLVII, 1946, p. 283; Gaston, *Portland*, I, p. 207.

18 Johansen and Gates, *Empire of the Columbia*, p. 272.

19 The five towns listed in the official publication of the census of 1850 are Astoria, Linn City, Milton City, Oregon City, and Portland. Jesse S. Douglas, in "Origins of the Population of Oregon in 1850," *Pacific Northwest Quarterly*, XLI, 1950, p. 100, corrects the figures for the population of Oregon's towns given in the official listing. His work is based upon a careful re-check of the original schedules. He notes, however, that it is impossible to determine the correct population of Astoria from an examination of the schedules.

20 Corning, *Williamette Landings*, pp. 43, 62; Mills, "A History of Transportation," *OHQ*, XLVII, 1946, p. 283.

21 Corning, *Williamette Landings*, pp. 28-29; George Gibbs to his mother, June 26, 1850, "Pacific Northwest Letters of George Gibbs," Vernon Carstensen, ed., *OHQ*, LIV, 1953, p. 201; *Oregonian*, Oct. 8, 1853.

22 Dorothy O. Johansen, Capitalism on the Far Western Frontier: The Oregon Steam Navigation Company (Ph.D. thesis, University of Washington, 1941), p. 59. (Hereafter cited Johansen, *Capitalism*.)

23 Corning, *Willamette Landings*, pp. 29-30; Gaston, *Portland*, I, pp. 207-208; Bancroft, *Oregon*, II, p. 251n; *Oregonian*, Dec. 4, 1850; *Lewis and Dryden's Marine History*, p. 31.

24 Gaston, *Portland*, I, p. 208; *Oregonian*, May 3, 17, 1851.

25 *Lewis and Dryden's Marine History*, pp. 33-45; Bancroft, *Oregon*, II, pp. 255-257; Irene Lincoln Poppleton, "Oregon's First Monopoly—The O. S. N. Co.," *OHQ*, IX, 1908, pp. 274-302; *Oregonian*, July 31, 1852 (adv.); *Oregon Spectator*, Sept. 2, 1853, cited by Johansen, *Capitalism*, p. 60n.

26 From a copy of the original schedules of the census of 1850, O.H.S.

27 McArthur, *Oregon Geographic Names*, *passim*; Corning, *Willamette Landings*, pp. 111-120; Johansen, *Capitalism*, pp. 1, 25-37; H. W. Scott, "Pioneer Character of Oregon Progress," *OHQ*, XVIII, 1917, p. 251.

28 Letters of the Rev. Ezra Fisher to Rev. B. M. Hill, Jan. 17, 1851, and Jan. 30, 1852, "Fisher Correspondence," *OHQ*, XVII, 1916, pp. 335, 449; Bushrod Wilson to Joseph P. Wilson, April 28, 1852, Bushrod Wilson Letters, Special Collections, University of Oregon Library.

29 Corning, *Willamette Landings*, pp. 37-52, 121.

30 Hezekiah Johnson to the editor of the *Western Christian Journal*, Jan. 25, 1849, "Letters of Hezekiah Johnson, 1838-1849," J. Orin Oliphant, ed., *PNQ*, XXXVII, 1946, pp. 28-30; Abernethy to Hines, Feb. 19, 1849, Abernethy Mss., O.H.S.; Atkinson, *Biography*, p. 441; George Gibbs to his mother, June 26, 1850, "Pacific Northwest Letters of George Gibbs," Carstensen, ed., *OHQ*, LIV, 1953, p. 200.

31 Lancaster Pollard, "The Pacific Northwest: A Regional Study," *OHQ*, LII, 1951, pp. 215-216.

Chapter VII

(pp. 124-141)

1 *The Eighth Census*, 1860, *Agriculture*, p. 222.

2 See introduction to Sidney Wallach, ed., *Narrative of an American Squadron to the China Seas and Japan Under the Command of Commodore M. C. Perry*, and Arthur Walworth, *Black Ships off Japan: The Story of Commodore Perry's Expedition*, introduction and pp. 14-18, for background and new significance of Manifest Destiny in the Pacific with America's expansion to the Pacific. For the immigration of Chinese coolies to San Francisco see Frank Soule', John H. Gihon, and James Nisbet, *Annals of San Francisco*, p. 413. (Hereafter, cited Soule', *Annals*.)

3 *Journal of Commerce* (Portland), April 20, 1853.

4 William L. Brewster, *William Mead Ladd of Portland, Oregon*, pp. 3-4.

5 Joseph Gaston, *Portland*, II, p. 106; Henry Failing, Statement, July 19, 1888, Pacific Manuscripts, Bancroft Library, University of California.

6 See H. H. Bancroft, *Chronicles of the Builders of the Commonwealth*, I, pp. 584-643 (hereafter cited Bancroft, *Chronicles*); Gaston, *Portland*, III, pp. 517-520; and Brewster, *William Mead Ladd*, pp. 3-26, for biographical sketches of William Sargent Ladd. Biographical histories like that of Gaston are highly eulogistic, but it is obvious that the factual data is derived from personal interviews.

7 Glenn Chesney Quiett, in *They Built the West*, pp. 350-351, refers to Portland as "a small edition of Boston."

8 Henry Failing, Statement, July 19, 1888, Pac. Mss., Bancroft Library, University of California; Bancroft, *Chronicles*, I, pp. 602-605, *passim*.

9 See Joseph A. Schumpeter, *The Theory of Economic Development*, pp. 74-78, 128-138.

10 H. W. Corbett, invoices, Corbett, Failing Co. records, Special Collections, University of Oregon Library. Business records for this period are generally scarce. There are various miscellaneous manuscripts, letter books, account books, etc. at the library of the Oregon Historical Society. Most of these are incomplete or for brief periods. Unfortunately the records for such firms as Allen and Lewis and Meier and Frank, the latter founded in 1855 and later to become Portland's great department store, are either unavailable or nonexistent. Only a few Ladd manuscripts are available. The most abundant set of business records the present writer has been able to find are those of Henry W. Corbett and Henry Failing. These span the period, 1851-91, but there are several disconcerting breaks. Prior to 1871 Corbett and Failing were competitors, but consolidated their firms in that year. The earlier records of both firms were thrown together haphazardly and those surviving have found three different depositories, and are classified as follows: (1) Corbett and Failing, Business Records, Oregon Historical Society, Portland, Oregon (hereafter cited CFOHS); (2) Corbett, Failing Co. Records, Special Collections, University of Oregon Library (hereafter cited CFUO); and (3) Corbett and Failing manuscripts, The Grace D. and R. R. Stuart Collection of Western Americana, College of the Pacific, Stockton, California (hereafter cited CFCOP). Short biographical sketches of Henry W. Corbett are contained in *Dictionary of American Biography*, IV, pp. 435-436; Bancroft, *Chronicles*, II, 572-593; and Gaston, *Portland*, II, pp. 22-27; and his early business career, which is treated in this and succeeding chapters, is summarized in the present author's "The Role of the Merchant on the Oregon Frontier: The Early Business Career of Henry W. Corbett, 1851-1869," *Journal of Economic History*, XVI, 1956, pp. 539-550.

11 Williams, Bradford & Co. to H. W. Corbett, Jan. 7, 1852, CFUO, "You must make your books conform to ours if our accounts are correct and then what is coming to us will be divided at the settlement. The commission accounts you will settle yourself and we will merely pay over as your agents & charge to you such sums as you may order. We do not wish to be known in these matters generally. The charges for freight, insurance &c &c you must make yourself . . ."

12 Bancroft, *Chronicles*, II, pp. 575-576; *Oregonian*, April 18, 1851; H. W. Corbett, day-book, 1851-52, CFCOP; Williams, Bradford & Co. to H. W. Corbett, Feb. 3, 1852, CFUO; Soule', *Annals*, pp. 366-367.

13 Sources for the prices given are H. W. Corbett, day-book, CFCOP, J. Failing and Company, Invoices, 1852, CFUO; C. H. Juergens, "Movement of Wholesale Prices in New York City, 1825-1863," *American Statistics Association Publications*, XII, 1910-1911, table opposite p. 544; *Wholesale Prices, Wages, and Transportation*, Senate Report, No. 1394, Part 2, 52nd Cong., 2nd Sess., pp. 155 and 195; and "Wholesale Prices Current," listed occasionally in the *Oregonian*. See *Oregonian*, May 24, July 25, Aug. 1, Oct. 4, 1851, March 20, and July 3, 1852.

14 H. W. Corbett, day-book, CFCOP: letters of Williams, Bradford & Co. to H. W. Corbett, Jan. 7, 24, Feb. 3, 1852, CFUO. The Jewish trade is also mentioned by R. N. & F. McLaren in a letter to H. W. Corbett in June, 1853, CFUO, in which Corbett was urged to send out clothing suitable for wholesaling only. "The Jews will always do the clothing trade," it was stated. By mid-decade an important coterie of Jewish merchants had appeared in Portland, among them Aaron Meier, who founded what is today one of the largest department stores in the Pacific Northwest. For a short biographical sketch of Aaron Meier, see Gaston, *Portland*, II, pp. 234-238.

15 Letters of Williams, Bradford & Co. to H. W. Corbett, Jan. 7 and Feb. 7, 1852, CFUO.

16 H. W. Corbett, day-book, CFCOP; letters of H. W. Corbett to Williams, Bradford & Co., Jan. 7, 1852 and to Samuel Roosevelt & Co., Jan. 20, 1858, CFUO; Bancroft, *Chronicles*, II, pp. 575-576; contract, H. W. Corbett and Williams, Bradford & Co., New York, Oct. 12, 1850, cancelled, Aug. 28, 1852, CFOHS; contract, H. W. Corbett and R. N. and F. McLaren, CFOHS.

17 R. N. and F. McLaren to H. W. Corbett, June 14, 1853; and R. N. and F. McLaren to Edward Sly, July 25, 1853, CFUO. *Oregon Statesman*, April 2, 1853, adv.

18 A financial statement, J. Failing & Co., Jan. 1, 1859, CFCOP, shows that the respective shares of the partners in 1857 were: C. W. Thomas, three-fifths; Josiah Failing, one-fifth; and Henry Failing, one-fifth.

19 C. W. Thomas to J. Failing & Co., Nov. 3, 1852, CFUO; Gaston, *Portland*, II, pp. 54, 66; Henry Failing, Statement, July 19, 1888, Pac. Mss., Bancroft Library, University of California.

20 See Soule', *Annals*, p. 367, for selling on commission or at auction in San Francisco. There are several references to this practice in the business records of R. N. & F. McLaren, CFUO. For example, there is an account sales of a consignment of merchandise received from the ship *Robert Burton* and sold for $2,184.95 for the account and risk of John S. Hill, New York City. There are several other accounts of this sort. The commission rate was ten per cent.

21 C. W. Thomas to J. Failing & Co. (date missing, but evidently 1852), CFUO.

22 C. W. Thomas to J. Failing & Co., Aug. 3, Nov. 3, 1852, CFUO

23 *Oregonian*, Feb. 7, 1852, Jan. 22, 29, Feb. 5, 1853; Gaston, *Portland*, II, p. 55; *Lewis and Dryden's Marine History*, pp. 19, 49, *passim*; James A. Gibbs, Jr., *Pacific Graveyard*, pp. 51-54; C. W. Thomas to J. Failing & Co., Sept. 4, 1852, CFUO.

24 C. W. Thomas to J. Failing & Co., Sept. 4, Nov. 3, 1852, Jan. 4, Feb. 22, March 21, 1853, CFUO.

25 Bancroft, *Chronicles*, I, p. 607.

26 Letters of C. W. Thomas to J. Failing & Co., Nov. 3, 1852 and April 20, 1853, CFUO; *Oregonian*, April 15, 1853.

27 Invoices of goods shipped by C. W. Thomas to J. Failing & Co. for 1852 and 1853, CFUO.

28 C. W. Thomas to J. Failing & Co., Nov. 19, 1853, Feb. 5, 1853; George Abernethy to A. S. Abernethy, Jan. 10, 1854, private collection of Miss Vara Caufield, McLoughlin House, Oregon City. Manifest of cargo of the bark *American* from New York, April 1, 1853, and filed at the Astoria Custom-House, Sept. 19, 1853, Astoria Custom-House Records (Microfilm, Oregon Historical Society). Abernethy mentions that the *American* was purchased sometime in 1853, but apparently at San Francisco and for the purpose of carrying lumber from Oak Point to San Francisco.

29 C. W. Thomas to J. Failing & Co., Feb. 22, 1853, CFUO.

30 This assumption is based only upon the fact that his advertisements in the Portland, Oregon City, and Salem papers were more extensive than those of any other wholesaler.

31 Letters of George Abernethy to A. S. Abernethy, Jan. 10, 1854, and March 18, 1855, private collection of Miss Vara Caufield, McLoughlin House, Oregon City.

32 Letters of C. W. Thomas to J. Failing & Co., Dec. 6, 1852, Feb. 5, April 20, 1853, CFUO.

33 Invoices, J. Failing & Co., 1852-54, CFUO.

Chapter VIII

(pp. 159-180)

1 *Oregonian*, April 24, May 8, June 26, July 17, 1852.

2 James H. Gilbert, *Trade and Currency in Early Oregon*, p. 76; *Oregonian*, May 24, July 26, August 2, Sept. 27, 1851.

3 *Oregonian*, Oct. 4, Dec. 20, 1851; Jan. 3, Feb. 14, March 13, June 26, and July 1, 1852.

4 *Oregonian*, April 24, and June 26, 1852. Also Soule', *Annals*, p. 413.

5 Thomas S. Kendall to Smith, Jan. 25, 1852, "Thomas S. Kendall's Letter on Oregon Agriculture, 1852," J. Orin Oliphant, ed., *Agricultural History*, IX, 1935, pp. 193, 195.

6 Bushrod Wilson to Joseph P. Wilson, April 28, 1852, Bushrod Wilson letters, Special Collections, University of Oregon Library.

7 *Oregonian*, Sept. 6, 20, 1851, Jan. 10, 1852; *History of Southern Oregon: Comprising Jackson, Josephine, Douglas, Curry and Coos Counties*, A. G. Walling, publisher and editor, pp. 335-339; William P. Tucker, The History of Jackson County, Oregon (M. A. thesis, University of Washington, 1931, copy, Oregon Historical Society), p. 33.

8 *Oregonian*, April 17, 24, May 15, July 3, 17, 31, and Aug. 14, 1852; Walling, *Southern Oregon*, p. 338; and Bancroft, *Oregon*, II, p. 738.

9 *Oregonian*, July 3, Aug. 21, 1852; Walling, *Southern Oregon*, pp. 338-339, 361.

10 *Oregonian*, May 14, Dec. 10, 1853; Walling, *Southern Oregon*, pp. 339-242, 360.

11 *History of the Willamette Valley*, H. O. Lang, ed., pp. 353 *et seq.* for the war of 1853; Carey, Bancroft, Walling, Lang and other general histories have accounts of the southern Oregon Indian wars.

12 Emil R. Peterson and Alfred Powers, *A Century of Coos and Curry: History of Southwest Oregon*, pp. 373-374; Verne Bright, "Randolph: Ghost Gold Town of the Oregon Beaches," *OHQ*, LVIII, 1957, pp. 293-306.

13 *Oregonian*, June 26, 1852.

14 Elaine Tanner, "A Study of the Underlying Causes of the Depression of 1854," *RCB*, XXV (April, 1947), p. 48; Binger Hermann, "Early Southern Oregon," *OHQ*, XIX, 1918, p. 63.

15 *Oregonian*, Aug. 21, Oct. 23, and Nov. 18, 1852; "Pacific Northwest Letters of George Gibbs," Vernon Carstensen, ed., *OHQ*, LIV, 1953, p. 225; C. H. Carey, *History of Oregon*, I, p. 509.

16 Soule', *Annals*, pp. 411-413; Paul, *California Gold*, p. 25; *Oregonian*, Sept. 12, Oct. 27, and Dec. 18, 1852.

17 Account book, W. H. Barnhart & Co., O.H.S.; H. W. Corbett, day-book, CFCOP; letters of C. W. Thomas to J. Failing & Co., Nov. 3, 19, 1852, CFUO. Barnhart's monthly sales are tabulated in Tanner, "Depression of 1854," *RCB*, XXV, 1947, pp. 62-63.

18 *Oregonian*, Jan. 22, 29, Feb. 19, 1853; *Journal of Commerce*, April 6, 16, 1853. Shipping manifests, S. S. *Fremont*, arrived Astoria, Jan. 17, 1853; S. S. *Columbia*, arrived Astoria, Jan. 29, 1853; S. S. *Columbia*, departing from San Francisco, April 10, 1853, Astoria Custom-House Records (Microfilm, O.H.S.); Tanner, "Depression of 1854," *RCB*, XXV, 1947, pp. 43-44.

19 W. H. Barnhart & Co., San Francisco, to W. H. Barnhart & Co., Portland, April 9, 1853, W. H. Barnhart papers, O.H.S., quoted by Tanner, "Depression of 1854," *RCB*, XXV, 1947, pp. 50-51; *Journal of Commerce*, May 14, 1853; shipping manifests, May and June, 1853, Astoria Custom-House Records (Microfilm, O.H.S.).

20 *Oregonian*, Feb. 19, March 19, May 7, 14, 1852; *Journal of Commerce*, April 1, 23, 1853; Oscar Osburn Winther, "Pack Animals for Transportation in the Pacific Northwest," *PNQ*, XXXIV, 1943, p. 132.

21 Walling, *Southern Oregon*, p. 325; the *Oregonian*, March 19, April 26, 1853.

22 Soule', *Annals*, pp. 497-500, 519-521, 543-544; Felix Reisenberg, Jr., *Golden Gate: The Story of San Francisco Harbor*, pp. 144-146; Kemble, *The Panama Route, 1848-1869*, p. 255.

23 Soule', *Annals*, pp. 241, 274, 277, 299, 407, 329ff; *Oregonian*, Dec. 20, 1851, Jan. 1, 31, March 13, 20, 27, Nov. 27, 1852, and Jan. 22, 1853.

24 *Journal of Commerce*, April 13, 16, 20, 1853; *Oregonian*, May 28, June 19, 25, 1853; *Portland Commercial*, Aug. 25, 1853; shipping manifests, Astoria Custom-House Records (Microfilm, O.H.S.) seem to give a complete record of shipping in and out of Astoria for the first half of 1853. Later in the year, however, manifests of the Pacific Mail Steamship Company's regular steamships, both inward and outward, and the outward manifests of the sailing vessels were either filed irregularly or not at all.

335

25 R. N. & F. McLaren to H. W. Corbett, June, 1853, and to John S. Hill, June 14, 1853, CFUO.

26 *Oregonian,* June 4, 1853. The lumber manifested at the Astoria Custom-House from June 1 through Dec. 31 for San Francisco shows the following pattern: June, 826.7 M; July, 497.09 M; Aug., 214.2 M; Sept., 235.8 M; Oct., 146 M; Nov., none; and Dec., 136.4 M. (Shipping manifests, Astoria Custom-House Records, Microfilm, O.H.S.) These figures may not give an entirely accurate picture, since some shipping manifests may not have been filed.

27 Shipping manifest, schooner *Spray,* Dec. 9, 1853, Astoria Custom-House Records (Microfilm, O.H.S.) ; *Oregonian,* Aug. 13, 1853; *Portland Commercial,* Aug. 25, 1853. The *Oregonian,* Oct. 22, 1853, reports the immigration, based upon the actual count of the Indian agent at Umatilla, as follows: "The whole number is 6449; of which 898 are wives, 1408 sons, 1513 daughters; leaving 2630 men." A complete list of the names of the immigrants is given in the *Oregonian,* Oct. 29, 1853.

28 Tanner, "The Depression of 1854," *RCB,* XXV, 1947, pp. 52 *et passim;* Allan, Lowe & Co. to James Birnie, May 23, 1853, Allan, Lowe-Birnie correspondence, O.H.S., quoted in *ibid.,* p. 53; Walling, *Southern Oregon,* p. 338.

29 W. H. Barnhart & Co. to Wells, Fargo & Co., June 1, 1853 (W. H. Barnhart Co. papers, O.H.S.), quoted by Tanner, "Depression of 1854," *RCB,* XXV, 1947, p. 54; R. N. & F. McLaren to H. W. Corbett, June, 1853, and to Page, Bacon and Co., San Francisco, June 28, 1853; *Oregon Spectator,* Oct. 20, 1853.

30 *Oregonian,* Oct. 1, 8, Nov. 5, 1853; *Oregon Spectator,* Aug. 19, 1853.

31 R. N. & F. McLaren to H. W. Corbett, Aug. 25, 1853, CFUO.

32 Wells, Fargo & Co. to W. H. Barnhart & Co., Sept. 8, 1853; Preston O'Neill & Co. to W. H. Barnhart & Co., Dec. 20, 1853, Barnhart papers, O. H. S., both quoted in Tanner, "Depression of 1854," *RCB,* XXV, 1947, p. 54; *Oregonian,* Dec. 31, 1853.

33 *Oregon Statesman,* Sept. 13, 1853.

34 *Oregonian,* Dec. 12, 1853, Feb. 14, March 4, 1854; letters of Corbett and Mc-Larens to John S. Hill, Dec. 12, 1853, Feb. 28, 1854, CFUO.

35 John Kelly, Deer Creek, O. T., to W. H. Barnhart & Co., Dec. 20, 1853 (Barnhart papers, O.H.S.), quoted by Tanner, "Depression of 1854," *RCB,* XXV, 1947, p. 55.

36 *Oregonian,* Feb. 15, 1854; letters of Corbett and McLarens to Hulet & Co. and to Moss, March 4, 1854, CFUO.

37 *Oregonian,* Feb. 15, 1854.

38 *Oregonian,* Oct. 22, 29, Nov. 19, Dec. 31, 1853, April 1, 1854; Corbett and Mc-Larens to H. W. Corbett, Nov. 12, 1853, CFUO.

39 Corbett and McLarens to Mr. Hayes, April 12, 1854, CFUO; H. W. Corbett, day-book, CFCOP; invoices, J. Failing and Co., 1853-54, CFUO; the *Oregonian,* Feb. 18, 1854.

40 Shipping manifests of the barks *Metropolis,* Sept. 12, Nov. 25, 1854; *Acadia,* April 10, 1854; *Louisiana,* Aug. 11, 1854; of the brig *Princess Louisa,* June 18, 1854; of the schooner *Endorus,* March 26, 1854; and the S. S. *Peytona,* Jan. and Feb., 1854. Astoria Custom-House Records (Microfilm, O. H. S.) ; invoices, J. Failing & Co., 1853-54, CFUO; Rydell, *Cape Horn,* pp. 139-140.

41 Elaine Tanner, "Depression of 1854," *RCB,* XXV, 1947, asserts that the trade between the commercial centers of northern Oregon and the southern Oregon mining region was the very basis of Oregon's prosperity during 1852 and the spring of 1853, and the principal factor in stimulating the heavy importation of provisions and merchandise into northern Oregon during the spring of 1853. The great increase in the population of the Willamette Valley owing to the immigration of 1852 is given little weight in this argument. It is based on the further premise that a severe business slump had existed in Oregon during 1851, and with Oregon exports declining in 1852 and 1853, that mining alone accounts for a second inflationary cycle. These are Miss Tanner's reasons for

336

dividing the period at 1851. Thus she challenges Gilbert's assertion in *Trade and Currency*, pp. 93-94, that trade and business conditions in Oregon from 1848 to 1854 were characterized by a single inflationary cycle caused by California gold. The assumption that there was a business depression in Oregon during 1851 is based upon the sales of W. H. Barnhart & Co. of Portland which were low during the summer months. As the sales for this company rose during the latter part of 1851 Miss Tanner assumes that recovery had begun to take place at that time. The monthly sales of H. W. Corbett for the same period during 1851 do not sustain this assumption. For comparison, the monthly sales of both are given as follows:

	H. W. Corbett	W. H. Barnhart & Co.
May	$ 14,832.57	$ ......
June	8,596.40	3,733.71
July	3,214.43	2,964.83
August	4,041.13	4,432.21
September	11,581.52	5,249.96
October	6,500.21	4,814.80
November	4,593.72	3,261.20
December	3,721.88	8,365.73

A seasonal slump in trade occurred in July and August rather than a general depression. Further, Miss Tanner assumes that business institutions were well established in Oregon prior to 1851. We have shown Portland's role as entrepôt to have just begun during that year. That southern Oregon gold was the basic factor stimulating business during 1852 and the spring of 1853 is a central idea in Miss Tanner's study. This gold did have a stimulating influence and when its supply was cut off in the summer and fall of 1853, it contributed to the contraction of the money supply. But the immigration of 1852, it seems, needs greater emphasis. That, far more than the few miners of southern Oregon, promised an expanding market for merchants. Miss Tanner over-emphasizes the attention the mining country actually received. She says that "every issue of the newspapers commented on the heavy supplies going up river to the miners . . ." (p. 50). There were references occasionally, but not in every issue, to shipments going to the "upper country" and they were almost always brief news items. The term "up country" or "upper country," as used in these items, furthermore, meant the entire hinterland south of Oregon City and did not apply to the mining area exclusively. As a result of questioning the assumptions contained in Miss Tanner's study, most of her primary sources have been re-examined. In the judgment of the present writer her central thesis is only partially sustained, and in general it seems that the earlier viewpoint of Gilbert concerning the period is sound. See pp. 39, 47, 51, 55, 62-63, particularly for the main points of her argument.

Chapter IX

(pp. 183-203)

1 Stanley S. Spaid, Joel Palmer and Indian Affairs in Oregon (Ph.D. thesis, University of Oregon, 1950), pp. 98-100, 108-111, 116-117, 141 (hereafter cited, Spaid, *Palmer*); Trimble, *Mining Advance*, pp. 18-19; and Bancroft, *Oregon*, II, pp. 205-246.

2 Spaid, *Palmer*, pp. 114-115, 137-142, 148-156.

3 Trimble, *Mining Advance*, pp. 19-21; *History of the Willamette Valley*, H. O. Lang, ed., pp. 381-384; Spaid, *Palmer*, pp. 163-164.

4 *Oregonian*, Sept. 3, 1853. See also the *Oregonian*, Aug. 11, 1855.

5 F. G. Young, "Financial History of Oregon," Part Two, *OHQ*, VIII, 1907, pp. 133n, 185n; Spaid, *Palmer*, pp. 221-222; Palmer to Manypenny, July 10, 1855, quoted in *ibid.*, p. 221; Palmer to Gen. John E. Wool, Dec. 1, 1855, *House Executive Document 93*, 34th Cong., 1st Sess., p. 24.

6 Matthew P. Deady to Asahel Bush, Nov. 5, 1855, cited by Spaid, *Palmer*, pp. 221-222; *Oregonian*, June 2, 1860 quoting Delazon Smith in 1855; F. G. Young, "Financial History," Part Two, *OHQ*, VIII, 1907, p. 133n, citing Applegate;

Ambrose to Deady, Oct. 11, 1855, quoted by Spaid, *Palmer*, pp. 221-222; William C. Hazlitt, *British Columbia and Vancouver Island*, p. 213.

7 Spaid, *Palmer*, p. 243; *House Executive Document 38,* 35th Cong., 1st Sess., p. 2.

8 *Senate Executive Document 24,* 35th Cong., 1st Sess., pp. 4-6; *Senate Executive Document 66,* 34th Cong., 1st Sess., pp. 55-60; General Wool to Col. George Wright, Jan. 29, 1856, *ibid.,* p. 63.

9 For the events and campaigns of these wars see Lang, *Willamette Valley,* Chaps. XII-XVII, and Frances Fuller Victor, *The Early Indian Wars of Oregon,* pp. 267-500. Spaid, *Palmer*, pp. 213-214.

10 *House Executive Document 11,* 36th Cong., 1 Sess., pp. 18-24; Gen. John E. Wool to R. J. Atkinson, July 15, 1859 and Capt. Cram to Atkinson, Aug. 29, 1859, *ibid.,* pp. 78, 88.

11 *Oregonian,* Nov. 3, 1855, C. W. Thomas to J. Failing & Co., Dec. 7, 1855, CFUO; Corbett, day-book, CFCOP.

12 *House Executive Document 11,* 36th Cong., 1st Sess., p. 95.

13 M. P. Deady, History and Progress of Oregon After 1845, ms., quoted by Trimble, *Mining Advance,* p. 23. See also Johansen, *Capitalism,* p. 62; H. W. Scott, *History of Portland,* pp. 142-143; and F. G. Young, "Financial History," Part Two, *OHQ,* VIII, 1907, p. 182.

14 Trimble, *Mining Advance,* pp. 22-23, 32-37; Lang, *Willamette Valley, pp. 467-*475.

15 Bancroft, *Oregon,* II, pp. 461-462; *Oregonian,* Nov. 20, 27, 1858, April 23, 1859; Johansen, *Capitalism,* pp. 64-65.

16 Spaid, *Palmer,* pp. 156, 243.

17 Letters of J. W. Nesmith to J. W. Denver, June 17, Sept. 1, 1857; to Charles E. Mix, Jan. 1, 1858, *House Executive Document 93,* 35th Cong., 1st Sess., pp. 2-4, 8-13, 18-26, 54-56.

18 J. W. Nesmith to J. W. Denver, Oct. 19, 1857, *ibid.,* p. 23.

19 Report of J. Ross Browne, Nov. 17, 1857, *House Executive Document 39,* 35th Cong., 1st Sess., pp. 41-42.

20 Henry Failing to John A. Hatt, Aug. 5, 1859; Failings and Hatt to John A. Hatt, Nov. 8, 1859, CFOHS. Letters of H. W. Corbett to W. P. Thompson and Friend Carter, Sept. 28, 1859, CFCOP.

21 *Senate Executive Document 24,* 35th Cong. 1st Sess., pp. 1-7; *House Executive Document 11,* 36th Cong., 1st Sess., pp. 1-3.

22 *House Executive Document 51,* 35th Cong., 1st Sess.

23 Gen. John E. Wool to R. J. Atkinson, July 15, 1859, *House Executive Document 11,* 36th Cong., 1st Sess., pp. 77-83; Gov. John Whiteaker to R. J. Atkinson, *ibid.,* pp. 92-93.

24 *House Executive Document 11,* 36th Cong., 1st Sess., pp. 39, 51-52, 108-109. *Oregonian,* June 25, Dec. 24, 1859; Nov. 3, 1860.

25 *Senate Executive Document 46,* 37th Cong., 2nd Sess., pp. 1-12; Failings and Hatt to C. W. Thomas, Sept. 4, 1861, CFOHS; G. F. Warren and F. A. Pearson, *Wholesale Prices for 213 Years, 1720 to 1932,* p. 76.

26 *History of Southern Oregon: Comprising Jackson, Josephine, Douglas, Curry and Coos Counties,* A. G. Walling, publisher, p. 342; Winther, *Old Oregon Country,* p. 138; Winther, "Pack Animals for Transportation in the Pacific Northwest," *PNQ,* XXXIV, 1943, pp. 131-132.

27 *Oregonian,* March 3, June 16, 23, 1855; Walling, *Southern Oregon,* pp. 325, 342; Trimble, *Mining Advance,* pp. 102-103; Territorial Papers of Oregon (microfilm, O.H.S. originals at Oregon State Archives, Salem).

28 *Oregonian,* June 23, Aug. 4, 11, 18, Sept. 1, 8, 22, 1855; *Oregon Argus,* July 21, 28, 1855; Trimble, *Mining Advance,* pp. 16-17.

29 *Oregonian,* Sept. 8, 1855. For the failure of the San Francisco financial houses see Felix Reisenberg, Jr., *Golden Gate: The Story of San Francisco Harbor,* pp. 144-146.

30 *Oregonian,* Sept. 20, 1856, May 11, July 11, 18, 25, 1857.

31 *Oregonian,* July 11, 1857. On July 9, 1859 the *Oregonian* reported bountiful crops in the Colvile Valley and that it was "pretty well" inhabited.

32 *Oregonian,* Sept. 26, Oct. 3, 1857.

33 *Oregonian,* April 24, May 1, 1858; *Lewis and Dryden's Marine History,* pp. 68-70; Hazlitt, *British Columbia,* pp. 146-148, 220.

34 See Trimble, *Mining Advance,* Chap. II for the Fraser River rush, and Chap. XI for the evolution of law and government in British Columbia. See Paul, *California Gold,* pp. 192-195 for the leadership of Californians in the development of new gold fields and F. W. Howay, W. N. Sage, and H. F. Angus, *British Columbia and the United States,* pp. 137-145.

35 Hazlitt, *British Columbia,* pp. 135-138; *Oregonian,* May 8, 15, June 19, 1858.

36 *Oregonian,* June 26, Aug. 28, Sept. 4, 1858.

37 Hazlitt, *British Columbia,* pp. 142, 219; *Oregonian,* July 5, 24, Oct. 16, and Nov. 20, 1858.

38 Hazlitt, *British Columbia,* p. 220; *Oregonian,* Oct. 9, 12, 30, 1858; Trimble, *Mining Advance,* p. 102; Howay, Sage, and Angus, *British Columbia and the United States,* pp. 137, 178, *passim.*

39 *Oregonian,* April 24, May 1, June 12, 26, July 3, 24, 1858.

40 *Oregonian,* April 24, 1858.

41 The *Oregonian,* 1858 and 1859 shows steamship announcements. Astoria Custom-House Records (Microfilm, O. H. S.) show a few outward manifests of cargoes for Victoria on board sailing vessels but none for the steamships. *Lewis and Dryden's Marine History,* pp. 69-70; *Oregonian,* Aug. 21, 1858; Trimble, *Mining Advance,* p. 26; J. Orin Oliphant, "The Cattle Trade on Puget Sound, 1858-1890," *Agricultural History,* VII, 1933, pp. 129-136.

42 *Oregonian,* April 24, May 1, 15, June 26, July 3, 17, 24, Aug. 14, 21, 1858, April 23, July 30, Sept. 3, 1859.

43 Stanley S. Spaid, "The Later Life and Activities of General Joel Palmer," *OHQ,* LV, 1954, pp. 313-315.

44 *Oregonian,* Aug. 7, 14, 1858; Failings and Hatt to John A. Hatt, Oct. 28, 1861, CFOHS.

Chapter X

(*pp. 204-228*)

1 Spaid, *Palmer,* p. 98; Delazon Smith, Speech in the Constitutional Convention, Aug. 24, 1857, in *The Oregon Constitution and Proceedings and Debates of the Constitutional Convention of 1857,* Charles H. Carey, ed., p. 149 (hereafter cited, Carey, *Constitution*) ; Bancroft, *Oregon,* II, pp. 268-275, 650.

2 *The Eighth Census,* 1860, *Agriculture,* pp. 120-121; *The Ninth Census,* 1870, *Population,* p. 57.

3 Wilson M. and Mary Ann Tigard to James and Nancy Winn, June 29, 1857, "Two Wilson M. Tigard Letters," Dorsey D. Jones, ed., *OHQ,* XLV, 1944, p. 236.

4 Bancroft, *Oregon,* II, pp. 255-256; *Lewis and Dryden's Marine History,* pp. 59-60; *Oregonian,* May 19, 1855, June 2, 1860; statements of Sigmund Rosenblatt and Jacob C. Spores, *House Executive Document 11,* 36th Cong., 1st Sess., pp. 96, 105.

5 Dorothy O. Johansen, Capitalism on the Far-Western Frontier: The Oregon Steam Navigation Company (unpublished Ph.D. thesis, University of Washington, 1941), pp. 61, 65-66, 71-79. (Hereafter cited, Johansen, *Capitalism.*)

6 Winther, *The Old Oregon Country*, pp. 138-142. See the *Oregonian*, Feb. 2 and July 17, 1858, for examples of the many complaints against the mail service. In 1858 mails arrived at Portland in 33 days from New York (*Oregonian*, Aug. 7, 1858), and in 1859, in 30 days (*Oregonian*, March 26, 1859).

7 *Oregonian*, Nov. 12, 1859.

8 *Oregonian*, Feb. 10, May 19, Sept. 29, Oct. 6, Nov. 9, 1855; manifest bark *Ocean Bird*, Nov. 15, 1855, Astoria Custom-House Records (Microfilm, O.H.S.). The barks *Metropolis, Ocean Bird, Charles Devens*, and *Susan Abigail*, the brig *Francisco*, and the schooner *Matthew Vassar* were on the San Francisco-Portland run irregularly during the year.

9 Price quotations for Oregon flour and produce used throughout this chapter are found under the heading "Market Review" in *Oregonian* from 1855 through 1860. Sometimes the heading reads "Prices Current," and this was used regularly during 1861. In the few cases where the upriver price of wheat is cited, the source is the *Oregon Statesman* for the same period.

10 *Oregonian*, April 4, 12, 19, 26, May 3, 1856.

11 *Oregonian*, April 18, June 13, 1857.

12 H. W. Corbett to Joseph Walker & Co., Boston, March 11, 1857, CFUO.

13 *Oregonian*, Feb. 19, 1859, March 30, 1857, April 10, 1858.

14 Joseph W. Ellison, "The Beginnings of the Apple Industry in Oregon." *Agricultural History*, XI, 1937. pp. 325-328, and quoting Luelling, *ibid.*, p. 327; Bancroft, *Oregon*, II, pp. 257-258, 637; Gaston, *Portland*, I, pp. 316-317, 351-353; Cleland and Hardy, *March of Industry*, pp. 44-45; *Oregonian*, June 9, 1860.

15 H. W. Corbett to J. W. Bingham, May 25, 1858, CFCOP; invoices, J. Failing & Company, 1855-1857, CFUO.

16 *Oregonian*, June 8, 20, 1857; invoice of goods shipped on board the *C. E. Tilton* to J. Failing & Company, March 9, 1857, CFUO.

17 *Oregonian*, May 14, 1859.

18 *Oregon Statesman*, Nov. 8, 1856, adv.; Astoria Custom-House Records (Microfilm, O.H.S.) ; George Abernethy to A. S. Abernethy, Oak Point W. T., May 2, 1855, Abernethy Mss., Private Collection of Miss Vara Caufield, McLoughlin House, Oregon City; *Oregonian*, Aug. 7, 1857; *Lewis and Dryden's Marine History*, p. 67.

19 Advertisements in the *Oregonian*, 1855 *et seq.*; H. W. Corbett's correspondence with D. Beach of Albany and Worth & Bro. of Corvallis, 1855-1860, CFUO and CFCOP.

20 *Oregon Statesman*, Feb. 10, 1857.

21 David Logan to his sister, Jan. 27, 1857, "22 Letters of David Logan, Pioneer Oregon Lawyer," Harry E. Pratt, ed., *OHQ*, XLIV, 1943, p. 273.

22 Astoria Custom-House Records (Microfilm, O.H.S.), 1854-59, particularly the shipping manifests of the brig *Francisco*, the barks *Metropolis, J. B. Lunt* and *Ocean Bird* during 1855, 1856, and 1857; *Eighth Census*, 1860, *Manufactures*, pp. 489-492; *Oregon Statesman*, 1857; *Oregonian*, 1855-56.

23 *Oregon Argus* (Oregon City), July 21, 1855, and frequent references to ships loading at Oak Point in the *Oregonian* during the later 1850s; George A. Abernethy to A. S. Abernethy, Oak Point, W. T., March 18, May 2, 1855, Abernethy Mss., Private Collection of Miss Vara Caufield, McLoughlin House, Oregon City; shipping manifests, Astoria Custom-House Records (Microfilm, O.H.S.).

24 *Lewis and Dryden's Marine History*, pp. 61, 88; *Eighth Census*, 1860, *Manufactures*, pp. 35-36, 489-492, 673.

25 *Oregonian*, March 28, Oct. 16, 1857, Feb. 27, April 10, 1858; letters of H. W. Corbett to Bosworth, Masters & Co., April 9, 1857; to Abernethy, Clark & Co., June 2, 1857; to several San Francisco houses, Feb. 18, 1858; to P. A. Burden, Feb. 14, 1859, CFCOP.

26 Advertisements for Abernethy, Clark & Co. and for George Abernethy & Co. are extensive in both the *Oregon Statesman* and the *Oregonian* until late in 1857. Astoria Custom-House Records (Microfilm, O.H.S.).

27 George Abernethy to A. S. Abernethy, Oak Point, March 18, 1855, Abernethy
Mss., Private Collection of Miss Vara Caufield, McLoughlin House, Oregon City;
Oregon Argus, Oct. 20, 1855; H. W. Corbett to Abernethy, Clark & Co., July 1,
1859, CFCOP.

28 *Oregon Statesman*, Feb. 11, 1861; James O'Meara, "An Early Steamboating Era
on the Willamette," *OHQ*, XLIV, 1943, p. 144; *Oregonian*, May 3, 1877, for an
obituary and eulogy of Abernethy; Frances Fuller Victor, *All Over Oregon and
Washington*, p. 64.

29 *Oregonian*, March 10, Nov. 27, 1858; Carey, *History of Oregon*, I, p. 540; Johansen, *Capitalism*, p. 66; *Eighth Census*, 1860, *Population*, pp. 405, 604; Carey,
Constitution, pp. 45-49.

30 Gaston, *Portland*, I, pp. 239-240; Scott, *Portland*, p. 141; H. W. Corbett to
Friend Bradford, July 26, 1858, CFUO; Failings and Hatt to John A. Hatt,
July 8, 1859, CFOHS.

31 Joseph Schafer, "The Western Ocean as a Determinant in Oregon History,"
The Pacific Ocean in History, H. Morse Stephens and Herbert E. Bolton, eds.,
pp. 294-295; *Eighth Census*, 1860, *Population*, p. 604; *Agriculture*, p. 222; *Manufactures*, pp. 492, 673.

32 L. E. Pratt, "The Origin and History of the Willamette Woolen Factory," *OHQ*,
III, 1902, pp. 248-253; *Oregon Argus*, March 6, 1858; *Oregonian*, Nov. 19, 1859;
Alfred L. Lomax, *Pioneer Woolen Mills in Oregon*, pp. 85-88, 118-126; H. W.
Corbett's extensive correspondence with the Willamette Woolens Manufacturing
Company, 1859 *et seq.*, CFOHS, CFUO, CFCOP; *Eighth Census*, 1860, *Manu-
factures*, pp. 490-492.

33 Bancroft, *Oregon*, II, pp. 331-334, 727-728, 743; H. H. Bancroft, *History of
Washington, Idaho and Montana*, p. 340.

34 *Eighth Census*, 1860, *Manufactures*, pp. 489-492; *Lewis and Dryden's Marine
History*, p. 61; Walker Allison Tompkins, "Oysterville, 1840-97," *OHQ*, XXXIII,
1932, pp. 160-162.

35 Wilson M. and Mary Ann Tigard to James and Nancy Winn, June 29, 1857,
"Two Wilson M. Tigard Letters," Dorsey D. Jones, ed., *OHQ*, XLV, 1944, p. 236;
R. C. Clark, *History of the Willamette Valley*, p. 459; H. W. Corbett, bill for
labor, July 1, 1858, CFUO; *House Executive Document 51*, 35th Cong., 2nd
Sess., pp. 5-8; Carey, *Constitution*, p. 370.

36 Carey, *Constitution*, pp. 232-265, 276-277, 339-341, 361, 370, 423-425. Article XI,
sec. 1, Oregon constitution prohibits all banks or monied institutions from
"making, issuing, or putting in circulation, any bill, check, certificate, promis-
sory note, or other paper, or the paper of any bank company, or person, to
circulate as money." Article XI, sec. 2, Oregon constitution says: "The stockholders of all corporations, and joint stock companies, shall be liable for the
indebtedness of said corporation to the amount of their stock subscribed, and
unpaid, and no more." The above sections in *ibid.*, p. 423; and the sections on
spending power and economy, nos. 5-10, in *ibid.*, pp. 424-425.

37 Winther, *The Old Oregon Country*, pp. 123-124; Waymire speech, Sept. 2, 1857,
Carey, *Constitution*, p. 261.

38 See speeches of Lafayette Grover and George H. Williams, Sept. 2, 1857, Carey,
Constitution, pp. 242-243, 252-256.

39 *Oregonian*, May 21, 1859.

40 *Oregonian*, April 2, 23, and July 30, 1859; letters of J. Failing & Company to
John A. Hatt, July 23, Aug. 5, 1859, CFOHS.

41 *Oregonian*, Nov. 5, 19, 1859, Jan. 14, 1860.

42 *Oregonian*, Jan. 14, June 30, July 7, 28, Nov. 10, 1860; Failings and Hatt to
John A. Hatt, Jan. 12, 1860, CFOHS; *Eighth Census*, 1860, *Agriculture*, pp.
xxix-xxx; Cleland and Hardy, *March of Industry*, pp. 39-41, 57.

43 *Oregonian*, June 30, 1860. (Quotation italicized in the source.)

44 Letters of Failings and Hatt to John A. Hatt, Feb. 6, 1860, July 5, Oct. 5, 16,
1861, Feb. 2, 1862, CFOHS.

45 Corning, *Willamette Landings,* pp. 49-51, 91; Failings and Hatt to John A. Hatt, Feb. 2, 1862, CFOHS.

46 For some of the effects of the panic of 1857, see Carl H. Juergens, "Movement of Wholesale Prices in New York City, 1825-1863," *Publications of the American Statistical Association,* XII, 1910-11, pp. 545-546, 553-554.

Chapter XI

(pp. 229-244)

1 Henry Failing to John A. Hatt, Nov. 25, 1859, CFOHS; *Oregonian,* Jan. 1, 1856. Other leading wholesale firms were George Abernethy & Co., Oregon City; Hull, Knapp & Co., W. S. Ladd & Co., and Allen and Lewis of Portland.

2 Contract, H. W. Corbett and R. N. and F. McLaren, CFOHS, and several other papers relating to the dissolution of this partnership, CFUO and CFCOP.

3 These statements are based upon a mass of Corbett correspondence with Hilliard, Hayes, Hopkins & Co., its successor, Hopkins, Hayes, Palmer & Co., Samuel Roosevelt & Co., and other New York firms concerning remittances, notes, interest, etc., 1855-59, CFCOP primarily, but also in CFUO and CFOHS.

4 H. W. Corbett to Samuel Roosevelt & Co., Jan. 3, 1859, CFCOP; numerous letters from H. W. Corbett to Abernethy, Clark & Co., 1856-58, and to William Alvord & Company, 1858-59, CFCOP and CFUO.

5 Letters of H. W. Corbett to William W. Wright & Co., New York, March 31, 1857, CFCOP; to Whitlock & Walker, Jan. 16, 1857, CFUO; to Walker & Co., Dec. 7, 1858; to Freeland, Squires & Co.. March 4, 1859, CFCOP.

6 Letters of H. W. Corbett to Hopkins, Hayes, Palmer & Co., Nov. 11, 1857, CFUO; to Abernethy, Clark & Co., Nov. 10, 1857, CFCOP; Nov. 24, 1857, CFUO; to Ira Jagger, Nov. 27, 1857, CFUO.

7 Letters of H. W. Corbett to Samuel Roosevelt & Co., Jan. 20, 1858, Nov. 27, 1857, CFUO, and March 1, 1858, CFCOP; to Hoyt, Tillinghast & Co., Aug. 26, 1858, CFUO.

8 Letters of H. W. Corbett to Croton Manufacturing Co., Feb. 8, 1858, CFCOP; to Nourse, Mason & Co., Dec. 11, 1857, CFUO.

9 Letters of H. W. Corbett to Lord, Warren, Evans and Co., Nov. 28, 1857, CFUO; to E. P. Clark & Co., Oct. 25, 1858; to Mason and Lawrence, April 19, 1858, CFCOP.

10 Letters of H. W. Corbett to Salter, Lord & Co., July 9, 1858; to Nourse, Mason & Co., April 17, 1858; to (addressee, illegible), Sept. 21, 1858; to Ira Jagger, Dec. 24, 1858; to Samuel Roosevelt & Co., Jan. 3, 1859; to Livingston and Copeland, Pittsburgh, Oct. 11, 1859; to Healy Atwater, May 23, 1859, CFCOP; to Lathrop, Ludington & Co., March 10, 1858, CFUO.

11 H. W. Corbett, day-book, CFCOP.

12 James H. Gilbert, "The Development of Banking in Oregon," *University of Oregon Bulletin* (New Series), IX, 1911, p. 9.

13 Letters of H. W. Corbett to Friend Bradford, July 26, 1858 and to Hoyt, Tillinghast & Co., Aug. 26, 1858, CFUO.

14 H. W. Corbett, day-book, CFCOP; *Oregonian,* 1855-60; *Wholesale Prices, Wages, and Transportation, Senate Report No. 1394,* 52nd Cong., 2nd Sess., known as the *Aldrich Report.*

15 Wilkes, *Narrative,* IV, pp. 350-351; *Oregon Spectator,* Oct. 18, 1849; Bancroft, *Oregon,* II, p. 258; advertisements, *Oregonian* and *Oregon Statesman,* 1855-58.

16 William T. Hutchinson, *Cyrus Hall McCormick,* II, pp. 66-67. See also *Eighth Census,* 1860, *Manufactures,* pp. ccxvii, ccxi-ccxii.

17 H. W. Corbett, memorandum, March, 1856; letters of H. W. Corbett to Ruggles, Nourse, Mason & Co., March 11, 1856; to A. B. McFadden, March 15, 1856, CFUO; H. W. Corbett, day-book, July, 1856, CFCOP; advertisement, George

Abernethy & Co., *Oregonian*, March 15, 1856, *et seq*. For the Chicago price of reapers, see Hutchinson, *McCormick*, I, p. 323.

18 Hutchinson, *McCormick*, II, p. 80; Corbett to McCormick, Aug. 24, 1858, CFCOP.

19 Hussey & Co. to Samuel Roosevelt & Co., Nov. 11, 1858, CFCOP.

20 Numerous Corbett letters, 1855-59, CFCOP, CFUO, CFOHS, contain produce accounts. The most extensive of these is the correspondence between Corbett and Worth & Bro., Corvallis. Many other Corbett letters are concerned with credit, interest, and collections. For specific examples see his letters to Friend Cole, Nov. 28, 1857; to Alexander Burns, Nov. 19, 1857, CFUO; to Friend Davis, Feb. 13, 1858; to Alexander Burns, Feb. 26, 1858; to Alberson & Co., Feb. 26, 1859, CFCOP.

21 Letters of H. W. Corbett to Worth & Bro., Dec. 3, 1857; to Wilson Blair, March 19, 1855; to Kelly and Wait, Attorneys, Oregon City, Nov. 17, 1857, and Feb. 18, 1858, CFUO; to Griswold & Co., Feb. 26, 1858, CFCOP.

22 *Sixty Milestones of Progress, 1859-1919, Ladd and Tilton Bank*, Martin F. Fitzgerald, ed., pp. 7-8, 15-19; Gilbert, "Development of Banking in Oregon," *U. of O. Bulletin* (New Series), IX, 1911, pp. 5-9. J. W. Ladd, brother of W. S. Ladd, and Simeon G. Reed took over W. S. Ladd's merchandising firm in 1859. Ladd, Reed & Co., the new firm, specialized in the wholesale liquor and grocery business.

23 Invoices, J. Failing and Co., CFUO; John Waymire to J. Failing & Co., Jan. 26, 1857, CFUO.

24 Financial statement, J. Failing & Co., CFUO; letters of J. Failing & Co. to C. W. Thomas, Oct. 25, 1858; to John A. Hatt, July 8, 1859; Failings and Hatt to John A. Hatt, Oct. 25, 1859, CFOHS.

25 Henry Failing to C. W. Thomas, Aug. 17, 1861; letters of Failings and Hatt to John A. Hatt, July 23, Sept. 12, Oct. 5, Oct. 12, 1861, CFOHS.

26 Letters of J. Failing & Co. to John A. Hatt, June 22, July 8, Aug. 5 and Aug. 20, 1859; letters of Henry Failing to John A. Hatt, Sept. 5 and Dec. 24, 1859, CFOHS; letters of H. W. Corbett to Anderson and Clark, Aug. 24, 1859; to Alexander and McEwan, Sept. 9, 1859; and to W. D. Bigelow, Oct. 8, 1859, CFCOP.

27 Failings and Hatt to John A. Hatt, Nov. 8, Dec. 24, 1859, Jan. 12, 1860.

Chapter XII

(pp. 247-276)

1 Trimble, *The Mining Advance Into the Inland Empire*, pp. 62-70.

2 Letters of Failings and Hatt to John A. Hatt, Nov. 11, Dec. 17, 1861, CFOHS. Trimble, *Mining Advance*, p. 71, states that Weiser took out $6,600 in one day.

3 Trimble, *Mining Advance*, pp. 70-71; Johansen, *Capitalism*, p. 81; Henry Failing to C. W. Thomas, Feb. 19, 1862, CFUO; *Oregonian*, March 14, 1862.

4 Dan E. Clark, "Movement to the Far West During the Decade of the Sixties," *WHQ*, XVII, 1926, p. 109; *Lewis and Dryden's Marine History*, pp. 86-87, 106; H. W. Scott, *History of the Oregon Country* (Leslie M. Scott, compiler), I, pp. 337-338; Johansen, *Capitalism*, p. 83.

5 *Oregonian*, April 19, 1862, May 25, 1861, March 14, 1862; letter from Medorem Crawford, 75 miles west of Omaha, June 20, 1862, in *Oregonian*, Aug. 2, 1862; Trimble, *Mining Advance*, p. 131.

6 John Hailey, *The History of Idaho*, pp. 29-32; Trimble, *Mining Advance*, pp. 70-72.

7 Trimble, *Mining Advance*, pp. 73-74, 107; Leslie M. Scott, "Pioneer Stimulus of Gold," *OHQ*, XVIII, 1917, pp. 151-152; H. W. Scott, *Oregon Country*, III, pp. 84-85; Verne Bright, "Auburn—The Story of an Oregon Ghost Town," *Commonwealth Review*, XXI, 1939, pp. 60-70. In the article cited Leslie M. Scott gives the amount of Portland capital invested in the Auburn ditch as $40,000, while H. W. Scott in *Oregon Country*, III, p. 84, gives the figure as $200,000.

8 Johansen, *Capitalism*, pp. 75-79; Dorothy O. Johansen, "The Oregon Steam Navigation Company, 1860-1880; An Example of Capitalism on the Frontier," *PHR*, X, 1941, pp. 179-181.

9 Johansen, *Capitalism*, pp. 86, 91-93, 98-100.

10 *Ibid.*, pp. 83-85.

11 P. W. Gillette, "A Brief History of the Oregon Steam Navigation Company," *OHQ*, V, 1904, pp. 125-127.

12 Johansen, *Capitalism*, p. 81, citing J. Ross Browne, who obtained the figures from the secretary of the Oregon Steam Navigation Company, in *Mineral Resources*, p. 579.

13 *Oregonian*, May 25, 1861. The editor emphasized the permanence of the Willamette Valley trade while referring to the temporary value of that of the upper Columbia.

14 Failings and Hatt to John A. Hatt, Oct. 28, 1861, CFOHS; Henry Failing to C. W. Thomas, Feb. 19, 1862, CFUO.

15 Johansen, *Capitalism*, pp. 114-120; *Lewis and Dryden's Marine History*, pp. 108-109; letters of Failings and Hatt to John A. Hatt, May 4, 12, July 3, 1863, CFOHS.

16 Failings and Hatt to John A. Hatt, June 1, 1863, CFOHS.

17 Hailey, *Idaho*, pp. 32-44, 61; Trimble, *Mining Advance*, pp. 74-75; *Oregonian*, April 15, 1863; letters of Failings and Hatt to John A. Hatt, June 12, 25, 1863, CFOHS.

18 *Oregonian*, March 10, 1863; *Sacramento Union*, April 2, 1863, quoted in the *Oregonian*, May 9, 1863; Dan E. Clark, "The Movement to the Far West During the Decade of the Sixties," *WHQ*, XVII, 1926, p. 106.

19 Hailey, *Idaho*, pp. 33, 61-63, 91-92; Failings and Hatt to John A. Hatt, June 25, 1863, CFOHS; Henry Failing to John A. Hatt, Dec. 19, 1864, CFUO; Winther, *The Old Oregon Country*, pp. 218-219, 257-259; H. H. Bancroft, *History of Washington, Idaho and Montana*, pp. 424-426, 436-437.

20 Price quotations given here and those given later are from the *Oregonian*.

21 *Oregonian*, June 8, 1864.

22 *Oregonian*, Sept. 27, 1862; Oct. 6, 1865.

23 J. Orin Oliphant, "The Cattle Herds and Ranches of the Oregon Country, 1860-1890," *Agricultural History*, XXI, 1947, p. 220; C. S. Kingston, "Introduction of Cattle Into the Pacific Northwest," *WHQ*, XIV, 1923, pp. 163-185. See also J. Orin Oliphant, "The Cattle Trade from the Far Northwest to Montana," *Agricultural History*, VI, 1932, pp. 69-70; and for a bibliographical essay on the entire subject see J. Orin Oliphant, "History of the Livestock Industry in the Pacific Northwest," *OHQ*, XLIX, 1948, pp. 3-29.

24 Letters of Failings and Hatt to John A. Hatt, Nov. 26, Oct. 5, 1861, CFOHS.

25 Letters of Failings and Hatt to John A. Hatt, Oct. 16, 28, Nov. 26, Dec. 17, 1861, CFOHS.

26 Letters of Failings and Hatt to John A. Hatt, Dec. 24, 1862, Jan. 2, and Feb. 13, 1863, CFOHS.

27 Gillette, "A Brief History of the Oregon Steam Navigation Company," *OHQ*, V, 1904, p. 128.

28 *Portland City Directory*, 1863, p. 13.

29 *Oregonian*, Oct. 25, 1862.

30 Letters of Failings and Hatt to John A. Hatt, Dec. 24, 1862, Jan. 2, March 4, April 25, June 25, 1863.

31 *Oregonian*, April 15, 1863.

32 Letters of Failings and Hatt to John A. Hatt, June 21, 1861, Jan. 2, April 25, June 1, 1863, CFOHS.

33 Johansen, *Capitalism,* pp. 89-91.

34 Failings and Hatt to John A. Hatt, July 14, 1863, CFOHS.

35 Failings and Hatt to John A. Hatt, June 12, 1863, CFOHS. See Rodman W. Paul, *California Gold,* pp. 186-188 for the importance of the production of mining machinery and placer tools in California. Trimble, *Mining Advance,* pp. 115-116, also deals with this subject and San Francisco's role as the emporium for the northern mining movement.

36 Letters of Failings and Hatt to John A. Hatt, March 23, Sept. 13, 1864, CFUO.

37 Winther, *The Old Oregon Country,* pp. 216-219; Bancroft, *Washington, Idaho and Montana,* pp. 425-427; Idaho *World,* Oct. 14, 1865, quoted by Trimble, *Mining Advance,* pp. 115-116.

38 *Oregonian,* Dec. 11, 1865.

39 Samuel Bowles, *Across the Continent, A Summer's Journey to the Rocky Mountains, the Mormons, and the Pacific States with Speaker Colfax,* p. 183.

40 Letters of Failings and Hatt to John A. Hatt, Aug. 20, Sept. 8, Oct. 3, 1863, CFOHS; letters of Henry Failing to John A. Hatt, May 3, 1864, March 14, April 17, and June 1, 1865, CFUO; Hailey, *Idaho,* p. 63; *Oregonian,* June 3, 1865 and Feb. 27, 1867.

41 Letter of an Oregon Observer, Oct. 1, 1865, "Supplementary Papers," in Bowles, *Across the Continent,* pp. 423, 427.

42 Trimble, *Mining Advance,* pp. 76-79; August C. Bolino, "The Role of Mining in the Economic Development of Idaho Territory," *OHQ,* LIX, 1958, pp. 119-123, 131-135.

43 Bowles, *Across the Continent,* p. 427.

44 Letters of Henry Failing to John A. Hatt, June 1, March 28, 1865, CFUO; Trimble, *Mining Advance,* p. 77n.

45 Trimble, *Mining Advance,* pp. 46-59; Failings and Hatt to John A. Hatt, Nov. 19, 1861, CFOHS; *Oregonian,* Jan. 14, 1865. The *Oregonian,* 1861-65 makes frequent references to the Victoria trade. Victoria was a regular port of call for the steamships on the northern route from San Francisco.

46 Trimble, *Mining Advance,* pp. 79-84; *Forty Years on the Frontier As Seen in the Journals and Reminiscenses of Granville Stuart,* Paul C. Phillips, ed., I, pp. 136-140, 205-272, *passim,* II, pp. 13-31; *Men and Trade on the Northwest Frontier as Shown by the Fort Owen Ledger,* George F. Weisel, ed., pp. 121-130, 159, 168n.

47 Oscar Osburn Winther, "Early Commercial Importance of the Mullan Road," *OHQ,* XLVI, 1945, pp. 22-31.

48 Albert J. Partoll, "Frank L. Worden, Pioneer Merchant, 1830-1887," *PNQ,* XL, 1949, pp. 191, 200-202. This article contains an important letter from Worden to Lyman Powers, dated Hellgate, W. T., Dec. 24, 1861. See Weisel, ed., *Men and Trade on the Northwest Frontier,* pp. xxx, 156n, *passim,* and Stuart, *Forty Years on the Frontier,* Phillips, ed., for references to Worden's store at Hellgate.

49 Johansen, *Capitalism,* pp. 185-186; Alton B. Oviatt, "Steamboat Traffic on the Upper Missouri River, 1859-1869," *PNQ,* XL, 1949, pp. 93-94; Winther, *The Old Oregon Country,* pp. 208-210; Trimble, *Mining Advance,* pp. 127-132.

50 Winther, *The Old Oregon Country,* pp. 207, 221, and quoting the *Oregonian,* Dec. 28, 1865, p. 223.

51 Stuart, *Forty Years,* Philips, ed., p. 239; Simeon G. Reed to J. W. Ladd and D. W. Bradford, Sept. 4, 1865, "A Chapter in the History of the Oregon Steam Navigation Company," Frank B. Gill and Dorothy O. Johansen, eds., *OHQ,* XXXVIII, 1937, p. 30; Johansen, *Capitalism,* pp. 185-186; Winther, "Pack Animals for Transportation in the Pacific Northwest," *PNQ,* XXXIV, 1943, p. 141.

52 Letters of Simeon G. Reed to J. W. Ladd, July 25, 1865, quoted in Johansen, *Capitalism,* p. 191, and to J. W. Ladd and D. F. Bradford, Sept. 4, 1865. "A Chapter in the History of the O.S.N.," Gill and Johansen, eds., *OHQ,* XXXVIII,

1937, pp. 29-30; H. D. Sanborn to W. S. Ladd, Sept. 30, 1865, *Oregonian*, Oct. 25, 1865.

53 *Oregonian*, Aug. 3, Sept. 12, Oct. 6, 27, Nov. 1, 3, 17, Dec. 19, 1865, Feb. 24, 26, March 10, 1866.

54 *Oregonian*, March 24, 1866; S. G. Reed to J. C. Ainsworth, March 19, 1866, quoted in Johansen, *Capitalism*, p. 187.

55 Johansen, *Capitalism*, pp. 93-95, 160, 173-182; Johansen, "The Oregon Steam Navigation Company, 1860-1880: An Example of Capitalism on the Frontier," *PHR*, X, 1941, pp. 185-188.

56 Johansen, *Capitalism*, pp. 188-189; *Lewis and Dryden's Marine History*, p. 145; *Oregonian*, June 2, 27, 1866.

57 Letters of Henry Failing to John A. Hatt, March 3, 12, May 1, 1866, CFUO; *Oregonian*, April 14, 1866.

58 *Oregonian*, May 19, June 8, July 28, Aug. 11, 1866; letters of Henry Failing to John A. Hatt, June 8, July 28, Aug. 7, 1866, CFUO.

59 Winther, *The Old Oregon Country*, p. 211; Johansen, *Capitalism*, p. 187.

60 *Oregonian*, April 19, June 8, 1866; A Letter from a Deer Lodge Merchant, Nov. 26, 1867, quoted in the *Oregonian*, Dec. 25, 1867.

61 *Sixteenth Annual Report of the Interstate Commerce Commission*, Dec. 15, 1902, Appendix G, part II, *House Document No. 253*, part 3, 58th Cong., 2nd Sess., pp. 50-51, for the rail rates. The Cape Horn and Panama rates are derived from the following sources: *Oregonian*, May 27, 1865, Nov. 17, 1866, April 27, 1867; Henry Failing to John A. Hatt, May 16, 1866, and Corbett and Failing, bills of lading, CFUO; *Lewis and Dryden's Marine History*, pp. 137, 150; "A Chapter in the History of the Oregon Steam Navigation Company," Johansen and Gill, eds., *OHQ*, XXXIX, 1938, pp. 56-57.

62 Alton B. Oviatt, "Steamboat Traffic on the Upper Missouri River, 1859-1869," *PNQ*, XL, 1949, pp. 97-103; Winther, *The Old Oregon Country*, p. 224.

63 *Montana Post*, May 2, 1868, quoted by Winther, *The Old Oregon Country*, pp. 194-195; and E. W. Carpenter, "A Glimpse of Montana," *The Overland Monthly*, II, April, 1869, p. 383, quoted by Winther, *The Old Oregon Country*, pp. 223-224.

64 Oviatt, "Steamboat Traffic on the Upper Missouri River, 1859-1869," *PNQ*, XL, 1949, pp. 104-109.

65 Trimble, *Mining Advance*, p. 102.

66 Bolino, "The Role of Mining in Economic Development of Idaho Territory," *OHQ*, LIX, 1958, pp. 119, 141.

67 Trimble, *Mining Advance*, pp. 102-106, 118.

Chapter XIII

(pp. 277-294)

1 Failing's complaints on this subject are contained in Failings and Hatt to John A. Hatt, June 6, 28, July 23, Aug. 17, Sept. 12, Oct. 5, 12, 28, Dec. 17, 27, 1861; and Henry Failing to C. W. Thomas, Aug. 17, 1861, CFOHS.

2 Failings and Hatt to John A. Hatt, Sept. 12, 1861, CFOHS.

3 Henry Failing to C. W. Thomas, Feb. 19, 1862; telegram, John A. Hatt to Failings and Hatt, c/o Ladd, Reed & Co., San Francisco, April 8, 1862, CFUO; Failings and Hatt to John A. Hatt, Feb. 2, 13, 1863, CFOHS, Jan. 23, Feb. 26, 27, 1864, CFUO. A notice of the dissolution of the partnership is in the *Oregonian*, May 4, 1864.

4 Henry Failing to John A. Hatt, April 14, 1864, CFUO.

5 Letters of Failings and Hatt to John A. Hatt, June 6, Nov. 8, Dec. 17, 1861, Dec. 4, 1862, Jan. 24, Feb. 2, 1863, CFOHS; Jagger & Co. to Failings and Hatt, April 17, 1862; Baldwin and Co. to Failings and Hatt, Sept. 17, 1862, CFUO.

6 Failings and Hatt to John A. Hatt, Dec. 12-13, 24, 1862, Feb. 13, 1863, CFOHS.

7 The *Oregonian* discontinued its quotation of the wholesale price of tobacco in June 1862. Failing mentions the higher price level in his letters to Hatt, Jan. 2, Feb. 13, 1863, CFOHS, and May 3 and Sept. 13, 1864, CFUO.

8 Gilbert, *Trade and Currency*, pp. 98-99, quoting the *Oregonian*, Aug. 8, 1862, and the San Francisco *Evening Bulletin*, Dec. 8, 1862.

9 Gilbert, *Trade and Currency*, pp. 98-102, 115; H. W. Corbett to A. C. Jones, Oct. 28, 1862, CFOHS; Failings and Hatt to John A. Hatt, Dec. 12, 13, 1862, CFOHS.

10 Ladd and Tilton to Hon. Benjamin Stark, U. S. Senator, Nov. 6, 1862. Stark papers, O.H.S.

11 Gilbert, *Trade and Currency*, pp. 101, 117; Failings and Hatt to John A. Hatt, Jan. 24, 1863; *Oregonian*, Jan. 24, 27, 1863.

12 *Oregonian*, March 13 (adv.), April 17, 1865, quoted in Scott, *Oregon Country*, III, pp. 167-168; a mass of bills in the Corbett and Failing records, CFUO, containing the phrase "Payable in U. S. Gold Coin"; Gilbert, *Trade and Currency*, pp. 104-105, 111-114, 117-118.

13 Bancroft, *Oregon*, II, p. 642. For a refutation of Bancroft's statement see Gilbert, *Trade and Currency*, pp. 120, 122.

14 See tables in *Wholesale Prices, Wages and Transportation, Senate Report No. 1394*, 52nd Cong., 2nd Sess., part 1, known as the *Aldrich Report*, pp. 91, 99, for yearly indexes, and G. F. Warren and F. A. Pearson's wholesale price index of all commodities in *Prices*, p. 12.

15 Failings and Hatt to John A. Hatt, Jan. 24, March 3, 1863, CFOHS.

16 *Aldrich Report*, part 2, pp. 135-136, 155.

17 Letters of Failings and Hatt to John A. Hatt, Feb. 2, Jan. 24, 1863, CFOHS.

18 See Chap. XIV, p. 299.

19 For a good analysis of this subject see Wesley C. Mitchell, *Gold, Prices, and Wages Under the Greenback Standard (University of California Publications in Economics*, I, 1908) , pp. 13-15.

20 Letters of Failings and Hatt to John A. Hatt, Feb. 13, May 4, 26, July 3, 14, and Aug. 20, 1863, CFOHS.

21 Letters of Failings and Hatt to John A. Hatt, Aug. 8, Sept. 24, Oct. 3, Nov. 13, 1863, CFOHS.

22 Letters of Failings and Hatt to John A. Hatt, Jan. 14, 23, Feb. 2, 12, March 17, 1864, and of Henry Failing to John A. Hatt, April 14, May 19, June 2, 13, 1864, CFUO.

23 Letters of Henry Failing to John A. Hatt, June 19, July 23, Aug. 22, Sept. 13, 23, 1864, CFUO.

24 Henry Failing to John A. Hatt, Oct. 7, 1864, CFUO.

25 Letters of Henry Failing to John A. Hatt, Oct. 17, 28, Dec. 7, 19, 27, 1864, Feb. 14, March 7, 14, 21, 28, 1865, CFUO.

26 Henry Failing to John A. Hatt, April 17, 1865, CFUO.

27 Letters of Henry Failing to John A. Hatt, April 6, 25, 29, May 2, 13, 23, June 24, July 5, 18, 25, Sept. 14, Oct. 2, 28, Nov. 11, Dec. 2, 1865, Feb. 1, July 7, 1866, CFUO.

28 *Oregonian*, April 14, 1860, July 15, 25, 1865.

29 Bowles, *Across the Continent*, pp. 342-343.

30 Letters of Failings and Hatt to John A. Hatt, July 7, 14, Aug. 22, Oct. 3, 1863, CFOHS.

31 Failings and Hatt to John A. Hatt, Oct. 16, July 14, 1863, CFOHS.

32 Failings and Hatt to John A. Hatt, Oct. 3, Nov. 13, 1863, CFOHS, Jan. 20, 1864; Henry Failing to John A. Hatt, Feb. 2, 1864; B. D. Godfrey to John A. Hatt,

Nov. 3, 1863, and B. D. Godfrey to Failings and Hatt, New York, April 15, 18, 1866, CFUO.

33 H. W. Corbett to Samuel T. House, Sept. 24, 1863, CFUO; letters of Failings and Hatt to John A. Hatt, July 25, Sept. 12, 24, Oct. 3, Nov. 28, 1863, CFOHS; letters of Henry Failing to John A. Hatt, June 19, 25, Sept. 23, 1864; Turner and Day to Failings and Hatt, New York, July 28, 1864, CFUO.

34 Henry Failing to John A. Hatt, Dec. 19, 1864, CFUO.

35 Letters of H. W. Corbett to Charles Pope and C. Holman, June 9, 1862, CFOHS. In the first of these letters Corbett wrote "there is money now on hand" and in the second, "money is more pleanty." Letters of Failings and Hatt to John A. Hatt, Feb. 25, April 1, June 1, 12, 1863, CFOHS.

36 Failings and Hatt to John A. Hatt, June 1, Aug. 20, 1863, CFOHS.

37 Henry Failing to John A. Hatt, Oct. 2, 1866, CFUO.

Chapter XIV

(pp. 295-315)

1 *Ninth Census*, 1870, *Population*, pp. 23, 46, 57, 71.

2 Winther, *The Old Oregon Country*, pp. 146-149, 264-266; Scott, *Oregon Country*, I, pp. 340-341; L. M. Scott, "The Pioneer Stimulus of Gold," *OHQ*, XVIII, 1917, pp. 159-160.

3 Much Corbett correspondence and other material concerning the stage business between Portland and Sacramento are in *My Playhouse Was a Concord Coach: An Anthology of Newspaper Clippings and Documents Relating to Those Who Made California History During the Years 1822-1888*, Helene Bacon Boggs, ed., pp. 430-519. See pp. 430-453 and 483-503 particularly. The *Oregonian*, July 20, 1866, adv., and Dec. 1, 1870; H. W. Corbett to Samuel T. House, Sept. 25, 1866, CFUO; records, mainly waybills, of the Oregon Stage Company for 1866 and 1867, are in the Special Collections, University of Oregon Library; Winther, *The Old Oregon Country*, pp. 255-257; Bancroft, *Chronicles*, II, p. 578.

4 *Oregonian*, Sept. 15, 1865.

5 Edward Hungerford, *Wells Fargo: Advancing the American Frontier*, pp. 87-92, 109 *passim*; Winther, *The Old Oregon Country*, pp. 267-270; Winther, "The Place of Transportation in the Early History of the Pacific Northwest," *PHR*, XI, 1942, pp. 393-394.

6 Scott, *Oregon Country*, I, p. 340n, III, pp. 187-188.

7 The *Oregonian* notes the arrivals and departures of the bark *Cambridge* to and from Honolulu during the decade. See *Oregonian*, June 20, 1864, for the editor's hope for a direct line of packets to Honolulu.

8 The *Oregonian*, 1863-65, reported gold shipments more or less regularly. See also Leslie M. Scott, "Pioneer Stimulus of Gold," *OHQ*, XVIII, 1917, pp. 165-166.

9 *Oregonian*, Nov. 16, 1867.

10 These statements are based upon financial and commercial news items in the *Oregonian*, 1861-65, which often published the shipping manifests.

11 Alfred L. Lomax, *Pioneer Woolen Mills*, pp. 88, 157.

12 Astoria Custom-House Records (Microfilm, O.H.S.). An account of the loss of the *Industry* is in the *Oregonian*, March 20, 1865. For other accounts of this and the loss of the *Scranton* see *Lewis and Dryden's Marine History*, pp. 143-144, 162, and James A. Gibbs, Jr., *Pacific Graveyard*, pp. 38-39, 186-187.

13 *Oregonian*, Jan. 21, Feb. 4, April 15, 22, July 8, 15, 29, Sept. 24, 1865; Edward Failing to H. W. Corbett, Sept. 5, 1865, CFCOP; Simeon G. Reed to J. W. Ladd and D. F. Bradford, Sept. 4, 1865, "A Chapter in the History of the Oregon Steam Navigation Company," Johansen and Gill, eds., *OHQ*, XXXVIII, 1937, p. 28; Henry Failing to John A. Hatt, May 16, 1866, CFUO.

14 *Lewis and Dryden's Marine History*, p. 100.

15 *Oregonian,* Feb. 11, 1864, Feb. 6, Aug. 14, 1865, and Jan. 6, 1866; Johansen, *Capitalism,* pp. 152-153; "A Chapter in the History of the O. S. N. Co.," Johansen and Gill, eds., *OHQ,* XXXVIII, 1937, pp. 3-4; *Lewis and Dryden's Marine History,* pp. 69, 86-87, 109.

16 Astoria Custom-House Records (Microfilm, O.H.S.), show the steamship entries per quarter beginning with the fourth quarter of 1861 through the first quarter of 1864. There are six entrances per quarter, except that the fourth quarter of 1861 shows nine; the second quarter of 1862, ten; and the first quarter of 1864, eight.

17 *Oregonian,* Aug. 2, 3, 1865. *Lewis and Dryden's Marine History,* pp. 131-134; "A Chapter in the History of O. S. N. Co.," Johansen and Gill, eds.; *OHQ,* XXXVIII, 1937, p. 19; Henry Failing to John A. Hatt, Aug. 16, 1865, CFUO.

18 Johansen, *Capitalism,* pp. 159, 172; *Oregonian,* July 10, 29, Aug. 16, 1865; S. G. Reed to J. W. Ladd, July 25, 1865, and Daniel Bradford to S. G. Reed, Aug. 16, 1865, "A Chapter in the History of the O. S. N. Co.," Johansen and Gill, eds., *OHQ,* XXXVIII, 1937, pp. 15-18, 25.

19 "A Chapter in the History of the O. S. N. Co.," Johansen and Gill, eds., *OHQ,* XXXVIII, 1937, pp. 24, 40-43, XXXIX, 1938, pp. 59-60; *Oregonian,* March 23, April 23, 1866, Feb. 22, 1867; *Lewis and Dryden's Marine History,* pp. 150-151.

20 *Ibid.,* pp. 137, 144, 150-152, 157-158; Astoria Custom-House Records (Microfilm, O.H.S.); *Oregonian,* April 27, 1867; Scott, *Oregon Country,* II, pp. 59-74, 263.

21 *Oregonian,* April 23, 27, 1867, quoted in "A Chapter in the History of the O. S. N. Co.," Johansen and Gill, eds., *OHQ,* XXXIX, 1938, pp. 57, 60.

22 *Oregonian,* Dec. 18, 1862, Sept. 2, 1867; Reisenberg, *Golden Gate,* pp. 174-175, 201; Cleland and Hardy, *March of Industry,* pp. 39, 73-74; Rydell, *Cape Horn,* pp. 145-149; Emory R. Johnson, *et al., History of the Domestic and Foreign Commerce of the United States,* II, pp. 46-47; Rodman W. Paul, "The Wheat Trade Between California and the United Kingdom," *MVHR,* XLV, 1958, pp. 391-396.

23 Bowles, *Across the Continent,* pp. 177-180.

24 *Oregonian,* Feb. 27, March 23, April 4, May 4, July 6, 27, Oct. 18, 1867.

25 *Portland City Directory,* 1867, 1868, 1869, 1870.

26 *Oregonian,* Nov. 23, 1867, Feb. 10, 1868.

27 *Oregonian,* May 17, 1865, Nov. 20, 1867; Johansen, *Capitalism,* pp. 232-234.

28 *Oregonian,* Nov. 2, 1863, Aug. 2, 1864, May 24, 27, June 13, Aug. 26, 1865, Feb. 27, Sept. 1, 1866, July 7, 23, Sept. 5, 1868, Feb. 8, 1870; Gaston, *Portland,* I, p. 319, quoting the *Portland Herald; Portland City Directory,* 1869, p. 12.

29 Dorothy D. Hirsch, "Study of the Foreign Wheat Trade of Oregon, 1869 to 1887," *RCB,* XXI (August, 1953), pp. 55-58; Rodman W. Paul, "The Wheat Trade Between California and the United Kingdom," *MVHR,* XLV, 1958, pp. 396-403; Donald W. Meinig, "Wheat Sacks out to Sea: The Early Export Trade from the Walla Walla Country," *PNQ,* XLV, 1954, pp. 13-18.

30 *Oregonian,* August 17, 1869.

31 *Ninth Census,* 1870, *Statistics of Wealth and Industry,* pp. 497, 508, 542, 580.

32 Scott, *Oregon Country,* III, pp. 22-25; Lomax, *Pioneer Woolen Mills,* p. 148, *passim;* Alfred L. Lomax, "Oregon Ctiy Woolen Mill," *OHQ,* XXXII, 1931, pp. 269-278.

33 Sister Mary de Sales McLellan, "William Hume, 1830-1902," *OHQ,* XXXV, 1934, pp. 270-273; Glenn Cunningham, "Oregon's First Salmon Canner, 'Captain' John West," *OHQ,* LIV, 1953, pp. 240-244.

34 Joseph Daniels, "Iron and Steel Manufacture in Washington, Oregon, California and Utah, "*Bulletin,* University of Washington, *Engineering Experiment Station Series, Report No. 2,* pp. 18-27; Joseph Daniels, "History of Pig Iron Manufacture on the Pacific Coast," *WHQ,* XVII, 1926, pp. 168-174; Herbert L. Hergert, "Early Iron Industry in Oregon," *RCB,* XXVI, (January, 1948), pp. 1-40;

Dorothy O. Johansen, "Organization and Finance of the Oregon Iron and Steel Company, 1880-1895," *PNQ*, XXXI, 1940, pp. 123-159.

35 W. Claude Adams, "History of Papermaking in the Pacific Northwest, I," *OHQ*, LII, 1951, pp. 21-31.

36 *Oregonian*, Feb. 3, 1866.

37 Gaston, *Portland*, I, pp. 280-294; Scott, *Oregon Country*, I, p. 108; IV, Chaps. XXXIX-XLIV; Bancroft, *Chronicle*, I, p. 592. For a good summary of the early development of railroads in the Pacific Northwest see Johansen, *Capitalism*, p. 194 *passim* and also John T. Ganoe, "The History of the Oregon and California Railroad," *OHQ*, XXV, 1924, pp. 236-283, 330-351.

38 H. W. Corbett and Company to Dupont deNemours & Co., Jan. 27, 1871, CFUO.

39 James H. Gilbert, "The Development of Banking in Oregon," *University of Oregon Bulletin*, New Series, IX, no. 1, 1911, p. 7; William L. Brewster, *William Mead Ladd*, p. 9.

40 Brewster, *William Mead Ladd*, pp. 19-20, 26.

41 Simeon G. Reed to J. W. Ladd and D. F. Bradford, Oct. 14, 1865, "A Chapter in the History of the O. S. N. Co.," Johansen and Gill, eds., *OHQ*, XXXVIII, 1937, p. 36.

42 Letters of Henry Failing to John A. Hatt, July 14, 23, Nov. 15, 1864; H. W. Corbett to Samuel T. House, June 3, 1864, CFUO; Brewster, *William Mead Ladd*, pp. 57-58; Gaston, *Portland*, I, pp. 592-593.

43 Corbett, Failing and Company to Samuel T. House, Jan. 28, 1885, CFOHS.

44 Johansen, *Capitalism*, pp. 269-276.

Bibliography

I. Guides and Bibliographies

Checklist of United States Public Documents, 1789-1909. Compiled under the Direction of the Superintendent of Documents. Third edition. Washington: Government Printing Office, 1911.

A Descriptive Catalogue of the Government Publications of the United States, September 5, 1774-March 4, 1881 (Senate Miscellaneous Document No. 67, 48th Cong., 2nd Sess.). Ben Perley Poore, compiler. Washington: Government Printing Office, 1885.

Douglas, Jesse S. "Guide to the Washington Historical Quarterly and the Pacific Northwest Quarterly, 1906-1938," *Pacific Northwest Quarterly*, XXIX, 1938, pp. 339-416.

Guide to the Manuscript Collections of the Oregon Historical Society. Portland, Oregon: Federal Works Agency, Work Projects Administration, Oregon Historical Records Survey, 1940.

Historical Statistics of the United States, 1789-1945. A Supplement to the Statistical Abstract of the United States *(Document No. 330, 80th Cong., 1st Sess.)*.

Koontz, Louis Knott, and Staff. "Guide to Articles and Documents in the Pacific Historical Review, 1932-43," *Pacific Historical Review*, XIII, 1944, pp. 174-191.

Pollard, Lancaster. "A Pacific Northwest Bibliography, 1942-1947," *Pacific Northwest Quarterly*, XXXIV, 1943, pp. 183-196; XXXV, 1944, pp. 157-164; XXXVI, 1945, pp. 132-142; XXXVII, 1946, pp. 143-154; XXXVIII, 1947, pp. 157-169; XXXIX, 1948, pp. 152-166.

Smith, Charles W. *Pacific Northwest Americana: A Check List of Books and Pamphlets Relating to the History of the Pacific Northwest* (Third edition). Portland: Binfords and Mort for the Oregon Historical Society, 1950.

Winther, Oscar Osburn. *The Trans-Mississippi West: A Guide To Its Periodical Literature* (1811-1938). Bloomington: Indiana University Publications, Social Science Series, 1942.

Winton, Harry N. M. "A Pacific Northwest Bibliography, 1940, 1941," *Pacific Northwest Quarterly*, XXXII, 1941, pp. 203-214; XXXIII, 1942, pp. 187-203.

II. Primary Sources: Manuscripts

A. Manuscripts of major importance to this study.

Abernethy, George. Letters. Oregon Historical Society.

————. Letters, Private Collection of Miss Vara Caufield, McLoughlin House, Oregon City.

Astoria Custom-House Records, 1848-68. Originals in the National Archives. (Microfilm, Oregon Historical Society.)

Corbett, Henry W. and Henry Failing. Business Records. The Grace D. and R. R. Stuart Collection of Western Americana, College of the Pacific.

————. Business Records. Oregon Historical Society.

————. Business Records. Special Collections, University of Oregon Library.

B. Other manuscript sources.

Bancroft, Hubert Howe, Pacific Manuscripts, Bancroft Library, University of California.

Abernethy, Mrs. Anne, Statement, June 21, 1878. (Microfilm, Oregon State Archives, Salem.)

Athey, James. Narrative on Workshops at Oregon City, 1843-53, June 18, 1878. (Microfilm, Oregon State Archives, Salem.)

Bacon, J. M. Statement on Mercantile Life at Oregon City, 1845-46, June 18, 1878. (Microfilm, Oregon State Archives, Salem.)

Failing, Henry. Statement, July 19, 1888.

Pettygrove, Francis W. Oregon in 1843. (Microfilm, Oregon Historical Society.)

351

Ross, Charles L. Experiences of a Pioneer of 1847 in California, 1878. A one-page biographical sketch of Ross in H. H. Bancroft's handwriting accompanies this document.

Barnhart, William H. & Co. Business Records. Oregon Historical Society.

Couch, John H. Journal. Oregon Historical Society.

Cox, Thomas and William. Day-book. Salem, Oregon, Oct. 17, 1847 through 1853, with intermittent entries to 1873. (Microfilm at Oregon Historical Society.)

Stark, Benjamin. Correspondence. Oregon Historical Society.

Territorial Papers of Oregon. Oregon State Archives, Salem. (Microfilm, Oregon Historical Society.)

U. S. Census. Copy of the Original Schedules for Oregon for 1850. Oregon Historical Society.

Wilson, Bushrod. Letters. Special Collections, University of Oregon Library.

III. Published Primary Sources
A. Government and semi-official documents.

British and American Joint Commission for the Settlement of the Claims of the Hudson's Bay & Puget Sound Agricultural Companies: Memorial and Argument, and Evidence on the part of the Hudson's Bay Company and Puget Sound Agricultural Company, 3 vols. Montreal: John Lovell, 1868.

Carey, Charles H., ed. The Oregon Constitution and Proceedings and Debates of the Constitutional Convention of 1857. Salem: State Printing Department, 1926.

Miller, Hunter. Treaties and Other International Acts of the United States of America, 8 vols. Washington: Government Printing Office, 1937.

McCormick, S. J., compiler. Portland City Directory, 1863-70.

Richardson, James D., ed. A Compilation of the Messages and Papers of the Presidents, 1789-1897, 10 vols. Washington: Government Printing Office, 1897.

United States. Census Report, 1850, 1860, 1870, 1890.

United States Congress. Congressional Globe. 1838-46.

_____. House Executive Documents.
Doc. 1, 34th Cong., 1st Sess. (Serial 840).
Doc. 93, 34th Cong., 1st Sess. (Serial 858).
Doc. 38, 35th Cong., 1st Sess. (Serial 955).
Doc. 39, 35th Cong., 1st Sess. (Serial 955).
Doc. 93, 35th Cong., 1st Sess. (Serial 957).
Doc. 51, 35th Cong., 2nd Sess. (Serial 1006).
Doc. 11, 36th Cong., 1st Sess. (Serial 1046).

_____. House Report No. 101, 25th Cong., 3rd Sess. (Serial 351).

_____. Senate Executive Documents.
Doc. 24, 25th Cong., 2nd Sess. (Serial 314).
Doc. 134, 25th Cong., 3rd Sess. (Serial 339).
Doc. 66, 34th Cong., 1st Sess. (Serial 822).
Doc. 24, 35th Cong., 1st Sess. (Serial 924).
Doc. 46, 37th Cong., 2nd Sess. (Serial 1122).

_____. Wholesale Prices, Wages and Transportation. Senate Report No. 1394, 52nd Cong., 2nd Sess. (Serial 3074).

United States Department of Labor, Bureau of Labor Statistics. Bulletin No. 367, Wholesale Prices, 1890-1923. Washington: Government Printing Office, 1925.

United States Interstate Commerce Commission. Sixteenth Annual Report of the Interstate Commerce Commission, December 15, 1902, Appendix G, Part II. House Document No. 253, Part 3, 58th Cong., 2nd Sess. (Serial 4699).

United States. The Statutes at Large and Treaties of the United States of America, From December 1, 1845, to March 3, 1851, vol. IX. Boston: Little and Brown, 1851.

Wilkes, Charles. Narrative of the United States Exploring Expedition During the Years 1838, 1839, 1840, 1841, 1842, 5 vols. Philadelphia: Lea and Blanchard, 1844.

B. Newspapers.

Journal of Commerce (Portland, Oregon). 1853.

Portland Commercial. 1853.

Oregon Argus (Oregon City). 1855.

Oregon Spectator (Oregon City). 1846-54.

Oregon Statesman (Salem, Oregon, except for brief periods at Oregon City and Corvallis). 1851-60.

Oregonian (Portland, Oregon). 1850-77.

C. Contemporary accounts: books.

Atkinson, Nancy B., compiler. *Biography of Rev. G. H. Atkinson, D.D. Journal of Sea Voyage to Oregon in 1848, and Selected Addresses and Printed Articles, and a Particular Account of his Churchwork in the Pacific Northwest.* Portland, Oregon: F. W. Bates & Co., 1893.

Barker, Burt Brown, ed. *The Letters of Dr. John McLoughlin Written at Fort Vancouver, 1829-32.* Portland, Oregon: Oregon Historical Society, 1948.

Boggs, Mae Helene Bacon, compiler. *My Playhouse Was a Concord Coach: An Anthology of Newspaper Clippings and Documents Relating to Those Who made California History During the Years 1822-1888.* Oakland, California: Howell-North Press, 1942.

Bowles, Samuel. *Across the Continent.* Springfield, Mass.: Samuel Bowles and Company, 1865.

Brown, J. Henry. *Brown's Political History of Oregon: Provisional Government.* Vol. I. Portland, Oregon: Press of the Lewis and Dryden Printing Co., 1892.

Dana, Richard Henry. *Two Years Before the Mast.* Charles M. Fuess, ed. New York: The Macmillan Company, 1926.

Gray, W. H. *A History of Oregon, 1792-1849, Drawn from Personal Observations and Authentic Information.* Portland, Oregon: Harris and Holman, 1870.

Hailey, John. *The History of Idaho.* Boise, Idaho: Syms-York Company, Inc., 1910.

Hazlitt, William C. *British Columbia and Vancouver Island.* London: G. Routledge & Co., 1858.

Landerholm, Carl, editor and translator. *Notices & Voyages of the Famed Quebec Mission to the Pacific Northwest, Being the Correspondence, Notices, etc., of Fathers Blanchet, Demers, together with those of Father Bolduc and Langlois.* Portland, Oregon: The Oregon Historical Society by the Champoeg Press, 1956.

Lee, Daniel and J. H. Frost. *Ten Years In Oregon.* New York: J. Collard, Printer, 1844.

Merk, Frederick, ed., *Fur Trade and Empire: George Simpson's Journal 1824-1825,* with an introduction by the editor. Cambridge: Harvard University Press, 1931.

Palmer, Joel. *Palmer's Journal of Travels Over the Rocky Mountains, 1845-1846,* Vol. XXX of *Early Western Travels, 1748-1846,* Reuben Gold Thwaites, ed. Cleveland, Ohio: Arthur H. Clark Company, 1906.

Phillips, Paul C., ed. *Forty Years on the Frontier as seen in the Journals and Reminiscences of Granville Stuart, Gold-miner, Trader, Merchant, Rancher and Politician,* 2 vols. Cleveland: The Arthur H. Clark Company, 1925.

Powell, Fred Wilbur, ed. *Hall J. Kelley on Oregon, A Collection of five of his published works and a number of hitherto unpublished letters.* Princeton: Princeton University Press, 1932.

Quaife, M. M., ed. *The Diary of James K. Polk,* 4 vols. Chicago: A. C. McClurg and Company, 1910.

Rich, E. E., ed. *The Letters of John McLoughlin From Fort Vancouver to the Governor and Committee,* First Series, 1825-38; Second Series, 1839-44; Third Series, 1844-46; with introductions to each series by W. Kaye Lamb. (Vol. IV, VI, and VII of *The Publications of the Hudson's Bay Record Society.*) London: The Champlain Society for the Hudson's Bay Record Society, 1941-44.

————, ed. *London Correspondence Inward from Eden Colvile, 1849-1852,* with an introduction by W. L. Morton. (Vol. XIX of *The Publications of the Hudson's Bay Record Society.*) London: The Hudson's Bay Record Society, 1956.

_____, ed. *Peter Skene Ogden's Snake Country Journals,* with an introduction by Burt Brown Barker. (Vol. XIII of *The Publications of the Hudson's Bay Record Society.*) London: The Hudson's Bay Record Society, 1950.

_____, ed. *Simpson's 1828 Journey to the Columbia,* with an introduction by W. Stewart Wallace. (Vol. X of *The Publications of the Hudson's Bay Record Society.*) London: The Champlain Society for the Hudson's Bay Record Society, 1947.

Soule', Frank, John H. Gihon, and James Nisbet. *The Annals of San Francisco.* New York: D. Appleton & Company, 1854.

Thornton, J. Quinn. *Oregon and California in 1848,* 2 vols. New York: Harper and Brothers, 1849.

deTocqueville, Alexis. *Democracy in America,* 2 vols. The Henry Reeve Text as edited by Phillips Bradley. New York: Alfred A. Knopf, 1945.

Wallach, Sidney, ed. *Narrative of an American Squadron to the China Seas and Japan Under the Command of Commodore M. C. Perry, United States Navy, Compiled at His Request and Under His Supervision by Francis L. Hawks.* New York: Coward-McCann, Inc., 1952.

Weisel, George F., ed. *Men and Trade on the Northwest Frontier as Shown by the Fort Owen Ledger* (vol. 2 of Montana State University Studies). Missoula: Montana State University Press, 1955.

Wyeth, John B. *Wyeth's Oregon, or a Short History of a Long Journey,* (Vol. XXI, *Early Western Travels,* Reuben Gold Thwaites, ed.), pp. 19-106. Cleveland, Ohio: The Arthur H. Clark Company, 1905.

Young, F. G., ed. *The Correspondence and Journals of Captain Nathaniel J. Wyeth, 1831-6.* (Vol. I of the *Sources of the History of Oregon.*) Eugene Oregon: University Press, 1899.

D. Contemporary accounts now published in periodicals.

Baker, Florence E., ed. "Letters of Tallmadge B. Wood," *Oregon Historical Quarterly,* III, 1902, pp. 394-398; IV, 1903, pp. 80-85.

Barker, Burt Brown. "The Estate of Dr. John McLoughlin: The Papers Discovered," *Oregon Historical Quarterly,* L, 1949, pp. 155-185.

_____, ed., "McLoughlin Proprietary Account With Hudson's Bay Company," *Oregon Historical Quarterly,* XLV, 1944, pp. 1-41.

Burnett, Peter H. "Recollections and Opinions of an Old Pioneer," *Oregon Historical Quarterly,* V, 1904, pp. 64-99, 151-198, 272-305, 370-401.

Carey, Charles H., ed. "Diary of Reverend George H. Gary," *Oregon Historical Quarterly,* XXIV, 1923, pp. 68-105, 151-185, 269-333, 386-433.

_____, ed. "Lee, Waller and McLoughlin," *Oregon Historical Quarterly,* XXXIII, 1932, pp. 187-213.

_____, ed. "Methodist Annual Reports Relating to the Willamette Mission, 1834-1848," *Oregon Historical Quarterly,* XXIII, 1922, pp. 303-364.

_____, ed., "The Oregon Mission Record Book," *Oregon Historical Quarterly,* XXIII, 1922, pp. 230-236.

Carstensen, Vernon, ed. "Pacific Northwest Letters of George Gibbs," *Oregon Historical Quarterly,* LIV, 1953, pp. 191-239.

Crawford, Medorem. "Gov. George Abernethy," *Transactions of the Oregon Pioneer Association,* 1886, pp 37-40.

Deady, Matthew P. "Annual Address," *Transactions of the Oregon Pioneer Association,* 1875.

Duniway, David C., and Neil R. Riggs, eds. "The Oregon Archives, 1841-1843," *Oregon Historical Quarterly,* LX, 1959, pp. 211-280.

Elliott, T. C., ed. "Journal of John Work, Covering Snake River Expedition of 1830-31," *Oregon Historical Quarterly,* XIII, 1912, pp. 363-371; XIV, 1913, pp. 280-314.

Gatke, Robert Moulton, ed. "A Document of Mission History, 1833-43," *Oregon Historical Quarterly,* XXXVI, 1935, pp. 71-94, 163-181.

_____, ed. "The Letters of the Rev. William M. Roberts, Third Superintendent of the Oregon Mission," *Oregon Historical Quarterly*, XXI, 1920, pp. 33-47; XXII, 1921, pp. 223-251; XXIII, 1922, pp. 163-191.

Gillette, P. W. "A Brief History of the Oregon Steam Navigation Company," *Oregon Historical Quarterly*, V, 1904, pp. 120-132.

Henderson, Sarah Fisher, Nellie Edith Latourette and Kenneth Scott Latourette, eds. "Correspondence of the Reverend Ezra Fisher," *Oregon Historical Quarterly*, XVII, 1916, pp. 55-76, 149-176, 267-339, 431-480.

Howison, Neil M. "Report of Lieutenant Neil M. Howison On Oregon, 1846," reprinted from *House Miscellaneous Documents No. 29*, 30th Cong., 1st Sess. *Oregon Historical Quarterly*, XIV, 1913, pp. 1-60.

Johannsen, Robert W., ed. "John Burkhart and Oregon Territory, 1849," *Oregon Historical Quarterly*, LIII, 1952, pp. 196-203.

Johansen, Dorothy O., and Frank B. Gill, eds. "A Chapter In the History of the Oregon Steam Navigation Company," *Oregon Historical Quarterly*, XXXVIII, 1937, pp. 1-43, 300-322, 398-410; XXXIX, 1938, pp. 50-64.

"John H. Couch," *Transactions of the Oregon Pioneer Association*, 1886, pp. 59-65.

Jones, Dorsey D., ed., "Two Wilson M. Tigard Letters," *Oregon Historical Quarterly*, XLV, 1944, pp. 228-237.

Knuth, Priscilla and Charles M. Gates, eds. "Oregon Territory in 1849-50," *Pacific Northwest Quarterly*, XL, 1949, pp. 3-23.

Lee, Jason. "Diary," *Oregon Historical Quarterly*, XVII, 1916, pp. 117-146, 240-266, 397-430.

Lyman, H. S., ed. "Reminiscences of Clement Adams Bradbury, 1846," *Oregon Historical Quarterly*, II, 1901, pp. 304-319.

McLoughlin, John. "Copy of a Document Found among the Private Papers of the late Dr. John McLoughlin," *Transactions of the Oregon Pioneer Association*, 1880, pp. 46-58.

_____. "Documents: Correspondence of McLoughlin, Wyeth, *et al.*," *Oregon Historical Quarterly*, I, 1900, pp. 105-109.

_____. Letter of Doctor John McLoughlin to Sir George Simpson, March 20, 1844, "Documentary," *Oregon Historical Quarterly*, XVII, 1916, pp. 215-239.

Minto, John. "Antecedents of the Oregon Pioneers and the Light These Throw on Their Motives," *Oregon Historical Quarterly*, V, 1904, pp. 38-63.

_____. "From Youth to Age As An American," *Oregon Historical Quarterly*, IX, 1908, pp. 127-178.

_____. "What I Know of Dr. John McLoughlin and How I Know It," *Oregon Historical Quarterly*, XI, 1910, pp. 177-200.

Oliphant, J. Orin, ed. "Letters of Hezekiah Johnson, 1838-1849," *Pacific Northwest Quarterly*, XXXVII, 1946, pp. 15-30.

_____, ed. "Thomas S. Kendall's Letter on Oregon Agriculture, 1852," *Agricultural History*, IX, 1935, pp. 187-197.

Pipes, Nellie B., ed. "Journal of John H. Frost, 1840-43," *Oregon Historical Quarterly*, XXXV, 1934, pp. 50-73, 139-167, 235-262, 348-375.

Pratt, Harry E., ed. "22 Letters of David Logan, Pioneer Oregon Lawyer," *Oregon Historical Quarterly*, XLIV, 1943, pp. 253-285.

Pratt, L. E. "The Origins and History of the Willamette Woolen Factory," *Oregon Historical Quarterly*, III, 1902, pp. 248-259.

Reed, Harry E., ed. "Lovejoy's Pioneer Narrative, 1842-48," *Oregon Historical Quarterly*, XXXI, 1930, pp. 236-260.

Rockwood, E. Ruth, ed. "Diary of Reverend George H. Atkinson, 1847-1858," *Oregon Historical Quarterly*, XL, 1939, pp. 52-63, 168-187, 265-282, 345-361; XLI, 1940, pp. 6-33, 212-226, 288-303, 386-404.

Schafer, Joseph, ed. "Letters of Sir George Simpson, 1841-1843," *American Historical Review*, XIV, 1908, pp. 70-94.

Scott, Leslie M., ed. "Report of Lieutenant Peel on Oregon in 1845-46," *Oregon Historical Quarterly*, XXIX, 1928, pp. 50-76.

Sylvester, Avery. "Voyages of the Pallas and Chenamus," *Oregon Historical Quarterly*, XXXIV, 1933, pp. 259-272, 359-371.

Sylvester, Edmund. "Edmund Sylvester's Narrative of the Founding of Olympia," *Pacific Northwest Quarterly*, XXXVI, 1945, pp. 331-339.

IV. Secondary Sources

A. Books.

Atherton, Lewis E. *The Pioneer Merchant in Mid-America*. (Vol. XIV, no. 2, *The University of Missouri Studies.*) Columbia, Missouri: University of Missouri Press, 1939.

Bancroft, Hubert Howe, *Chronicles of the Builders of the Commonwealth*, 6 vols. San Francisco: The History Company, 1891.

————. *History of California*. 7 vols. (Vols. XVIII-XXIV of *Bancroft's Works*). San Francisco: The History Company, 1884-1890.

————. *History of Oregon*. 2 vols. (Vols. XXIX-XXX of *Bancroft's Works*). San Francisco: The History Company, 1886 and 1888.

————. *History of Washington, Idaho and Montana*, 1845-1889 (Vol. XXXI of *Bancroft's Works*). San Francisco: The History Company, 1890.

Brewster, William L. *William Mead Ladd of Portland, Oregon*. Portland, Oregon: Metropolitan Press, 1933.

Brosnan, Cornelius J. *Jason Lee, Prophet of the New Oregon*. New York: The Macmillan Company, 1932.

Carey, Charles Henry. *History of Oregon*, 3 vols. Author's Edition. Chicago and Portland: The Pioneer Historical Publishing Company, 1922.

Caughey, John Walton. *California*. Second edition. New York: Prentice-Hall, Inc., 1953.

————. *Gold is the Cornerstone*. Berkeley and Los Angeles: University of California Press, 1948.

Childs, Marquis W. and Douglas Cater. *Ethics in a Business Society*, New York: Harper and Brothers, 1954.

Clark, Arthur H. *The Clipper Ship Era, 1843-1869*. New York and London: G. P. Putnam's Sons, 1910.

Clark, Robert C. *History of the Willamette Valley, Oregon*, 3 vols. Chicago: S. J. Clarke Publishing Co., 1927.

Cleland, Robert O. and Osgood Hardy. *March of Industry*. Los Angeles, San Francisco: Powell Publishing Co., 1929.

Corning, Howard McKinley. *Willamette Landings: Ghost Towns of the River*. Portland, Oregon: Binfords and Mort for the Oregon Historical Society, 1947.

Drury, Clifford Merrill. *Marcus Whitman M. D.* Caldwell, Idaho: Caxton Printers, 1937.

Fitzgerald, Martin F., ed. *Sixty Milestones of Progress 1859-1919, Ladd and Tilton Bank*. Portland, Oregon: Printed for Ladd and Tilton Bank by James, Kerns, & Abbott Company, 1919.

Fuller, George W. *A History of the Pacific Northwest, with Special Emphasis on the Inland Empire*. Second revised edition. New York: Alfred A. Knopf, 1948.

Galbraith, John S. *The Hudson's Bay Company as an Imperial Factor*. Berkeley and Los Angeles: University of California Press, 1957.

Gaston, Joseph. *Portland, Oregon, Its History and Builders*, 3 vols. Chicago and Portland: The S. J. Clarke Publishing Co., 1911.

Ghent, W. J. *The Road to Oregon: A Chronicle of the Great Emigrant Trail*. London: Longmans, Green and Company, 1929.

Gibbs, James A., Jr. *Pacific Graveyard: A Narrative of the Ships Lost Where the Columbia River Meets the Pacific Ocean*. Portland, Oregon: Binfords & Mort, Publishers, 1950.

Gilbert, James Henry. *Trade and Currency in Early Oregon* (vol. XXVI, *Studies in History, Economics and Public Law*, edited by the Faculty of Political Science of Columbia University). New York: The Columbia University Press, 1907.

Graebner, Norman A. *Empire on the Pacific: A Study in American Continental Expansion*. New York: The Ronald Press Company, 1955.

Holman, Frederick V. *Dr. John McLoughlin: the Father of Oregon*. Cleveland, Ohio: The Arthur H. Clarke Company, 1907.

Howay, F. W., W. N. Sage, and H. F. Angus. *British Columbia and the United States*. Toronto: The Ryerson Press, 1942.

Hungerford, Edward. *Wells Fargo: Advancing the American Frontier*. New York: Random House, 1949.

Hussey, John A. *The History of Fort Vancouver and Its Physical Structure*. Tacoma: Washington State Historical Society in Cooperation with the National Park Service, United States Department of Interior, 1957.

Hutchinson, William T. *Cyrus Hall McCormick*, 2 vols. New York and London: The Century Company and D. Appleton-Century Company, 1930 and 1935.

Jacobs, Melvin Clay. *Winning Oregon: A Study of an Expansionist Movement*. Caldwell, Idaho: Caxton Printers, 1938.

Johannsen, Robert W. *Frontier Politics and the Sectional Conflict: The Pacific Northwest on the Eve of the Civil War*. Seattle: University of Washington Press, 1955.

Johansen, Dorothy O. and Charles M. Gates. *Empire of the Columbia: A History of the Pacific Northwest*. New York: Harper and Brothers, 1957.

Johnson, Allen, ed. *Dictionary of American Biography*, 20 vols. New York: Charles Scribner's Sons, 1928-36.

Johnson, Emory R., T. W. Van Metre, G. G. Huebner, and D. S. Hanchett. *History of the Domestic and Foreign Commerce of the United States*, 2 vols. Washington, D. C.: The Carnegie Institution of Washington, 1915.

Kemble, John Haskell. *The Panama Route, 1848-1869*. Berkeley and Los Angeles: University of California Press, 1943.

Lang, H. O., ed. *History of the Willamette Valley*. Portland, Oregon: Himes and Lang, 1885.

Lomax, Alfred L. *Pioneer Woolen Mills in Oregon: History of Wool and the Woolen Textile Industry, 1811-1875*. Portland, Oregon: Binfords & Mort, 1941.

Mack, Gerstle. *The Land Divided: A History of the Panama Canal and Other Isthmian Canal Projects*. New York: Alfred A. Knopf, 1944.

McArthur, Lewis A. *Oregon Geographic Names*. Second edition. Portland, Oregon: Binfords and Mort for the Oregon Historical Society, 1944.

Merk, Frederick. *Albert Gallatin and the Oregon Problem*. Cambridge: Harvard University Press, 1950.

Mitchell, Wesley O. *Gold, Prices, and Wages under the Greenback Standard* (vol. I, *University of California Publications in Economics*, March 27, 1908). Berkeley: The University Press, 1908.

Morison, Samuel E. *The Maritime History of Massachusetts*. Boston and New York: Houghton Mifflin Company, 1921.

Morrell, W. P. *The Gold Rushes*. New York: The Macmillan Company, 1941.

Morton, Arthur S. *Sir George Simpson: Overseas Governor of the Hudson's Bay Company*. Portland, Oregon: Binfords & Mort for the Oregon Historical Society, 1944.

Paul, Rodman W. *California Gold: The Beginning of Mining in the Far West*. Cambridge: Harvard University Press, 1947.

Peterson, Emil R. and Alfred Powers. *A Century of Coos and Curry: History of Southwest Oregon*. Portland, Oregon: Binfords & Mort, 1952.

Powell, Fred Wilbur. *Hall Jackson Kelley, Prophet of Oregon*. Portland, Oregon: The Ivy Press, 1917.

Quiett, Glen Chesney. *They Built the West*. New York: D. Appleton-Century Co., 1934.

Riesenberg, Felix, Jr. *Golden Gate: The Story of San Francisco Harbor*. New York and London: Alfred A. Knopf, 1940.

357

Rydell, Raymond A. *Cape Horn to the Pacific: The Rise and Decline of an Ocean Highway*. Berkeley: University of California Press, 1952.

Schafer, Joseph. *A History of the Pacific Northwest*. Revised ed., New York: The Macmillan Co., 1921.

Schumpeter, Joseph A. *The Theory of Economic Development*. Trans. from the German by Redvers Opie. Cambridge: Harvard University Press, 1934.

Scott, Harvey W. *History of the Oregon Country*. Leslie M. Scott, compiler. 6 vols. Cambridge: Riverside Press, 1924.

_____, ed. *History of Portland, Oregon*. Syracuse, N. Y.: D. Mason & Co., 1890.

Semple, Ellen Churchill. *American History and Its Geographic Conditions*. Boston and New York: Houghton, Mifflin and Company, 1903.

Trimble, William J. *The Mining Advance Into the Inland Empire. (Bulletin of the University of Wisconsin No. 638,* History Series, Vol. 3, No. 2, pp. 137-392.) Madison: 1914.

Turner, Frederick Jackson. *The Frontier in American History*. New York: Henry Holt & Co., 1920.

Victor, Frances Fuller. *All Over Oregon and Washington*. San Francisco: John H. Carmany & Co., 1872.

_____. *Early Indian Wars of Oregon*. Salem, Oregon: Frank C. Baker, State Printer, 1894.

Walling, A. G., publisher and compiler. *History of Southern Oregon: Comprising Jackson, Josephine, Douglas, Curry and Coos Counties*. Portland, Oregon: Lithographing House of A. G. Walling, 1884.

Walworth, Arthur. *Black Ships off Japan, The Story of Commodore Perry's Expedition*. New York: Alfred A. Knopf, 1946.

Warren, George F. and Frank A. Pearson. *Prices*. New York: John Wiley & Sons, 1933.

_____. *Wholesale Prices for 213 Years, 1720-1932*. Cornell University Agricultural Experiment Station, *Memoir 142*, part 1. Ithaca, 1932.

Winther, Oscar Osburn. *The Great Northwest*. New York: Alfred A. Knopf, 1950.

_____. *The Old Oregon Country: A History of Frontier Trade, Transportation, and Travel*. Stanford, California: Stanford University Press, 1950.

Wright, E. W., ed. *Lewis and Dryden's Marine History of the Pacific Northwest*. Portland, Oregon: The Lewis and Dryden Printing Co., 1895.

B. Theses.

Johansen, Dorothy O. "Capitalism on the Far-Western Frontier: The Oregon Steam Navigation Company." Ph.D. thesis in history, University of Washington, 1941.

Meany Edmond Stephen, Jr. "The History of the Lumber Industry in the Pacific Northwest to 1917." Ph.D. thesis, Harvard University, 1935.

Spaid, Stanley S. "Joel Palmer and Indian Affairs in Oregon." Ph.D. thesis, University of Oregon, 1950.

Throckmorton, Arthur L. "The Oregon Boundary Controversy, 1818-1846." M.A. thesis, University of North Carolina, 1947.

Tucker, William Pierce. "The History of Jackson County, Oregon." M.A. thesis, University of Washington, 1931.

C. Articles.

Adams, W. Claude. "History of Papermaking in the Pacific Northwest: I," *Oregon Historical Quarterly*, LII, 1951, pp. 21-37.

Atkin, W. T. "Snake River Fur Trade, 1816-24," *Oregon Historical Quarterly*, XXXV, 1934, pp. 295-312.

Beidleman, Richard G. "Nathaniel Wyeth's Fort Hall," *Oregon Historical Quarterly*, LVIII, 1957, pp. 197-250.

Bibler, Stephen H. "Specimen of Abernethy Rock: A Medium of Exchange," *Oregon Historical Quarterly*, XLIV, 1943, pp. 249-252.

Bolino, August C. "The Role of Mining in the Economic Development of Idaho Territory," *Oregon Historical Quarterly*, LIX, 1958, pp. 116-151.

Bowers, Helen. "Trade and Administrative Policies and Practices of McLoughlin," *Reed College Bulletin*, XXI (November, 1942), pp. 5-16.

Bright, Verne. "Auburn—The Story of an Oregon Ghost Town," *The Commonwealth Review*, XXI, 1939, pp. 60-70.

————. "The Folklore and History of the 'Oregon Fever'," *Oregon Historical Quarterly*, LII, 1951, pp. 241-253.

————. "Randolph: Ghost Gold Town of the Oregon Beaches," *Oregon Historical Quarterly*, LVIII, 1957, pp. 293-306.

Clark, Dan Elbert. "Manifest Destiny and the Pacific," *Pacific Historical Review*, I, 1932, pp. 1-17.

————. "The Movement to the Far West During the Decade of the Sixties," *Washington Historical Quarterly*, XVII, 1926, pp. 105-113.

Cunningham, Glenn. "Oregon's First Salmon Canner, 'Captain' John West," *Oregon Historical Quarterly*, LIV, 1953, pp. 240-248.

Daniels, Joseph. "History of Pig Iron Manufacture on the Pacific Coast," *Washington Historical Quarterly*, XVII, 1926, pp. 168-189.

————. "Iron and Steel Manufacture in Washington, Oregon, California and Utah," *Bulletin, University of Washington Engineering Experiment Station* (Engineering Experiment Station Series, Report No. 2, Dec. 15, 1929), pp. 1-69.

Deutsch, Herman J. "Economic Imperialism in the Early Pacific Northwest," *Pacific Historical Review*, IX, 1940, pp. 377-388.

Douglas, Jesse S. "Origins of the Population of Oregon in 1850," *Pacific Northwest Quarterly*, XLI, 1950, pp. 95-108.

Eaton, W. Clement. "Nathaniel Wyeth's Oregon Expeditions," *Pacific Historical Review*, IV, 1935, pp. 101-113.

Ellison, Joseph W. "The Beginnings of the Apple Industry in Oregon," *Agricultural History*, XI, 1937, pp. 322-343.

Galbraith, John S. "The Early History of the Puget Sound Agricultural Company, 1838-1843," *Oregon Historical Quarterly*, LV, 1954, pp. 234-259.

————. "George N. Sanders, 'Influence Man' For the Hudson's Bay Company," *Oregon Historical Quarterly*, LIII, 1952, p. 159-176.

Ganoe, John Tilson. "The History of the Oregon and California Railroad," *Oregon Historical Quarterly*, XXV, 1924, pp. 236-283, 330-351.

Gilbert, James Henry. "The Development of Banking in Oregon," *University of Oregon Bulletin* (New Series), IX, no. 1, Sept., 1911, pp. 5-30.

Grant, L. S. "Fort Hall Under the Hudson's Bay Company, 1837-1856," *Oregon Historical Quarterly*, XLI, 1940, pp. 34-39.

Haines, Francis D., Jr. "The Relations of the Hudson's Bay Company with the American Fur Traders in the Pacific Northwest," *Pacific Northwest Quarterly*, XL, 1949, pp. 273-294.

Hergert, Herbert L. "Early Iron Industry in Oregon," *Reed College Bulletin*, XXVI (January, 1948), pp. 1-40.

Hermann, Binger. "Early Southern Oregon," *Oregon Historical Quarterly*, XIX, 1918, pp. 53-68.

Hirsch, Dorothy D. "Study of the Foreign Wheat Trade of Oregon, 1869 to 1887," *Reed College Bulletin*, XXI (August, 1953), pp. 47-85.

Howay, F. W. "The Brig Owyhee in the Columbia, 1829-30," *Oregon Historical Quarterly*, XXV, 1934, pp. 10-21.

Johansen, Dorothy O. "The Oregon Steam Navigation Company: 1860-1880. An Example of Capitalism on the Frontier," *Pacific Historical Review*, X, 1941, pp. 179-188.

————. "Organization and Finance of the Oregon Iron and Steel Company," *Pacific Northwest Quarterly*, XXXI, 1940, pp. 123-159.

Juergens, Carl H. "Movement of Wholesale Prices in New York City, 1825-1863," *Publications of the American Statistical Association*, XII, 1910-1911, pp. 544-557.

Kingston, C. S. "Introduction of Cattle Into the Pacific Northwest," *Washington Historical Quarterly*, XIV, 1923, pp. 163-185.

Knuth, Priscilla. "Nativism In Oregon," *Reed College Bulletin*, XXIV (January, 1946), pp. 1-25.

Kroll, Helen B. "The Books That Enlightened the Emigrants," *Oregon Historical Quarterly*, XLV, 1944, pp. 103-123.

Lazenby, Marie. "Down-Easters Out West," *Reed College Bulletin*, XXV (April, 1947), pp. 1-33.

Loehr, Rodney C. "Business Records," Chap. V of *Local History: How to Gather It, Write It, and Publish It*. Donald Dean Parker and Bertha E. Josephson, eds. (New York: The Social Science Research Council, 1944), pp. 70-79.

Lomax, Alfred L. "Hawaii-Columbia River Trade in Early Days," *Oregon Historical Quarterly*, XLIII, 1942, pp. 328-338.

————. "Oregon City Woolen Mill," *Oregon Historical Quarterly*, XXXII, 1931, pp. 240-261.

Ludington, Flora Belle. "The Newspapers of Oregon, 1846-1870," *Oregon Historical Quarterly*, XXVI, 1925, pp. 229-262.

Martig, Ralph Richard. "Hudson's Bay Company Claims, 1846-69," *Oregon Historical Quarterly*, XXXVI, 1935, pp. 60-70.

McLellan, Sister Mary de Sales. "William Hume, 1830-1902," *Oregon Historical Quarterly*, XXXV, 1934, pp. 269-278.

Meinig, Donald W. "Wheat Sacks out to Sea," *Pacific Northwest Quarterly*, XLV, 1954, pp. 13-18.

Merk, Frederick. "The British Corn Crisis and the Oregon Treaty," *Agricultural History*, VIII, 1934, pp. 95-134.

————. "British Government Propaganda and the Oregon Treaty," *American Historical Review*, XL, 1934, pp. 38-63.

————. "British Party Politics and the Oregon Treaty," *American Historical Review*, XXXVII, 1932, pp. 653-677.

————. "The Genesis of the Oregon Question," *Mississippi Valley Historical Review*, XXXVI, 1950, pp. 593-612.

————. "Oregon Pioneers and the Boundary," *American Historical Review*, XXIX, 1924, pp. 681-699.

————. "Snake Country Expedition, 1824-25," *Oregon Historical Quarterly*, XXXV, 1934, pp. 93-122.

Mills, Randall V. "A History of Transportation in the Pacific Northwest," *Oregon Historical Quarterly*, XLVII, 1946, pp. 281-312.

Morison, Samuel Eliot. "New England and the Opening of the Columbia River Salmon Trade, 1830," *Oregon Historical Quarterly*, XXVIII, 1927, pp. 111-132.

Oliphant, J. Orin. "The Cattle Herds and Ranches of the Oregon Country, 1860-1890," *Agricultural History*, XXI, 1947, pp. 217-238.

————. "The Cattle Trade from the Far Northwest to Montana," *Agricultural History*, VI, 1932, pp. 69-83.

————. "The Cattle Trade on Puget Sound, 1858-1890," *Agricultural History*, VII, 1933, pp. 129-149.

————. "George Simpson and Oregon Missions," *Pacific Historical Review*, VI, 1937, pp. 213-248.

————. "History of the Livestock Industry in the Pacific Northwest," *Oregon Historical Quarterly*, XLIX, 1948, pp. 171-191.

O'Meara, James. "An Early Steamboating Era on the Willamette," *Oregon Historical Quarterly*, XLIV, 1943, pp. 140-146.

Overmeyer, Philip Henry. "Members of the First Wyeth Expedition," *Oregon Historical Quarterly*, XXXVI, 1935, pp. 95-101.

_____. "Nathaniel Jarvis Wyeth, *Washington Historical Quarterly*, XXIV, 1933, pp. 28-48.

Oviatt, Alton B. "Steamboat Traffic on the Upper Missouri River, 1859-1869," *Pacific Northwest Quarterly*, XL, 1949, pp. 93-105.

Paul, Rodman W. "The Wheat Trade Between California and the United Kingdom," *Mississippi Valley Historical Review*, XLV, 1958, pp. 391-412.

Partoll, Albert J. "Frank L. Worden, Pioneer Merchant, 1830-1887," *Pacific Northwest Quarterly*, XL, 1949, pp. 189-202.

Pike, C. J. "Petitions of Oregon Settlers," *Oregon Historical Quarterly*, XXXIV, 1933, pp. 216-235.

"A Pocket Full of Rocks," *Oregon Native Son*, I, 1899-1900, p. 90.

Pollard, Lancaster. "The Pacific Northwest: A Regional Study," *Oregon Historical Quarterly*, LII, 1951, pp. 211-234.

Poppleton, Irene Lincoln. "Oregon's First Monopoly—The O. S. N. Co.," *Oregon Historical Quarterly*, IX, 1908, pp. 274-304.

Ross, Frank E. "The Retreat of the Hudson's Bay Company In the Pacific Northwest," *Canadian Historical Review*, XVIII, 1937, pp. 262-280.

Sage, Walter N. "The Place of Fort Vancouver in the History of the Northwest," *Pacific Northwest Quarterly*, XXXIX, 1948, pp. 83-102.

Schafer, Joseph. "The Western Ocean as a Determinant in Oregon History," *The Pacific Ocean In History, Papers and Addresses Presented at the Panama-Pacific Historical Congress, Held at San Francisco, Berkeley, and Palo Alto, California, July 19-23, 1915,* H. Morse Stephens and Herbert E. Bolton, eds. (New York: The Macmillan Company, 1917), pp. 287-297.

Scott, Harvey W. "The Pioneer Character of Oregon Progress," *Oregon Historical Quarterly*, XVIII, 1917, pp. 245-270.

Scott, Leslie M. "Influence of American Settlement Upon the Oregon Boundary Treaty of 1846," *Oregon Historical Quarterly*, XXIX, 1928, pp. 1-19.

_____. "Pioneer Gold Money," *Oregon Historical Quarterly*, XXXIII, 1932, pp. 25-30.

_____. "The Pioneer Stimulus of Gold," *Oregon Historical Quarterly*, XVIII, 1917, pp. 147-166.

Shippee, Lester Burrell. "The Federal Relations of Oregon," *Oregon Historical Quarterly*, XIX, 1918, pp. 89-133, 189-230, 283-331.

Spaid, Stanley S. "The Later Life and Activities of General Joel Palmer," *Oregon Historical Quarterly*, LV, 1954, pp. 311-332.

Spence, Clark G. "British Investment and Oregon Mining, 1860-1900," *Oregon Historical Quarterly*, LVIII, 1957, pp. 101-112.

Tanner, Elaine. "A Study of the Underlying Causes of the Depression of 1854," *Reed College Bulletin*, XXV (April, 1947), pp. 35-65.

Thomas, Russell B. "Truth and Fiction of the Champoeg Meeting," *Oregon Historical Quarterly*, XXX, 1929, pp. 218-237.

Throckmorton, Arthur L. "George Abernethy, Pioneer Merchant," *Pacific Northwest Quarterly*, XLVIII, 1957, pp. 76-88.

_____. "The Role of the Merchant on the Oregon Frontier: The Early Business Career of Henry W. Corbett, 1851-1869," *Journal of Economic History*, XVI, 1956, pp. 539-550.

Tompkins, Walker Allison. "Oysterville, 1840-97," *Oregon Historical Quarterly*, XXXIII, 1932, pp. 160-163.

Troxel, Kathryn. "Food of the Overland Emigrants," *Oregon Historical Quarterly*, LVI, 1955, pp. 12-26.

Van Alstyne, Richard W. "International Rivalries in the Pacific Northwest," *Oregon Historical Quarterly*, XLVI, 1945, pp. 185-218.

Wardell, M. L. "Oregon Immigration Prior to 1846," *Oregon Historical Quarterly*, XXVII, 1926, pp. 41-64.

Winther, Oscar Osburn. "California Stage Company in Oregon," *Oregon Historical Quarterly*, XXXV, 1934, pp. 131-138.

_____. "Commercial Routes from 1792 to 1843 by Sea and Overland," *Oregon Historical Quarterly*, XLII, 1941, pp. 230-246.

_____. "Early Commercial Importance of the Mullan Road," *Oregon Historical Quarterly*, XLVI, 1945, pp. 22-43.

_____. "Pack Animals for Transportation in the Pacific Northwest," *Pacific Northwest Quarterly*, XXXIV, 1943, pp. 131-146.

_____. "The Place of Transportation in the Early History of the Pacific Northwest," *Pacific Historical Review*, XI, 1942, pp. 383-396.

_____. "Roads and Transportation in Territorial Oregon," *Oregon Historical Quarterly*, XLI, 1940, pp. 40-52.

Young, F. G. "Financial History of Oregon," *Oregon Historical Quarterly*, VII, 1906, pp. 360-432; VIII, 1907, pp. 129-200.

_____. "The Oregon Trail," *Oregon Historical Quarterly*, I, 1900, pp. 340-370.

INDEX

California, 3, 9, 22, 32, 41, 62, 68, 85-86,
   87, 89-90, 92-93, 95, 98, 103, 104, 108,
   110, 111-12, 113, 115, 119, 128, 132,
   140, 159, 160, 163, 165, 168-69, 172-73,
   175, 179-80, 199-200, 202, 204, 207,
   216, 220, 225-26, 227, 231-32, 247, 249,
   255, 259, 262, 265, 281, 296, 302,
   304-306, 308, 309, *see also* Gold mines
   and mining, Prices, Trade and
   commerce
California (ship), 109
California, Oregon & Mexico
   Steamship Co., 303, 304
California Stage Co., 295-97
California Steam Navigation Co., 249,
   253, 301, 303, 304
Canemah, Ore., 112, 205
Canton, China, 7
Cape Horn, *see* Shipping and
   freighting—routes
Caroline (steamship), 112
Carpenter shops, 57
Carrie Ladd (steamer), 206
Cathlamet, Wash., 81
Cattle, 9, 16, 210, 256-57, 273
Celilo Falls, 251, 252
Centerville, Ida., 255
Central Overland California & Pike's
   Peak Express Co., 295
Central Pacific Railroad, 267, 298-99
Champoeg, Ore., 38, 40, 58, 63, 121, 227
Chapman, W. W., 120
Charles Devens (bark), 213, 340
Chemeketa, 24, 25
Chenamus (ship), 30, 39, 39n, 57n
Chicago, Ill., 274
Chippewa (steamboat), 268-69
Civil War, 80, 195, 222, 226, 277,
   285-86, 296, 299, 304
Clackamas River, 116, 311
Clackamas River Manufacturing
   Co., 311
Clark, Hiram, 89, 103, 104, 214, 217, 218
Clarke, N. S., 190
Clatsop, 24, 25-26
Clatsop mission, 24, 25
Clearwater River, 247, 248
Coal mining, 222
Coe, Lawrence, 250
Coffin, Stephen, 120
Colonel Wright (steamship), 190, 251
Columbia (river steamer), 118-19,
   120, 129
Columbia (side-wheeler), 112, 113
Columbia (steamship), 170
Columbia Barracks, 79, 80
Columbia River, 5, 6, 8, 10, 11, 13, 29,
   55, 57, 96, 97, 105, 107, 112, 136, 214,
   217, 301, 308, 310:
   Cascades of, 120, 165, 190, 206, 251,
   253-54; Clark's Fork, 270, 271, 272;
   see also Boundary controversy,

Shipping and freighting, Trade and
   commerce, Transportation
Columbia River Navigation Co., 206
Columbia River Paper Co., 311
Columbia Valley, 185, 205
Colvile, Eden, 75
Commerce, *see* Trade and commerce
Commodore (ship), 199
Communications, 298:
   telegraph, 223, 224, 285, 295, 299
Convoy (ship), 8
Cook & Burbank, 240
Coos Bay, Ore., 164, 222
Corbett, Elijah, 297
Corbett, Henry W., 126-27, 128, 129-30,
   131, 132-33, 140, 166, 171, 174, 175,
   176, 178, 189, 201, 208-10, 212, 214,
   218, 220, 221, 229, 230-38, 239-40, 241,
   253, 261, 291, 292-93, 294, 297, 299,
   312-13, 314, 333, 337
Corbett, Failing & Co., 312, 314-15
Corbett, H. W., & Co., 310, 330
Corbitt & Macleay, 308
Corrine, Utah, 275
Corvallis, Ore., 121, 122, 161, 162, 164,
   205, 206, 223, 240
Couch, John H., 29-30, 32, 34, 35, 39,
   40, 55, 58, 60, 90, 97, 101, 128
Cowelitz (bark), 39n
Cowlitz Farm, 11, 18
Cowlitz Valley, 11, 125
Cox, Thomas, 63-64
Credit, 27, 35, 36-37, 48, 49, 60, 90,
   101-102, 132, 175, 176, 187, 189,
   191-92, 230, 234-35, 239, 243,
   259-60, 278, 281:
   interest, 36, 50, 102, 230, 232, 233,
   234, 235, 239, 278
Crescent City, Calif., 163, 168, 172,
   173, 196, 207, 302
Crichton, E. W., 311
Crosby, Nathaniel, 57, 90, 101
Crown-Zellerbach Corp., 312
Culloma (bark), 105, 139, 173
Curry, George L., 67, 91n, 187
Cushing, Caleb, 21, 22
Cushing, J. P., & Co., 29, 30, 32, 39, 40
Customs duties, 76-77

Dallas, A. G., 80
Dallas, Ore., 121, 310
Dart, Anson, 76
Davis, W. T. A., 229
Day, Eph, 252
Day, H. I., 281
Dayton, Ore., 121
Deady, Matthew P., 186, 189
Deer Lodge, Mont., 273
Deer Lodge Valley, 267
Demers, Modeste, 17-18
Denver, Colo., 298
Deschutes Landing, 190
Desdemona (ship), 213

364

General Warren (steamship), 136, 138
George Raynes (ship), 216
Gibbs, George, 123
Gill, J. K., 311
Gillette, P. W., 252, 258
Godfrey, B. D., 291
Gold Beach, Ore., 164
Gold Hunter (steamship), 120
Gold mines and mining:
  British Columbia, 198-99, 200-203,
  266-67—
    yield, 199, 200, 201
  California, 53, 69, 85-88, 92-93,
  109, 115, 162—
    yield, 85, 88, 91, 169
  Colvile region, 190, 196, 197-98—
    yield, 196-97, 198
  gold bullion, 110, 276; gold dust, 169,
  170; gold production, 1860s, 275-76
  Idaho, 226-27, 247-50, 254-55, 264-65,
  266, 267—
    yield, 248, 255
  mining tools, 261-62, 291; Montana,
  267, 268-71
  Southern Oregon, 89, 93, 125, 135,
  162-63, 164, 196-97—
    yield, 162-63, 168, 196-97
Grande Ronde Valley, 250
Grasshopper Creek, 267
Gray, Robert, 8
Greathouse & Co., 256
Grimes, George, 254

Hailey & Greathouse, 296
Hailey & Ish, 255, 256
Halsted, Samuel, 102
Halsted, S. & S., 102
Hapgood, Andrew S., 310
Hapgood, Hume & Co., 310
Hargraves, Edward, 87
Harney, W. S., 80, 190
Hassalo (steamer), 202
Hatt, John A., 195n, 242, 243, 277, 278,
  286, 288, 290, 291, 292, 312, see also
  Failings & Hatt
Hawaiian Islands, 11, 39, 40, 46, 54,
  58-59, 62, 90, 179, 215, 299
Hazlitt, William C., 186-87, 201
Helen Angier (ship), 308
Helen W. Almy (bark), 301
Helena, Mont., 267, 269, 270, 273, 274
Hell Gate, Mont., 268
Henry (ship), 57, 63, 64, 88, 89, 90
Hide and tallow trade, 9, 62, 128
Higgins, C. P., 268
Hillsboro, Ore., 121
Holladay, Ben, 295, 296, 298, 301-302,
  303, 304, 312, 314
Holladay & Flint, 301
Holman, J., 240
Honolulu (schooner), 87, 90
Hopkins, Hayes, Palmer & Co., 230,
  231, 233

House, Samuel T., 278, 310, 312, 315
Howison, Neil M., 52-56, 57, 58, 60
Hudson's Bay Company:
  in California, 7, 41, 62; claims, 70-81;
  Columbia Dept., 3-4, 5, 8, 10, 11, 38,
  40-41, 45; competition, 6, 7, 8-9, 11,
  28, 29, 40, 41, 46, 59, 62; exclusive
  trade privileges, 6, 10, 81; New
  Caledonia dist., 7; Northern Dept.,
  5n; partnership shares in, 5n;
  possessory rights, 70-81; settler
  relationships, 6, 7, 8, 10, 13, 14, 15, 17,
  18-19, 23, 25, 27, 28, 29, 34, 36-37,
  40, 42, 43, 50-51, 55, 59
Hull, Knapp & Co., 238
Hume, George W., 310
Hume, William, 310
Humiston, C. H., 281
Hunt, Henry H., 38-39
Hunt, Thomas & Co., 241, 242
Hurricane (clipper ship), 133, 139, 241
Hussey Co., 239

Idaho, see Gold mines and mining,
  Prices, Trade and commerce
Idaho (steamship), 303, 304
Idaho & California Wagon
  Road Co., 262
Idaho City, Ida., 263-64
Illinois River, 163
Independence, Ore., 121
Indian war claims, 192-93, 194-95
Indians, 15, 19, 66, 72, 76, 79, 81, 324:
  treaties with, 184-85, 186, 190; wars,
  164, 183, 184-88, 189, 190, 192-93, 198
Industry (bark), 213, 289, 301
Industry and manufacturing, 92,
  161-62, 173, 175, 221, 309-11, 315
Insurance, 55, 102, 135, 136, 213
Iron manufacturing, 310-11
Island Milling Co., 28-29, 50
Isthmus of Panama, see Panama

J. B. Lunt (bark), 213, 340
J. Merrithew (bark), 136
Jacksonville, Ore., 162, 163, 164, 166,
  167-68, 175, 195, 206, 241
Jagger, I. E., 249
Jane A. Falkenburg (bark), 214, 301
Jennie Clark (steamer), 206
Jennings, Berryman, 119
John Day River, 250
Josephine (bark), 77

Kamm, Jacob, 119, 206, 271
Kelley, Hall J., 21-22
Kendrick, John, 8
Kilbourne, William K., 63, 64, 90,
  99, 115n
Kilbourne, Lawton & Co., 89-90
Kingston, C. S., 257
Kone, W. W., 25

Labor, 92, 96, 160-62, 305, see also
  Employment, Wages

Mindora (bark), 136
Mineral resources, Oregon, 89, see also Gold mines and mining
Mississippi River, 31, 88, 119, 123
Mississippi Valley, 32, 64, 123, 304, 219, 220, 257
Missoula, Mont., 268
Missoula (steamer), 272
Missouri, 31, 32, 48, 94
Missouri River, 192, 267, 268, 269, 270, 273, 274
Modeste (sloop), 36
Money:
    Abernethy rocks, 60; barter of goods, 34, 56, 59, 64; beaver money, 99-100; bills of exchange, 102, 135; currency, 53-54, 59, 60, 63, 67-68, 87, 99, 100, 102, 105, 192, 196, 279-80, 281-82, 283-85; discounts, 60, 68; drafts, 59, 63, 192, 231, 233; gold and gold dust, 98, 99-100, 102, 172-73, 227, 278; gold premium, 195n, 280-82, 283-90; legal tender, 59, 60, 63, 68, 195, 279-82; orders on solvent merchants, 59, 60, 63; scrip, 68, 187-88, 189, 190, 193-95; wheat as medium of exchange, 14, 46-47, 53, 56, 59, 60-61, 68; see also Credit
Montana, see Gold mines and mining, Trade and commerce
Montana (steamship), 303
Montana Post (newspaper), 274-75
Montieth, Thomas, 115n, 121
Montieth, Walter, 115n, 121
Mountain Buck (steamer), 202
Mullan, John, 192, 226, 268, 269, 292n
Multnomah (steamer), 177

Nahumkeag (bark), 213
Nelson, Judge —, 314
Nesmith, James W., 191
Nevada, 86, 290
New England, 21, 22, 23, 114n, 125, 127, 263, 291
New Orleans, La., 31, 123
New Westminster, B. C., 266-67, 299
New York, 23, 27, 57, 65, 86, 90, 92, 108, 109, 110, 111, 112, 125, 127, 129, 132, 133, 134, 135, 137, 140, 166, 168-69, 194, 226, 230-31, 232, 233-36, 241, 242, 243, 257, 261, 265-66, 273, 277, 278, 281, 284, 288, 299, 304-305, 315, see also Prices, Shipping and freighting
New York & Owyhee Co., 265
Newburyport, Mass., 21, 29, 30, 63, 90
Newell, Capt. —, 87
Newport, Ore., 222
Nisqually, 24, 25
Nisqually mission, 24, 25
North Bend, Ore., 222
North Pacific Transportation Co., 304
North West Company, 3, 5, 6
Northern Pacific Railroad, 312, 314, 315

Northerner (steamship), 225
Northrup, Nelson, 222
Northrup & Simonds, 222

Oak Point, 96-97, 215-16, 219
Ocean Bird (ship), 207, 213, 340
Ogden, Peter Skene, 4, 6, 11, 13, 42, 66-67, 74, 77, 115n
Okanogan (steamboat), 252
Okanogan River, 201, 202
Olmstead, H., 271
Oregon:
    Provisional Govt., 33-34, 52, 59, 63, 67, 74, 99, 114; Territorial Govt., 66, 68-69, 72
Oregon (ship), 109
Oregon & California Packet Line, 108, 213, 217
Oregon & California Railroad, 312
Oregon & California Stage Co., 297
Oregon & Montana Transportation Co., 272
Oregon Central Railroad, 312
Oregon City, 30, 38, 47, 57, 64, 88, 91-92, 95-96, 99, 104, 108, 115-17, 118, 119, 120, 121, 126, 140, 174, 197, 204, 205, 206, 212, 214, 218, 227, 240, 311: land claims, 42-46, 51; see also Mercantile stores
Oregon City Woolen Manufacturing Co., 310
Oregon Exchange Co., 99
Oregon Iron & Steel Co., 311
Oregon Iron Co., 310
Oregon Provisional Emigration Society, 22
Oregon question, 72-74
Oregon Spectator, quoted, 89, 91n, 93, 105, 172-73
Oregon Stage Co., 297
Oregon Statesman, quoted, 113, 174, 175, 218
Oregon Steam Navigation Co., 206, 248, 250-54, 255-56, 260, 261, 265, 267-68, 270, 271-72, 276, 295, 296, 302-303, 307, 312, 315
Oregon Telegraph Co., 299
Oregon Trail, 31, 63, 128, 249
Oregon treaty, see Boundary controversy
Oregonian (Portland), quoted, 136, 159, 160, 162, 163-64, 165, 166, 173, 174, 176-77, 185-86, 188, 194, 197, 201, 203, 211, 219, 225, 249, 254, 256, 258, 259, 262, 269, 270-71, 272, 273, 279, 281, 283, 290, 297, 298, 299, 303, 304, 306, 308-309, 311, 312
Oregonian (steamship), 303, 304
Oriflamme (steamship), 303, 304
Orizaba (ship), 302
Orofino, Ida., 248
Oswego, Ore., 310
Oswego Iron Co., 311

Willamette Falls, 28, 35, 36, 38, 42, 44, 46, 47, 48, 55, 59, *see also* Oregon City, Ore.
Willamette Falls mission, 24, 28-29
Willamette River, 29, 58, 96, 107, 108, 116-17, 118-21, 161, 173, 177, 205, 214, 267:
  flood, 218-19, 227;
  see also Shipping and freighting, Trade and commerce, Transportation
Willamette Valley, 10, 11, 14-15, 16, 19, 27, 31-32, 33, 42, 47, 53, 63-64, 67, 81, 107, 114, 116, 121, 122, 123, 124-25, 129, 130, 159-61, 163, 164-65, 168, 169, 172, 173, 176, 196, 199, 201, 202, 204-205, 207, 210, 211, 215, 225, 226, 227, 228, 229, 244, 247-48, 250, 256-57, 278, 291, 295, 300, 305, 308, 309, 314
Willamette Woolen Manufacturing Co., 221-22, 310
William and Ann (brig), 8

Williams, Charles, 234
Williams, Bradford & Co., 129, 132, 133, 134, 234
Willapa Bay, 222
Wilson, Albert E., 39
Wilson, Bushrod, 161-62
Winchester, Ore., 206
Wolff, Mr. —, 202
Wood, Tallmadge B., 38-39
Wool, John E., 187, 190, 194, 198
Woolen industry, 221, 300-301, 310
Worden, Frank L., 268-69
Work, John, 6, 75
Worth & Bro., 240
Wrangell, Ferdinand, 9
Wright, George, 190
Wycoff & Co., 134, 137

Yakima Valley, 201
Yreka, Calif., 285, 299
Young, Ewing, 22, 33